ASPEN PUBLISHERS

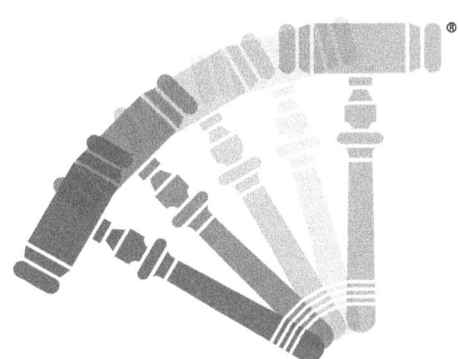

Casenote™ *Legal Briefs*

COPYRIGHT

Keyed to Courses Using

**Cohen, Loren, Okediji, and O'Rourke
Copyright in a Global Information Economy**

Third Edition

AUSTIN   BOSTON   CHICAGO   NEW YORK   THE NETHERLANDS

This publication is designed to provide accurate and authoritative information in regard to the subject matter covered. It is sold with the understanding that the publisher is not engaged in rendering legal, accounting, or other professional services. If legal advice or other expert assistance is required, the services of a competent professional person should be sought.

> — From a Declaration of Principles adopted jointly by a Committee of the American Bar Association and a Committee of Publishers and Associates

© 2010 Aspen Publishers. All Rights Reserved.
www.AspenLaw.com

No part of this publication may be reproduced or transmitted in any form or by any means, electronic or mechanical, including photocopy, recording, or any information storage and retrieval system, without permission in writing from the publisher. Requests for permission to make copies of any part of this publication should be mailed to:

> Aspen Publishers
> Attn: Permissions Dept.
> 76 Ninth Avenue, 7th Floor
> New York, NY 10011-5201

To contact Customer Care, e-mail customer.service@aspenpublishers.com, call 1-800-234-1660, fax 1-800-901-9075, or mail correspondence to:

> Aspen Publishers
> Attn: Order Department
> P.O. Box 990
> Frederick, MD 21705

Printed in the United States of America.

1 2 3 4 5 6 7 8 9 0

ISBN 978-0-7355-9457-9

About Wolters Kluwer Law & Business

Wolters Kluwer Law & Business is a leading provider of research information and workflow solutions in key specialty areas. The strengths of the individual brands of Aspen Publishers, CCH, Kluwer Law International and Loislaw are aligned within Wolters Kluwer Law & Business to provide comprehensive, in-depth solutions and expert-authored content for the legal, professional and education markets.

CCH was founded in 1913 and has served more than four generations of business professionals and their clients. The CCH products in the Wolters Kluwer Law & Business group are highly regarded electronic and print resources for legal, securities, antitrust and trade regulation, government contracting, banking, pension, payroll, employment and labor, and health-care reimbursement and compliance professionals.

Aspen Publishers is a leading information provider for attorneys, business professionals and law students. Written by preeminent authorities, Aspen products offer analytical and practical information in a range of specialty practice areas from securities law and intellectual property to mergers and acquisitions and pension/benefits. Aspen's trusted legal education resources provide professors and students with high-quality, up-to-date and effective resources for successful instruction and study in all areas of the law.

Kluwer Law International supplies the global business community with comprehensive English-language international legal information. Legal practitioners, corporate counsel and business executives around the world rely on the Kluwer Law International journals, loose-leafs, books and electronic products for authoritative information in many areas of international legal practice.

Loislaw is a premier provider of digitized legal content to small law firm practitioners of various specializations. Loislaw provides attorneys with the ability to quickly and efficiently find the necessary legal information they need, when and where they need it, by facilitating access to primary law as well as state-specific law, records, forms and treatises.

Wolters Kluwer Law & Business, a unit of Wolters Kluwer, is headquartered in New York and Riverwoods, Illinois. Wolters Kluwer is a leading multinational publisher and information services company.

Format for the Casenote Legal Brief

Nature of Case: This section identifies the form of action (e.g., breach of contract, negligence, battery), the type of proceeding (e.g., demurrer, appeal from trial court's jury instructions), or the relief sought (e.g., damages, injunction, criminal sanctions).

Fact Summary: This is included to refresh your memory and can be used as a quick reminder of the facts.

Rule of Law: Summarizes the general principle of law that the case illustrates. It may be used for instant recall of the court's holding and for classroom discussion or home review.

Facts: This section contains all relevant facts of the case, including the contentions of the parties and the lower court holdings. It is written in a logical order to give the student a clear understanding of the case. The plaintiff and defendant are identified by their proper names throughout and are always labeled with a (P) or (D).

Palsgraf v. Long Island R.R. Co.

Injured bystander (P) v. Railroad company (D)

N.Y. Ct. App., 248 N.Y. 339, 162 N.E. 99 (1928).

NATURE OF CASE: Appeal from judgment affirming verdict for plaintiff seeking damages for personal injury.

FACT SUMMARY: Helen Palsgraf (P) was injured on R.R.'s (D) train platform when R.R.'s (D) guard helped a passenger aboard a moving train, causing her package to fall on the tracks. The package contained fireworks which exploded, creating a shock that tipped a scale onto Palsgraf (P).

RULE OF LAW
The risk reasonably to be perceived defines the duty to be obeyed.

FACTS: Helen Palsgraf (P) purchased a ticket to Rockaway Beach from R.R. (D) and was waiting on the train platform. As she waited, two men ran to catch a train that was pulling out from the platform. The first man jumped aboard, but the second man, who appeared as if he might fall, was helped aboard by the guard on the train who had kept the door open so they could jump aboard. A guard on the platform also helped by pushing him onto the train. The man was carrying a package wrapped in newspaper. In the process, the man dropped his package, which fell on the tracks. The package contained fireworks and exploded. The shock of the explosion was apparently of great enough strength to tip over some scales at the other end of the platform, which fell on Palsgraf (P) and injured her. A jury awarded her damages, and R.R. (D) appealed.

ISSUE: Does the risk reasonably to be perceived define the duty to be obeyed?

HOLDING AND DECISION: (Cardozo, C.J.) Yes. The risk reasonably to be perceived defines the duty to be obeyed. If there is no foreseeable hazard to the injured party as the result of a seemingly innocent act, the act does not become a tort because it happened to be a wrong as to another. If the wrong was not willful, the plaintiff must show that the act as to her had such great and apparent possibilities of danger as to entitle her to protection. Negligence in the abstract is not enough upon which to base liability. Negligence is a relative concept, evolving out of the common law doctrine of trespass on the case. To establish liability, the defendant must owe a legal duty of reasonable care to the injured party. A cause of action in tort will lie where harm, though unintended, could have been averted or avoided by observance of such a duty. The scope of the duty is limited by the range of danger that a reasonable person could foresee. In this case, there was nothing to suggest from the appearance of the parcel or otherwise that the parcel contained fireworks. The guard could not reasonably have had any warning of a threat to Palsgraf (P), and R.R. (D) therefore cannot be held liable. Judgment is reversed in favor of R.R. (D).

DISSENT: (Andrews, J.) The concept that there is no negligence unless R.R. (D) owes a legal duty to take care as to Palsgraf (P) herself is too narrow. Everyone owes to the world at large the duty of refraining from those acts that may unreasonably threaten the safety of others. If the guard's action was negligent as to those nearby, it was also negligent as to those outside what might be termed the "danger zone." For Palsgraf (P) to recover, R.R.'s (D) negligence must have been the proximate cause of her injury, a question of fact for the jury.

ANALYSIS
The majority defined the limit of the defendant's liability in terms of the danger that a reasonable person in defendant's situation would have perceived. The dissent argued that the limitation should not be placed on liability, but rather on damages. Judge Andrews suggested that only injuries that would not have happened but for R.R.'s (D) negligence should be compensable. Both the majority and dissent recognized the policy-driven need to limit liability for negligent acts, seeking, in the words of Judge Andrews, to define a framework "that will be practical and in keeping with the general understanding of mankind." The Restatement (Second) of Torts has accepted Judge Cardozo's view.

Quicknotes

FORESEEABILITY A reasonable expectation that change is the probable result of certain acts or omissions.

NEGLIGENCE Conduct falling below the standard of care that a reasonable person would demonstrate under similar conditions.

PROXIMATE CAUSE The natural sequence of events without which an injury would not have been sustained.

Party ID: Quick identification of the relationship between the parties.

Concurrence/Dissent: All concurrences and dissents are briefed whenever they are included by the casebook editor.

Analysis: This last paragraph gives you a broad understanding of where the case "fits in" with other cases in the section of the book and with the entire course. It is a hornbook-style discussion indicating whether the case is a majority or minority opinion and comparing the principal case with other cases in the casebook. It may also provide analysis from restatements, uniform codes, and law review articles. The analysis will prove to be invaluable to classroom discussion.

Issue: The issue is a concise question that brings out the essence of the opinion as it relates to the section of the casebook in which the case appears. Both substantive and procedural issues are included if relevant to the decision.

Holding and Decision: This section offers a clear and in-depth discussion of the rule of the case and the court's rationale. It is written in easy-to-understand language and answers the issue presented by applying the law to the facts of the case. When relevant, it includes a thorough discussion of the exceptions to the case as listed by the court, any major cites to the other cases on point, and the names of the judges who wrote the decisions.

Quicknotes: Conveniently defines legal terms found in the case and summarizes the nature of any statutes, codes, or rules referred to in the text.

Note to Students

Aspen Publishers is proud to offer *Casenote Legal Briefs*—continuing thirty years of publishing America's best-selling legal briefs.

Casenote Legal Briefs are designed to help you save time when briefing assigned cases. Organized under convenient headings, they show you how to abstract the basic facts and holdings from the text of the actual opinions handed down by the courts. Used as part of a rigorous study regimen, they can help you spend more time analyzing and critiquing points of law than on copying bits and pieces of judicial opinions into your notebook or outline.

Casenote Legal Briefs should never be used as a substitute for assigned casebook readings. They work best when read as a follow-up to reviewing the underlying opinions themselves. Students who try to avoid reading and digesting the judicial opinions in their casebooks or online sources will end up shortchanging themselves in the long run. The ability to absorb, critique, and restate the dynamic and complex elements of case law decisions is crucial to your success in law school and beyond. It cannot be developed vicariously.

Casenote Legal Briefs represents but one of the many offerings in Aspen's Study Aid Timeline, which includes:

- *Casenote Legal Briefs*
- *Emanuel Law Outlines*
- *Examples & Explanations* Series
- *Introduction to Law* Series
- Emanuel *Law in a Flash* Flash Cards
- Emanuel *CrunchTime* Series

Each of these series is designed to provide you with easy-to-understand explanations of complex points of law. Each volume offers guidance on the principles of legal analysis and, consulted regularly, will hone your ability to spot relevant issues. We have titles that will help you prepare for class, prepare for your exams, and enhance your general comprehension of the law along the way.

To find out more about Aspen Study Aid publications, visit us online at *www.AspenLaw.com* or email us at *legaledu@wolterskluwer.com*. We'll be happy to assist you.

Get this Casenote Legal Brief as an AspenLaw Studydesk eBook today!

By returning this form to Aspen Publishers, you will receive a complimentary eBook download of this Casenote Legal Brief and AspenLaw Studydesk productivity software.* Learn more about AspenLaw Studydesk today at *www.AspenLaw.com/Studydesk*.

Name	Phone ( )
Address	**Apt. No.**
City	**State**	**ZIP Code**
Law School	**Graduation Date** Month _____ Year _____

Cut out the UPC found on the lower left corner of the back cover of this book. Staple the UPC inside this box. Only the original UPC from the book cover will be accepted. (No photocopies or store stickers are allowed.)

Attach UPC inside this box.

Email (Print legibly or you may not get access!)

Title of this book (course subject)

ISBN of this book (10- or 13-digit number on the UPC)

Used with which casebook (provide author's name)

Mail the completed form to: Aspen Publishers, Inc.
Legal Education Division
130 Turner Street, Bldg 3, 4th Floor
Waltham, MA 02453-8901

* Upon receipt of this completed form, you will be emailed a code for the digital download of this book in AspenLaw Studydesk eBook format and a free copy of the software application, which is required to read the eBook.

For a full list of eBook study aids available for AspenLaw Studydesk software and other resources that will help you with your law school studies, visit *www.AspenLaw.com*.

Make a photocopy of this form and your UPC for your records.

For detailed information on the use of the information you provide on this form, please see the PRIVACY POLICY at *www.AspenLaw.com*.

How to Brief a Case

A. Decide on a Format and Stick to It

Structure is essential to a good brief. It enables you to arrange systematically the related parts that are scattered throughout most cases, thus making manageable and understandable what might otherwise seem to be an endless and unfathomable sea of information. There are, of course, an unlimited number of formats that can be utilized. However, it is best to find one that suits your needs and stick to it. Consistency breeds both efficiency and the security that when called upon you will know where to look in your brief for the information you are asked to give.

Any format, as long as it presents the essential elements of a case in an organized fashion, can be used. Experience, however, has led *Casenotes* to develop and utilize the following format because of its logical flow and universal applicability.

NATURE OF CASE: This is a brief statement of the legal character and procedural status of the case (e.g., "Appeal of a burglary conviction").

There are many different alternatives open to a litigant dissatisfied with a court ruling. The key to determining which one has been used is to discover *who is asking this court for what.*

This first entry in the brief should be kept as *short as possible.* Use the court's terminology if you understand it. But since jurisdictions vary as to the titles of pleadings, the best entry is the one that addresses who wants what in this proceeding, not the one that sounds most like the court's language.

RULE OF LAW: A statement of the general principle of law that the case illustrates (e.g., "An acceptance that varies any term of the offer is considered a rejection and counteroffer").

Determining the rule of law of a case is a procedure similar to determining the issue of the case. Avoid being fooled by red herrings; there may be a few rules of law mentioned in the case excerpt, but usually only one is *the* rule with which the casebook editor is concerned. The techniques used to locate the issue, described below, may also be utilized to find the rule of law. Generally, your best guide is simply the chapter heading. It is a clue to the point the casebook editor seeks to make and should be kept in mind when reading every case in the respective section.

FACTS: A synopsis of only the essential facts of the case, i.e., those bearing upon or leading up to the issue.

The facts entry should be a short statement of the events and transactions that led one party to initiate legal proceedings against another in the first place. While some cases conveniently state the salient facts at the beginning of the decision, in other instances they will have to be culled from hiding places throughout the text, even from concurring and dissenting opinions. Some of the "facts" will often be in dispute and should be so noted. Conflicting evidence may be briefly pointed up. "Hard" facts must be included. Both must be *relevant* in order to be listed in the facts entry. It is impossible to tell what is relevant until the entire case is read, as the ultimate determination of the rights and liabilities of the parties may turn on something buried deep in the opinion.

Generally, the facts entry should not be longer than three to five *short* sentences.

It is often helpful to identify the role played by a party in a given context. For example, in a construction contract case the identification of a party as the "contractor" or "builder" alleviates the need to tell that that party was the one who was supposed to have built the house.

It is always helpful, and a good general practice, to identify the "plaintiff" and the "defendant." This may seem elementary and uncomplicated, but, especially in view of the creative editing practiced by some casebook editors, it is sometimes a difficult or even impossible task. Bear in mind that the *party presently* seeking something from this court may not be the plaintiff, and that sometimes only the cross-claim of a defendant is treated in the excerpt. Confusing or misaligning the parties can ruin your analysis and understanding of the case.

ISSUE: A statement of the general legal question answered by or illustrated in the case. For clarity, the issue is best put in the form of a question capable of a "yes" or "no" answer. In reality, the issue is simply the Rule of Law put in the form of a question (e.g., "May an offer be accepted by performance?").

The major problem presented in discerning what is *the* issue in the case is that an opinion usually purports to raise and answer several questions. However, except for rare cases, only one such question is really the issue in the case. Collateral issues not necessary to the resolution of the matter in controversy are handled by the court by language known as *"obiter dictum"* or merely *"dictum."* While dicta may be included later in the brief, they have no place under the issue heading.

To find the issue, ask *who wants what* and then go on to ask *why did that party succeed or fail in getting it.* Once this is determined, the "why" should be turned into a question.

The complexity of the issues in the cases will vary, but in all cases a single-sentence question should sum up the issue. *In a few cases,* there will be two, or even more rarely, three issues of equal importance to the resolution of the case. Each should be expressed in a single-sentence question.

Since many issues are resolved by a court in coming to a final disposition of a case, the casebook editor will reproduce the portion of the opinion containing the issue or issues most relevant to the area of law under scrutiny. A noted law professor gave this advice: "Close the book; look at the title on the cover." Chances are, if it is Property, you need not concern yourself with whether, for example, the federal government's treatment of the plaintiff's land really raises a federal question sufficient to support jurisdiction on this ground in federal court.

The same rule applies to chapter headings designating sub-areas within the subjects. They tip you off as to what the text is designed to teach. The cases are arranged in a casebook to show a progression or development of the law, so that the preceding cases may also help.

It is also most important to remember to *read the notes and questions* at the end of a case to determine what the editors wanted you to have gleaned from it.

HOLDING AND DECISION: This section should succinctly explain the rationale of the court in arriving at its decision. In capsulizing the "reasoning" of the court, it should always include an application of the general rule or rules of law to the specific facts of the case. Hidden justifications come to light in this entry: the reasons for the state of the law, the public policies, the biases and prejudices, those considerations that influence the justices' thinking and, ultimately, the outcome of the case. At the end, there should be a short indication of the disposition or procedural resolution of the case (e.g., "Decision of the trial court for Mr. Smith (P) reversed").

The foregoing format is designed to help you "digest" the reams of case material with which you will be faced in your law school career. Once mastered by practice, it will place at your fingertips the information the authors of your casebooks have sought to impart to you in case-by-case illustration and analysis.

B. Be as Economical as Possible in Briefing Cases

Once armed with a format that encourages succinctness, it is as important to be economical with regard to the time spent on the actual reading of the case as it is to be economical in the writing of the brief itself. This does not mean "skimming" a case. Rather, it means reading the case with an "eye" trained to recognize into which "section" of your brief a particular passage or line fits and having a system for quickly and precisely marking the case so that the passages fitting any one particular part of the brief can be easily identified and brought together in a concise and accurate manner when the brief is actually written.

It is of no use to simply repeat everything in the opinion of the court; record only enough information to trigger your recollection of what the court said. Nevertheless, an accurate statement of the "law of the case," i.e., the legal principle applied to the facts, is absolutely essential to class preparation and to learning the law under the case method.

To that end, it is important to develop a "shorthand" that you can use to make marginal notations. These notations will tell you at a glance in which section of the brief you will be placing that particular passage or portion of the opinion.

Some students prefer to underline all the salient portions of the opinion (with a pencil or colored underliner marker), making marginal notations as they go along. Others prefer the color-coded method of underlining, utilizing different colors of markers to underline the salient portions of the case, each separate color being used to represent a different section of the brief. For example, blue underlining could be used for passages relating to the rule of law, yellow for those relating to the issue, and green for those relating to the holding and decision, etc. While it has its advocates, the color-coded method can be confusing and time-consuming (all that time spent on changing colored markers). Furthermore, it can interfere with the continuity and concentration many students deem essential to the reading of a case for maximum comprehension. In the end, however, it is a matter of personal preference and style. Just remember, whatever method you use, underlining must be used sparingly or its value is lost.

If you take the marginal notation route, an efficient and easy method is to go along underlining the key portions of the case and placing in the margin alongside them the following "markers" to indicate where a particular passage or line "belongs" in the brief you will write:

N   (NATURE OF CASE)
RL (RULE OF LAW)
I   (ISSUE)
HL (HOLDING AND DECISION, relates to the RULE OF LAW behind the decision)
HR (HOLDING AND DECISION, gives the RATIONALE or reasoning behind the decision)
HA (HOLDING AND DECISION, APPLIES the general principle(s) of law to the facts of the case to arrive at the decision)

Remember that a particular passage may well contain information necessary to more than one part of your brief, in which case you simply note that in the margin. If you are using the color-coded underlining method instead of marginal notation, simply make asterisks or checks in the margin next to the passage in question in the colors that indicate the additional sections of the brief where it might be utilized.

The economy of utilizing "shorthand" in marking cases for briefing can be maintained in the actual brief writing process itself by utilizing "law student shorthand" within the brief. There are many commonly used words and phrases for which abbreviations can be substituted in your briefs (and in your class notes also). You can develop abbreviations that are personal to you and which will save you a lot of time. A reference list of briefing abbreviations can be found on page xii of this book.

C. Use Both the Briefing Process and the Brief as a Learning Tool

Now that you have a format and the tools for briefing cases efficiently, the most important thing is to make the time spent in briefing profitable to you and to make the most advantageous use of the briefs you create. Of course, the briefs are invaluable for classroom reference when you are called upon to explain or analyze a particular case. However, they are also useful in reviewing for exams. A quick glance at the fact summary should bring the case to mind, and a rereading of the rule of law should enable you to go over the underlying legal concept in your mind, how it was applied in that particular case, and how it might apply in other factual settings.

As to the value to be derived from engaging in the briefing process itself, there is an immediate benefit that arises from being forced to sift through the essential facts and reasoning from the court's opinion and to succinctly express them in your own words in your brief. The process ensures that you understand the case and the point that it illustrates, and that means you will be ready to absorb further analysis and information brought forth in class. It also ensures you will have something to say when called upon in class. The briefing process helps develop a mental agility for getting to the *gist* of a case and for identifying, expounding on, and applying the legal concepts and issues found there. The briefing process is the mental process on which you must rely in taking law school examinations; it is also the mental process upon which a lawyer relies in serving his clients and in making his living.

Abbreviations for Briefs

acceptance	acp
affirmed	aff
answer	ans
assumption of risk	a/r
attorney	atty
beyond a reasonable doubt	b/r/d
bona fide purchaser	BFP
breach of contract	br/k
cause of action	c/a
common law	c/l
Constitution	Con
constitutional	con
contract	K
contributory negligence	c/n
cross	x
cross-complaint	x/c
cross-examination	x/ex
cruel and unusual punishment	c/u/p
defendant	D
dismissed	dis
double jeopardy	d/j
due process	d/p
equal protection	e/p
equity	eq
evidence	ev
exclude	exc
exclusionary rule	exc/r
felony	f/n
freedom of speech	f/s
good faith	g/f
habeas corpus	h/c
hearsay	hr
husband	H
injunction	inj
in loco parentis	ILP
inter vivos	I/v
joint tenancy	j/t
judgment	judgt
jurisdiction	jur
last clear chance	LCC
long-arm statute	LAS
majority view	maj
meeting of minds	MOM
minority view	min
Miranda rule	Mir/r
Miranda warnings	Mir/w
negligence	neg
notice	ntc
nuisance	nus
obligation	ob
obscene	obs
offer	O
offeree	OE
offeror	OR
ordinance	ord
pain and suffering	p/s
parol evidence	p/e
plaintiff	P
prima facie	p/f
probable cause	p/c
proximate cause	px/c
real property	r/p
reasonable doubt	r/d
reasonable man	r/m
rebuttable presumption	rb/p
remanded	rem
res ipsa loquitur	RIL
respondeat superior	r/s
Restatement	RS
reversed	rev
Rule Against Perpetuities	RAP
search and seizure	s/s
search warrant	s/w
self-defense	s/d
specific performance	s/p
statute	S
statute of frauds	S/F
statute of limitations	S/L
summary judgment	s/j
tenancy at will	t/w
tenancy in common	t/c
tenant	t
third party	TP
third party beneficiary	TPB
transferred intent	TI
unconscionable	uncon
unconstitutional	unconst
undue influence	u/e
Uniform Commercial Code	UCC
unilateral	uni
vendee	VE
vendor	VR
versus	v
void for vagueness	VFV
weight of authority	w/a
weight of the evidence	w/e
wife	W
with	w/
within	w/i
without	w/o
without prejudice	w/o/p
wrongful death	wr/d

Table of Cases

A
A&M Records, Inc. v. Napster, Inc. *132*
A.A. Hoehling v. Universal City Studios, Inc. *15*
Aalmuhammed v. Lee.............................. *25*
Abend v. MCA, Inc. *187*
Alfred Bell & Co. v. Catalda Fine Arts, Inc. *9*
American Dental Association v. Delta Dental
 Plans Association *16*
American Geophysical Union v. Texaco, Inc. *133*
Apple Computer, Inc. v. Franklin Computer Corp. ... *43*
Arista Records, LLC v. Launch Media, Inc. *103*
Arnstein v. Porter *64*
Asset Marketing Systems, Inc. v. Gagnon......... *136*
Aymes v. Bonelli *27*

B
Baker v. Selden...................................... *14*
Baltimore Orioles, Inc. v. Major League Baseball
 Players Association *167*
Bassett v. Mashantucket Pequot Tribe............ *177*
BellSouth Advertising & Publishing Corp. v.
 Donnelley Information Publishing, Inc. *53*
Bill Graham Archives v. Dorling
 Kindersley Ltd. *124*
Bleistein v. Donaldson Lithographing Co. *8*
Bobbs-Merrill Company v. Straus *76*
Boisson v. Banian, Ltd. *66*
Bonito Boats, Inc. v. Thunder Craft Boats, Inc. ... *163*
Boosey & Hawkes Music Publishers, Ltd. v.
 The Walt Disney Company *140*
Bouchat v. Baltimore Ravens Football Club, Inc. *194*
Bowers v. Baystate Technologies, Inc. *172*
Brandir International, Inc. v. Cascade Pacific
 Lumber Co. *42*
Bridgeman Art Library, Ltd. v. Corel Corp. *186*
Bridgeport Music, Inc. v. Dimension Films *102*
Brown v. Ames *168*
Bryan Ashley International, Inc. v. Shelby Williams
 Industries, Inc. *182*
Burrow-Giles Lithographic Co. v. Sarony............ *7*

C
CCC Information Services, Inc. v. Maclean Hunter
 Market Reports, Inc. *54*
CDN Inc. v. Kapes..................................... *55*
Campbell v. Acuff-Rose Music, Inc. *121*
Capitol Records, Inc. v. Thomas..................... *73*
Carol Barnhart Inc. v. Economy Cover Corp. *41*
Cartoon Network LP v. CSC Holdings, Inc. *95*
Castle Rock Entertainment, Inc. v. Carol
 Publishing Group, Inc. *79, 122*
Cavalier v. Random House, Inc. *70*
Chamberlain Group, Inc. v. Skylink Tech., Inc. ... *152*
Chavez v. Arte Publico Press *183*
Christopher Phelps & Associates, LLC v.
 Galloway *188*
Columbia Pictures Indus. v. Redd Horne, Inc. *94*
Community for Creative Non-Violence v. Reid *26*
Computer Associates International, Inc. v.
 Altai, Inc. *44, 72*

D
Dastar Corp. v. Twentieth Century Fox Film
 Corp. *92*

E
Eden Toys, Inc. v. Florelee Undergarment Co. ... *181*
Eldred v. Ashcroft.................................... *33*
Entertainment Research Group, Inc. v. Genesis
 Creative Group, Inc. *18*
Erickson v. Trinity Theatre, Inc. *24*

F
Fantasy, Inc. v. Fogerty *201*
Feist Publications, Inc. v. Rural Telephone
 Service Co. *5*
Feist Publications, Inc. v. Rural Telephone
 Service Co. *19*
Feltner v. Columbia Pictures Television, Inc. *184*
Fonovisa, Inc. v. Cherry Auction, Inc. *108*
Frank Music Corp. v. Metro-Goldwyn-Mayer
 Inc. *193*

G
Gilliam v. American Broadcasting Companies,
 Inc. *88*
Goldstein v. California............................ *161*

H
Harper & Row, Publishers, Inc. v. Nation
 Enterprises................................. *120, 164*

I
International News Service v. Associated Press... *170*
Intervest Construction, Inc. v. Canterbury
 Estate Homes, Inc. *49*
IQ Group, Ltd. v. Wiesner Publishing, LLC........ *156*
Itar-Tass Russian News Agency v. Russian
 Kurier, Inc. *185*

J
Jacobsen v. Katzer................................ *144*

K
Kelly v. Arriba Soft Corp. *158*
Kewanee Oil Co. v. Bicron Corp. *162*
Kieselstein-Cord v. Accessories by Pearl, Inc. *40*

L
L. Batlin & Son, Inc. v. Snyder..................... *17*
LaMacchia, United States v. *117*
Lee v. A.R.T. Company *84*
Lewis Galoob Toys, Inc. v. Nintendo of
 America, Inc. *85*
Lexmark International, Inc. v. Static Control
 Components, Inc. *154*
Lilley v. Stout *89*
Lindsay v. The Wrecked and Abandoned
 Vessel R.M.S. Titanic 52 U. *23*
Los Angeles News Service v. Reuters
 Television International, Ltd. *197*
Lotus Development Corporation v. Borland
 International, Inc. *47*

xiii

M MAI Systems Corp. v. Peak Computer, Inc. 4
Mannion v. Coors Brewing Company 12, 67
Martin v. City of Indianapolis 91
Martin Luther King, Jr., Inc., Estate of v.
　　CBS, Inc. 32
Mason v. Montgomery Data, Inc. 22
Matthew Bender & Co. v. West Publishing Co. 56
Mazer v. Stein 39
Meshwerks, Inc. v. Toyota Motor Sales
　　U.S.A., Inc. 10
Metro-Goldwyn-Mayer, Inc. v. American Honda
　　Motor Co. 51
Metro-Goldwyn-Mayer Studios, Inc. v.
　　Grokster, Ltd. 114, 190
Micro Star v. FormGen Inc. 86
Mirage Editions, Inc. v. Albuquerque A.R.T.
　　Company.. 83
Moran, United States v. 116

N Napster, Inc. Copyright Litigation, In re 148
National Basketball Association v.
　　Motorola, Inc. 171
Nelson-Salabes, Inc. v. Morningside Holdings 48
Newton v. Diamond 101
New York Times Company v. Tasini............... 138
Nichols v. Universal Pictures Corp. 63
Núñez v. Caribbean International News Corp.
　　(El Vocero de Puerto Rico).................... 123

P Perfect 10, Inc. v. Amazon.com, Inc. 97, 109, 129
Perfect 10, Inc. v. Visa International
　　Service Association 112
Positive Black Talk Inc. v. Cash Money
　　Records Inc. 202

Q Quality King Distributors, Inc. v. L'anza
　　Research International, Inc. 77

R Random House v. Rosetta Books, LLC............ 141
Reed Elsevier, Inc. v. Muchnick 178

Religious Technology Center v. Netcom On-Line
　　Communication Services, Inc. 106
Roeslin v. District of Columbia...................... 28
Roley v. New World Pictures, Ltd. 180
Roth Greeting Cards v. United Card Co. 21

S Sears, Roebuck & Co. v. Stiffel Co. 160
Sega Enterprises Ltd. v. Accolade, Inc. 127
Selle v. Gibb 61
Sid & Marty Krofft Television Productions, Inc. v.
　　McDonald's Corp. 69
Softel, Inc. v. Dragon Medical and Scientific
　　Communications, Inc. 46
Sony Computer Entertainment, Inc. v.
　　Connectix Corp. 128
Sony Corporation of America v. Universal City
　　Studios, Inc. 131
Steinberg v. Columbia Pictures Industries, Inc. 65
Stewart v. Abend 35
Swirsky v. Carey 71

T Three Boys Music Corp. v. Michael Bolton 60
Titan Sports, Inc. v. Turner Broadcasting
　　Systems, Inc. 52
Ty, Inc. v. GMA Accessories, Inc. 62

U Universal City Studios, Inc. v. Reimerdes..... 150, 192

V Vernor v. Autodesk, Inc. 142
Video Pipeline, Inc. v. Buena Vista Home
　　Entertainment, Inc. (2002)...................... 165
Video Pipeline, Inc. v. Buena Vista Home
　　Entertainment, Inc. (2004)...................... 146

W Warner Bros. Entertainment, Inc. v. RDR Books 80
White v. Samsung Electronics America, Inc. 169
Williams Electronics, Inc. v. Artic
　　International, Inc. 3

Z Zomba Enterprises, Inc. v. Panorama
　　Records, Inc. 198

Note: There are no principal cases in Chapter 1.

CHAPTER 2

Authors, Writings, and Progress

Quick Reference Rules of Law

	PAGE

1. **Fixation.** The fixation requirement of § 101 of the Copyright Act is met where the work is of a sufficiently permanent nature that it may be reproduced or communicated for more than a transitory period. (Williams Electronics, Inc. v. Artic International, Inc.) — 3

2. **Fixation.** Copying of a computer program occurs when the program is transferred to the computer's random access memory (RAM). (MAI Systems Corp. v. Peak Computer, Inc.) — 4

3. **Originality.** To be copyrightable, a work must be original to the author and possess at least some minimal degree of creativity. (Feist Publications, Inc. v. Rural Telephone Service Co.) — 5

4. **Originality.** Photographs evidencing originality and creativity, in features such as selection of costume, pose, and so on, are copyrightable. (Burrow-Giles Lithographic Co. v. Sarony) — 7

5. **Originality.** Chromolithographs are entitled to copyright protection even if designed for advertising purposes. (Bleistein v. Donaldson Lithographing Co.) — 8

6. **Originality.** A "copy" of something in the public domain may itself be copyrighted if the author thereof has contributed something of his own thereto, that is, more than a "trivial" variation. (Alfred Bell & Co. v. Catalda Fine Arts, Inc.) — 9

7. **Originality.** A digital model that merely replicates an object in digital form, without adding any original elements to the object, is not copyrightable. (Meshwerks, Inc. v. Toyota Motor Sales U.S.A., Inc.) — 10

8. **Originality.** A photograph is original, and can therefore be protected by copyright, where the entire image, as a whole, has been orchestrated by the photographer. (Mannion v. Coors Brewing Company) — 12

9. **The "Idea/Expression Distinction."** The protection afforded by a copyright on a book explaining an art or system extends only to the author's unique explanation thereof and does not preclude others from using the system or the forms necessarily incidental to such use. (Baker v. Selden) — 14

10. **The "Idea/Expression Distinction."** Interpretations of historical events are not copyrightable. (A.A. Hoehling v. Universal City Studios, Inc.) — 15

11. **The "Idea/Expression Distinction."** Classification guides are original works of authorship, not records of processes or systems, and are thus entitled to copyright protection. (American Dental Association v. Delta Dental Plans Association) — 16

12. **Derivative Works and Compilations.** A replica of a work not subject to copyright protection must be more than a mere copy to gain copyright protection. (L. Batlin & Son, Inc. v. Snyder) — 17

13. **Derivative Works and Compilations.** Inflatable three-dimensional costumes based on copyrighted cartoon characters are not sufficiently original to be copyrighted as separate derivative works. (Entertainment Research Group, Inc. v. Genesis Creative Group, Inc.) — 18

CHAPTER 2

14. **Derivative Works and Compilations.** A telephone "white pages" directory does not contain the minimal degree of creativity necessary to be original and copyrightable. (Feist Publications, Inc. v. Rural Telephone Service Co.) — 19

15. **Derivative Works and Compilations.** Works should be considered as wholes when determining whether they are original and copyrightable. (Roth Greeting Cards v. United Card Co.) — 21

16. **Derivative Works and Compilations.** Compilations of pictorial information gain originality such as to allow them to be copyrighted if the selection, coordination, and arrangement of the information depicted is sufficiently creative. (Mason v. Montgomery Data, Inc.) — 22

17. **Sole Authorship.** An individual who exercises a high degree of control over a photograph may be considered the "author," even when that individual does not physically shoot the photograph. (Lindsay v. The Wrecked and Abandoned Vessel R.M.S. Titanic 52 U.) — 23

18. **Joint Authorship.** A product is a "joint work" only if the collaborators can be considered as authors. (Erickson v. Trinity Theatre, Inc.) — 24

19. **Who Is an Author?: Joint Authorship.** A person claiming to be a co-owner of a joint work must prove that both parties intended the work to be a joint work. (Aalmuhammed v. Lee) — 25

20. **Works Made for Hire.** Under common-law agency principles, one who creates an artwork at the behest of another retains the copyright, unless he was an employee of that other. (Community for Creative Non-Violence v. Reid) — 26

21. **Works Made for Hire.** Although no one factor is dispositive, the lack of benefits extended to an individual or the failure to pay taxes on an individual's behalf is indicative of independent contractor status. (Aymes v. Bonelli) — 27

22. **Works Made for Hire.** A work is not "made for hire" where an employee creates the work for use in connection with his job, but does so on his time and at his own expense; the work is not in the line of work the employee has been hired to do; the employee is not compensated for the work; and the employee's motivation in creating the work is to show that the work can be created and to create job opportunities for himself. (Roeslin v. District of Columbia) — 28

Williams Electronics, Inc. v. Artic International, Inc.

Video game manufacturer (P) v. Competitor (D)

685 F.2d 870 (3d Cir. 1982).

NATURE OF CASE: Appeal from final injunction and order restraining copyright infringement.

FACT SUMMARY: Williams Electronics, Inc. (P) brought an action to enforce three copyright registrations relating to its Defender video game, covering the computer program, audiovisual effects displayed during the game's "attract mode," and audiovisual effects displayed during the game's "play mode."

RULE OF LAW
The fixation requirement of § 101 of the Copyright Act is met where the work is of a sufficiently permanent nature that it may be reproduced or communicated for more than a transitory period.

FACTS: Williams Electronics, Inc. (Williams) (P) had three copyright registrations covering its Defender video game. One covered the computer program itself and the other two covered the audiovisual effects displayed during the game's "attract mode" and "play mode," respectively. Artic International, Inc. (Artic) (D), a competitor of Williams (P), sold a video game incorporating a computer program almost identical to that of Defender. The district court found that Artic (D) infringed Williams' (P) copyrights on the Defender game.

ISSUE: Will copyright protection extend to images in video games?

HOLDING AND DECISION: (Sloviter, J.) Yes. Features in a video game that repeat themselves over and over are sufficiently permanent to be considered more than transitory. This is true even though player interaction with the machine during a game causes the audiovisual presentation to change. These player-instigated changes take place within a context of repeating audiovisual elements. Affirmed.

ANALYSIS

Under § 101 a work is "fixed" if it is "sufficiently permanent or stable to permit it to be perceived, reproduced or otherwise communicated for a period of more than transitory duration."

Quicknotes

COPYRIGHT INFRINGEMENT A violation of one of the exclusive rights granted to an artist pursuant to Article I, section 8, clause 8 of the United States Constitution over the reproduction, display, performance, distribution, and adaptation of his work for a period prescribed by statute.

INJUNCTION A court order requiring a person to do or prohibiting that person from doing a specific act.

MAI Systems Corp. v. Peak Computer, Inc.

Software company (P) v. Technicians (D)

991 F.2d 511 (9th Cir. 1993), cert. dismissed, 510 U.S. 1033 (1994).

NATURE OF CASE: Appeal of injunction against copyright infringement and unfair competition with computer systems manufacturer.

FACT SUMMARY: Peak Computer, Inc. (D) used MAI Systems Corp. (P) operating system software to maintain its customers' computers.

RULE OF LAW
Copying of a computer program occurs when the program is transferred to the computer's random access memory (RAM).

FACTS: MAI Systems Corp. (MAI) (P) licenses software to its customers. The terms of the license allow customers to use the software for internal information processing, but the license does not extend to the use or copying of the software by third parties. Peak Computer, Inc. (Peak) (D) maintains computer systems for its customers and uses MAI's (P) operating software to the extent necessary for repairs and maintenance. The services provided by Peak (D) to its customers require it to turn on the computer, during which time MAI's (P) operating system is automatically loaded onto the computer's RAM. The Peak (D) technicians also run MAI's (P) operating system to view error logs and diagnose problems. The district court granted summary judgment in favor of MAI (P) and found that Peak (D) violated MAI's (P) copyright in the software by running MAI (P) software on Peak (D) customers' computers.

ISSUE: Does the loading of copyrighted computer software onto a computer's RAM create a copy that is sufficiently "fixed" under the Copyright Act?

HOLDING AND DECISION: (Brunetti, J.) Yes. The loading of copyrighted software onto a computer's RAM creates a copy under the Copyright Act. Here, because the copy of the software loaded into the computer's RAM could be "perceived, reproduced, or otherwise communicated," a copy was created in violation of MAI's (P) copyright. Affirmed.

ANALYSIS

As noted by Justice Brunetti, it is generally accepted that loading software into a computer creates a copy under the Copyright Act.

Quicknotes

COPYRIGHT ACT Copyright Act of 1976 extends copyright protection to "original works of authorship fixed in any tangible medium of expression, now known or later developed, from which they can be perceived, reproduced, or otherwise communicated, either directly or with the aid of a machine or device." 17 U.S.C. § 102.

COPYRIGHT INFRINGEMENT A violation of one of the exclusive rights granted to an artist pursuant to Article I, section 8, clause 8 of the United States Constitution over the reproduction, display, performance, distribution, and adaptation of his work for a period prescribed by statute.

INJUNCTION A court order requiring a person to do or prohibiting that person from doing a specific act.

SUMMARY JUDGMENT Judgment rendered by a court in response to a motion by one of the parties, claiming that the lack of a question of material fact in respect to an issue warrants disposition of the issue without consideration by the jury.

Feist Publications, Inc. v. Rural Telephone Service Co.

Public telephone utility (P) v. Publisher of telephone directories (D)

499 U.S. 340 (1991).

NATURE OF CASE: Appeal from grant of summary judgment to plaintiff in suit for copyright infringement.

FACT SUMMARY: After Feist Publications, Inc. (Feist) (D) took 1,309 listings from Rural Telephone Service Co.'s (Rural) (P) white pages when compiling Feist's (D) own white pages, Rural (P) filed suit for copyright infringement.

RULE OF LAW
To be copyrightable, a work must be original to the author and possess at least some minimal degree of creativity.

FACTS: As a certified telephone service utility provided in northwest Kansas, Rural Telephone Service Co. (Rural) (P) published a typical telephone directory as a condition of its monopoly franchise. The white pages alphabetically listed the names, towns, and telephone numbers of Rural's (P) subscribers. Feist Publications, Inc. (Feist) (D) was a publishing company specializing in area-wide telephone directories. The Feist (D) published a directory that covered 11 different telephone service areas in 15 counties and contained 46,878 white pages listings, compared to Rural's (P) approximately 7,700 listings. Feist (D) approached the 11 northwest Kansas telephone companies and offered to pay for the right to use their respective white pages listings. When only Rural (P) refused to license its listings, Feist (D) used them without Rural's (P) consent. A typical Feist (D) listing included each individual's street address, while most of Rural's (P) did not. Of the 46,878 listings in Feist's (D) 1983 directory, 1,309 of those listings were identical to listings in Rural's (P) white pages. Rural (P) sued for copyright infringement in the district court, arguing that Feist (D), in compiling its own directory, could not use the information contained in Rural's (P) white pages. The district court granted summary judgment to Rural (P), and the court of appeals affirmed. The Supreme Court granted certiorari.

ISSUE: To be copyrightable, must a work be original to the author and possess at least some minimal degree of creativity?

HOLDING AND DECISION: (O'Connor, J.) Yes. To be copyrightable, a work must be original to the author and possess at least some minimal degree of creativity. Here, two well-established propositions—that facts are not copyrightable and that compilations of facts generally are—collide. To resolve the tension between these positions requires an understanding of why facts are not copyrightable. Facts, which do not originate with authors, cannot be said to possess originality, which is a constitutional sine qua non of copyrightability. To be original, a work must be created (rather than copied) by the author and must contain a minimal degree of creativity. The threshold of creativity is extremely low. The disparate treatment of facts and compilations under copyright law rests on the distinction between creation and discovery; while one may by the first to discover a fact and report the discovery, the discoverer has not created the fact. On the other hand, factual compilations may contain the requisite originality because, usually, the compilation author exercises some minimal degree of creativity in assembling the factual data. However, not every compilation contains even this minimal level of creativity, since not every selection, coordination, or arrangement of facts will be done in "such a way" as to be thought of as original. Even if the method of selection or arrangement is not novel, it will pass muster if the author has made it independently, without copying that selection or arrangement from another work. Nevertheless, there is a narrow category of works in which the creative spark is utterly lacking or so trivial as to be virtually nonexistent. Works that fall into that category do not merit copyright protection. [Reversed.]

ANALYSIS

In the words of the Court, copyright assures authors the right to their original expression, but encourages others to build freely upon the ideas and information conveyed by a work. This principle, known as the idea/expression or fact/expression dichotomy, applies to all works of authorship. As applied to a factual compilation, assuming the absence of original written expression, only the compiler's selection and arrangement may be protected; the raw facts may be copied at will. This is the means by which copyright advances the progress of science and art by encouraging creativity with the reward of exclusive rights for the original creation.

Quicknotes

COPYRIGHT Refers to the exclusive rights granted to an artist pursuant to Article I, section 8, clause 8 of the United States Constitution over the reproduction, display, performance, distribution, and adaptation of his work for a period prescribed by statute.

COPYRIGHT INFRINGEMENT A violation of one of the exclusive rights granted to an artist pursuant to Article I, section

Continued on next page.

8, clause 8 of the United States Constitution over the reproduction, display, performance, distribution, and adaptation of his work for a period prescribed by statute.

SUMMARY JUDGMENT Judgment rendered by a court in response to a motion by one of the parties, claiming that the lack of a question of material fact in respect to an issue warrants disposition of the issue without consideration by the jury.

Burrow-Giles Lithographic Co. v. Sarony

Photographer (P) v. Lithographic Company (D)

111 U.S. 53 (1884).

NATURE OF CASE: Action for damages for copyright infringement.

FACT SUMMARY: Burrow-Giles Lithographic Co. (D) sold copies it made of a posed photograph of Oscar Wilde taken by Sarony (P).

RULE OF LAW
Photographs evidencing originality and creativity, in features such as selection of costume, pose, and so on, are copyrightable.

FACTS: A lithographic company, Burrow-Giles Lithographic Co. (Burrow-Giles) (D), sold copies of a posed photograph of Oscar Wilde on which Sarony (P), the original photographer, had secured a copyright. Sarony (P) sued for copyright infringement and was awarded damages. On appeal, Burrow-Giles (D) argued that copyrights cannot be granted for photographs because they do not fall within the constitutional power given Congress to grant protection to "authors and inventors" for their "respective writings and discoveries."

ISSUE: Are photographs copyrightable?

HOLDING AND DECISION: (Miller, J.) Yes. Photographs that reflect originality and creativity in the photographer's selection of features such as costumes, pose, lighting, expression, and so on, can be copyrighted as the "writing or production" of an "author." As is evidenced by the decisions allowing the copyrighting of charts, maps, engravings, cuts, etchings, and so on, the words "author" and "writing or production" are used in their broad sense in that part of the Constitution dispensing the power to grant copyrights. An "author" is, then, "he to whom anything owes its origin," and a "writing" is any literary production of such an originator. A photograph that evidences the photographer's originality and creativity is certainly well within such terms. Here, the photograph obviously possessed those characteristics and was copyrightable. Affirmed.

ANALYSIS

Artistic input is no longer a consideration in granting protection to photographs under English law. In this country, it is still considered a basis for copyrightability of photographs, but courts have been willing to find such input in the slightest things, such as one's choice of the type of camera or film to use.

Quicknotes

COPYRIGHT Refers to the exclusive rights granted to an artist pursuant to Article I, section 8, clause 8 of the United States Constitution over the reproduction, display, performance, distribution, and adaptation of his work for a period prescribed by statute.

COPYRIGHT INFRINGEMENT A violation of one of the exclusive rights granted to an artist pursuant to Article I, section 8, clause 8 of the United States Constitution over the reproduction, display, performance, distribution, and adaptation of his work for a period prescribed by statute.

Bleistein v. Donaldson Lithographing Co.

Advertising company (P) v. Lithographic company (D)

188 U.S. 239 (1903).

NATURE OF CASE: Appeal from an affirmation of a decision for a direct verdict in a suit to recover penalties for copyright infringement.

FACT SUMMARY: Donaldson Lithographing Co. (D) copied in reduced form three chromolithographs that Bleistein (P) had prepared to advertise Wallace's circus.

RULE OF LAW
Chromolithographs are entitled to copyright protection even if designed for advertising purposes.

FACTS: In order to advertise his circus, Wallace hired Bleistein (P), who produced three chromolithographs depicting Wallace in the corner, and some of the circus acts and including lettering announcing the act depicted. When Donaldson Lithographing Co. (Donaldson) (D) subsequently produced reduced copies of these three advertisement chromolithographs, Bleistein (P) sued to recover penalties for copyright infringement. Arguing that chromolithographs were not entitled to protection under federal statutes allowing a copyright to the "author, designer, or proprietor . . . of any engraving, cut, print . . . (or) chrome," Donaldson (D) obtained a directed verdict that was upheld on appeal. On this further appeal, Donaldson (D) again asserted that chromolithographs do not meet the criteria for copyright protection, because a provision in the act of 1874 states that the words "engraving," "cut," and "print" apply only to "pictorial illustrations or works connected with the fine arts."

ISSUE: Are chromolithographs, designed for advertising purposes, barred from copyright protection?

HOLDING AND DECISION: (Holmes, J.) No. The fact that a chromolithograph was produced as an advertisement vehicle does not alter the fact that such "pictorial illustrations" are copyrightable. Even if the Court were to hold that the act of 1874 limits the words "engraving," "cut," and "print" to pictorial illustrations connected with the fine arts or to works connected with the fine arts (instead of viewing the qualifying phrase "connected with the fine arts" as applicable only to the word "works"), this decision would not change. The antithesis to "illustrations or works connected with the fine arts" is not works of little merit or humble degree or illustrations addressed to the less educated classes; it is "print or labels designed to be used for any other articles of manufacture." To hold otherwise would be to set up the judiciary as an arbiter of artistic quality. Some works of genius would be sure to miss appreciation because they spoke in a new language not yet appreciated. The fact that a picture might have broad appeal to a public less educated than the judge should not be a bar to protecting the work, whose public appreciation makes its value obvious. In this case, the very fact that there was a desire to reproduce the chromolithographs outside the advertisement framework shows that they had their worth. As protection should have been afforded, the judgment below is reversed.

ANALYSIS

Under previous decisions, the chromolithographs would have been copyrightable had they been designed for no purpose beyond artistic expression. Whatever artistic value was inherent then is hardly changed by the subsequent use.

Quicknotes

COPYRIGHT Refers to the exclusive rights granted to an artist pursuant to Article I, section 8, clause 8 of the United States Constitution over the reproduction, display, performance, distribution, and adaptation of his work for a period prescribed by statute.

COPYRIGHT INFRINGEMENT A violation of one of the exclusive rights granted to an artist pursuant to Article I, section 8, clause 8 of the United States Constitution over the reproduction, display, performance, distribution, and adaptation of his work for a period prescribed by statute.

Alfred Bell & Co. v. Catalda Fine Arts, Inc.

Fine art engraver (P) v. Lithographic company (D)

191 F.2d 99 (2d Cir. 1951).

NATURE OF CASE: Action for damages for copyright infringement.

FACT SUMMARY: Alfred Bell & Co. (P) produced mezzotint engravings of paintings by the old masters, which Catalda Fine Arts, Inc. (D) then copied by lithographic process and sold.

RULE OF LAW
A "copy" of something in the public domain may itself be copyrighted if the author thereof has contributed something of his own thereto, that is, more than a "trivial" variation.

FACTS: Alfred Bell & Co. (Bell) (P) had produced mezzotint engravings of paintings by the old masters, which resulted in fairly accurate replicas thereof. The process involved required the engraver to exercise considerable personal judgment, conception, and execution in fashioning the plates to resemble the original painting being copied. Hence, no two engravers ever produce identical "copies" of a subject painting, and the original itself is never precisely copied in all its details. Catalda Fine Arts, Inc. (Catalda) (D) used a lithographic process to produce copies of Bell's (P) engravings. On appeal from a decision finding that this constituted copyright infringement, Catalda (D) argued that the mezzotint engravings were uncopyrightable because, as mere copies of the original paintings of the old masters, they lacked the requisite originality.

ISSUE: If one who "copies" a work in the public domain contributes something of his own to the "copy," something more than a "mere trivial" variation, can the "copy" be copyrighted?

HOLDING AND DECISION: (Frank, J.) Yes. A "copy" of something in the public domain may itself be copyrighted if the author thereof contributes something of his own to the "copy," that is, something more than a "mere trivial" variation. Copyrightability requires that an author contribute to the work something originating with him, but there is no requirement that it be novel. That is why one who independently creates what turns out to be an exact duplicate of the painting or work of another could nonetheless receive a copyright on his own work. Here, Bell's (P) mezzotint engravings made more than trivial personal contributions to his "copies" of old masters' paintings. The fact that such personal input may have been unintended or an inadvertent byproduct of the copying process used is inconsequential. The mezzotints were copyrightable, and the copying thereof constituted infringement. Affirmed.

ANALYSIS
The courts still adhere to the view that novelty is no prerequisite to copyrightability. Many, including Justice Douglas, have urged such a requirement, feeling that those thereby left without copyright protection could turn to suits based on unfair competition or conversion.

Quicknotes

CONVERSION The act of depriving an owner of his property without permission or justification.

COPYRIGHT Refers to the exclusive rights granted to an artist pursuant to Article I, section 8, clause 8 of the United States Constitution over the reproduction, display, performance, distribution, and adaptation of his work for a period prescribed by statute.

COPYRIGHT INFRINGEMENT A violation of one of the exclusive rights granted to an artist pursuant to Article I, section 8, clause 8 of the United States Constitution over the reproduction, display, performance, distribution, and adaptation of his work for a period prescribed by statute.

PUBLIC DOMAIN Works that are not protected by copyright and are free for the public to utilize.

UNFAIR COMPETITION Any dishonest or fraudulent rivalry in trade and commerce, particularly imitation and counterfeiting.

Meshwerks, Inc. v. Toyota Motor Sales U.S.A., Inc.

Digital modeler (P) v. Automobile manufacturer (D)

528 F.3d 1258 (10th Cir. 2008).

NATURE OF CASE: Appeal from summary judgment in action for copyright infringement.

FACT SUMMARY: Meshwerks, Inc. (P) contended that Toyota Motor Sales U.S.A., Inc. (Toyota) (D) and others infringed Meshwerks' (P) copyright in digitized wire-mesh models of cars manufactured by Toyota (D) that Meshwerks (P) had prepared for a Toyota (D) ad campaign.

RULE OF LAW
A digital model that merely replicates an object in digital form, without adding any original elements to the object, is not copyrightable.

FACTS: Toyota Motor Sales U.S.A., Inc. (Toyota) (D), an automobile manufacturer, had an annual ad campaign, and Meshwerks, Inc. (P) was hired as a subcontractor to create digital models of Toyota's (D) vehicles. To that end, Meshwerks (P) collected data points for each model, mapped those data points onto a computerized grid, and used modeling software to create an unadorned, two-dimensional digital wire frame of each vehicle that appeared three-dimensional. Meshwerks' (P) employees then had to manually fine-tune, or "sculpt" the models based on photographs to more accurately render details, such as tires and logos. However, the wire-frame models lacked color, shading, and other details, which were later added by a different company. Meshwerks (P) subsequently brought a copyright infringement suit against Toyota (D) and others, claiming that it had contracted for only a single use of its models and that the digital models created from Meshwerks' (P) wire-frames were not permitted by the contract to be used in other advertisements. The district court granted summary judgment to Toyota (D) and other defendants, and the court of appeals granted review.

ISSUE: Is a digital model that merely replicates an object in digital form, without adding any original elements to the object, copyrightable?

HOLDING AND DECISION: (Gorsuch, J.) No. A digital model that merely replicates an object in digital form, without adding any original elements to the object, is not copyrightable. Based on received copyright doctrine, developed in the context of photographs, ideas and facts cannot be copyrighted, whereas the expression of those ideas and facts can—where there has been an incremental contribution by the author. In the case of photographs—which the digital wire-mesh models here were intended to substitute—such contribution consists of elements such as pose, lighting, angle, etc. Here, Meshwerks' (P) models are merely very good copies of Toyota (D) vehicles. They do not contain the elements that represent an author's incremental contributions to an object, and an accurate portrayal of an unadorned object cannot be copyrighted. In other words, an unadorned object that is not attributable to an author's creativity must be filtered out of the copyright analysis to see what copyrightable elements remain. Because Meshwerks' (P) digital wire-frame models depict only those unadorned vehicles, having stripped away all lighting, angle, perspective, and "other ingredients" associated with an original expression, no copyrightable matter is left. This conclusion is confirmed by the fact that Meshwerks (P) was hired expressly to create unadorned models, which others would adorn and imbue with creative elements, as well as determine how the models would be used. While Meshwerks' (P) renderings were skillful and labor-intensive, they are not entitled to copyright, which only looks at the final product and not the amount of effort necessary to get there. Because there is no doubt that Meshwerks (P) intended to merely copy Toyota's (D) vehicles, and because the originality requirement tests the putative author's state of mind, the models, which conformed to Meshwerks' (P) intent, are not original, and, therefore, not entitled to copyright protection. Affirmed.

ANALYSIS

The court emphasized that its opinion left open the possibility that, like photography, digital modeling could produce copyrightable works. Just as photographs can be, but are not per se, copyrightable, the same holds true for digital models, and there is little dispute that digital models can contain copyrightable features, whether by virtue of unique shading, lighting, angle, background scene, or other choices. The problem for Meshwerks (P) in this particular case was simply that the uncontested facts revealed that it was not hired to, and did not, add such features to its models.

Quicknotes

COPYRIGHT Refers to the exclusive rights granted to an artist pursuant to Article I, Section 8, clause 8 of the United States Constitution over the reproduction, display, performance, distribution, and adaptation of his work for a period prescribed by statute.

COPYRIGHT INFRINGEMENT A violation of one of the exclusive rights granted to an artist pursuant to Article I, Section

Continued on next page.

8, clause 8 of the United States Constitution over the reproduction, display, performance, distribution, and adaptation of his work for a period prescribed by statute.

SUMMARY JUDGMENT Judgment rendered by a court in response to a motion made by one of the parties, claiming that the lack of a question of material fact in respect to an issue warrants disposition of the issue without consideration by the jury.

Mannion v. Coors Brewing Company

Copyright holder (P) v. Alleged infringer (D)

377 F. Supp. 2d 444 (S.D.N.Y. 2006).

NATURE OF CASE: Cross motions for summary judgment in copyright infringement action.

FACT SUMMARY: Mannion (P) contended that a photograph used by Coors Brewing Company (Coors) (D) in billboard advertisements for Coors Light beer violated his copyright in a photograph of the basketball star Kevin Garnett because the two images were substantially similar.

RULE OF LAW
A photograph is original, and can therefore be protected by copyright, where the entire image, as a whole, has been orchestrated by the photographer.

FACTS: Mannion (P), a freelance photographer, took a photograph of the basketball star Kevin Garnett (Garnett Photograph) that was a three-quarter-length portrait of Garnett against a backdrop of clouds with some blue sky shining through. The view is up and across the right side of Garnett's torso, so that he appears to be towering above earth. He wears a white T-shirt, white athletic pants, a black close-fitting cap, and a large amount of platinum, gold, and diamond jewelry. His head is cocked, his eyes are closed, and his heavily-veined hands, nearly all of which are visible, rest over his lower abdomen, with the thumbs hooked on the waistband of the trousers. The light is from the viewer's left, so that Garnett's right shoulder is the brightest area of the photograph and his hands cast slight shadows on his trousers. Most of Garnett's left arm is cut off. Carol H. Williams Advertising (CHWA) (D) began developing ideas for outdoor billboards that would advertise Coors Light beer to young black men in urban areas. One of CHWA's (D) "comp boards"—a "comp board" is an image created by an advertising company to convey a proposed design—used a manipulated version of the Garnett Photograph and superimposed on it the words "Iced Out" ("ice" being slang for diamonds) and a picture of a can of Coors Light beer (the "Iced Out Comp Board"). CHWA (D) obtained authorization from Mannion's (P) representative to use the Garnett Photograph for this purpose. The Coors Brewing Company (Coors) (D) billboard, based on the Iced Out Comp Board, depicted in black-and-white the torso of a muscular black man, albeit a model other than Garnett, shot against a cloudy backdrop. The pose was similar to that in the Garnett Photograph, and the view also was up and across the left side of the torso. The model in the billboard photograph also wore a white T-shirt and white athletic pants. The model's jewelry was prominently depicted, and the light came from the viewer's right, so that the left shoulder was the brightest part of the photograph, and the right arm and hand cast slight shadows on the trousers. Mannion (P) sued Coors (D) and CHWA (D) for infringement. Each party moved for summary judgment.

ISSUE: Is a photograph original, and can it therefore be protected by copyright, where the entire image, as a whole, has been orchestrated by the photographer?

HOLDING AND DECISION: (Kaplan, J.) Yes. A photograph is original, and can therefore be protected by copyright, where the entire image, as a whole, has been orchestrated by the photographer. The first issue is in what respects the Garnett Photograph is protectible by copyright, i.e., in what respects is it original. There are three respects in which a photograph may be original. First, there is rendition, which does not depend on the creation of the scene or object to be photographed, but instead involves such specialties as angle of shot, light and shade, exposure, effects achieved by means of filters, developing techniques, etc. In this instance, copyright protects not what is depicted, but how it is depicted. Second, there is timing, where a photograph is created when the author is at the right place at the right time to capture a specific image. In practice, originality in timing gives rise to the same type of protection as originality in the rendition. In each case, the image that exhibits the originality, but not the underlying subject, qualifies for copyright protection. Third, a photograph may be original to the extent that the photographer created "the scene or subject to be photographed." Insofar as a photograph is original in the rendition or timing, copyright protects the image but does not prevent others from photographing the same object or scene. By contrast, to the extent that a photograph is original in the creation of the subject, copyright extends also to that subject. Thus, an artist who arranges and then photographs a scene often will have the right to prevent others from duplicating that scene in a photograph or other medium. Applying these principles here, there is no doubt that the Garnett Photograph is an original work. The photograph does not result from slavishly copying another work and therefore is original in the rendition. Mannion's (P) relatively unusual angle and distinctive lighting strengthen that aspect of the photograph's originality. His composition—posing man against sky—evidences originality in the creation of the subject. Furthermore, he instructed Garnett to wear simple and plain clothing and as much jewelry as possible, and "to look 'chilled out.'" His orchestration of the scene contributes additional originality in the creation of the subject. Although, as Coors/CHWA (D) correctly observe, there are limits to the photograph's originality—so that others may photograph Garnett or a man posed against a cloudy sky—the originality

Continued on next page.

of the photograph extends beyond the individual clothing, jewelry, and pose viewed in isolation. It is the entire image, depicting man, sky, clothing, and jewelry in a particular arrangement, that is at issue here, not its individual components. [Summary judgment motions denied.]

ANALYSIS

The court's analysis may be limited to film photography and not digital photography, where through ready manipulation any photographer may easily arrange or orchestrate a subject, thus putting into issue the degree of originality brought by the photographer to the image.

Quicknotes

COPYRIGHT INFRINGEMENT A violation of one of the exclusive rights granted to an artist pursuant to Article I, section 8, clause 8 of the United States Constitution over the reproduction, display, performance, distribution, and adaptation of his work for a period prescribed by statute.

SUMMARY JUDGMENT Judgment rendered by a court in response to a motion made by one of the parties, claiming that the lack of a question of material fact in respect to an issue warrants disposition of the issue without consideration by the jury.

Baker v. Selden

Author of bookkeeping system (P) v. Printer of bookkeeping forms (D)

101 U.S. 99 (1879).

NATURE OF CASE: Appeal from award of damages for copyright infringement.

FACT SUMMARY: Baker (D) sold forms similar to those Selden (P) had in his copyrighted book setting forth his system of bookkeeping.

RULE OF LAW
The protection afforded by a copyright on a book explaining an art or system extends only to the author's unique explanation thereof and does not preclude others from using the system or the forms necessarily incidental to such use.

FACTS: Selden (P) copyrighted a book in which he used an introductory essay to explain his system of bookkeeping after which he included the forms needed to put the system to use. He had arranged the columns and headings so that the entire operation of a day, week, or month was on a single page or on two facing pages. Baker (D) subsequently began selling forms with differently arranged columns and headings that achieved the same result. He argued that forms were noncopyrightable.

ISSUE: Does a copyright on a book explaining an art or system preclude others from using the system or the forms incidental to such use?

HOLDING AND DECISION: (Bradley, J.) No. A copyright on a book explaining an art or system protects only the author's unique explanation thereof and does not preclude others from using the system or the forms incidental to such use. To find that a copyright protected against use of the system itself or the forms necessary to such use would be to grant patent-type protection without requiring a showing of novelty. Copyright is based on originality, not novelty, and protects the explanation and not the use of the system explained. Here, therefore, the copyright Selden (P) obtained could not give him the exclusive right to use the bookkeeping system or the forms necessary to such use.

ANALYSIS

Many have interpreted this case as allowing copying for use as opposed to copying for explanatory purposes. However, in applying this rule, some courts have gone a bit far and have allowed something to pass as copying for use when there were other arrangements of words available that could just as easily have been used to convey the noncopyrightable system or art. This has engendered much criticism of this interpretation of the rule of this case.

Quicknotes

COPYRIGHT Refers to the exclusive rights granted to an artist pursuant to Article I, section 8, clause 8 of the United States Constitution over the reproduction, display, performance, distribution, and adaptation of his work for a period prescribed by statute.

COPYRIGHT INFRINGEMENT A violation of one of the exclusive rights granted to an artist pursuant to Article I, section 8, clause 8 of the United States Constitution over the reproduction, display, performance, distribution, and adaptation of his work for a period prescribed by statute.

PATENT A limited monopoly conferred on the invention or discovery of any new or useful machine or process that is novel and nonobvious.

A.A. Hoehling v. Universal City Studios, Inc.

Book author (P) v. Motion picture studio (D)

618 F.2d 972 (2d Cir.), cert. denied, 449 U.S. 841 (1980).

NATURE OF CASE: Appeal from summary judgment in favor of alleged copyright infringer.

FACT SUMMARY: A.A. Hoehling (P) sued a competing author and motion picture studio for copyright infringement claiming they copied the plot of his book.

RULE OF LAW
Interpretations of historical events are not copyrightable.

FACTS: A.A. Hoehling (P) wrote a book about the destruction of the Hindenburg, advancing as the primary theory of the book the idea that sabotage caused the disaster and that a rigger on the Hindenburg, Eric Spehl, was most likely the saboteur responsible. Ten years after Hoehling's (P) book was published, another author, Michael MacDonald Mooney (D), published a book advancing the same theory. The rights to Mooney's (D) book were sold to Universal City Studios (D). Hoehling (P) sued for copyright infringement, claiming Mooney (D) copied the plot of his book. The district court granted summary judgment in favor of the defendants.

ISSUE: Are interpretations of historical events copyrightable?

HOLDING AND DECISION: (Kaufman, J.) No. Neither factual information nor interpretations of it can be subject to copyright. Here, Hoehling's (P) theory was based on interpretation of historical facts, and such facts are not protected by copyright. Affirmed.

the lack of a question of material fact in respect to an issue warrants disposition of the issue without consideration by the jury.

ANALYSIS

The court granted wide latitude to works based on historical subjects, including the selection and order of facts and the use of interpretations and stock narrative devices, suggesting that only works explicitly duplicating prior works will infringe.

Quicknotes

COPYRIGHT INFRINGEMENT A violation of one of the exclusive rights granted to an artist pursuant to Article I, section 8, clause 8 of the United States Constitution over the reproduction, display, performance, distribution, and adaptation of his work for a period prescribed by statute.

SUMMARY JUDGMENT Judgment rendered by a court in response to a motion by one of the parties, claiming that

American Dental Association v. Delta Dental Plans Association

Author of taxonomy of dental procedures (P) v. Alleged infringer (D)

126 F.3d 977 (7th Cir. 1997).

NATURE OF CASE: Appeal from order finding a taxonomy was not copyrightable.

FACT SUMMARY: American Dental Association sought enforcement of copyright on a catalog of dental procedures.

RULE OF LAW
Classification guides are original works of authorship, not records of processes or systems, and are thus entitled to copyright protection.

FACTS: The American Dental Association (ADA) (P) created the *Code on Dental Procedures and Nomenclatures*. The code classifies different dental procedures into groups and assigns each procedure a code number; brief and long descriptions are attached to each. Delta Dental Plans Association (D) subsequently published a work entitled *Universal Coding and Nomenclature*, using most of the same numbers and descriptions as are in the ADA's (P) code. The ADA (P) brought action to enforce its copyright in the code. The district court held that the code was not copyrightable. The ADA (P) appealed.

ISSUE: Is a classification guide copyrightable?

HOLDING AND DECISION: (Easterbrook, J.) Yes. Classifications require creativity and are original literary works that may be copyrighted. The level of originality required to make a work copyrightable is low and is met here. The ADA (P) could have classified the dental procedures in many ways, i.e., according to complexity, type of tools used, parts of the mouth involved, and so on. The multiplicity of possible choices renders the ultimate selection among them sufficiently creative and original. The long descriptions, short descriptions, and numbers assigned by the ADA (P) are all results of creative endeavor, making the whole an original work of authorship. Reversed.

ANALYSIS

Courts have held that other types of taxonomies are subject to copyright protection, including blueprints, car repair instruction manuals, used car value guides, dictionaries, encyclopedias, maps, architectural plans, and computer programs.

Quicknotes

COPYRIGHT Refers to the exclusive rights granted to an artist pursuant to Article I, section 8, clause 8 of the United States Constitution over the reproduction, display, performance, distribution, and adaptation of his work for a period prescribed by statute.

L. Batlin & Son, Inc. v. Snyder

Importer of mechanical bank (P) v. Copyright holder in plastic bank (D)

536 F.2d 486 (2d Cir.) (en banc), *cert. denied*, 429 U.S. 857 (1976).

NATURE OF CASE: Appeal of grant of preliminary injunction restraining the enforcement of a copyright.

FACT SUMMARY: An importer of novelty Uncle Sam mechanical banks (P) filed suit against the holder of a copyright on plastic Uncle Sam banks (D).

RULE OF LAW
A replica of a work not subject to copyright protection must be more than a mere copy to gain copyright protection.

FACTS: Snyder (D) obtained a patent on a plastic Uncle Sam bank that was a replica of an antique cast iron model in the public domain. The plastic bank was shorter than the cast iron original, the base of the bank was shortened, and the shapes of a carpet bag and an umbrella on the bank were changed for functional purposes. L. Batlin & Son, Inc. (Batlin) (P) also produced a replica of the antique bank, making other changes and producing it in cast iron. Batlin (P) commenced suit to enjoin the enforcement of Snyder's (D) copyright after the U.S. Customs Service refused entry to a shipment of Batlin's (P) banks.

ISSUE: Does copyright protection extend to a replica of a work of art in the public domain, where the replica makes only minuscule variations from the original?

HOLDING AND DECISION: (Oakes, J.) No. Although the test for originality is a low one, a replica must be more than a mere copy to gain copyright protection. Some degree of skill must be demonstrated to make the reproduction copyrightable. Here, the plastic model made only subtle variations that were not sufficient for copyright protection. Affirmed.

DISSENT: (Meskill, J.) Even inadvertent variations to a work in the public domain can form the basis of a valid copyright. Courts should not dwell on the purpose for such changes, be they aesthetic or functional.

ANALYSIS

Originality in a reproduction will be found where the reproduction is created by a skilled artist, where such reproduction took many hours to create, and where the reproduction conveys a public benefit.

Quicknotes

COPYRIGHT Refers to the exclusive rights granted to an artist pursuant to Article I, section 8, clause 8 of the United States Constitution over the reproduction, display, performance, distribution, and adaptation of his work for a period prescribed by statute.

PRELIMINARY INJUNCTION An order issued by the court at the commencement of an action, requiring a party to refrain from conducting a specified activity that is the subject of the controversy, until the matter is determined.

Entertainment Research Group, Inc. v. Genesis Creative Group, Inc.

Costume maker (P) v. Competitor (D)

122 F.3d 1211 (9th Cir. 1997), cert. denied, 523 U.S. 1021 (1998).

NATURE OF CASE: Appeal of summary judgment in favor of alleged copyright infringer.

FACT SUMMARY: Entertainment Research Group, Inc. (ERG) (P) sued Genesis Creative Group, Inc. (Genesis) (D) for copyright infringement. Genesis (D) marketed and sold costumes created by ERG (P) as well as costumes created by an ERG (P) competitor.

RULE OF LAW
Inflatable three-dimensional costumes based on copyrighted cartoon characters are not sufficiently original to be copyrighted as separate derivative works.

FACTS: Entertainment Research Group, Inc. (ERG) (P) designs and manufactures inflatable costumes that are purchased by third parties to promote their products, i.e., an inflatable Pillsbury Dough Boy or Toucan Sam. ERG (P) and Genesis Creative Group, Inc. (Genesis) (D) entered into an agreement to market ERG's (P) costumes. Subsequently, Genesis (D) also entered into agreement to distribute inflatable costumes produced by an ERG (P) competitor. ERG (P) sued for copyright infringement. The district court granted summary judgment in favor of Genesis (D) on the copyright claim.

ISSUE: Are inflatable costumes depicting copyrighted characters sufficiently original to be extended copyright protection?

HOLDING AND DECISION: (Rea, J.) No. When considering the originality of costumes based on copyrighted cartoons, any differences based on functionality or mechanics should not be considered. Any original aspects of a derivative work should be more than trivial and must not affect the scope of any copyright protection in the existing material. Here, any differences in the derivative work, i.e., proportions, were driven by functional considerations and did not render the inflatable costumes original. Affirmed.

ANALYSIS

A distinction is drawn between the copyrightability of a derivative work based on noncopyrighted work in the public domain and a derivative work based on a preexisting copyrighted work. In *Doran v. Sunset House Distributing Corp.*, 197 F. Supp. 940 (S.D. Cal. 1961), the district court held that where a derivative work is based on work in the public domain the proper test for copyrightability is whether the form of the original work and that of the derivative work differ sufficiently; if so, the derivative work is copyrightable.

Quicknotes

COPYRIGHT INFRINGEMENT A violation of one of the exclusive rights granted to an artist pursuant to Article I, section 8, clause 8 of the United States Constitution over the reproduction, display, performance, distribution, and adaptation of his work for a period prescribed by statute.

DERIVATIVE WORK A work of authorship that is based on a previous work.

SUMMARY JUDGMENT Judgment rendered by a court in response to a motion by one of the parties, claiming that the lack of a question of material fact in respect to an issue warrants disposition of the issue without consideration by the jury.

Feist Publications, Inc. v. Rural Telephone Service Co.

Public telephone utility (P) v. Publisher of telephone directories (D)

499 U.S. 340 (1991).

NATURE OF CASE: Appeal from affirmance of grant of summary judgment to plaintiff in suit for copyright infringement.

FACT SUMMARY: After Feist Publications, Inc. (Feist) (D) took 1,309 listings from Rural Telephone Service Co.'s (Rural) (P) white pages when compiling Feist's (D) own white pages, Rural (P) filed suit for copyright infringement.

RULE OF LAW
A telephone "white pages" directory does not contain the minimal degree of creativity necessary to be original and copyrightable.

FACTS: As a certified telephone service utility provided in northwest Kansas, Rural Telephone Service Co. (Rural) (P) published a typical telephone directory as a condition of its monopoly franchise. The white pages alphabetically listed the names, towns, and telephone numbers of Rural's (P) subscribers. Feist Publications, Inc. (Feist) (D) was a publishing company specializing in area-wide telephone directories. The Feist (D) published a directory that covered 11 different telephone service areas in 15 counties and contained 46,878 white pages listings, compared to Rural's (P) approximately 7,700 listings. Feist (D) approached the 11 northwest Kansas telephone companies and offered to pay for the right to use their respective white pages listings. When only Rural (P) refused to license its listings, Feist (D) used them without Rural's (P) consent. A typical Feist (D) listing included each individual's street address, while most of Rural's (P) did not. Of the 46,878 listings in Feist's (D) 1983 directory, 1,309 of those listings were identical to listings in Rural's (P) white pages. Rural (P) sued for copyright infringement in the district court, arguing that Feist (D), in compiling its own directory, could not use the information contained in Rural's (P) white pages. The district court granted summary judgment to Rural (P), and the Court of Appeals affirmed. The Supreme Court granted certiorari.

ISSUE: Does a telephone "white pages" directory contain the minimal degree of creativity necessary to be original and copyrightable?

HOLDING AND DECISION: (O'Connor, J.) No. A telephone "white pages" directory does not contain the minimal degree of creativity necessary to be original and copyrightable. Here, two well-established propositions—that facts are not copyrightable and that compilations of facts generally are—collide. To resolve the tension between these positions requires an understanding of why facts are not copyrightable. Facts, which do not originate with authors, cannot be said to possess originality, which is a constitutional sine qua non of copyrightability. To be original, a work must be created (rather than copied) by the author and must contain a minimal degree of creativity. The threshold of creativity is extremely low. The disparate treatment of facts and compilations under copyright law rests on the distinction between creation and discovery; while one may by the first to discover a fact and report the discovery, the discoverer has not created the fact. On the other hand, factual compilations may contain the requisite originality because, usually, the compilation author exercises some minimal degree of creativity in assembling the factual data. However, not every compilation contains even this minimal level of creativity, since not every selection, coordination, or arrangement of facts will be done in "such a way" as to be thought of as original. Even if the method of selection or arrangement is not novel, it will pass muster if the author has made it independently, without copying that selection or arrangement from another work. Nevertheless, there is a narrow category of works in which the creative spark is utterly lacking or so trivial as to be virtually nonexistent. Works that fall into that category do not merit copyright protection. The Copyright Act of 1976 and its predecessor, the Copyright Act of 1909, leave no doubt that originality is the touchstone of copyright protection in directories and other fact-based works. The 1976 Act explains that copyright extends to "original works of authorship," 17 U.S.C. § 102(a), and that there can be no copyright in facts, § 102(b). A compilation is not copyrightable per se, but is copyrightable only if its facts have been "selected, coordinated, or arranged in such a way that the resulting work as a whole constitutes an original work of authorship." Thus, the statute envisions that some ways of selecting, coordinating, and arranging data are not sufficiently original to trigger copyright protection. Even a compilation that is copyrightable receives only limited protection, for the copyright does not extend to facts contained in the compilation. Lower courts that adopted a "sweat of the brow" or "industrious collection" test—which extended a compilation's copyright protection beyond selection and arrangement to the facts themselves—misconstrued the 1909 Act and eschewed the fundamental axiom of copyright law that no one may copyright facts or ideas. Rural's (P) white pages do not meet the constitutional or statutory requirements for copyright protection. There is nothing original in Rural's (P) white pages. The raw data are uncopyrightable facts, and the way in which Rural (P) selected, coordinated, and arranged those

Continued on next page.

facts is not original in any way. Rural's (P) selection of listings—subscribers' names, towns, and telephone numbers—could not be more obvious and lacks the modicum of creativity necessary to transform mere selection into copyrightable expression. In fact, it is plausible to conclude that Rural (P) did not truly "select" to publish its subscribers' names and telephone numbers, since it was required to do so by state law. Rural (P) expended sufficient effort to make the white pages directory useful, but insufficient creativity to make it original—and, therefore, copyrightable. Reversed.

ANALYSIS

The factual compilation cases decided since *Feist* seem to indicate that while courts are primarily guided by the doctrine of creative originality to grant copyrightability to compilations that do not simply repackage pre-existing information in predictable ways but that add content, in the form of useful subjective evaluations, to unprotectable facts, courts still seem to reward sweat of the brow efforts to retain incentives for authors—despite *Feist's* express rejection of that doctrine. Some commentators believe that the courts have done so by equating originality with effort. See Denise R. Polivy, "*Feist* Applied: Imagination Protects, But Perspiration Persists—the Bases of Copyright Protection for Factual Compilations," 8 *Fordham Intell. Prop. Media & Ent. L.J.* 773.

Quicknotes

COPYRIGHT Refers to the exclusive rights granted to an artist pursuant to Article I, section 8, clause 8 of the United States Constitution over the reproduction, display, performance, distribution, and adaptation of his work for a period prescribed by statute.

COPYRIGHT INFRINGEMENT A violation of one of the exclusive rights granted to an artist pursuant to Article I, section 8, clause 8 of the United States Constitution over the reproduction, display, performance, distribution, and adaptation of his work for a period prescribed by statute.

SUMMARY JUDGMENT Judgment rendered by a court in response to a motion by one of the parties, claiming that the lack of a question of material fact in respect to an issue warrants disposition of the issue without consideration by the jury.

Roth Greeting Cards v. United Card Co.

Greeting card maker (P) v. Competitor (D)

429 F.2d 1106 (9th Cir. 1970).

NATURE OF CASE: Action for infringement of copyrighted greeting cards.

FACT SUMMARY: A maker of greeting cards sued a competitor for copyright infringement.

RULE OF LAW
Works should be considered as wholes when determining whether they are original and copyrightable.

FACTS: Roth Greeting Cards (Roth) (P) produces and distributes greeting cards. Roth (P) brought an action for copyright infringement against United Card Co. (D), a competitor. In its decision, the trial court viewed the greeting cards in terms of their separate components, considering the artwork and the text in isolation from one another. It found that the artwork was copyrightable but not infringed and that the text was not copyrightable. Roth (P) appealed.

ISSUE: Should works be considered as a whole when determining copyrightability?

HOLDING AND DECISION: (Hamley, J.) Yes. The proper analysis of a work is as a whole. Here, the greeting cards should be viewed as wholes, i.e., with the artwork and the text taken together. Of significance is the association between the artwork and the text. Viewed in that way, the greeting cards are copyrightable as wholes, and the same concept and feel captured by a competitor would infringe on that copyright. Reversed.

DISSENT: (Kilkenny, J.) The text and artwork are separate elements and copyright protection should not extend where neither text nor artwork have been infringed.

ANALYSIS

The court agreed that if the text of the greeting card was considered separately from the artwork it would not be copyrightable.

Quicknotes

COPYRIGHT INFRINGEMENT A violation of one of the exclusive rights granted to an artist pursuant to Article I, section 8, clause 8 of the United States Constitution over the reproduction, display, performance, distribution, and adaptation of his work for a period prescribed by statute.

Mason v. Montgomery Data, Inc.

Map maker (P) v. Competitor (D)

967 F.2d 135 (5th Cir. 1992).

NATURE OF CASE: Appeal from grant of partial summary judgment in favor of alleged infringer.

FACT SUMMARY: A maker of maps (P) that included legal and factual information sued a competitor (D) for copyright infringement.

RULE OF LAW
Compilations of pictorial information gain originality such as to allow them to be copyrighted if the selection, coordination, and arrangement of the information depicted is sufficiently creative.

FACTS: Using deeds, tax and survey records, and other public information, Mason (P) created and published real estate ownership maps for all of Montgomery County. The maps identified deeds, acreage, and ownership of the various parcels, as well as topographical features. Landata (D) purchased a Mason (P) map and by cutting, pasting, reorganizing, and updating the information, created its own maps. Mason (P) sued for copyright infringement. The district court found that Mason's (P) copyright was limited to the actual maps he created. Mason (P) appealed, arguing that his copyright protected his idea to create the maps based on legal information and the expression of that idea in different ways.

ISSUE: Can an author gain copyright protection in a map that is based on a compilation of public information?

HOLDING AND DECISION: (Reavley, J.) Yes. The selection of information and the coordination and arrangement of that information can render a map based on public information sufficiently original as to merit copyright protection. Here, Mason's (P) maps were sufficiently creative to make them original compilations and thus to merit copyright protection. Reversed.

ANALYSIS

Section 101 of the Copyright Act defines a compilation as "a work formed by the collection and assembling of preexisting materials or of data that are selected, coordinated, or arranged in such a way that the resulting work as a whole constitutes an original work of authorship."

Quicknotes

COPYRIGHT ACT SECTION 101 Section 101 of the Copyright Act of 1976, setting forth the definitions for purposes of the act.

COPYRIGHT INFRINGEMENT A violation of one of the exclusive rights granted to an artist pursuant to Article I, section 8, clause 8 of the United States Constitution over the reproduction, display, performance, distribution, and adaptation of his work for a period prescribed by statute.

PARTIAL SUMMARY JUDGMENT Judgment rendered by a court in response to a motion by one of the parties, claiming that the lack of a question of material fact in respect to one of the issues warrants disposition of that issue without going to the jury.

Lindsay v. The Wrecked and Abandoned Vessel R.M.S. Titanic

Documentary film maker (P) v. Film crew (D)

52 U.S.P.Q. 2d 1609 (S.D.N.Y. 1999).

NATURE OF CASE: Claim for copyright infringement.

FACT SUMMARY: Lindsay (P) asserted a copyright infringement claim based on the defendants' licensing of footage of the Titanic, shot at his direction, to the Discovery Channel.

RULE OF LAW
An individual who exercises a high degree of control over a photograph may be considered the "author," even when that individual does not physically shoot the photograph.

FACTS: Lindsay (P) developed a film project to explore the Titanic using high illumination lighting equipment. To further the project, he created story boards consisting of a series of drawings in which specific camera angles and shooting sequences were identified, and he constructed the needed light towers. Lindsay (P) then acted as director, producer, and cinematographer of the footage shot. The defendants, who actually shot the footage, licensed it to the Discovery Channel. Lindsay (P) asserted a claim for copyright infringement. The lower court denied defendants' motion to dismiss, and they appealed.

ISSUE: Must an individual physically shoot a photographic image to be considered its author and to have a copyrightable interest?

HOLDING AND DECISION: (Baer, J.) No. An author, for copyright purposes, must show originality, conception, or intellectual production. Here, Lindsay's (P) storyboards, designs, and specific directions for the taking of the images is sufficient to demonstrate his control and conception. The final images show his visions, and he is thus an author under the Copyright Act. Affirmed.

ANALYSIS

Commentators have noted that the increasingly abstract concept of "authorship" under copyright law has created a tension between protecting the actual creators of a work and protecting economic interests in the work.

Quicknotes

COPYRIGHT Refers to the exclusive rights granted to an artist pursuant to Article I, section 8, clause 8 of the United States Constitution over the reproduction, display, performance, distribution, and adaptation of his work for a period prescribed by statute.

COPYRIGHT ACT Copyright Act of 1976 extends copyright protection to "original works of authorship fixed in any tangible medium of expression, now known or later developed, from which they can be perceived, reproduced, or otherwise communicated, either directly or with the aid of a machine or device." 17 U.S.C. § 102.

COPYRIGHT INFRINGEMENT A violation of one of the exclusive rights granted to an artist pursuant to Article I, section 8, clause 8 of the United States Constitution over the reproduction, display, performance, distribution, and adaptation of his work for a period prescribed by statute.

MOTION TO DISMISS Motion to terminate a trial based on the adequacy of the pleadings.

Erickson v. Trinity Theatre, Inc.

Author of copyrighted plays (P) v. Alleged infringer (D)

13 F.3d 1061 (7th Cir. 1994).

NATURE OF CASE: Copyright infringement suit.

FACT SUMMARY: Trinity Theatre, Inc. (D) argued that three plays prepared by Karen Erickson (P) constituted a "joint work" by Erickson (P) and Trinity Theatre (D) because several of Trinity's (D) actors made suggestions that were incorporated into the plays during their development, thereby making Trinity Theatre (D) a co-author of the copyright with Erickson (P).

RULE OF LAW
A product is a "joint work" only if the collaborators can be considered as authors.

FACTS: Karen Erickson (P), a play writer and founding member of Trinity Theatre, Inc. (D), wrote three plays for the company. After a dispute between the two, Trinity (D) stopped royalty payments to Erickson (P), arguing that it was a co-author and co-owner of the copyright to the plays because various of Trinity's (D) actors had made suggestions that Erickson (P) incorporated during development of the plays.

ISSUE: May a product be deemed a "joint work" only if the collaborators can be considered as authors?

HOLDING AND DECISION: (Ripple, J.) Yes. A product is a "joint work" only if the collaborators can be considered as authors. Even if several persons collaborate with the intention to create a work which is unitary, a "joint work," within the meaning of the Copyright Statute, arises only if all collaborators are deemed authors in the sense that each of the individuals must supply something more tangible than mere direction or ideas. The viewpoint of Professor Nimmer, expressed in the so-called de minimis test, that requires only that the combined product of joint efforts be copyrightable, has not found judicial support. The premise of the Copyright Act is that ideas and concepts standing alone should not receive copyright protection. Because the creative process necessarily involves the development of existing concepts into new forms, any restriction on the free exchange of ideas stifles creativity to some extent. Furthermore, contribution of an idea is an exceedingly ambiguous concept, and Professor Nimmer provides little guidance regarding when a contribution rises to the level of joint authorship. On the other hand, Professor Goldstein's copyrightability test, which requires that each author's contribution be copyrightable, provides a far more workable test of when joint authorship has been achieved. Here, because Trinity (D) is unable to identify any specific copyrightable contributions made by its purported authors, Trinity (D) cannot qualify as a joint author of the plays.

ANALYSIS
A "joint work" is defined by Section 101 of the Copyright Act as a work prepared by two or more authors with the intention that their contributions be merged into inseparable or independent parts of the unitary whole. Persons accorded joint authorship status enjoy significant benefits since each joint author holds undivided interests in the work, no matter how minor their contribution. As a co-owner, each author has the right to use or license the use of the work, subject to an accounting to the other co-owners for profits.

Quicknotes

COPYRIGHT Refers to the exclusive rights granted to an artist pursuant to Article I, section 8, clause 8 of the United States Constitution over the reproduction, display, performance, distribution, and adaptation of his work for a period prescribed by statute.

COPYRIGHT ACT Copyright Act of 1976 extends copyright protection to "original works of authorship fixed in any tangible medium of expression, now known or later developed, from which they can be perceived, reproduced, or otherwise communicated, either directly or with the aid of a machine or device." 17 U.S.C. § 102.

COPYRIGHT ACT SECTION 101 Section 101 of the Copyright Act of 1976, setting forth the definitions for purposes of the act.

COPYRIGHT INFRINGEMENT A violation of one of the exclusive rights granted to an artist pursuant to Article I, section 8, clause 8 of the United States Constitution over the reproduction, display, performance, distribution, and adaptation of his work for a period prescribed by statute.

DE MINIMIS Insignificant; trivial; not of sufficient significance to resort to legal action.

ROYALTY Payment to the owner of property for the use or sale of such property either as a percentage of profits or per unit sold.

Aalmuhammed v. Lee

Alleged co-author (P) v. Copyright holder (D)

202 F.3d 1227 (9th Cir. 1999).

NATURE OF CASE: Appeal from dismissal of a case for declaratory relief under the Copyright Act.

FACT SUMMARY: Aalmuhammed (P) sought a declaratory judgment that he was a co-owner of the copyright in a movie and thus entitled to an accounting of the profits from the movie.

RULE OF LAW
A person claiming to be a co-owner of a joint work must prove that both parties intended the work to be a joint work.

FACTS: Aalmuhammed (P) worked as a consultant on Lee's (D) film about Malcolm X. Aalmuhammed (P) reviewed the script, suggested revisions, and rewrote certain portions. When the film was released, Aalmuhammed (P) was listed in the credits as an "Islamic Technical Consultant." Aalmuhammed (P) sought a declaratory judgment that the movie was a "joint work" and that he was a co-owner of the copyright and entitled to an accounting of profits. Aalmuhammed (P) did not claim to be a co-author. The district court granted summary judgment to the defendants.

ISSUE: Does the contribution of independently copyrightable material to a work intended to be an inseparable whole make the work a joint work?

HOLDING AND DECISION: (Kleinfeld, J.) No. A joint work is one that was intended by both parties to be a joint work. That determination is fact specific. The courts will look to, among other things, the apportionment of decision making authority and the billing accorded the various parties. Here, none of the parties made any objective manifestations of intent to be co-authors. Specifically, Aalmuhammed (P) had no supervisory authority over the film and signed a "work for hire" agreement that precluded him from being a co-author. Affirmed.

ANALYSIS

A social consideration underlies limitations in the definitions of author and of joint work. The ability of an author to collaborate or consult with others without the risk of losing ownership in the work favors the progress of knowledge.

Quicknotes

COPYRIGHT Refers to the exclusive rights granted to an artist pursuant to Article I, section 8, clause 8 of the United States Constitution over the reproduction, display, performance, distribution, and adaptation of his work for a period prescribed by statute.

COPYRIGHT ACT Copyright Act of 1976 extends copyright protection to "original works of authorship fixed in any tangible medium of expression, now known or later developed, from which they can be perceived, reproduced, or otherwise communicated, either directly or with the aid of a machine or device." 17 U.S.C. § 102.

DECLARATORY JUDGMENT A judgment of the court establishing the rights of the parties.

SUMMARY JUDGMENT Judgment rendered by a court in response to a motion by one of the parties, claiming that the lack of a question of material fact in respect to an issue warrants disposition of the issue without consideration by the jury.

Community for Creative Non-Violence v. Reid

Art buyer (P) v. Artist (D)

490 U.S. 730 (1989).

NATURE OF CASE: Review of order adjudicating copyrights with respect to a sculpture.

FACT SUMMARY: Reid (D), who had created a sculpture on commission from the Community for Creative Non-Violence (CCNV) (P), contended that since he had not been an employee of it under common-law agency principles, he owned the copyright.

RULE OF LAW
Under common-law agency principles, one who creates an artwork at the behest of another retains the copyright, unless he was an employee of that other.

FACTS: The Community for Creative Non-Violence (CCNV) (P) was a nonprofit organization dedicated to advocacy for the cause of the homeless in the United States. It negotiated with Reid (D), a sculptor, for the latter to fashion a variation on the classic Nativity scene, depicting homeless individuals. Agreement was finally made, and Reid (D) fashioned the sculpture out of a bronze-like material. The work was done by Reid (D) in his studio, with minimal direction from CCNV (P). After the unveiling, Reid (D) registered a copyright on the work. Subsequent to this, a disagreement arose between CCNV (P) and Reid (D), who had taken custody of the sculpture, over its future exhibition. CCNV (P) filed an action seeking to obtain possession of the work. The district court held CCNV (P) to have the right to exhibit the statute. The Federal Circuit of the Court of Appeals reversed, and the Supreme Court granted review.

ISSUE: Under common-law agency principles, does one who creates an artwork at the behest of another retain the copyright?

HOLDING AND DECISION: (Marshall, J.) Yes. Under common-law agency principles, one creating an artwork at the behest of another retains copyright thereon unless he had been an employee of that other. 17 U.S.C. § 201(a) provides that copyright ownership vests initially in the work's author, something Reid (D) in this instance indisputably was. Section 101 of the 1976 Copyright Act creates an exception to this in the case of works created "for hire." Section 101(2) mandates copyright vestiture in the case where the author is an independent contractor of another, in specific instances not applicable here. Section 101(1) provides that the work is one created "for hire" if the work is created by an employee within the scope of his employment, and this subsection is the only one which can divest Reid (D) of copyright therein. "Employee" is not defined in the section. This being so, the rule comes into play that words used in a statute will be presumed to possess their normal meanings. Contrary to CCNV's (P) assertions, "employee" is a narrower term than one over whom another exercises a measure of control. Rather, "employee" has a particular meaning, derived from common-law agency principles, wherein one party performs labor for another under circumstances in which that other exerts substantial control over the work environment on the laborer, as well as the manner of performance. Numerous factors figure in this equation, such as the level of skill required, tax treatment of the putative employee, the singleness of the assignment, and the source of the instrumentalities of the labor. Here, the work was highly skilled, Reid (D) was retained only for this single assignment, was not treated as an employee for tax purposes, and supplied his own tools and work area. The conclusion is mandated that, under agency principles, Reid (D) was not an employee of CCNV (P). Therefore, the § 101(1) exception to § 201(a) does not apply, and the copyright belongs to Reid (D). Affirmed.

ANALYSIS

Sections 101(1) and 101(2) were the result of lengthy debate and compromise in Congress. Prior to 1955, any commissioned work belonged to the hiring party. For the next several years, changes in this rule were proposed numerous times. Not until 1965 was the substantive embodiment of current law enacted.

Quicknotes

COPYRIGHT Refers to the exclusive rights granted to an artist pursuant to Article I, section 8, clause 8 of the United States Constitution over the reproduction, display, performance, distribution, and adaptation of his work for a period prescribed by statute.

COPYRIGHT ACT SECTION 101 Section 101 of the Copyright Act of 1976, setting forth the definitions for purposes of the act.

Aymes v. Bonelli

Employee (P) v. Employer (D)

980 F.2d 857 (2d Cir. 1992).

NATURE OF CASE: Appeal from dismissal of a case for copyright infringement.

FACT SUMMARY: Aymes (P) who had been hired by Bonelli (D) to create computer programs for Bonelli's (D) swimming pool business, contended that he was the owner of the copyright in those programs.

RULE OF LAW
Although no one factor is dispositive, the lack of benefits extended to an individual or the failure to pay taxes on an individual's behalf is indicative of independent contractor status.

FACTS: Bonelli (D) hired Aymes (P) to create computer programs for Bonelli's (D) pool business. Aymes (P) worked primarily in Bonelli's (D) offices, but generally worked alone. Aymes (P) had significant autonomy, limited only by the functionality Bonelli (D) wanted from the programs. Aymes (P) was generally paid by the project and received bonuses for finishing projects on time. Bonelli (D) never paid an employer's portion of Ayme's (P) payroll taxes and never withheld any salary for state or federal taxes.

ISSUE: Will an individual generally be an independent contractor where the employer pays no benefits or taxes?

HOLDING AND DECISION: (Altimari, J.) Yes. Although no one factor spelled out in *Community Center for Non-Violence v. Reid*, 490 U.S. 730 (1989), is dispositive as to whether an individual is an employee or an independent contractor, typically, where the hiring party pays no benefits or taxes on the individual's behalf, the individual is deemed to be an independent contractor. Here, because Bonelli (D) paid no benefits to Aymes (P) and did not pay an employer's portion of taxes, Aymes (P) is deemed to be an independent contractor. Affirmed.

ANALYSIS

Copyright law regarding software and the use of independent contractors to write software continues to evolve. Because software is often the result of the efforts of many programmers, one commentator proposes that their efforts be treated as contributions to a compilation.

Quicknotes

COPYRIGHT Refers to the exclusive rights granted to an artist pursuant to Article I, section 8, clause 8 of the United States Constitution over the reproduction, display, performance, distribution, and adaptation of his work for a period prescribed by statute.

COPYRIGHT INFRINGEMENT A violation of one of the exclusive rights granted to an artist pursuant to Article I, section 8, clause 8 of the United States Constitution over the reproduction, display, performance, distribution, and adaptation of his work for a period prescribed by statute.

Roeslin v. District of Columbia

Employee-author (P) v. Employer (D)

921 F. Supp. 793 (D.D.C. 1995).

NATURE OF CASE: Copyright infringement action brought by employee against employer.

FACT SUMMARY: Roeslin (P), an economist for the Department of Employment Services (D.O.E.S.) of the District of Columbia (District) (D), contended that a software program he created (the "DC-790" system) was not a work made for hire and that he therefore owned the copyright in it.

RULE OF LAW

A work is not "made for hire" where an employee creates the work for use in connection with his job, but does so on his time and at his own expense; the work is not in the line of work the employee has been hired to do; the employee is not compensated for the work; and the employee's motivation in creating the work is to show that the work can be created and to create job opportunities for himself.

FACTS: Roeslin (P) was an economist for the Department of Employment Services (D.O.E.S.) of the District of Columbia (District) (D). Although he used a computer on occasion to assist with his work, he was not a computer programmer. He was responsible for improving data collection for the District's (D) Current Employment Service (CES) survey. When Roeslin (P) started with D.O.E.S., data was collected manually and then was entered into a mainframe computer by data processing staff. The District (D) anticipated the future development of the Automated Current Employment Statistics (ACES) mainframe system. After attending a CES seminar, Roeslin (P) became convinced that a personal computer (PC)-based system could be developed for the CES surveys, and shared his idea with his supervisor, Groner, who told Roeslin (P) not to pursue it, in part because D.O.E.S. had already decided to eventually implement ACES and because Groner thought such a system was neither feasible nor desirable. Roeslin (P) informed Groner that he would create the program on his own time, and Groner told him that the program would be "in the public domain." Roeslin (P) pursued this to create job opportunities for himself and to prove that the system could be created. To this end, he purchased a PC and software using his own funds and spent around 3000 hours creating and testing the program (the "DC-790" system) at home. He was not offered compensation for the creation of the system. After testing each module at home, Roeslin (P) brought each module into work to test with actual data. Some of the testing and debugging of various modules was done during office hours. Once each module worked properly, he incorporated the modules into the PC system operating at D.O.E.S. Shortly after the DC-790 system became operational, D.O.E.S. personnel ceased using the former manual recording system. Roeslin (P) also created an operating manual for the DC-790 system and received positive performance appraisals based, in part, on his development of the DC-790 system. Around a year later, Roeslin (P) learned that the District (D) had asserted a proprietary interest in the system. He met with Groner to discuss this, asserting that if anyone owned a proprietary interest in the system, he did, and requested recognition by the District (D) that he had independent ownership of the program, in exchange for which the District (D) would be allowed free use and distribution of the software. He also requested a promotion. He then placed a copyright notice on the initial screen of the DC-790 system, and, through counsel, he notified the District (D) of his claim of copyright ownership. He also demanded that the District (D) stop using the system, and filed for and received a copyright registration for the program. Despite Roeslin's (P) notice of copyright ownership, District (D) employees continued using the system, as Groner never instructed them to stop using it. Roeslin (P) sued for copyright infringement, and the District (D) defended by claiming that the DC-790 system was a work made for hire, so that it owned the copyright in it.

ISSUE: Is a work "made for hire" where an employee creates the work for use in connection with his job, but does so on his time and at his own expense; the work is not in the line of work the employee has been hired to do; the employee is not compensated for the work; and the employee's motivation in creating the work is to show that the work can be created and to create job opportunities for himself?

HOLDING AND DECISION: (Greene, J.) No. A work is not "made for hire" where an employee creates the work for use in connection with his job, but does so on his time and at his own expense; the work is not in the line of work the employee has been hired to do; the employee is not compensated for the work; and the employee's motivation in creating the work is to show that the work can be created and to create job opportunities for himself. The key issue here is which party owns the copyright in the DC-790 system. The copyright statute defines a work made for hire as "a work prepared by an employee within the scope of his or her employment." Because Roeslin (P) has received a copyright registration for the DC-790 system, the presumption is that he owns the copyright, and the District (D) bears the burden to establish that the system is a work made for hire. The law

Continued on next page.

of agency determines whether an employee has created a work within the scope of his employment. Under the Restatement (Second) of Agency, § 228, conduct of an employee is within the scope of employment if (a) it is within the kind he is employed to perform; (b) it occurs substantially within the authorized time and space limits; and (c) it is actuated, at least in part, by a purpose to serve the employer. As to the first requirement, developing computer software was not the kind of work Roeslin (P) was employed to perform. Even though he used computers in his work, he was not hired as a computer programmer, and his job description was for a labor economist. While work that is incidental to the conduct authorized by the employer, even if it is not central to the employee's job duties, also falls within the scope of employment, developing the DC-790 system was not the type of activity in which Roeslin (P) would be reasonably expected to engage, even if the system ultimately did help D.O.E.S. Further, Groner discouraged him from developing the system, and the District (D) had already decided to implement ACES. As to the second requirement, the development of the system did not occur substantially within the authorized time and space limits. Even though Roeslin (P) tested each module at work, and once each module was operational, it was used in the work place, the substantial amount of time he spent creating the DC-790 system was done on his own time, at his own expense, outside of the office. Finally, as to the third requirement, Roeslin's (P) primary motivation for creating the system was to create job opportunities for himself and to prove it could be done. Thus, he was primarily motivated by self-fulfilling purposes, notwithstanding that the system helped his employer. Therefore, on the whole, the DC-790 system was not a work made for hire, and the District (D) does not have any copyright interests therein. Judgment for Roeslin (P).

ANALYSIS

The test for whether an employee's conduct is within the scope of his or her employment has been modified in The Restatement (Third) of Agency, § 7.07(2). The new test provides that "An employee acts within the scope of employment when performing work assigned by the employer or engaging in a course of conduct subject to the employer's control." An employee's act is not within the scope of employment when it occurs within an independent course of conduct not intended by the employee to serve any purpose of the employer. The key difference between the Second and Third Restatement is the degree to which the employee must intend his or her actions to be in service of his or her employer before liability can attach. In the Second Restatement, the conduct is not within the scope of employment if it is "too little actuated by a purpose to serve the master." Restatement (Second) of Agency § 228(2). However, as quoted above, in the Third Restatement, conduct is not within the scope of employment "when it occurs within an independent course of conduct not intended by the employee to serve any purpose of the employer." Restatement (Third) of Agency § 7.07(2). Under this revised formulation, the District (D) arguably could have shown that Roeslin (P) intended his conduct to serve some purpose of the D.O.E.S., since the DC-790 system was created to help with the CES, and did in fact help the D.O.E.S.

Quicknotes

COPYRIGHT INFRINGEMENT A violation of one of the exclusive rights granted to an artist pursuant to Article I, Section 8, clause 8 of the United States Constitution over the reproduction, display, performance, distribution, and adaptation of his work for a period prescribed by statute.

CHAPTER 3

Acquiring and Maintaining Copyright

Quick Reference Rules of Law

	PAGE

1. **What Is Publication?** The release of a speech to the news media for coverage of a newsworthy event is a limited publication under the Copyright Act of 1909 and does not destroy common-law copyright protection. (Estate of Martin Luther King, Jr., Inc. v. CBS, Inc.) — *32*

2. **The Policy Behind Copyright Duration.** Congress has the authority to enact legislation that extends copyright terms for both existing and future copyrights. (Eldred v. Ashcroft) — *33*

3. **Renewals.** The owner of the copyright of a derivative work infringes the copyright of the underlying, preexisting work on which the derivative work is based if he continues to use the derivative work once his grant of rights in the preexisting work has lapsed. (Stewart v. Abend) — *35*

Estate of Martin Luther King, Jr., Inc. v. CBS, Inc.

Copyright owner (P) v. Documentary film producer (D)

194 F.3d 1211 (11th Cir. 1999).

NATURE OF CASE: Appeal from summary judgment in favor of alleged infringer.

FACT SUMMARY: The Estate of Martin Luther King, Jr., Inc. (the Estate) (P), brought suit for copyright infringement against CBS, Inc. (D) for airing a documentary that featured Dr. King's famous "I have a dream" speech from 1963 without permission from the Estate (P).

RULE OF LAW
The release of a speech to the news media for coverage of a newsworthy event is a limited publication under the Copyright Act of 1909 and does not destroy common-law copyright protection.

FACTS: In October 1963, Dr. King was granted a certificate of registration to copyright his famous "I have a dream" speech. In 1994, CBS, Inc. (D) produced a documentary that had a segment devoted to Dr. King and featured extensive footage of the Speech. CBS (D) did not seek permission from the Estate of Martin Luther King, Jr., Inc. (the Estate) (P) to include the footage, and it paid no royalties. The Estate (P) sued for copyright infringement. The district court granted summary judgment in favor of CBS (D), holding that the wide and unlimited reproduction and dissemination of the Speech was a general publication that put the Speech in the public domain. The Estate (P) appealed.

ISSUE: Does the release of a newsworthy speech to the media for news coverage constitute a general publication, destroying common-law copyright protection?

HOLDING AND DECISION: (Anderson, J.) No. A general publication only occurs in two situations: (1) where tangible copies of the work are distributed to the public in a way that allows the public to exercise control over the work; and (2) where the work is exhibited in a way that permits unrestricted copying by the general public. Here, the mere performance of the Speech, no matter the size of the audience, is not a general publication. The significance of the Speech does not enter into the analysis. Reversed.

ANALYSIS

The distinction between "general publication" and "limited publication" is a court-created distinction designed to soften the rule that any publication destroys common-law copyright protection. Only general publication divests rights.

Quicknotes

COPYRIGHT ACT Copyright Act of 1976 extends copyright protection to "original works of authorship fixed in any tangible medium of expression, now known or later developed, from which they can be perceived, reproduced, or otherwise communicated, either directly or with the aid of a machine or device." 17 U.S.C. § 102.

COPYRIGHT INFRINGEMENT A violation of one of the exclusive rights granted to an artist pursuant to Article I, section 8, clause 8 of the United States Constitution over the reproduction, display, performance, distribution, and adaptation of his work for a period prescribed by statute.

ROYALTY Payment to the owner of property for the use or sale of such property either as a percentage of profits or per unit sold.

SUMMARY JUDGMENT Judgment rendered by a court in response to a motion by one of the parties, claiming that the lack of a question of material fact in respect to an issue warrants disposition of the issue without consideration by the jury.

Eldred v. Ashcroft

Businesses (P) v. Attorney General (D)

537 U.S. 186 (2003).

NATURE OF CASE: Appeal of action challenging the authority of Congress (D) to legislate.

FACT SUMMARY: Eldred (P) challenged the authority of Congress (D) to enlarge the term for published works with existing copyrights.

RULE OF LAW
Congress has the authority to enact legislation that extends copyright terms for both existing and future copyrights.

FACTS: In 1790, the nation's first copyright statute was enacted and its term of years applied to both existing works and future works. Similarly, in 1831, 1909, and l976, Congress (D) extended the duration of copyrights to existing and future copyrights. Again in 1998, Congress (D), with the Copyright Term Extension Act (CTEA), enlarged the duration of copyrights from life plus 50 years to life plus 70 years and the new term applied to both existing and future copyrights. Eldred (P) builds off of copyrighted works after they go into the public domain and sued Ashcroft (D) contending that the provisions of CTEA violated the Constitution. Eldred (P) alleges that Congress (D) did not have the power to enlarge the term for published works with existing copyrights and that CTEA is a content-neutral regulation of speech that fails inspection under heightened judicial scrutiny. The district court and the court of appeals found CTEA to be valid and Eldred (P) appealed.

ISSUE:
(1) Do the provisions of CTEA, which enlarge the term for published works with existing copyrights, violate the Constitution's "limited Times" prescription?
(2) Does CTEA, which extends the term for both existing and future copyrights, violate the First Amendment?

HOLDING AND DECISION: (Ginsburg, J.)
(1) No. The provisions of CTEA, which enlarge the term for published works with existing copyrights, do not violate the Constitution's "limited Times" prescription because the text of the Constitution, as well as history and precedent allow for such an extension and CTEA is a rational exercise of legislative authority. Pursuant to the Constitution, Congress (D) has the right to secure to authors "for limited Times ... the exclusive Right to their ... Writings." The word "limited" does not mean that a time span once set becomes inalterable. Thus a new time span can apply to both future and existing copyrights. Moreover, throughout history, beginning with the first Copyright Act in 1790, and continuing through term extensions made in 1831, 1909, and 1976, Congress (D) has consistently granted to authors of works with existing copyrights and future copyrights the benefit of term extensions. In addition, CTEA is a rational exercise of legislative authority conferred by the Constitution. Congress (D) usually makes the kind of judgments as those in CTEA, such as ones based on international concerns, demographic, economic and technological changes, and such judgments are not outside of its domain. Eldred's (P) argument that CTEA does not "promote the Progress of Science," which is the primary objective of copyright, because it does not stimulate the creation of new works fails because it is for Congress (D), not the courts, to decide how best to pursue the Copyright Clause's objectives. Moreover, the reasons for the enactment of CTEA provide a rational basis for the conclusion that CTEA promotes the Progress of Science.

(2) No. CTEA, which extends the terms for both existing and future copyrights, does not violate the First Amendment because strict scrutiny should not be applied. Strict scrutiny should not be applied because the Copyright Clause already incorporates its own speech-protective safeguards. For instance, it makes only expression eligible for protection, thus every idea in a copyrighted work is available for public exploitation. Moreover, the fair use defense allows the public to use the expression contained in a copyrighted work in some circumstances. Affirmed.

DISSENT: (Stevens, J.) That Congress (D) exercised its constitutional authority in the enactment of the Copyright Act of 1790, does not provide support for the proposition that Congress (D) can extend pre-existing federal protections retroactively. Here, by failing to protect the public interest in free access to the products of inventive genius and by virtually ignoring the central purpose of the Copyright/Patent Clause, this Court has quitclaimed to Congress (D) its principal responsibility in this area of the law. Such result cannot be squared with the basic tenets of our constitutional structure.

DISSENT: (Breyer, J.) CTEA lacks the constitutionally necessary rational support since the significant benefits it bestows are private, not public; it threatens seriously to undermine the expressive values which the Copyright Clause embodies; and it cannot find justification in any significant Clause-related objective.

ANALYSIS

The Court found the argument that Congress's (D) extensions create invalid perpetual copyrights and that Congress (D) may not extend an existing copyright absent

Continued on next page.

new consideration from the author to be unpersuasive. Moreover, it found that the author of a work would expect that not only would he receive a copyright now, but that his rights would be extended in the future if so legislated. Thus the author does not have to give new consideration in order to get the extension.

Quicknotes

COPYRIGHT Refers to the exclusive rights granted to an artist pursuant to Article I, section 8, clause 8 of the United States Constitution over the reproduction, display, performance, distribution, and adaptation of his work for a period prescribed by statute.

COPYRIGHT ACT Copyright Act of 1976 extends copyright protection to "original works of authorship fixed in any tangible medium of expression, now known or later developed, from which they can be perceived, reproduced, or otherwise communicated, either directly or with the aid of a machine or device." 17 U.S.C. § 102.

FIRST AMENDMENT Prohibits Congress from enacting any law respecting an establishment of religion, prohibiting the free exercise of religion, abridging freedom of speech or the press, the right of peaceful assembly and the right to petition for a redress of grievances.

QUITCLAIM A deed whereby the grantor conveys whatever interest he or she may have in the property without any warranties or covenants as to title.

STRICT SCRUTINY Method by which courts determine the constitutionality of a law, when a law affects a fundamental right. Under the test, the legislature must have a compelling interest to enact the law and measures prescribed by the law must be the least restrictive means possible to accomplish its goal.

Stewart v. Abend

Literary rightsholder (P) v. Movie rightsholder (D)

495 U.S. 207 (1990).

NATURE OF CASE: Appeal from reversal of summary judgment denying damages for copyright infringement.

FACT SUMMARY: Stewart (D) made and starred in a motion picture named "Rear Window," which was based on a Cornell Woolrich story to which he held, as assignee, the derivative movie rights; Abend (P), the assignee of Woolrich's rights in the copyright in the original story, sued to recover damages for the unauthorized rerelease of "Rear Window" during the story's renewal copyright term.

RULE OF LAW
The owner of the copyright of a derivative work infringes the copyright of the underlying, preexisting work on which the derivative work is based if he continues to use the derivative work once his grant of rights in the preexisting work has lapsed.

FACTS: In 1942, Cornell Woolrich wrote the story "It Had to Be Murder," which was published in a magazine. In 1945, Woolrich assigned the motion picture rights to the story to a production company and agreed to renew the story's copyright at the end of the original 28-year term and to reassign the movie rights to the production company. In 1953, the company assigned its rights to Stewart (D) and director Alfred Hitchcock, constituted as Patron, Inc. The next year Patron, Inc., and Paramount Pictures made and distributed the movie "Rear Window," based on "It Had to Be Murder." Woolrich died, without surviving spouse or children, in 1968, before he could exercise his rights in the renewal term of the copyright on the story. His property was left in trust to Chase Manhattan Bank for the benefit of Columbia University. Chase then assigned the renewal rights in "It Had to Be Murder" to Abend (P) for $650 and 10% of all proceeds from the story's exploitation. After "Rear Window" was aired on television in 1971 and again in 1974 over his protest, Abend (P) filed suit against Stewart (D), Hitchcock, and MCA, Inc., for copyright infringement. Abend (P) settled that claim for $25,000 but filed a new suit in the early 1980s when Stewart (D) and MCA (D) rereleased "Rear Window" in theaters, on videocassettes, and over cable television. The district court granted Stewart's (D) motion for summary judgment, the court of appeals reversed, and Stewart (D) appealed.

ISSUE: Does the owner of the copyright of a derivative work infringe the copyright of the underlying, preexisting work on which the derivative work is based if he continues to use the derivative work past the time his grant of rights in the preexisting work has lapsed?

HOLDING AND DECISION: (O'Connor, J.) Yes. The owner of the copyright of a derivative work infringes the copyright of the underlying, preexisting work on which the derivative work is based if he continues to use the derivative work past the time his grant of rights in the preexisting work has lapsed. This Court held in *Miller Music Corp. v. Charles N. Daniels, Inc.*, 362 U.S. 373 (1960), that the assignment of renewal rights by an author before the time for renewal arrives cannot defeat the right of the author's statutory successor to the renewal rights if the author dies before the right to renewal accrues. An assignee of the renewal rights takes only an expectancy. Here, Stewart (D) received from Woolrich's assignee only an expectancy that he would receive an additional assignment of rights to use the preexisting work embodied in the derivative work during the renewal term of the "It Had to Be Murder" copyright. This expectancy did not mature because Woolrich died before he could exercise his renewal right. This right of renewal then inhered by statute in Woolrich's wife, children, or next of kin, who could not have been divested of the renewal right unless Woolrich had been alive at the commencement of the renewal period. This policy was enacted to permit the author, or his heirs, originally in a poor bargaining position, to renegotiate the terms of the grant of the right to use the preexisting work after the preexisting work had been tested and more accurately evaluated through exploitation. Thus, although the aspects of a derivative work added by the derivative author are that author's property, the element drawn from the preexisting work remains on grant from the owner of the preexisting work, here Abend (P). The holding of the Second Circuit in *Rohauer v. Killiam Shows, Inc.*, 551 F.2d 484 (1977), which attempted to balance the equities between the preexisting work's author's rights to renewal and the derivative work's author's right to exploitation, which allowed the derivative author to exploit the derivative work during the renewal term of the preexisting work copyright without consent of the preexisting author, is expressly overruled. Affirmed.

ANALYSIS

Despite its holding of copyright infringement, the Ninth Circuit refused to issue an injunction against sale or distribution of "Rear Window," noting the "injustice" that a ban on exhibition would cause. This decision, however, seemed to deprive Abend (P) of his remedy. Also, the result might have been different had this case been decided under the 1976 Act, which in § 101(c)(6)(A) provides: "A derivative

Continued on next page.

work prepared under authority of the grant before its termination may continue to be utilized under the terms of the grant after its termination."

Quicknotes

COPYRIGHT Refers to the exclusive rights granted to an artist pursuant to Article I, section 8, clause 8 of the United States Constitution over the reproduction, display, performance, distribution, and adaptation of his work for a period prescribed by statute.

COPYRIGHT INFRINGEMENT A violation of one of the exclusive rights granted to an artist pursuant to Article I, section 8, clause 8 of the United States Constitution over the reproduction, display, performance, distribution, and adaptation of his work for a period prescribed by statute.

DERIVATIVE WORK A work of authorship that is based on a previous work.

INJUNCTION A court order requiring a person to do or prohibiting that person from doing a specific act.

REMEDY Compensation for violation of a right or injuries sustained.

SUMMARY JUDGMENT Judgment rendered by a court in response to a motion by one of the parties, claiming that the lack of a question of material fact in respect to an issue warrants disposition of the issue without consideration by the jury.

CHAPTER 4

Protected Works and Boundary Problems

Quick Reference Rules of Law

                                                                                                                                             PAGE

1. **"Kitsch" or "Progress"?** An article having a utilitarian application may be copyrighted. (Mazer v. Stein)   *39*

2. **Defining Useful Articles and Determining Separability.** Useful articles are copyrightable only to the extent that their designs incorporate artistic features that can be identified separately from the functional elements of the articles. (Kieselstein-Cord v. Accessories by Pearl, Inc.)   *40*

3. **Defining Useful Articles and Determining Separability.** An article with ornamental features inseparable from its functional features is not copyrightable. (Carol Barnhart Inc. v. Economy Cover Corp.)   *41*

4. **Defining Useful Articles and Determining Separability.** If the design elements of a work are predominantly functional considerations that trump the artistic elements of the work, the work is not copyrightable. (Brandir International, Inc. v. Cascade Pacific Lumber Co.)   *42*

5. **Computer Software.** There is no merit to the contention that computer operating system programs, as distinguished from application programs, are per se not copyrightable. (Apple Computer, Inc. v. Franklin Computer Corp.)   *43*

6. **Computer Software.** To warrant a finding of copyright infringement, the protectable, nonliteral elements of one computer program must be substantially similar to those same elements in the second program. (Computer Associates International, Inc. v. Altai, Inc.)   *44*

7. **Computer Software.** Similarity of computer programs can constitute copyright infringement. (Softel, Inc. v. Dragon Medical and Scientific Communications, Inc.)   *46*

8. **Computer Software.** A computer menu command hierarchy is not copyrightable subject matter. (Lotus Development Corporation v. Borland International, Inc.)   *47*

9. **Architectural Works.** A combination of common structural building features can constitute a unique, copyrightable design. (Nelson-Salabes, Inc. v. Morningside Holdings)   *48*

10. **Architectural Works.** To determine whether an architectural floor-plan infringes another, only the differences between the arrangement and coordination of non-protectible elements should be compared to determine if there is substantial similarity between the two plans. (Intervest Construction, Inc. v. Canterbury Estate Homes, Inc.)   *49*

11. **Characters.** A movie character can be copyrightable where he has specific character traits that are developed through a series of films. (Metro-Goldwyn-Mayer, Inc. v. American Honda Motor Co.)   *51*

12. **Characters.** The owner of a copyright in works embodying a character can obtain a copyright in the character itself if the character is specifically delineated in the work and is sufficiently unique. (Titan Sports, Inc. v. Turner Broadcasting Systems, Inc.)   *52*

13. **Databases.** The names, addresses, telephone numbers, and business types listed in a yellow pages directory are not original elements of a work and are not copyrightable. (BellSouth Advertising & Publishing Corp. v. Donnelley Information Publishing, Inc.)   *53*

37

CHAPTER 4

14. Databases. Copyright protection does not extend to ideas but does extend to compilations and the expression of those ideas. (CCC Information Services, Inc. v. Maclean Hunter Market Reports, Inc.) — *54*

15. Databases. A compilation of information that distills and extrapolates from factual data can demonstrate creativity and originality sufficient to make that compilation copyrightable. (CDN Inc. v. Kapes) — *55*

16. Databases. Elements of a compilation that are determined by a computer program do not entail a modicum of creativity and are unprotected. (Matthew Bender & Co. v. West Publishing Co.) — *56*

Mazer v. Stein

Statuette manufacturer (P) v. Copyright owner (D)

347 U.S. 201 (1954).

NATURE OF CASE: Review of order enjoining copyright infringement and awarding damages.

FACT SUMMARY: Mazer (D) contended that an article having a utilitarian application could not be copyrighted.

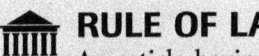

RULE OF LAW
An article having a utilitarian application may be copyrighted.

FACTS: Stein (P) obtained a copyright on a statuette. The statuette was put into mass production and was used as a base for table lamps. Mazer (D) began producing duplicate statuettes for use in table lamps. Stein (P) brought an action alleging copyright infringement, seeking damages and injunctive relief. The district court found infringement and awarded damages and enjoined further infringement. Mazer (D) appealed, contending that a practically useful article could be protected only by a patent, not by a copyright. The court of appeals affirmed, and the Supreme Court granted certiorari.

ISSUE: Can an article having a utilitarian application be copyrighted?

HOLDING AND DECISION: (Reed, J.) Yes. An article having a utilitarian application may be copyrighted. A subsequent utilization of a work of art in an article of manufacture in no way affects the right of the copyright owner to be protected against infringement of the work of art itself. Verbal distinctions between purely aesthetic articles and useful works of art have long ago ended insofar as statutory copyright language is concerned. The economic philosophy behind the Copyright Clause is the conviction that encouragement of individual effort by personal gain is the best way to advance public welfare through the talent of authors and inventors. Affirmed.

CONCURRENCE: (Douglas, J.) There is a long list of articles which have been copyrighted, hence the time has come to place this case for reargument.

ANALYSIS

The Court did not address the issue of whether the statuette was patentable, as its conclusion that the statuette was copyrightable made the issue moot. Generally speaking, patentability is more difficult to achieve than copyrightability. It is questionable whether the patentability requirements of novelty, utility, and originality would have existed here.

Quicknotes

CERTIORARI A discretionary writ issued by a superior court to an inferior court in order to review the lower court's decisions; the Supreme Court's writ ordering such review.

COPYRIGHT Refers to the exclusive rights granted to an artist pursuant to Article I, section 8, clause 8 of the United States Constitution over the reproduction, display, performance, distribution, and adaptation of his work for a period prescribed by statute.

COPYRIGHT INFRINGEMENT A violation of one of the exclusive rights granted to an artist pursuant to Article I, section 8, clause 8 of the United States Constitution over the reproduction, display, performance, distribution, and adaptation of his work for a period prescribed by statute.

INJUNCTIVE RELIEF A court order issued as a remedy, requiring a person to do, or prohibiting that person from doing, a specific act.

PATENT A limited monopoly conferred on the invention or discovery of any new or useful machine or process that is novel and nonobvious.

Kieselstein-Cord v. Accessories by Pearl, Inc.

Jewelry designer/manufacturer (P) v. Accessories manufacturer (D)

632 F.2d 989 (2d Cir. 1980).

NATURE OF CASE: Action for copyright infringement of a belt buckle design.

FACT SUMMARY: Kieselstein-Cord (P) sued Accessories by Pearl, Inc. (D) for copyright infringement on a belt buckle design, and the defendant argued that belt buckles were utilitarian objects and hence not copyrightable.

RULE OF LAW
Useful articles are copyrightable only to the extent that their designs incorporate artistic features that can be identified separately from the functional elements of the articles.

FACTS: Kieselstein-Cord (P) obtained copyrights for two belt buckles featuring sculptured designs cast in precious metals. The buckles were decorative in nature and used for ornamentation. They were accepted by the Metropolitan Museum of Art for its permanent collection. Kieselstein-Cord (P) was given a Coty American Fashion Critics' Award for his work in jewelry design and was elected to the Council of Fashion Designers of America. He brought suit for copyright infringement against Accessories by Pearl, Inc. (D), which argued that the buckles were "useful articles" with no "pictorial, graphic or sculptural features that can be identified separately from, and are capable of existing independently of, [their] utilitarian aspects." Kieselstein-Cord (P) appealed. District court decided for the Defendant.

ISSUE: Are utilitarian articles copyrightable only to the extent that their designs incorporate artistic features that can be identified separately from the functional elements of the articles?

HOLDING AND DECISION: (Oakes, J.) Yes. The 1976 copyright statute does not provide for the copyrighting of useful articles except to the extent that their designs incorporate artistic features that can be identified separately from the functional elements of the articles. Thus, in cases such as this, the primary object is to determine when a pictorial, graphic, or sculptured feature "can be identified separately from, and is capable of existing independently of, the utilitarian aspects of the article." Such separability may occur either "physically or conceptually." In this instance, the buckles have conceptually separable sculptural elements. Their primary ornamental aspect is conceptually separable from their subsidiary utilitarian function. Thus, they are copyrightable. Reversed.

DISSENT: (Weinstein, J.) The form of the buckles is inseparable from their function. Congress specifically declined to enact legislation that would have extended copyright protection to useful articles. Although the result may be the unfortunate occurrence of commercial piracy, the buckles are useful articles and not copyrightable.

ANALYSIS

Professor Nimmer has illustrated separability using the example of "conceptual art," which by its nature utilizes objects to make a statement. He notes that Christo's "Running Fence" "did not contain sculptural features that were physically separable from the utilitarian aspects of the fence, but the whole point of the work was that the artistic aspects of the work were conceptually separable." 1 Nimmer on Copyright § 2.08(B)(3), (1986).

Quicknotes

COPYRIGHT Refers to the exclusive rights granted to an artist pursuant to Article I, section 8, clause 8 of the United States Constitution over the reproduction, display, performance, distribution, and adaptation of his work for a period prescribed by statute.

COPYRIGHT INFRINGEMENT A violation of one of the exclusive rights granted to an artist pursuant to Article I, section 8, clause 8 of the United States Constitution over the reproduction, display, performance, distribution, and adaptation of his work for a period prescribed by statute.

Carol Barnhart, Inc. v. Economy Cover Corp.

Mannequin designer and manufacturer (P) v. Mannequin manufacturer (D)

773 F.2d 411 (2d Cir. 1985).

NATURE OF CASE: Appeal of summary judgment dismissing copyright infringement action.

FACT SUMMARY: Carol Barnhart, Inc. (P) sought copyright protection of certain mannequins, the ornamental features of which were inseparable from their functional features.

RULE OF LAW
An article with ornamental features inseparable from its functional features is not copyrightable.

FACTS: Carol Barnhart, Inc. (Barnhart) (P) began marketing certain distinctive mannequins for sale to clothing retailers. Economy Cover Corp. (D) began selling duplicates. Upon learning of this, Barnhart (P) applied for and received a copyright on the mannequin design. It then sued for infringement. The district court held that the mannequins' ornamental qualities were inseparable from their function and were therefore uncopyrightable. The court granted summary judgment dismissing the case, and Barnhart (P) appealed.

ISSUE: Is an article with ornamental features inseparable from its functional features copyrightable?

HOLDING AND DECISION: (Mansfield, J.) No. An article with ornamental features inseparable from its functional features is not copyrightable. While the evidence may indicate that the instant torso forms are in fact aesthetically satisfying and valuable, it is insufficient to show that the forms possess aesthetic or artistic features that are physically or conceptually separable from the forms' use as utilitarian objects to display clothes. Here, the features claimed to be aesthetic or artistic, e.g., the life-size configuration of the breasts and the width of the shoulders, are inextricably intertwined with the utilitarian feature, the display of clothes. Affirmed.

DISSENT: (Newman, J.) The separateness between function and aesthetics necessary for copyrightability is not physical, but conceptual. If, to the ordinary reasonable observer, function and aesthetics would be conceptually distinct, the ornamental features are copyrightable. Here, such an observer could admire the ornamental features without contemplating the function of the mannequins, so these features should be copyrightable.

ANALYSIS

It is rather difficult to reconcile the instant case with *Mazer v. Stein*, 347 U.S. 201 (1954). In that case, certain decorative statuettes were held to be copyrightable. It is difficult indeed to see the difference between the statuettes in *Mazer* and the mannequins here. It is possible that the focus of each case was different: in *Mazer*, the Court was occupied more with the issue of whether patentability precluded copyrightability than with the issue of copyrightability itself.

Quicknotes

COPYRIGHT INFRINGEMENT A violation of one of the exclusive rights granted to an artist pursuant to Article I, section 8, clause 8 of the United States Constitution over the reproduction, display, performance, distribution, and adaptation of his work for a period prescribed by statute.

SUMMARY JUDGMENT Judgment rendered by a court in response to a motion by one of the parties, claiming that the lack of a question of material fact in respect to an issue warrants disposition of the issue without consideration by the jury.

Brandir International, Inc. v. Cascade Pacific Lumber Co.

Bicycle rack maker (P) v. Alleged infringer (D)

834 F.2d 1142 (2d Cir. 1987).

NATURE OF CASE: Appeal from judgment in favor of competitor on a copyright and trademark infringement action.

FACT SUMMARY: Brandir International, Inc. (Brandir) (P) created a bicycle rack made of bent metal tubing, which Cascade Pacific Lumber Co. (D) then copied. The Copyright Office denied Brandir (P) copyright registration.

RULE OF LAW
If the design elements of a work are predominantly functional considerations that trump the artistic elements of the work, the work is not copyrightable.

FACTS: The owner of Brandir International, Inc. (Brandir) (P) designed a bicycle rack made of metal tubing. The design of the rack evolved from wire sculptures created by Brandir's (P) owner, but these had been significantly adapted to serve as functional bike racks. Cascade Pacific Lumber Co. (D) copied the bike rack design. The Copyright Office denied registration to Brandir (P). The district court agreed and granted summary judgment to Cascade (D) on Brandir's (P) claim for copyright infringement.

ISSUE: Will a work be copyrightable where its design is significantly influenced by utilitarian concerns that trump the aesthetic elements of the work?

HOLDING AND DECISION: (Oakes, J.) No. Under the test articulated by Denicola, if the design elements of a work reflect a merger of aesthetic and functional considerations, the artistic elements are not separable and thus the work is not copyrightable. Here, although the bike rack was based on an artistic design, the original design had been significantly adapted to serve the utilitarian function of a bike rack. Affirmed.

DISSENT: (Winter, J.) The true focus should be on whether the work is perceived as being artistic or merely functional, not on the development process behind the product.

ANALYSIS

Commentators have noted that the idea of "conceptual separability" often requires a judgment call as to what is or is not art. There are differences of opinion as to how much leeway should be afforded the courts in making these judgment calls.

Quicknotes

COPYRIGHT Refers to the exclusive rights granted to an artist pursuant to Article I, section 8, clause 8 of the United States Constitution over the reproduction, display, performance, distribution, and adaptation of his work for a period prescribed by statute.

COPYRIGHT INFRINGEMENT A violation of one of the exclusive rights granted to an artist pursuant to Article I, section 8, clause 8 of the United States Constitution over the reproduction, display, performance, distribution, and adaptation of his work for a period prescribed by statute.

SUMMARY JUDGMENT Judgment rendered by a court in response to a motion by one of the parties, claiming that the lack of a question of material fact in respect to an issue warrants disposition of the issue without consideration by the jury.

Apple Computer, Inc. v. Franklin Computer Corp.

Computer company (P) v. Computer programmer (D)

714 F.2d 1240 (3d Cir. 1983), *cert. dismissed*, 464 U.S. 1033 (1984).

NATURE OF CASE: Appeal from denial of motion to enjoin copyright infringement.

FACT SUMMARY: Franklin Computer Corp.'s (D) response to Apple Computer, Inc.'s (Apple's) (P) allegation that it was infringing the copyrights on 14 computer programs was that Apple (P) operating systems were not capable of copyright protection.

RULE OF LAW
There is no merit to the contention that computer operating system programs, as distinguished from application programs, are per se not copyrightable.

FACTS: The district court denied Apple Computer, Inc.'s (Apple's) (P) motion to preliminarily enjoin Franklin Computer Corp. (Franklin) (D) from infringing the copyrights Apple (P) held on 14 computer programs. On appeal, the central contention made by Franklin (D) was that computer operating system programs, as distinguished from application programs, are per se uncopyrightable because such programs are either a "process," "system," or "method of operation." The district court had been persuaded by Franklin's (D) argument that an operating system program is part of a machine.

ISSUE: Are computer operating system programs per se uncopyrightable?

HOLDING AND DECISION: (Sloviter, J.) No. The copyrightability of computer programs is firmly established after the 1980 amendment to the Copyright Act directed toward that issue. It defines a "computer program" as "sets of statements or instructions to be used directly or indirectly in a computer in order to bring about a certain result." There is nothing to suggest that computer operating system programs, as distinguished from application programs, are per se uncopyrightable. By copyrighting an operating system program, Apple (P) did not seek to copyright the method by which the computer is instructed to perform its operating functions. It sought only to copyright the instructions themselves. It makes no difference in the copyright context whether the instructions tell the computer to help prepare an income tax return, which an application program would do, or to translate a high-level language program from a source code into its binary language object code form, which is the task of an operating system program. It is only the instructions that are protected. There is no reason to afford any less copyright protection to the instructions in an operating system program than to the instructions in an application program. Franklin's (D) attack on operating system programs as "methods" or "processes" is inconsistent with its concession that application programs are an appropriate subject of copyright. Both types of programs instruct the computer to do something. The medium is not the message. The mere fact that the operating system program may be etched on a ROM does not make the program either a machine, part of a machine, or its equivalent. Furthermore, the statutory definition of a computer program, makes no distinction between application programs and operating programs. Reversed and remanded.

ANALYSIS

In his concurring opinion in the Final Report of the National Commission on New Technological Uses of Copyrighted Works, Professor Nimmer wrote that it might prove useful at some point to "limit copyright protection for software to those computer programs which produce works which themselves would qualify for copyright protection." For example, under such an approach, one could copyright the program for a computer-video game or an information retrieval system because the output would constitute a work in itself, but one could not copyright programs for computer-controlled functions, such as a building's heating and cooling system or fuel flow to an engine.

Quicknotes

COPYRIGHT Refers to the exclusive rights granted to an artist pursuant to Article I, section 8, clause 8 of the United States Constitution over the reproduction, display, performance, distribution, and adaptation of his work for a period prescribed by statute.

COPYRIGHT INFRINGEMENT A violation of one of the exclusive rights granted to an artist pursuant to Article I, section 8, clause 8 of the United States Constitution over the reproduction, display, performance, distribution, and adaptation of his work for a period prescribed by statute.

ENJOIN The ordering of a party to cease the conduct of a specific activity.

Computer Associates International, Inc. v. Altai, Inc.

Software designer (P) v. Competitor (D)

982 F.2d 693 (2d Cir. 1992).

NATURE OF CASE: Appeal from award of damages for copyright infringement.

FACT SUMMARY: Upon discovering that Altai, Inc. (D) may have appropriated parts of its "Adapter" computer program, Computer Associates International, Inc. (CA) (P) sued Altai (D) for copyright infringement and trade secret misappropriation.

RULE OF LAW
To warrant a finding of copyright infringement, the protectable, nonliteral elements of one computer program must be substantially similar to those same elements in the second program.

FACTS: Computer Associates International, Inc. (CA) (P) designed, developed, and marketed various types of computer programs, including "CA-Scheduler," a job scheduling program containing a sub-program entitled "Adapter." Adapter was a wholly integrated component of CA-Scheduler with no capacity for independent use. In 1982, Altai, Inc. (D) began marketing its own job scheduling program entitled "Zeke." Subsequently, Altai (D) decided to rewrite Zeke to run in conjunction with a different operating system, and approached Arney, a computer programmer who worked for CA (P), about working for Altai (D). When Arney left CA (P) to work for Altai (D), he took with him copies of the source code for two versions of Adapter. No one at Altai (D) knew that Arney had the Adapter codes and was using them to design Altai's (D) new component-program, "Oscar" (Version 3.4). Arney copied approximately 30% of Oscar's code from CA's (P) Adapter program. When CA (P) first learned that Altai (D) may have appropriated parts of Adapter, it brought this copyright and trade secret misappropriation action against Altai (D), which then initiated a rewrite of Oscar, entitled Oscar 3.5. From that point on, Altai (D) shipped only Oscar 3.5 to new customers and provided a free 3.5 upgrade to all customers who had previously purchased version 3.4. The district court awarded CA (P) $364,444 in actual damages and apportioned profits for copyright infringement regarding Oscar 3.4. However, the court denied relief on CA's (P) second claim, finding that Oscar 3.5 was not substantially similar to Adapter. The court further concluded that CA's (P) state law trade secret misappropriation claim against Altai (D) was preempted by the federal copyright act. On appeal, Altai (D) conceded liability for the copying of Adapter into Oscar 3.4 and raised no challenge to the award of damages. Thus, only CA's (P) second and third claims were addressed on appeal.

ISSUE: To warrant a finding of copyright infringement, must the protectable, nonliteral elements of one computer program be substantially similar to those elements in a second program?

HOLDING AND DECISION: (Walker, J.) Yes. To warrant a finding of copyright infringement, the protectable, nonliteral elements of one computer program must be substantially similar to those elements in a second program. It is now well settled that the literal elements of computer programs, i.e., their source and object codes, are the subject of copyright protection. Altai (D) made sure that the literal elements of its revamped Oscar program were no longer substantially similar to the literal elements of CA's (P) Adapter. If the nonliteral structures of literary works are protected by copyright, then the nonliteral structures of computer programs are also protected by copyright. However, it is a fundamental principle of copyright law that a copyright does not protect an idea, but only the expression of the idea. A three-step procedure, based on that utilized by the district court, should be used to determine whether the nonliteral elements of two or more computer programs are substantially similar. The first step in the examination for substantial similarity is abstraction. It is necessary to retrace and map each of the designer's steps in the opposite order in which they were taken during the program's creation. Once the program's abstraction levels have been discovered, the substantial similarity inquiry moves from the conceptual to the concrete. This process, termed filtration, entails examining the structural components at each level of abstraction to determine whether their particular inclusion at that level was dictated by considerations of efficiency; required by factors external to the program itself; or taken from the public domain, thus making them nonprotectable. Once a court has sifted out all those elements of the allegedly infringed program, there may remain a core of protectable expression. At this point, the court's substantial similarity inquiry turns to comparison, focusing on whether Altai (D) copied any aspect of this protected expression, as well as an assessment of the copied portion's relative importance with respect to CA's (P) overall program. The three-step approach outlined here not only comports with, but advances the constitutional policies underlying the copyright act. The court found no error on the part of the district court judge and affirmed.

ANALYSIS

One of the doctrines discussed by the court is the doctrine of merger. The doctrine's underlying principle is that when there is essentially only one way to express an idea, the idea and its expression are inseparable and copyright is no bar to copying that expression. In the computer context,

Continued on next page.

this means that when specific instructions, even though previously copyrighted, are the only and essential means of accomplishing a given task, their later use by another will not amount to infringement. When one considers the fact that programmers generally strive to create programs "that meet the user's needs in the most efficient manner," the applicability of the merger doctrine to computer programs becomes compelling.

Quicknotes

COPYRIGHT ACT Copyright Act of 1976 extends copyright protection to "original works of authorship fixed in any tangible medium of expression, now known or later developed, from which they can be perceived, reproduced, or otherwise communicated, either directly or with the aid of a machine or device." 17 U.S.C. § 102.

COPYRIGHT INFRINGEMENT A violation of one of the exclusive rights granted to an artist pursuant to Article I, section 8, clause 8 of the United States Constitution over the reproduction, display, performance, distribution, and adaptation of his work for a period prescribed by statute.

Softel, Inc. v. Dragon Medical and Scientific Communications, Inc.

Software maker (P) v. Customer (D)

118 F.3d 955 (2d Cir. 1997), cert. denied, 523 U.S. 1020 (1998).

NATURE OF CASE: Action for copyright infringement and misappropriation of trade secrets.

FACT SUMMARY: Softel, Inc. (P) sued a former customer (D) for copyright infringement after the former customer used Softel's (P) software to create new programs.

RULE OF LAW
Similarity of computer programs can constitute copyright infringement.

FACTS: Softel, Inc. (P) provided imaging software to Dragon Medical and Scientific Communications, Inc. (Dragon) (D). After the relationship between the parties ended, Softel (P) attempted to remove all of its software from Dragon's (D) computers but was unable to remove it completely. Dragon (D) used some of the remaining software to create new programs. Softel (P) sued for copyright infringement. During the litigation, Dragon (D) created additional programs from Softel's (P) software, but in different languages and to run on different hardware. The judge found that the pre-litigation programs infringed Softel's (P) copyright, but that the post-litigation ones did not. Softel (P) appealed.

ISSUE: Will copyright protection extend to a work where the individual design elements of the work cannot be independently protected?

HOLDING AND DECISION: (Parker, J.) Yes. A compilation of non-protectable elements can enjoy copyright protection. Examining the individual elements here, Softel's (P) copyright could have been infringed. Here, the manner in which Softel (P) combined computer design elements could be considered original and may be entitled to copyright protection. Vacated and remanded.

ANALYSIS

This decision is in line with cases such as *Feist Publications, Inc. v. Rural Telephone Service Co.*, 499 U.S. 340 (1991), and *Computer Assocs. International, Inc. v. Altai, Inc.*, 755 F. Supp. 544 (E.D.N.Y. 1991), in which courts have recognized the protectability of compilations.

Quicknotes

COPYRIGHT Refers to the exclusive rights granted to an artist pursuant to Article I, section 8, clause 8 of the United States Constitution over the reproduction, display, performance, distribution, and adaptation of his work for a period prescribed by statute.

COPYRIGHT INFRINGEMENT A violation of one of the exclusive rights granted to an artist pursuant to Article I, section 8, clause 8 of the United States Constitution over the reproduction, display, performance, distribution, and adaptation of his work for a period prescribed by statute.

Lotus Development Corporation v. Borland International, Inc.

Software designer (P) v. Competitor (D)

49 F.3d 807 (1st Cir. 1995), *aff'd by an equally divided court*, 516 U.S. 233 (1996).

NATURE OF CASE: Appeal from finding of copyright infringement.

FACT SUMMARY: Borland International, Inc. (Borland) (D) included in its own spreadsheet programs the commands used by the computer program Lotus 1-2-3 so that spreadsheet users who were already familiar with 1-2-3 could easily switch to the Borland (D) programs without learning new commands.

RULE OF LAW
A computer menu command hierarchy is not copyrightable subject matter.

FACTS: Lotus Development Corp. (Lotus) (P) marketed a computer spreadsheet program, Lotus 1-2-3. The program incorporated 469 menu commands, such as "Copy," "Print," etc. The program also enabled the user to write macros that would designate a series of commands with a single macro keystroke. Borland International, Inc. (Borland) (D) subsequently released two versions of its own spreadsheet programs, called Quattro and Quattro Pro. Borland (D) included a virtually identical copy of the entire 1-2-3 menu tree in its Quattro programs. It did not copy any of Lotus's (P) underlying computer code, but it did copy the words and structures of Lotus's (P) menu command hierarchy so that consumers who used Borland's (D) programs would not have to relearn any commands or rewrite their Lotus (P) macros. Lotus (P) sued for copyright infringement and received a judgment in its favor. Borland (D) appealed, contending that the Lotus (P) menu command hierarchy was not copyrightable because it was a system, method of operation, process, or procedure foreclosed from protection by the Copyright Act.

ISSUE: Is a computer menu command hierarchy copyrightable subject matter?

HOLDING AND DECISION: (Stahl, J.) No. A computer menu command hierarchy is not copyrightable subject matter. A menu command hierarchy is an uncopyrightable "method of operation" as that term is used in § 102(b) of the Copyright Act. It provides the means by which users control and operate a program's functional capabilities. Just as it would be impossible to operate a VCR without buttons, it would be impossible to operate Lotus 1-2-3 without employing its menu command hierarchy. Thus, the Lotus (P) command terms are equivalent to the buttons themselves, which are an uncopyrightable method of operating the VCR. Therefore, Borland (D) did not infringe Lotus's (P) copyright when it copied its menu command hierarchy. Reversed.

CONCURRENCE: (Boudin, J.) If a better spreadsheet comes along, there is no reason why those customers who have learned the Lotus (P) menu and devised macros for it should be forced to remain captive of Lotus (P) merely because of an investment in learning made by them and not by Lotus (P).

ANALYSIS
Judge Boudin suggested that an alternative analysis would be to say that Borland's (D) use of Lotus's (P) menu was privileged because it was merely trying to assist former Lotus (P) customers, not attract them. The closest analogy to that approach would be the fair use doctrine employed in conventional copyright law. However, he also admitted that a privileged use doctrine would cause a host of administrative problems and would also reduce the ability of the industry to predict outcomes.

Quicknotes

COPYRIGHT Refers to the exclusive rights granted to an artist pursuant to Article I, section 8, clause 8 of the United States Constitution over the reproduction, display, performance, distribution, and adaptation of his work for a period prescribed by statute.

COPYRIGHT ACT Copyright Act of 1976 extends copyright protection to "original works of authorship fixed in any tangible medium of expression, now known or later developed, from which they can be perceived, reproduced, or otherwise communicated, either directly or with the aid of a machine or device." 17 U.S.C. § 102.

COPYRIGHT INFRINGEMENT A violation of one of the exclusive rights granted to an artist pursuant to Article I, section 8, clause 8 of the United States Constitution over the reproduction, display, performance, distribution, and adaptation of his work for a period prescribed by statute.

Nelson-Salabes, Inc. v. Morningside Holdings

Architects (P) v. Developer (D)

2001 W.L. 419002 (D. Md. 2001), aff'd in part, rev'd in part on other grounds, 284 F.3d 505 (4th Cir. 2002).

NATURE OF CASE: Action for copyright infringement of an architectural design.

FACT SUMMARY: Nelson-Salabes, Inc. (P) sued Morningside Holdings (D) for infringement of copyright in the architectural designs of an assisted-living facility.

RULE OF LAW
A combination of common structural building features can constitute a unique, copyrightable design.

FACTS: Nelson-Salabes, Inc. (P) was hired by developers to provide architectural designs for a proposed assisted-living facility. The designs were submitted to the Baltimore County board for approval. Prior to approval of the designs, the original developers sold the site to Morningside Holdings (D). Nelson-Salabes (P) were told they would not be retained by Morningside (D). Nelson-Salabes (P) agreed to step aside, but they told Morningside (D) that it could not use Nelson-Salabes's (P) designs, including the footprint and elevations. New plans were submitted to the county by Morningside's (D) architects, with only minor changes from the Nelson-Salabes's (P) footprint and elevation designs.

ISSUE: Are the designs for the footprints and elevations of a building copyrightable?

HOLDING AND DECISION: (Black, J.) Yes. Although the use of common architectural features is not copyrightable, the combination of such common features can form a unique design that is copyrightable. Here, Nelson-Salabes's (P) combination is unique. Moreover, the footprint and elevation designs by Nelson-Salabes (P) are not the only designs feasible. Therefore, Nelson-Salabes (P) had a valid copyright that was infringed by Morningside (D).

section 8, clause 8 of the United States Constitution over the reproduction, display, performance, distribution, and adaptation of his work for a period prescribed by statute.

ANALYSIS

Under section 101 of the Copyright Act of 1976, an "architectural work" includes "the overall form as well as the arrangement and composition of spaces and elements in the design, but does not include individual standard features."

Quicknotes

COPYRIGHT ACT SECTION 101 Section 101 of the Copyright Act of 1976, setting forth the definitions for purposes of the act.

COPYRIGHT INFRINGEMENT A violation of one of the exclusive rights granted to an artist pursuant to Article I,

Intervest Construction, Inc. v. Canterbury Estate Homes, Inc.

Construction company (P) v. Construction company (D)

554 F.3d 914 (11th Cir. 2008).

NATURE OF CASE: Appeal from judgment for defendant in action for copyright infringement of an architectural work.

FACT SUMMARY: Intervest Construction, Inc. (Intervest) (P) contended that its floor-plan for a house, The Westminster, was infringed by Canterbury Estate Homes, Inc.'s (Canterbury's) (D) floor-plan for a similar house, The Kensington.

RULE OF LAW
To determine whether an architectural floor-plan infringes another, only the differences between the arrangement and coordination of non-protectible elements should be compared to determine if there is substantial similarity between the two plans.

FACTS: Intervest Construction, Inc. (Intervest) (P) created a floor-plan for a house, The Westminster. Canterbury Estate Homes, Inc. (Canterbury) (D) created a floor-plan for a similar house, The Kensington. Each floor-plan depicted a house with the same types of spaces, e.g., a two-car garage, four bedrooms, porch/patio, nooks, etc., and similar square footage. Each plan also reflected certain "elements" common to most houses, e.g., doors, windows, walls, bathroom and kitchen fixtures, etc. Intervest (P) brought suit, claiming that Canterbury's (D) plan infringed Intervest's (P) plan. The district court, after identifying all of these unassigned spaces and elements of the floor-plans, undertook a detailed comparative analysis of the selection, coordination, and arrangement of these common components and elements, focusing upon the dissimilarities in such coordination and arrangement. The district court concluded that no reasonable observer could conclude that the copyrightable elements of the two floor-plans were substantially similar. Intervest (P) appealed, arguing that the district court erred in focusing on the dissimilarities between the two floor-plans at issue. The court of appeals granted review.

ISSUE: To determine whether an architectural floor plan infringes another, should only the differences between the arrangement and coordination of non-protectible elements be compared to determine if there is substantial similarity between the two plans?

HOLDING AND DECISION: (Birch, J.) Yes. To determine whether an architectural floor plan infringes another, only the differences between the arrangement and coordination of non-protectible elements should be compared to determine if there is substantial similarity between the two plans. At issue is an architectural work, which is defined by the Copyright Act as "the design of a building as embodied in any tangible medium of expression, including a building, architectural plans or drawings. The work includes the overall form as well as the arrangement and composition of spaces and elements in the design, but does not include individual standard features." The "individual standard features" refers to unprotectible elements such as windows and doors. The definition reflects Congress's belief that the creative elements in the work are the "arrangement and coordination" of the unprotectible elements. Thus, the definition of an architectural work closely parallels that of a "compilation," since the compiler's choices as to selection coordination, or arrangement are the only portions of a compilation that are even entitled to copyright protection. Accordingly, any similarity comparison of the works must be accomplished at the level of protected expression, i.e., the arrangement and coordination of the common, unprotectible elements. When making such a comparison, it must be kept in mind that copyright protection in a compilation is "thin," so that the substantial similarity test in case of a compilation is modified to accentuate the narrower scope of protection available. Applying such a narrowed test here, the district court did not err in emphasizing the plans' dissimilarities. Given that the differences in the protectible expression were so significant, as a matter of law, no reasonable properly-instructed jury of lay observers could find the works substantially similar. Affirmed.

ANALYSIS

There are three types of work that are entitled to copyright protection—creative, derivative, and compiled. Copyrights in these three distinct works are known as creative, derivative, and compilation copyrights. An example of a creative work is a novel. An example of a derivative work is a screenplay based on a novel; it is called "derivative" because it is based on a preexisting work that has been recast, transformed, or adapted. An example of a compilation is the floor-plans at issue in this case. The Copyright Act has thus created a hierarchy in terms of the protection afforded to these different types of copyrights. A creative work is entitled to the most protection, followed by a derivative work, and finally by a compilation. This is why the copyright protection in a factual compilation is "thin."

Quicknotes

COPYRIGHT ACT Copyright Act of 1976 extends copyright protection to "original works of authorship fixed in any

Continued on next page.

tangible medium of expression, now known or later developed, from which they can be perceived, reproduced, or otherwise communicated, either directly or with the aid of a machine or device." 17 U.S.C. § 102.

COPYRIGHT INFRINGEMENT A violation of one of the exclusive rights granted to an artist pursuant to Article I, Section 8, clause 8 of the United States Constitution over the reproduction, display, performance, distribution, and adaptation of his work for a period prescribed by statute.

Metro-Goldwyn-Mayer, Inc. v. American Honda Motor Co.

Copyright holder (P) v. Alleged infringer (D)

900 F. Supp. 1287 (C.D. Cal. 1995).

NATURE OF CASE: Action for copyright infringement of a movie character.

FACT SUMMARY: Metro-Goldwyn-Mayer (P) sought to enjoin American Honda Motor Co. (D) from running an ad campaign for its Honda del Sol, alleging that the ads infringed on certain copyrights related to sixteen James Bond films.

RULE OF LAW
A movie character can be copyrightable where he has specific character traits that are developed through a series of films.

FACTS: Honda (D) produced a commercial promoting their Honda del Sol model that depicted a well-dressed couple in a Honda del Sol being chased by a villain in a helicopter. Plaintiffs brought suit for copyright infringement and sought to enjoin the commercial, claiming that the commercial infringed various copyrights to sixteen James Bond films and the James Bond character.

ISSUE: Are movie characters copyrightable?

HOLDING AND DECISION: (Kenyon, J.) Yes. Although no one test for copyrightability of movie characters has been delineated in the Ninth Circuit, movie characters may be copyrighted in certain circumstances. Those circumstances include (1) where the character represents the story actually being told in the film and is not merely a "chessman" in that story; (2) where the character is graphically depicted; or (3) where the character is especially distinctive. Here, the James Bond character is determined to be copyrightable in that he represents the story being told and is especially distinctive.

ANALYSIS
Individual film scenes may also be copyrightable, especially where they incorporate a copyrightable character that brings specific elements of his character to the scene.

Quicknotes

COPYRIGHT Refers to the exclusive rights granted to an artist pursuant to Article I, section 8, clause 8 of the United States Constitution over the reproduction, display, performance, distribution, and adaptation of his work for a period prescribed by statute.

COPYRIGHT INFRINGEMENT A violation of one of the exclusive rights granted to an artist pursuant to Article I, section 8, clause 8 of the United States Constitution over the reproduction, display, performance, distribution, and adaptation of his work for a period prescribed by statute.

ENJOIN The ordering of a party to cease the conduct of a specific activity.

Titan Sports, Inc. v. Turner Broadcasting Systems, Inc.

Wrestling promoter (P) v. Cable network (D)

981 F. Supp. 65 (D. Conn. 1997).

NATURE OF CASE: Action for copyright infringement of wrestling characters.

FACT SUMMARY: Titan Sports, Inc. (P) alleged copyright infringement against Turner Broadcasting Systems, Inc. (D), a competitor, for infringement of wrestling characters.

RULE OF LAW
The owner of a copyright in works embodying a character can obtain a copyright in the character itself if the character is specifically delineated in the work and is sufficiently unique.

FACTS: Titan Sports, Inc. (Titan) (P) promotes professional wrestling under the name World Wrestling Federation (WWF). Turner Broadcasting Systems, Inc. (D) owns several cable networks and has as one of its subsidiaries World Championship Wrestling, Inc. (WCW), which competes with the WWF. Two former WCW wrestlers contracted with the WWF to wrestle for it. The WWF developed characters, including a specific costume and persona for each wrestler. Subsequently, the wrestlers were enticed back to WCW, where they continued to wrestle in their WWF personas, but under different names. Titan (P) alleged copyright infringement of the characters it had created for the wrestlers.

ISSUE: Is copyright protection available for characters?

HOLDING AND DECISION: (Dorsey, J.) Yes. The owner of a copyright in works embodying a character can acquire copyright protection for the character itself. The plaintiff, however, bears the burden of demonstrating that the character is specifically delineated in the plaintiff's work and that that delineation was copied and that the character must have been uniquely developed. Here, Titan (P) has sufficiently shown that the characters were developed by it and were distinctive and unique and thus worthy of copyright protection. The characters, with their distinctive costumes, hairstyles, and dress, were unique and immediately recognizable to wrestling fans. Defendant's motion to dismiss denied.

ANALYSIS
The key to the copyrightability of characters is in their specific delineation in the copyrighted work. Not all characters appearing in a copyrighted work will automatically be protected. The character must be sufficiently developed in the work, distinctly delineated, and unique.

Quicknotes

COPYRIGHT INFRINGEMENT A violation of one of the exclusive rights granted to an artist pursuant to Article I, section 8, clause 8 of the United States Constitution over the reproduction, display, performance, distribution, and adaptation of his work for a period prescribed by statute.

… Copyright

BellSouth Advertising & Publishing Corp. v. Donnelley Information Publishing, Inc.

Telephone book publisher (P) v. Competitor (D)

999 F.2d 1436 (11th Cir. 1993), cert. denied, 510 U.S. 1101 (1994).

NATURE OF CASE: Action for copyright infringement of a telephone directory.

FACT SUMMARY: BellSouth Advertising & Publishing Corp. (BellSouth) (P) alleged copyright infringement against Donnelley Information Publishing, Inc. (D) for copying information from BellSouth's yellow pages directory.

RULE OF LAW
The names, addresses, telephone numbers, and business types listed in a yellow pages directory are not original elements of a work and are not copyrightable.

FACTS: BellSouth Advertising & Publishing Corp. (BellSouth) (P) published a yellow pages directory for the Greater Miami area. Donnelley Information Publishing, Inc. (Donnelley) (D) began promoting a competing directory. Donnelley (D) generated a list of businesses to solicit for its directory from the BellSouth directory and created a computer database using telephone numbers, addresses, and business types taken from the BellSouth directory. Relying on this information, Donnelley (D) published a competing directory. The district court granted summary judgment in favor of BellSouth (P) on its copyright infringement claim, and the court of appeals affirmed. On petition for certiorari, the Supreme Court vacated the decision and remanded to the district court for reconsideration, given the Supreme Court's ruling in *Feist Publications, Inc. v. Rural Tel. Serv. Co.*, 499 U.S. 340 (1991).

ISSUE: Are the names, addresses, telephone numbers, and business types listed in a yellow pages directory protected by a registered copyright in the directory as a whole?

HOLDING AND DECISION: (Birch, J.) No. The copyright protection extended to a compilation does not go deep and depends on whether the compiler has demonstrated originality in the selection, arrangement, and coordination of the information compiled. The arrangement of the information in the BellSouth (P) directory is typical of such directories, and Donnelley (D) did not photocopy or reproduce the page by page arrangement of BellSouth's (P) directory, its typeface, or the accompanying advertisements. Donnelley's (D) directory does not, therefore, infringe BellSouth's (P) copyright in its yellow pages directory.

DISSENT: (Hatchett, J.) The original selection of headings used in BellSouth's (P) directory demonstrates that BellSouth's (P) directory was original and should be protected.

ANALYSIS

The Copyright Act does not protect facts contained within a particular work. Therefore, the only protection afforded to databases of factual information is in the selection and arrangement of those facts.

Quicknotes

CERTIORARI A discretionary writ issued by a superior court to an inferior court in order to review the lower court's decisions; the Supreme Court's writ ordering such review.

COPYRIGHT ACT Copyright Act of 1976 extends copyright protection to "original works of authorship fixed in any tangible medium of expression, now known or later developed, from which they can be perceived, reproduced, or otherwise communicated, either directly or with the aid of a machine or device." 17 U.S.C. § 102.

COPYRIGHT INFRINGEMENT A violation of one of the exclusive rights granted to an artist pursuant to Article I, section 8, clause 8 of the United States Constitution over the reproduction, display, performance, distribution, and adaptation of his work for a period prescribed by statute.

SUMMARY JUDGMENT Judgment rendered by a court in response to a motion by one of the parties, claiming that the lack of a question of material fact in respect to an issue warrants disposition of the issue without consideration by the jury.

CCC Information Services, Inc. v. Maclean Hunter Market Reports, Inc.

Publisher (P) v. Publisher (D)

44 F.3d 61 (2d Cir. 1994), *cert. denied*, 516 U.S. 817 (1995).

NATURE OF CASE: Suit for declaratory judgment.

FACT SUMMARY: Maclean Hunter Market Reports (Maclean) (D) alleged that CCC Information Services, Inc. (P) infringed its copyright by copying portions of Maclean's (D) Red Book into its computer database and selling it.

RULE OF LAW
Copyright protection does not extend to ideas but does extend to compilations and the expression of those ideas.

FACTS: Maclean Hunter Market Reports (Maclean) (D) is the publisher of the Automobile Red Book (the Red Book), which sets forth the editors' predictions of the values of used cars. CCC Information Services, Inc. (CCC) (P) also provides such information through a computer database. Since 1988, CCC (P) has systematically loaded portions of the Red Book into its computer network and republished it in various forms for resale. Many of the Red Book's customers canceled their subscriptions with Maclean (D), choosing instead to utilize CCC's (P) services. CCC (P) brought action seeking a declaratory judgment that it incurred no liability under copyright law by republishing the material from the Red Book. Maclean (D) counterclaimed alleging copyright infringement. Both parties moved for summary judgment. Judgment was entered for CCC (P), and Maclean (D) appealed.

ISSUE: Does copyright protection extend to ideas?

HOLDING AND DECISION: (Leval, J.) No. Copyright protection does not extend to ideas, but it does extend to compilations and the expression of those ideas. CCC (P) argued that it only copied Maclean's (D) ideas, which are not entitled to protection under copyright law. CCC (P) further argued that to the extent such ideas constituted expression, since the expression is indispensable to the idea, it merges with the idea so that the method of expression is not protectable. It has long been recognized that copyright protection does not extend to ideas, but only to the means of expression of such ideas. When the particular expression is essential to the statements of the idea, however, the expression will also be unprotected in order to insure public access to the idea. In the case of compilations, the original contributions of compilers will almost always consist of ideas. Originality in selection, for example, will involve the compiler's idea as to the utility of the particular data selected. The original contribution of the compiler may also include the ideas as to the arrangement of the data presented. This court considered this issue in *Kregos v. Associated Press*, 937 F.2d 700 (1991). There the court articulated different categories of ideas, including those that attempt to further the solution of problems in contrast to those that express the author's opinion. The court stated that the first categories of ideas are entitled to greater freedom from ownership on the basis that they assist future thinkers. Applying this analysis to the present case, the court should not have applied the merger doctrine and should have extended protection to Maclean's (D) Red Book. First, CCC (P) took virtually the entire Red Book and then attempted to sell it to Maclean's (D) customers. Second, the ideas in the Red Book fall into the latter category of opinion. Reversed and remanded.

ANALYSIS

The "idea/expression dichotomy," which holds that an expression and not its underlying idea is copyrightable, was first set forth in *Baker v. Seldi*, 101 U.S. 99 (1879), and subsequently codified in 17 U.S.C. § 102(b). Under the "merger doctrine," if there only exists one or a few means of expressing an idea, then the expression is not protected either. The rationale supporting the merger doctrine is that no one should be entitled to the monopolization of an idea.

Quicknotes

COPYRIGHT Refers to the exclusive rights granted to an artist pursuant to Article I, section 8, clause 8 of the United States Constitution over the reproduction, display, performance, distribution, and adaptation of his work for a period prescribed by statute.

COPYRIGHT INFRINGEMENT A violation of one of the exclusive rights granted to an artist pursuant to Article I, section 8, clause 8 of the United States Constitution over the reproduction, display, performance, distribution, and adaptation of his work for a period prescribed by statute.

COUNTERCLAIM An independent cause of action brought by a defendant to a lawsuit in order to oppose or deduct from the plaintiff's claim.

DECLARATORY JUDGMENT An adjudication by the courts which grants not relief but is binding over the legal status of the parties involved in the dispute.

SUMMARY JUDGMENT Judgment rendered by a court in response to a motion by one of the parties, claiming that the lack of a question of material fact in respect to an issue warrants disposition of the issue without consideration by the jury.

CDN Inc. v. Kapes

Newsletter publisher (P) v. Website developer (D)

197 F.3d 1256 (9th Cir. 1999).

NATURE OF CASE: Suit for copyright infringement.

FACT SUMMARY: CDN Inc. (P) sued Kapes (D) for copyright infringement for using CDN's (P) published wholesale prices for coins as a baseline for compiling retail prices for coins.

RULE OF LAW
A compilation of information that distills and extrapolates from factual data can demonstrate creativity and originality sufficient to make that compilation copyrightable.

FACTS: CDN Inc. (P) publishes a weekly newsletter containing wholesale prices for collectible U.S. coins. CDN (P) compiles the wholesale prices by obtaining retail price information from other coin publications, retaining only that information it finds most accurate and significant; and reviewing bid and asking prices from online sites; considering results of public auctions and private sales; and analyzing the impact of the economy and foreign policies on coin prices. Kapes (D), who operates a coin business, began developing an online retail price list based on CDN's (P) newsletter prices and a computer program he developed to estimate retail prices based on wholesale prices. CDN (P) sued Kapes (D) for copyright infringement. The district court granted summary judgment for CDN (P), and the court of appeals affirmed.

ISSUE: Is a compilation of prices listed in a price guide sufficiently original to sustain a copyright?

HOLDING AND DECISION: (O'Scannlain, J.) Yes. Although facts themselves are not copyrightable, compilations of facts are copyrightable. In order to warrant protection, compilations of facts must contain a minimal amount of originality. Here, CDN's (P) list of coin prices is based not only on facts but on CDN's (P) judgment and expertise in setting prices. By infusing its own judgment into the process, CDN (P) has demonstrated originality and creativity sufficient to make its lists copyrightable.

ANALYSIS

The key to drawing the distinction between a fact and information based on expertise or judgment, that is, between what is copyrightable and what is not, is the degree of originality and creativity brought to bear by the compiler. Compilers merely discover facts, but by exerting the force of their expertise, creativity, and originality, they can achieve copyright status for their information.

Quicknotes

COPYRIGHT Refers to the exclusive rights granted to an artist pursuant to Article I, section 8, clause 8 of the United States Constitution over the reproduction, display, performance, distribution, and adaptation of his work for a period prescribed by statute.

COPYRIGHT INFRINGEMENT A violation of one of the exclusive rights granted to an artist pursuant to Article I, section 8, clause 8 of the United States Constitution over the reproduction, display, performance, distribution, and adaptation of his work for a period prescribed by statute.

SUMMARY JUDGMENT Judgment rendered by a court in response to a motion by one of the parties, claiming that the lack of a question of material fact in respect to an issue warrants disposition of the issue without consideration by the jury.

Matthew Bender & Co. v. West Publishing Co.

Publisher (P) v. Publisher (D)

158 F.3d 693 (2d Cir. 1998), *cert. denied*, 526 U.S. 1154 (1999).

NATURE OF CASE: Appeal from decision granting summary judgment of noninfringement.

FACT SUMMARY: Matthew Bender & Co. (P) and intervenor HyperLaw, Inc., seek judgment declaring that the use of star pagination references to West Publishing Co.'s (West's) (D) case reporters will not infringe West's (D) copyrights in compilations of judicial opinions.

RULE OF LAW
Elements of a compilation that are determined by a computer program do not entail a modicum of creativity and are unprotected.

FACTS: West Publishing Co. (West) (D) obtains the text of judicial opinions directly from courts and alters these texts to create a case report, which it publishes in the form of the Supreme Court Reporter and Federal Reporter. Matthew Bender & Co. (Bender) (P) and intervenor Hyper-Law, Inc., manufacture and market compilations of judicial opinions stored on CD-ROM in which they embed citations to the page location of the relevant text in West's (D) printed version of the case. Such references are called "star pagination." Bender (P) and HyperLaw seek a judgment declaring that their insertion of star pagination references to West's (D) case reporters does not infringe West's (D) copyright. The district court judge entered judgment for the Plaintiffs and the Defendants appealed.

ISSUE: Are non-original elements of a compilation copyrightable?

HOLDING AND DECISION: (Jacobs, J.) No. Copyright protection in compilations extends only to the original components of the compilation. The originality requirement has two elements. First, the element must be independently created. Second, the element must involve at least a modicum of creativity. Here, West (D) admits that pagination in its reporters is determined by a computer program and does not entail even a modicum of creativity. Therefore, volume and page numbers are unprotected features of West's (D) compilations, and Bender (P) and HyperLaw did not infringe by inserting those numbers on their disks. Affirmed.

DISSENT: (Sweet, J.): West's (D) case arrangements, include page citations, are original works of authorship and are copyrightable. Page numbers, although arbitrarily determined, are the result of West's (D) arrangement, including syllabi, headnotes, key numbering, citations, and descriptions.

ANALYSIS
In deciding the issue of originality, the court dissected each element of West's (D) editorial process and then extrapolated the cumulative effect of their citations decisions as either obvious or trivial. In his dissent, Judge Sweet criticized the analytical method (which the court had in previous cases warned against) as ignoring protectible expression within an unprotectible element.

Quicknotes
SUMMARY JUDGMENT Judgment rendered by a court in response to a motion by one of the parties, claiming that the lack of a question of material fact in respect to an issue warrants disposition of the issue without consideration by the jury.

CHAPTER 5

The Statutory Rights of Copyright Owners

Quick Reference Rules of Law

		PAGE
1.	**Infringement.** The access element of a claim for copyright infringement may be shown by demonstrating that the alleged infringer had reasonable access to the copyrighted work. (Three Boys Music Corp. v. Michael Bolton)	60
2.	**Infringement.** Inference of access giving rise to copyright infringement may not be based on mere conjecture, speculation, or a bare possibility of access. (Selle v. Gibb)	61
3.	**Infringement.** Access and copying may be inferred when two works are so similar to each other and not to anything in the public domain that it is likely that the creator of the second work copied the first; but the inference can be rebutted by disproving access or otherwise showing independent creation. (Ty, Inc. v. GMA Accessories, Inc.)	62
4.	**Reproduction.** Copyright protection of literary property is not limited to protecting merely the literal text of the work. (Nichols v. Universal Pictures Corp.)	63
5.	**Reproduction.** The question of whether two musical compositions are substantially similar is generally a question for a jury and should not be determined on summary judgment. (Arnstein v. Porter)	64
6.	**Reproduction.** A visual image that would be recognized by the average person as having been appropriated from a copyright work infringes on that copyright. (Steinberg v. Columbia Pictures Industries, Inc.)	65
7.	**Reproduction.** Where a copyright holder's work is not wholly original but incorporates elements from the public domain, infringement may be shown only by a substantial similarity to the elements properly copyrightable. (Boisson v. Banian, Ltd.)	66
8.	**Reproduction.** To determine whether a photograph is substantially similar to a copyrighted photograph, the protectible elements of the copyrighted photograph, when taken together and not in isolation, must be compared with similar elements of the allegedly infringing photograph, regardless of whether an "ordinary observer" or a "more discerning observer" test is used. (Mannion v. Coors Brewing Company)	67
9.	**Reproduction.** Works which capture the "total concept and feel" of copyrighted material may constitute infringement of such material. (Sid & Marty Krofft Television Productions, Inc. v. McDonald's Corp.)	69
10.	**Reproduction.** Random similarities scattered throughout a work do not constitute copyright infringement. (Cavalier v. Random House, Inc.)	70
11.	**Reproduction.** Summary judgment may not be granted on the basis of scenes a faire without independent evidence unless the allegation of *scènes à faire* is uncontested. (Swirsky v. Carey)	71
12.	**Reproduction.** When assessing the substantial similarity of nonliteral computer components, the proper procedure is to filter out the unprotected aspects of the program allegedly infringed and to compare the end product to the structure of the allegedly infringing program. (Computer Associates International, Inc. v. Altai, Inc.)	72

CHAPTER 5

13. **Distribution.** Merely making files available for sharing via a peer-to-peer network does not violate the distribution right that a copyright owner has in those files. (Capitol Records, Inc. v. Thomas) — 73

14. **Distribution.** Absent privity of contract, the sole right to vend granted to copyright holders does not create a right to impose limitations on the right of sale of future purchasers. (Bobbs-Merrill Company v. Straus) — 76

15. **Distribution.** The right of a copyright owner to prohibit the unauthorized importation of copies of its work is subject to the first sale doctrine of § 109(a). (Quality King Distributors, Inc. v. L'anza Research International, Inc.) — 77

16. **Derivative Works.** A derivative work in a different medium can be substantially similar to the copyrighted work when the derivative work is based on original, protectable expression in the copyrighted work. (Castle Rock Entertainment, Inc. v. Carol Publishing Group, Inc.) — 79

17. **Derivative Works.** (1) A prima facie copyright infringement case is established where a copyright owner shows that an alleged infringer has incorporated into the allegedly infringing work a quantitatively and qualitatively substantial portion of the original work. (2) An allegedly infringing work that contains a substantial amount of material from an original work is not a derivative work where the allegedly infringing work gives the copyrighted material a purpose that differs from the purpose the material has in the original. (Warner Bros. Entertainment, Inc. v. RDR Books) — 80

18. **Derivative Works.** A person cannot commercially transfer copyrighted artworks onto other surfaces without authorization. (Mirage Editions, Inc. v. Albuquerque A.R.T. Company) — 83

19. **Derivative Works.** In order for a work of authorship to constitute a derivative work, it must possess a sufficient level of creativity. (Lee v. A.R.T. Company) — 84

20. **Derivative Works.** A derivative work does not need to be fixed, as defined by the Copyright Act, to infringe on a valid copyright. (Lewis Galoob Toys, Inc. v. Nintendo of America, Inc.) — 85

21. **Derivative Works.** The unauthorized commercial exploitation of copyrighted computer games, even highly complex games in which the user actually participates in manipulating the game levels, may constitute infringement. (Micro Star v. FormGen Inc.) — 86

22. **Moral Rights: Theories for the Protection of Moral Rights Under U.S. Law.** Unauthorized editing for rebroadcasting of a televised program constitutes copyright infringement. (Gilliam v. American Broadcasting Companies, Inc.) — 88

23. **The Visual Artists Rights Act of 1990 (VARA).** A photographic work is not a "work of visual art" as defined by VARA where the work is created for multiple purposes. (Lilley v. Stout) — 89

24. **The Visual Artists Rights Act of 1990 (VARA).** For the purposes of VARA protection, two elements must be satisfied for a work to be of "recognized stature." First, the work must have merit or intrinsic worth, and, second, the work must be recognized by art experts, members of the artistic community, or society. (Martin v. City of Indianapolis) — 91

25. **Attribution.** Section 43(a) of the Lanham Act does not prevent the unaccredited copying of an uncopyrighted work. (Dastar Corp. v. Twentieth Century Fox Film Corp.) — 92

26. **Public Performance and Public Display.** A video rental proprietor may not exhibit videos to the public without authorization. (Columbia Pictures Indus. v. Redd Horne, Inc.) — 94

CHAPTER 5

27. **Public Performance and Public Display.**   A cable operator does not violate the public performance rights of the copyright owner of a motion picture or other audiovisual work by transmitting the work to a single customer who has pre-selected the work for playback. (Cartoon Network LP v. CSC Holdings, Inc.) — 95

28. **Public Performance and Public Display.**   (1) A computer owner that stores an image as electronic information and serves that electronic information directly to a user displays the electronic information in violation of a copyright holder's exclusive display right in the image. (2) A computer owner that in-line links to or frames a full-size image does not infringe the distribution right of the image's copyright owner when the image is displayed on a user's computer screen. (3) A search engine's owner's appropriation of a copyrighted image for use as an indexed thumbnail picture is a protected "fair use" under the copyright law where the balance of the statutory fair use factors favors the search engine owner. (Perfect 10, Inc. v. Amazon.com, Inc.) — 97

29. **Sampling Musical Works and Sound Recordings.**   The de minimis use of a copyrighted musical composition does not constitute infringement. (Newton v. Diamond) — 101

30. **Sampling Musical Works and Sound Recordings.**   When an alleged infringer does not dispute that it sampled a copyrighted sound recording, a substantial similarity or de minimis argument may not be used. (Bridgeport Music, Inc. v. Dimension Films) — 102

31. **Public Performance of Musical Works.**   An internet radio webcasting service does not "specially create" programs for users within the meaning of 17 U.S.C. § 114(j)(7) where the user does not have sufficient control over the interactive service to be able to predict the songs the user will hear. (Arista Records, LLC v. Launch Media, Inc.) — 103

Three Boys Music Corp. v. Michael Bolton

Songwriters (P) v. Alleged infringer (D)

212 F.3d 477 (9th Cir. 2000), *cert. denied*, 531 U.S. 1126 (2001).

NATURE OF CASE: Suit for copyright infringement of a song.

FACT SUMMARY: Three Boys Music Corp. (P) sued Michael Bolton (D) and his songwriting partner (D) for infringing on the song "Love Is a Wonderful Thing," written and recorded by the Isley Brothers.

RULE OF LAW
The access element of a claim for copyright infringement may be shown by demonstrating that the alleged infringer had reasonable access to the copyrighted work.

FACTS: In 1964, the Isley Brothers wrote and recorded the song "Love Is a Wonderful Thing." The song was released in 1966 as single and was listed at 110 in a chart titled "Bubbling Under the Hot 100," but it never made it to the top 100. In 1990, Michael Bolton (D) and his songwriting partner wrote a song also entitled "Love Is a Wonderful Thing," that reached 49 on the top 100 charts. Three Boys Music Corp. (P), the owner of the copyright in the Isley Brothers' song, sued Bolton (D), his partner, and their record companies for copyright infringement. A jury awarded Three Boys Music Corp. (P) $5.4 million on its claim for copyright infringement.

ISSUE: May reasonable access be found where the copyright holder argues that the infringer had access to the work because it was widely disseminated and thus could be subconsciously copied?

HOLDING AND DECISION: (Nelson, J.) Yes. Reasonable access can be shown by circumstantial evidence where (1) a particular chain between the protected work and the allegedly infringing work can be shown; and (2) where the protected work has been widely distributed. The burden is on the plaintiff. Here, plaintiff presented evidence supporting the argument that its song was widely distributed and that defendants subconsciously copied the work. Although the plaintiffs' reasonable access arguments were not persuasive to this court, the court did find that there was sufficient evidence to support the jury's finding of infringement, and the jury's decision would not be disturbed.

ANALYSIS

There are two elements to a prima facie case for copyright infringement. First, the plaintiff must show proof of ownership of a valid copyright. Second, the plaintiff must show that the defendant violated one of the rights protected in § 106 of the Copyright Act, that is, the right to reproduce or publicly perform.

Quicknotes

COPYRIGHT Refers to the exclusive rights granted to an artist pursuant to Article I, section 8, clause 8 of the United States Constitution over the reproduction, display, performance, distribution, and adaptation of his work for a period prescribed by statute.

COPYRIGHT ACT Copyright Act of 1976 extends copyright protection to "original works of authorship fixed in any tangible medium of expression, now known or later developed, from which they can be perceived, reproduced, or otherwise communicated, either directly or with the aid of a machine or device." 17 U.S.C. § 102.

COPYRIGHT INFRINGEMENT A violation of one of the exclusive rights granted to an artist pursuant to Article I, section 8, clause 8 of the United States Constitution over the reproduction, display, performance, distribution, and adaptation of his work for a period prescribed by statute.

Selle v. Gibb

Copyright owner (P) v. Alleged infringer (D)

741 F.2d 896 (7th Cir. 1984).

NATURE OF CASE: Appeal from a judgment notwithstanding the verdict.

FACT SUMMARY: Selle (P) alleged that the Gibb brothers (D), known as the Bee Gees (D), had infringed the copyright of his song.

RULE OF LAW
Inference of access giving rise to copyright infringement may not be based on mere conjecture, speculation, or a bare possibility of access.

FACTS: Selle (P) composed a song in 1975 and obtained a copyright for it later that year. He played his song with his small band two or three times in Chicago and sent a tape of the music to eleven music recording and publishing companies. Eight of the companies returned the materials and three did not respond. When Selle (P) heard the Bee Gees' (D) song "How Deep Is Your Love," in 1978, he thought he recognized the music as his own, although the lyrics were different. When Selle (P) sued for infringement, Gibb (D) and the Bee Gees (D) presented testimony that they had independently composed their song. Although Selle (P) presented evidence that the two songs were substantially similar, there was no direct evidence of access. The jury returned a verdict in Selle's (P) favor on the issue of liability in a bifurcated trial. The district court judge granted Gibb's (D) motion for judgment notwithstanding the verdict and in the alternative for a new trial. Selle (P) appealed.

ISSUE: May inference of access giving rise to copyright infringement be based on mere conjecture, speculation, or a bare possibility of access?

HOLDING AND DECISION: (Cudahy, J.) No. Inference of access giving rise to copyright infringement may not be based on mere conjecture, speculation, or a bare possibility of access. The judge's conclusions that there was no more than a bare possibility that Gibbs (D) could have had access to Selle's (P) song and that this was an insufficient basis from which the jury could have reasonably inferred the existence of access seem correct. Although proof of striking similarity may permit an inference of access, Selle (P) must still meet some minimum threshold of proof which demonstrates that the inference of access is reasonable. In this case, the availability of Selle's (P) song was virtually de minimis. In order to bolster the expert's conclusion that independent creation was not possible, there should be some testimony or other evidence of the relative complexity or uniqueness of the two compositions. The evidence of striking similarity was not sufficiently compelling to make the case when the proof of access must otherwise depend largely upon speculation and conjecture. Affirmed.

ANALYSIS

To establish a claim of copyright infringement of a musical composition, the plaintiff must prove ownership of a copyright, originality of the work, copying of the work by the defendant, and a substantial degree of similarity between the two works. The third element was at issue in this case. If the plaintiff presents evidence of striking similarity sufficient to raise an inference of access, then copying is presumably proved simultaneously.

Quicknotes

COPYRIGHT Refers to the exclusive rights granted to an artist pursuant to Article I, section 8, clause 8 of the United States Constitution over the reproduction, display, performance, distribution, and adaptation of his work for a period prescribed by statute.

COPYRIGHT INFRINGEMENT A violation of one of the exclusive rights granted to an artist pursuant to Article I, section 8, clause 8 of the United States Constitution over the reproduction, display, performance, distribution, and adaptation of his work for a period prescribed by statute.

DE MINIMIS Insignificant; trivial; not of sufficient significance to resort to legal action.

Ty, Inc. v. GMA Accessories, Inc.

Toy manufacturer (P) v. Copyright infringer (D)

132 F.3d 1167 (7th Cir. 1997).

NATURE OF CASE: Appeal from decision granting preliminary injunction for copyright infringement.

FACT SUMMARY: Ty, Inc. (P) contends that GMA Accessories, Inc. (GMA) (D) copied its toy pig, Squealer, in making GMA's (D) own toy pig, Preston.

RULE OF LAW
Access and copying may be inferred when two works are so similar to each other and not to anything in the public domain that it is likely that the creator of the second work copied the first; but the inference can be rebutted by disproving access or otherwise showing independent creation.

FACTS: Ty, Inc. (P) is the manufacturer of the "Beanie Babies" line of stuffed animals. Ty (P) began selling this line, including its stuffed pig, Squealer, in 1993. The popularity of the line induced GMA Accessories, Inc. (GMA) (D) to bring out its own line of bean-bag stuffed animals three years later. GMA's (D) stuffed pig, Preston the Pig, looks almost identical to Ty's (P) stuffed pig, Squealer. Ty (P) contended that GMA's (D) pig was a copy of Ty's (P) copyrighted pig. Ty (P) obtained a preliminary injunction under the Copyright Act against the sale by GMA (D) of Preston the Pig. GMA (D) appealed.

ISSUE: May access and copying be inferred when two works are strikingly similar to each other and not to anything else in the public domain?

HOLDING AND DECISION: (Posner, J.) Yes. Access and copying may be inferred when two works are so similar to each other and not to anything in the public domain that it is likely that the creator of the second work copied the first; but the inference can be rebutted by disproving access or otherwise showing independent creation. The more a work is both like an already copyrighted work and unlike anything that is in the public domain, the less likely it is to be an independent creation. The issue of copying can be broken down into two subissues. The first is whether the alleged copier had access to the work that he is claimed to have copied; the second is whether, if so, he used his access to copy. A similarity that is so close as to be highly unlikely to have been an accident of independent creation is evidence of access. GMA's (D) pig is strikingly similar to Ty's (P) pig but not to anything in the public domain, such as a real pig. GMA (D) has also not pointed to any fictional pig in the public domain that Preston resembles. Preston resembles only Squealer, and he resembles him so closely as to warrant an inference that GMA (D) copied Squealer. The affidavit of GMA's (D) designer attesting that she never looked at a Squealer before submitting her design of Preston is only weak evidence of independent creation. The absence of any evidence of how the designer's drawing was translated into the Squealer-resembling production model of Preston, combined with the similarity of that model to Squealer (and to nothing in the public domain) overbore the weak evidence of the affidavit at trial. Affirmed.

ANALYSIS

Once a plaintiff has offered convincing indirect evidence of copying, the burden of persuasion shifts to the defendant, who can then attempt to persuade the trier-of-fact that such factors as independent creation, coincidence, or prior common source, rather than copying, explain the similarity between the two works.

Quicknotes

AFFIDAVIT A declaration of facts written and affirmed before a witness.

COPYRIGHT ACT Copyright Act of 1976 extends copyright protection to "original works of authorship fixed in any tangible medium of expression, now known or later developed, from which they can be perceived, reproduced, or otherwise communicated, either directly or with the aid of a machine or device." 17 U.S.C. § 102.

COPYRIGHT INFRINGEMENT A violation of one of the exclusive rights granted to an artist pursuant to Article I, section 8, clause 8 of the United States Constitution over the reproduction, display, performance, distribution, and adaptation of his work for a period prescribed by statute.

PRELIMINARY INJUNCTION An order issued by the court at the commencement of an action, requiring a party to refrain from conducting a specified activity that is the subject of the controversy, until the matter is determined.

Nichols v. Universal Pictures Corp.

Writer (P) v. Movie producer (D)

45 F.2d 119 (2d Cir. 1930), cert. denied, 282 U.S. 902 (1931).

NATURE OF CASE: Appeal from dismissal of suit for copyright infringement.

FACT SUMMARY: Universal Pictures Corp.'s (D) movie about a marriage between a Jewish and an Irish family, prompted Nichols (P) to bring suit for copyright infringement of her play "Abie's Irish Rose."

RULE OF LAW
Copyright protection of literary property is not limited to protecting merely the literal text of the work.

FACTS: Nichols (P) authored and copyrighted the play "Abie's Irish Rose." This work depicted the marriage between a Jewish boy and an Irish Catholic girl, their deception of their religious fathers, and the eventual acceptance and reconciliation. Universal Pictures Corp. (D) produced "The Cohens and the Kellys," a movie about the marriage between an Irish boy and a Jewish girl. While not emphasizing the religious, the movie centered on the interactions of the two families. Nichols (P) brought suit for copyright infringement and the district court dismissed; Nichols (P) appealed.

ISSUE: Is copyright protection of literary property limited merely to protecting the literal text of the work?

HOLDING AND DECISION: (Hand, J.) No. Copyright protection cannot be limited to the literal text, else a plagiarist could escape liability by immaterial variations; however, protection cannot extend to the "ideas" of the copyrighted work. Every work can be abstracted on several levels. These abstractions range from the most general statement of what the work is about to the very specific reproduction of the work. Between this series of abstractions lies the boundary between protection and non-protectable "ideas." Nobody has ever been able to fix that boundary and nobody ever can. In the case at bar, the only matter common to the two works is a quarrel between a Jewish and an Irish father, the marriage of their children, the birth of grandchildren, and a reconciliation. This is too generalized an abstraction from what Nichols (P) wrote, and thus was only a part of her "ideas." Affirmed.

ANALYSIS

Copyright protects an author from infringement of his "expression" but not from appropriation of his mere "ideas." The problem is to draw the line between idea and expression, and several methods are utilized. The *Nichols* court utilized the "abstractions test," a test still popular among courts. Other possible approaches include the Content Analysis test [counting the number of times identical words or phrases appear; see 37 Cornell L.Q. 638 (1952)] and the "Patterns test" (comparing the sequence of events and the interplay of characters; see 45 Colum. L. Rev. 503 (1945)].

Quicknotes

COPYRIGHT Refers to the exclusive rights granted to an artist pursuant to Article I, section 8, clause 8 of the United States Constitution over the reproduction, display, performance, distribution, and adaptation of his work for a period prescribed by statute.

COPYRIGHT INFRINGEMENT A violation of one of the exclusive rights granted to an artist pursuant to Article I, section 8, clause 8 of the United States Constitution over the reproduction, display, performance, distribution, and adaptation of his work for a period prescribed by statute.

Arnstein v. Porter

Composer (P) v. Alleged infringer (D)

154 F.2d 464 (2d Cir. 1946), cert. denied, 330 U.S. 851 (1947).

NATURE OF CASE: Appeal from summary judgment in favor of alleged copyright infringer.

FACT SUMMARY: Arnstein (P), a composer, brought a claim for copyright infringement against Porter (D), for allegedly plagiarizing several of Arnstein's (P) compositions.

RULE OF LAW
The question of whether two musical compositions are substantially similar is generally a question for a jury and should not be determined on summary judgment.

FACTS: Arnstein (P) alleged that Porter (D) infringed on several of his original compositions. Arnstein (P) claimed that Porter (D) had access to these compositions because they were widely sold and others were publicly performed. Porter (D) denied that he had ever heard or seen any of Arnstein's (P) publications.

ISSUE: Does the trier of fact determine whether similarities in two compositions by separate authors are sufficiently similar to prove copying?

HOLDING AND DECISION: (Frank, J.) Yes. Once there is evidence of access and similarities, it is up to the trier of fact to determine whether the similarities are sufficient to prove copying. Proof of copying alone is not sufficient. The plaintiff must show that the copying was illicit, that is, that so much of the original composition was copied that it constitutes a wrongful appropriation. The plaintiff may call witnesses and experts, but the ultimate decision is for the jury. Summary judgment for the defendant reversed and the case remanded.

ANALYSIS

A plaintiff in a copyright infringement claim must show that a work was copied, that the work was protectible under copyright law, and that the two works are "substantially similar." The "substantial similarity" test has been difficult to apply because an element of similarity must also be addressed at the initial stage when determining if the work has been copied.

Quicknotes

COPYRIGHT INFRINGEMENT A violation of one of the exclusive rights granted to an artist pursuant to Article I, section 8, clause 8 of the United States Constitution over the reproduction, display, performance, distribution, and adaptation of his work for a period prescribed by statute.

SUMMARY JUDGMENT Judgment rendered by a court in response to a motion by one of the parties, claiming that the lack of a question of material fact in respect to an issue warrants disposition of the issue without consideration by the jury.

Steinberg v. Columbia Pictures Industries, Inc.

Illustrator (P) v. Movie studio (D)

663 F. Supp. 706 (S.D.N.Y. 1987).

NATURE OF CASE: Motion for summary adjudication of liability in a copyright infringement action.

FACT SUMMARY: Columbia Pictures Industries, Inc. (D) used, in a clearly recognizable fashion, an illustration by Steinberg (P) as a model for a film poster.

RULE OF LAW
A visual image that would be recognized by the average person as having been appropriated from a copyright work infringes on that copyright.

FACTS: In 1976, Steinberg (P) created a drawing which was used as a cover illustration by *The New Yorker* magazine. The drawing depicted, in humorous fashion, New York's self-perceived image as the center of the world. Specifically, it depicted a westward-looking landscape which featured portions of Manhattan Island in relative detail, and depicted in increasingly minimalist fashion, the rest of the nation, the Pacific Ocean and the Asian land mass. In 1984, Columbia Pictures Industries, Inc. (D), as an advertising campaign promoting the film "Moscow on the Hudson," distributed a poster showing in similar fashion a relatively detailed Manhattan in the foreground and, in the background, looking eastward, a less detailed Atlantic Ocean and Europe, with a large Kremlin in the background. The Manhattan buildings in the foreground were stylistically similar to those in Steinberg's (P) drawing. Steinberg (P) sued for infringement. He moved summary adjudication as to liability.

ISSUE: Does a visual image that would be recognized by the average person as having been appropriated from a copyrighted work infringe on that copyright?

HOLDING AND DECISION: (Stanton, J.) Yes. A visual image that would be recognized by the average person as having been appropriated from a copyrighted work infringes on that copyright. To prevail in a copyright infringement action concerning a visual representation, a plaintiff must prove copying. The standard for determining whether a copying occurred is whether there is a "substantial similarity" between the works. The test for determining whether such similarity exists is whether an average lay observer would recognize the alleged copy as having been appropriated from the copyrighted work. It is not necessary that every detail be similar; as long as the appropriation is apparent, infringement exists. Here, it is more than evident that the Columbia (D) poster appropriates from the Steinberg (P) drawing. They both feature a detailed Manhattan backed by an increasingly less-detailed rest of the world in the background. Even the detailed buildings in the foreground are similar. Finally, this is not an instance of an improper attempt by Steinberg (P) to copyright the idea of New York as the center of the world. The drawing was Steinberg's (P) expression of that idea, which was a proper subject of copyright. Motion granted.

ANALYSIS

The Second Circuit, the circuit in which the district court here sat, once had a different test. This was called the "ordinary observer" test. As articulated by Learned Hand, the test would be met if, to an ordinary observer, the pictures had the same aesthetic appeal. The test as it is now stated would appear to be somewhat more favorable to plaintiffs.

Quicknotes

COPYRIGHT INFRINGEMENT A violation of one of the exclusive rights granted to an artist pursuant to Article I, section 8, clause 8 of the United States Constitution over the reproduction, display, performance, distribution, and adaptation of his work for a period prescribed by statute.

Boisson v. Banian, Ltd.

Quilt manufacturer (P) v. Alleged copyright infringer (D)

273 F.3d 262 (2d Cir. 2001).

NATURE OF CASE: Appeal from a plaintiff's judgment in a copyright infringement suit.

FACT SUMMARY: When Boisson (P) sued Banian, Ltd. (D) for copyright infringement of its alphabet quilts, Banian (D) argued that the quilts contained uncopyrightable matter such as the alphabet.

RULE OF LAW
Where a copyright holder's work is not wholly original but incorporates elements from the public domain, infringement may be shown only by a substantial similarity to the elements properly copyrightable.

FACTS: Boisson (P) designed and produced certain alphabet quilts, consisting of square blocks containing the capital letters of the alphabet, displayed in order. The letters and blocks were made up of different colors, set off by a white border and colored edging. Banian, Ltd. (D) imported from India various alphabet quilts which contained colored alphabet blocks whose pattern and placement closely resembled the quilts of Boisson (P). Boisson (P) sued Banian (D) for copyright infringement. The federal district court found in favor of Boisson (P) on the grounds that, although the alphabet itself was not copyrightable, Boisson's (P) layout was. Banian (D) appealed.

ISSUE: Where a copyright holder's work is not wholly original but incorporates elements from the public domain, may infringement be shown only by a substantial similarity to the elements properly copyrightable?

HOLDING AND DECISION: (Cardamone, J.) Yes. Where a copyright holder's work is not wholly original but incorporates elements from the public domain, infringement may be shown only by a substantial similarity to the elements properly copyrightable. In applying this test, however, a court is not to dissect the works at issue into separate components and compare only the copyrightable items. To do so would result in almost nothing being copyrightable because original works broken down into their composite parts would usually be little more than basic elements like letters, colors, and symbols. Here, while use of the alphabet may not provide a basis for infringement, one must compare Banian's (D) quilts and Boisson's (P) quilts on the basis of the arrangement and shapes of the letters, the colors chosen to represent the letters and other parts of the quilts, the quilting patterns, and the particular icons chosen and their placement. This court's analysis of the "total concept and feel" of these works should be instructed by common sense. The court must consider "the arrangement of the whole" when comparing the two works. After detailed examination of both works, this court finds Banian's (D) quilts to be sufficiently similar to Boisson's (P) design as to demonstrate illegal copying. In particular, the overwhelming similarities in color choices lean toward a finding of infringement. Affirmed as to these quilts, but reversed as to some other of the quilts.

ANALYSIS

In the *Boisson* decision, although the icons chosen for each quilt were, for the most part, different, the differences were not sufficient to cause even a discerning observer to think that the quilts were other than substantially similar.

Quicknotes

COPYRIGHT Refers to the exclusive rights granted to an artist pursuant to Article I, section 8, clause 8 of the United States Constitution over the reproduction, display, performance, distribution, and adaptation of his work for a period prescribed by statute.

COPYRIGHT INFRINGEMENT A violation of one of the exclusive rights granted to an artist pursuant to Article I, section 8, clause 8 of the United States Constitution over the reproduction, display, performance, distribution, and adaptation of his work for a period prescribed by statute.

Mannion v. Coors Brewing Company

Copyright holder (P) v. Alleged infringer (D)

377 F. Supp. 2d 444 (S.D.N.Y. 2005).

NATURE OF CASE: Cross motions for summary judgment in copyright infringement action.

FACT SUMMARY: Mannion (P) contended that a photograph used by Coors Brewing Company (D) in billboard advertisements for Coors Light beer violated his copyright in a photograph of the basketball star Kevin Garnett because the two images were substantially similar.

RULE OF LAW
To determine whether a photograph is substantially similar to a copyrighted photograph, the protectible elements of the copyrighted photograph, when taken together and not in isolation, must be compared with similar elements of the allegedly infringing photograph, regardless of whether an "ordinary observer" or a "more discerning observer" test is used.

FACTS: Mannion (P), a freelance photographer, took a photograph of the basketball star Kevin Garnett (Garnett Photograph) that was a three-quarter-length portrait of Garnett against a backdrop of clouds with some blue sky shining through. The view is up and across the right side of Garnett's torso, so that he appears to be towering above earth. He wears a white T-shirt, white athletic pants, a black close-fitting cap, and a large amount of platinum, gold, and diamond jewelry. His head is cocked, his eyes are closed, and his heavily-veined hands, nearly all of which are visible, rest over his lower abdomen, with the thumbs hooked on the waistband of the trousers. The light is from the viewer's left, so that Garnett's right shoulder is the brightest area of the photograph and his hands cast slight shadows on his trousers. Most of Garnett's left arm is cut off. Carol H. Williams Advertising (CHWA) (D) began developing ideas for outdoor billboards that would advertise Coors Light beer to young black men in urban areas. One of CHWA's (D) "comp boards"—a "comp board" is an image created by an advertising company to convey a proposed design—used a manipulated version of the Garnett Photograph and superimposed on it the words "Iced Out" ("ice" being slang for diamonds) and a picture of a can of Coors Light beer (the "Iced Out Comp Board"). CHWA (D) obtained authorization from Mannion's (P) representative to use the Garnett Photograph for this purpose. The Coors Brewing Company (Coors) (D) billboard, based on the Iced Out Comp Board, depicted in black-and-white the torso of a muscular black man, albeit a model other than Garnett, shot against a cloudy backdrop. The pose was similar to that in the Garnett Photograph, and the view also was up and across the left side of the torso. The model in the billboard photograph also wore a white T-shirt and white athletic pants. The model's jewelry was prominently depicted, and the light came from the viewer's right, so that the left shoulder was the brightest part of the photograph, and the right arm and hand cast slight shadows on the trousers. Mannion (P) perfected his copyright in the Garnett Photograph and sued Coors (D) and CHWA (D) for infringement. Each party moved for summary judgment.

ISSUE: To determine whether a photograph is substantially similar to a copyrighted photograph, must the protectible elements of the copyrighted photograph, when taken together and not in isolation, be compared with similar elements of the allegedly infringing photograph, regardless of whether an "ordinary observer" or a "more discerning observer" test is used?

HOLDING AND DECISION: (Kaplan, J.) Yes. To determine whether a photograph is substantially similar to a copyrighted photograph, the protectible elements of the copyrighted photograph, when taken together and not in isolation, must be compared with similar elements of the allegedly infringing photograph, regardless of whether an "ordinary observer" or a "more discerning observer" test is used. For copyright to inhere in any work, there must be components that are original to the author. There are three respects in which a photograph may be original. First, there is rendition, which does not depend on the creation of the scene or object to be photographed, but instead involves such specialties as angle of shot, light and shade, exposure, effects achieved by means of filters, developing techniques, etc. In this instance, copyright protects not what is depicted, but how it is depicted. Second, there is timing, where a photograph is created when the author is at the right place at the right time to capture a specific image. In practice, originality in timing gives rise to the same type of protection as originality in the rendition. In each case, the image that exhibits the originality, but not the underlying subject, qualifies for copyright protection. Third, a photograph may be original to the extent that the photographer created "the scene or subject to be photographed." Insofar as a photograph is original in the rendition or timing, copyright protects the image but does not prevent others from photographing the same object or scene. By contrast, to the extent that a photograph is original in the creation of the subject, copyright extends also to that subject. Thus, an artist who arranges and then photographs a scene often will have the right to prevent others from duplicating that scene in a photograph or other medium. Applying these principles here, there is no doubt that the Garnett Photograph is an

Continued on next page.

original work. The photograph does not result from slavishly copying another work and therefore is original in the rendition. Mannion's (P) relatively unusual angle and distinctive lighting strengthen that aspect of the photograph's originality. His composition—posing man against sky—evidences originality in the creation of the subject. Furthermore, he instructed Garnett to wear simple and plain clothing and as much jewelry as possible, and "to look 'chilled out.'" His orchestration of the scene contributes additional originality in the creation of the subject. Although, as Coors/CHWA (D) correctly observe, there are limits to the photograph's originality—so that others may photograph Garnett or a man posed against a cloudy sky—the originality of the photograph extends beyond the individual clothing, jewelry, and pose viewed in isolation. It is the entire image, depicting man, sky, clothing, and jewelry in a particular arrangement, that is at issue here, not its individual components. While it is also true that copyright does not protect "ideas" but only their expression, here, the "idea" of the photograph—a young African American man wearing a white T-shirt and a large amount of jewelry—postulated by Coors/CHWA (D) does not even come close to accounting for all the similarities between the two works, which extend at least to angle, pose, background, composition, and lighting. It is possible to imagine any number of depictions of a black man wearing a white T-shirt and "bling bling" that look nothing like either of the photographs at issue here. This alone is sufficient to dispose of the defendants' contention that Mannion's (P) claims must be rejected because he seeks to protect an idea rather than its expression. Nonetheless, it should be said that the idea/expression dichotomy is appropriate in the literary context, but not in the visual arts. There is little to be gained by attempting to distinguish an unprotectible "idea" from its protectible "expression" in a photograph or other work of visual art, since the work's elements could be characterized as one or the other. It is nonsensical to speak of one photograph being substantially similar to another in the rendition and creation of the subject but somehow not infringing because of a shared idea. If the two photographs at issue are not substantially similar in the rendition and creation of the subject, the idea/expression distinction becomes irrelevant. Regardless whether an "ordinary observer" or a "more discerning observer" test is used to determine whether, as a matter of fact, the Coors/CHWA (D) billboard is substantially similar to the Garnett Photograph, the inquiry is identical: the relevant comparison is between the protectible elements in the Garnett Photograph and the Coors/CHWA (D) billboard, when those elements are not viewed in isolation. The question comes down to whether the aesthetic appeal of the two images is the same, since some elements, such as Garnett's likeness, a cloudy sky, a white shirt, and similar elements are not protectible in isolation, but when combined, and when photographed a certain way, are. Thus, the two photographs share a similar composition, angle, lighting, and cloudy sky. The subjects are wearing similar clothing and similar jewelry arranged in a similar way. Based on the agglomeration of these elements, it seems that Coors/CHWA (D) have recreated much of the subject that Mannion (P) had created and then, through imitation of angle and lighting, rendered it in a similar way. However, there are also differences that are in the nature of changes: "One image is black and white and dark, the other is in color and bright. One is the mirror image of the other. One depicts only an unidentified man's torso, the other the top three-fourths of Kevin Garnett's body. The jewelry is not identical. One T-shirt appears to fit more tightly than the other." Such differences may be weighed in determining substantial similarity because "if the points of dissimilarity not only exceed the points of similarity, but indicate that the remaining points of similarity are, within the context of plaintiff's work, of minimal importance . . . then no infringement results." Because a reasonable jury could find substantial similarity, or the absence thereof, the parties' summary judgment motions must be denied.

ANALYSIS

Because the photographs at issue in this case were sufficiently similar, the court denied summary judgment to both sides, concluding that a trier of fact would be in the best position to determine if the works' similarities—and differences—would require a finding of infringement. Essentially, the court was concluding that it was too close a factual call to rule that infringement occurred, or did not occur, as a matter of law.

Quicknotes

COPYRIGHT INFRINGEMENT A violation of one of the exclusive rights granted to an artist pursuant to Article I, section 8, clause 8 of the United States Constitution over the reproduction, display, performance, distribution, and adaptation of his work for a period prescribed by statute.

SUMMARY JUDGMENT Judgment rendered by a court in response to a motion made by one of the parties, claiming that the lack of a question of material fact in respect to an issue warrants disposition of the issue without consideration by the jury.

Sid & Marty Krofft Television Productions, Inc. v. McDonald's Corp.

Television program producer (P) v. Alleged copyright infringer (D)

562 F.2d 1157 (9th Cir. 1977).

NATURE OF CASE: Appeal from a plaintiff's judgment in a copyright infringement suit.

FACT SUMMARY: When McDonald's Corp. (D) aired TV commercials which allegedly used a fantasyland and costumed characters similar to those created by Sid and Marty Krofft Television Productions, Inc. (P) for their TV commercials, Sid and Marty Krofft (P) sued McDonalds's (D) for copyright infringement.

RULE OF LAW
Works which capture the "total concept and feel" of copyrighted material may constitute infringement of such material.

FACTS: Sid and Marty Krofft (P) created a TV show for children that featured a fantasyland and costumed characters. McDonald's Corp. (D) produced and used a TV commercial to appeal to children, which allegedly featured the same fantasyland and same costumed characters. The Kroffts (P) sued McDonald's (D) for copyright infringement, and the federal district court rendered judgment for the Kroffts (P). McDonald's (D) appealed.

ISSUE: May works which capture the "total concept and feel" of copyrighted material constitute infringement of such material?

HOLDING AND DECISION: (Carter, J.) Yes. Works which capture the "total concept and feel" of copyrighted material may constitute infringement of such material. The real task in a copyright infringement action is to determine whether there has been copying of the expression of an idea rather than just the idea itself. There must be a substantial similarity not only of the general ideas, but of their expression. Obviously no simple principle can be stated as to when an imitator has gone beyond copying the "idea" and has borrowed its "expression." Decisions must therefore inevitably be made ad hoc. The test of substantial similarity to be applied is properly labeled an intrinsic test because the answer depends on the response of the ordinary reasonable person. Because this is an intrinsic test, analytic dissection and expert testimony are not appropriate. Affirmed.

ANALYSIS

As the court in the *Krofft* case makes clear, the two works involved should be considered and tested, not hypocritically or with meticulous scrutiny, but rather by the observations and impressions of the average reasonable reader or spectator.

Quicknotes

AD HOC DECISION A decision made for a specific purpose.

COPYRIGHT Refers to the exclusive rights granted to an artist pursuant to Article I, section 8, clause 8 of the United States Constitution over the reproduction, display, performance, distribution, and adaptation of his work for a period prescribed by statute.

COPYRIGHT INFRINGEMENT A violation of one of the exclusive rights granted to an artist pursuant to Article I, section 8, clause 8 of the United States Constitution over the reproduction, display, performance, distribution, and adaptation of his work for a period prescribed by statute.

Cavalier v. Random House, Inc.

Authors (P) v. Publishing company (D)

297 F.3d 815 (9th Cir. 2002).

NATURE OF CASE: Appeal from a defense summary judgment in a copyright infringement suit.

FACT SUMMARY: When the Cavaliers (P) sued Random House, Inc. (D) for copyright infringement of an anthropomorphic moon character, Random House (D) argued that random similarities scattered throughout a work do not constitute copyright infringement.

RULE OF LAW
Random similarities scattered throughout a work do not constitute copyright infringement.

FACTS: A character called Nicky Moonbeam (an anthropomorphic moon) was developed by the Cavaliers (P) who submitted over 280 pages of materials, including their concededly copyrighted works, to Random House, Inc. (D) to make a pitch for a childrens' book based on the character. Random House (D) rejected the submissions. Shortly afterward, Random House (D) published several childrens' books containing the concept of moon characters. The Cavaliers (P) sued Random House (D) for copyright infringement. The trial court granted Random House's (D) motion for summary judgment on the grounds, inter alia, that the moon-type characters in the two works, including various illustrations, were not substantially similar. The Cavaliers (P) appealed.

ISSUE: Do random similarities scattered throughout a work constitute copyright infringement?

HOLDING AND DECISION: (Fletcher, J.) No. Random similarities scattered throughout a work do not constitute copyright infringement. This argument is especially strong in the instant case since the alleged similarities were selected from over 280 pages of submissions. Further, consideration of the total concept and feel of a work, rather than specific inquiry into plot and character development, is especially appropriate in an infringement action involving childrens' works. Here, the total concept and feel of the Cavaliers' (P) stories are more serious and instructional than the works produced by Random House (D). The pace, dialogue, mood, and theme of the Random House (D) works differ markedly from those of the Cavalier (P) books. The principal setting in the *Good Night* books [Random House (D)] is the night sky, which is also prevalent in the *Nicky Moonbeam* stories [Cavalier (P)]. However, this setting naturally and necessarily flows from the basic plot premise of a child's journey through the night sky; therefore, the night sky setting constitutes *scènes à faire* and cannot support a finding of substantial similarity. Furthermore, neither of the *Good Night* books involves the beach or the North Pole, the venues for significant parts of the *Nicky Moonbeam* stories. The main characters in the *Good Night* books are also different. Affirmed.

ANALYSIS

The *Cavalier* court noted that the two works (the *Nicky Moonbeam* stories and the *Good Night* books) did not share any detailed sequence of events.

Quicknotes

COPYRIGHT INFRINGEMENT A violation of one of the exclusive rights granted to an artist pursuant to Article I, section 8, clause 8 of the United States Constitution over the reproduction, display, performance, distribution, and adaptation of his work for a period prescribed by statute.

INTER ALIA Among other things.

SCÈNES À FAIRE DOCTRINE Elements of a work that are not subject to copyright protection since they are indispensable to the particular genre.

SUMMARY JUDGMENT Judgment rendered by a court in response to a motion by one of the parties, claiming that the lack of a question of material fact in respect to an issue warrants disposition of the issue without consideration by the jury.

Swirsky v. Carey

Copyright owner of music (P) v. Alleged infringer (D)

376 F.3d 841 (9th Cir. 2004).

NATURE OF CASE: Appeal from a defense summary judgment in a copyright infringement suit.

FACT SUMMARY: When Seth Swirsky (P) sued Mariah Carey (D) for the copyright infringement of a song, and Carey (D) argued *scènes à faire*, Swirsky (P) countered that substantial similarity, hence infringement, can be found in a combination of elements, even if some of those elements are individually unprotected.

RULE OF LAW
Summary judgment may not be granted on the basis of *scènes à faire* without independent evidence unless the allegation of *scènes à faire* is uncontested.

FACTS: Seth Swirsky (P) composed and recorded an R&B song entitled "One of Those Love Songs" ("One"). Another R&B song, entitled "Thank God I Found You" ("Thank God") was composed and recorded by Mariah Carey (D). "One" and "Thank God" have dissimilar lyrics and verse melodies, but they share a similar chorus. Swirsky (P) sued Carey (D) and others for copyright infringement in the federal district court. Notwithstanding the expert testimony of the chair of the Musicology Department at UCLA that the two songs had substantially similar choruses, the court granted Carey's (D) motion for summary judgment. Swirsky (P) appealed.

ISSUE: May summary judgment be granted on the basis of *scènes à faire* without independent evidence where the allegation of *scènes à faire* is contested?

HOLDING AND DECISION: (Canby, J.) No. Summary judgment may not be granted on the basis of *scènes à faire* without independent evidence unless the allegation of *scènes à faire* is uncontested. The district court erred by basing its comparison of the two choruses almost entirely on a measure-by-measure comparison of melodic note sequences from the full transcriptions of the choruses. Objective analysis of music does not mean that a court may simply compare the numerical representations of pitch sequences and the visual representation of notes to determine that two choruses are not substantially similar, without regard to other elements of the compositions. No approach can completely divorce pitch sequences and rhythm from harmonic cord progression, tempo, and key, and thereby support a conclusion that compositions are dissimilar as a matter of law. It is these elements that determine what notes and pitches are heard in a song and at what point in the song they are found. To pull these elements out of a song individually, without also looking at them in combination, is to perform an incomplete and distorted musicological analysis. Thus, here, although the cord progressions may not be individually protected, if in combination with rhythm and pitch sequence, they show the chorus of "Thank God" to be substantially similar to the chorus of "One," infringement can be found. Reversed.

ANALYSIS

In analyzing musical compositions, courts have never announced a uniform set of factors to be used. Music, like software programs and art objects, is not capable of ready classification into only five or six constituent elements. As made clear in the *Swirsky* decision, to disregard cord progression, key, tempo, rhythm, and genre is to ignore the fact that a substantial similarity can be found in a combination of elements, even if some of those elements are individually unprotected.

Quicknotes

COPYRIGHT INFRINGEMENT A violation of one of the exclusive rights granted to an artist pursuant to Article I, section 8, clause 8 of the United States Constitution over the reproduction, display, performance, distribution, and adaptation of his work for a period prescribed by statute.

SCÈNES À FAIRE DOCTRINE Elements of a work that are not subject to copyright protection since they are indispensable to the particular genre.

SUMMARY JUDGMENT Judgment rendered by a court in response to a motion by one of the parties, claiming that the lack of a question of material fact in respect to an issue warrants disposition of the issue without consideration by the jury.

Computer Associates International, Inc. v. Altai, Inc.

Software designer (P) v. Competitor (D)

982 F.2d 693 (2d Cir. 1992).

NATURE OF CASE: Appeal from award of damages for copyright infringement.

FACT SUMMARY: Upon discovering that Altai, Inc. (D) may have appropriated parts of its "Adapter" computer program, Computer Associates International, Inc. (CA) (P) sued Altai (D) for copyright infringement and trade secret misappropriation.

RULE OF LAW
When assessing the substantial similarity of nonliteral computer components, the proper procedure is to filter out the unprotected aspects of the program allegedly infringed and to compare the end product to the structure of the allegedly infringing program.

FACTS: Computer Associates International, Inc. (CA) (P) designed, developed, and marketed various types of computer programs including "CA-Scheduler," a job scheduling program containing a subprogram entitled "Adapter." Adapter was a wholly integrated component of CA-Scheduler, with no capacity for independent use. In 1982, Altai, Inc. (D) began marketing its own job scheduling program entitled "Zeke." Subsequently, Altai (D) decided to rewrite Zeke to run in conjunction with a different operating system, and approached Arney, a computer programmer who worked for CA (P), about working for Altai (D). When Arney left CA (P) to work for Altai (D), he took with him copies of the source code for two versions of Adapter. No one at Altai (D) knew that Arney had the Adapter codes and was using them to design Altai's (D) new component-program, "Oscar" (Version 3.4). Arney copied approximately 30% of Oscar's code from CA's (P) Adapter program. When CA (P) first learned that Altai (D) may have appropriated parts of Adapter, it brought this copyright and trade secret misappropriation action against Altai (D), which then initiated a rewrite of Oscar, entitled Oscar 3.5. From that point on, Altai (D) shipped only Oscar 3.5 to new customers and sent a free 3.5 upgrade to all customers who had previously purchased version 3.4. The district court awarded CA (P) $364,444 in actual damages and apportioned profits for copyright infringement regarding Oscar 3.4. However, the court denied relief on CA's (P) second claim, finding that Oscar 3.5 was not substantially similar to Adapter. The court further concluded that CA's (P) state law trade secret misappropriation claim against Altai (D) was preempted by the federal copyright act. On appeal, Altai (D) conceded liability for the copying of Adapter into Oscar 3.4 and raised no challenge to the award of damages. The reverse order used by the district court, however, had no material impact on the outcome of this case. Denial of infringement affirmed.

ISSUE: When comparing non-literal computer programs, should the court filter out the non-copyrightable aspects of the allegedly infringed program before comparing it to the allegedly infringing program.

HOLDING AND DECISION: (Walker, J.) Yes. The third part of the test for substantial similarity of non-literal computer program components necessitates a comparison. The proper way to make that comparison is first to filter out the unprotected aspects of the program allegedly infringed and then to compare what remains to the structure of the allegedly infringing program. The district court's analysis was backwards because it filters out the uncopyrightable aspects of the infringing program instead. The focus should be on the infringed work and not the other way around. This analysis necessitates a good deal of evidentiary review.

ANALYSIS

The approach adopted by the court here, filtering out unprotected elements before conducting a comparison, has been widely adopted by subsequent courts, especially those dealing with high-technology issues.

Quicknotes

COPYRIGHT ACT Copyright Act of 1976 extends copyright protection to "original works of authorship fixed in any tangible medium of expression, now known or later developed, from which they can be perceived, reproduced, or otherwise communicated, either directly or with the aid of a machine or device." 17 U.S.C. § 102.

COPYRIGHT INFRINGEMENT A violation of one of the exclusive rights granted to an artist pursuant to Article I, section 8, clause 8 of the United States Constitution over the reproduction, display, performance, distribution, and adaptation of his work for a period prescribed by statute.

Capitol Records, Inc. v. Thomas

Recording company (P) v. Peer-to-peer file sharer (D)

579 F. Supp. 2d 1210 (D. Minn. 2008).

NATURE OF CASE: Court's sua sponte reconsideration of jury instruction in action for copyright infringement.

FACT SUMMARY: Recording companies (P) brought suit against Thomas (D) for copyright infringement based on her illegal downloading and distribution of recordings via a peer-to-peer file sharing network, and a jury convicted Thomas (D). The court sua sponte reconsidered a jury instruction it had permitted to be given as to what constituted illegal distribution, believing the instruction was manifestly erroneous.

RULE OF LAW
Merely making files available for sharing via a peer-to-peer network does not violate the distribution right that a copyright owner has in those files.

FACTS: Recording companies (P) brought suit against Thomas (D) for copyright infringement. Thomas (D) had allegedly made copies of 24 of the recording companies' (P) copyrighted sound recordings available for copying via a peer-to-peer network, and she allegedly violated both the distribution right under § 106(3) of the Copyright Act and the reproduction right under § 106(1). The only evidence of actual dissemination of the sound recording was that the recording companies' (P) agent, MediaSentry, acting as an investigator, copied songs from a shared folder on the peer-to-peer network. Jury Instruction No. 15 regarding distribution stated that the act of making copyrighted recordings available on a peer-to-peer network without a license violated the distribution right regardless of whether actual distribution had been shown. A jury found infringement as to all 24 recordings and awarded statutory damages to the recording companies (P). The court then sua sponte raised the issue of whether it had committed a manifest error of law in giving Jury Instruction No. 15 to determine whether to grant a new trial.

ISSUE: Does merely making files available for sharing via a peer-to-peer network violate the distribution right that a copyright owner has in those files?

HOLDING AND DECISION: (Davis, C.J.) No. Merely making files available for sharing via a peer-to-peer network does not violate the distribution right that a copyright owner has in those files. First, the recording companies' (P) argue that even if Jury Instruction No. 15 was erroneous, it did not prejudice Thomas (D) because in any event the recording companies' (P) had a valid reproduction claim. This argument must be rejected because it cannot be known whether the jury reached its verdict on permissible or impermissible grounds or whether the jury would have granted the same high statutory damage award based solely on violation of the reproduction right. Second, Thomas' (D) argument that dissemination to an investigator acting as an agent for a copyright owner cannot constitute infringement must be rejected. Although a lawful owner of a copyright cannot infringe its own copyright, it is established law that the owner's investigator does not validate unlawful copying by a third party. Thus, because the use of investigators is approved by the law, distribution to MediaSentry can form the basis of an infringement claim. Here, even if Thomas (D) did not directly make the copy, she substantially assisted in its making by providing the copyrighted works for copying and placing them on a network specifically designed for easy, unauthorized copying. However, even though distribution to an investigator, such as MediaSentry, can constitute unauthorized distribution, if the court determines that Jury Instruction No. 15 was incorrect, it will grant a new trial. The Copyright Act does not define "distribute" in § 106(3), and whether making a work available for copying constitutes distribution is the key issue that needs to be resolved. Looking to the language of the statute itself, Congress explains the manners in which distribution can be effected: sale, transfer of ownership, rental, lease, or lending. The provision does not state that an offer to do any of these acts, or making a work available for any of these activities, constitutes distribution. Thus, the statute's language favors Thomas (D), as does the dictionary meaning of "distribute," which necessarily entails a transfer of ownership or possession from one person to another. Moreover, the leading copyright treatises conclude that making a work available is insufficient to establish distribution. On the other hand, the Register of Copyrights has opined that making a work available for copying violates the distribution right. It is also true that in other provisions of federal copyright law, Congress has explicitly defined "distribute" to include offers to distribute. This fact, however, shows that there is not a uniform definition of "distribute" in the Act, and that when Congress intends distribution to encompass making available or offering to transfer, it has demonstrated that it is quite capable of explicitly providing that definition within the statute. Thus, its failure to do so in § 106(3) demonstrates that it intended that an actual distribution or dissemination is required. Similarly, although Congress added "offers to sell" in the Patent Act, its failure to amend the Copyright Act to include offers further supports the finding that it intended to require actual distribution or dissemination. Accordingly, based on the legislative history, the plain

Continued on next page.

meaning of the term "distribute" does not encompass "making available." Another sub-issue is whether "distribution" is synonymous with "publication," which includes in its definition the "offering" to distribute copies. Although Committee Reports used the terms "distribution" and "publication" interchangeably, these snippets of legislative history are not dispositive of the definition of distribution, as the legislative history does not demonstrate that Congress intended that distribution should be given the same broad meaning as publication. Simply because all distributions within the meaning of § 106(3) are publications does not mean that all publications within the meaning of § 101 are distributions. To the contrary, the use of both terms within the Copyright Act demonstrates an intent that the terms have different meanings. In addition, the recording companies (P) contend that authorizing distribution is an exclusive right protected by the Copyright Act. If this is correct, then Thomas' (D) making sound recordings available on the peer-to-peer network would have violated the recording companies' (P) exclusive right to authorize distribution. However, the authorization clause on which the recording companies (P) base this argument merely provides a statutory foundation for secondary liability, not a means of expanding the scope of direct infringement liability. Also rejected is the deemed-distribution liability approach of the Fourth Circuit as embodied in its decision of *Hotaling v. Church of Jesus Christ of Latter-Day Saints*, 118 F.3d 199 (4th Cir. 1997). In that case, the Fourth Circuit held that "a library distributes a published work ... when it places an unauthorized copy of the work in its collection, includes the copy in its catalog or index system, and makes the copy available to the public." Some courts have applied the principle articulated in *Hotaling* to conclude that merely making a work available for others to download over a peer-to-peer network may constitute a distribution, since a contrary rule would reward infringers who use technology configured to not retain direct evidence of wrongdoing. However, *Hotaling* was not supported by an analysis of case law, legislative history or the statute's plain meaning, but merely by equitable principles; in fact, it is inconsistent with such an analysis. However, the rejection of *Hotaling's* deemed distribution approach in favor of the plain meaning of § 106(3) does not leave copyright holders without redress, since they can still pursue violations of the reproduction right, whether through direct or indirect infringement, and do not have to directly prove actual dissemination, but may do so through circumstantial evidence. Lastly, it has been argued that recording companies (P) enjoy a making-available right because the United States is a party to international treaties that recognize a making-available right that is not dependent on proof that copies were actually transferred to particular individuals. These include the World Intellectual Property Organization (WIPO) Copyright Treaty (WCT) and the WIPO Performances and Phonograms Treaty (WPPT), as well as various Free Trade Agreements (FTAs). It is argued that the court must adopt any reasonable interpretation of the Copyright Act that would grant the recording companies (P) a making-available right to ensure that the U.S. complies with its treaty obligations, since an act of Congress ought never to be construed to violate the law of nations if any other possible construction is available. However, the WIPO treaties are not self-executing and lack any binding legal authority separate from their implementation through the Copyright Act. Thus, the contents of the WIPO (and FTAs) treaties are only relevant insofar as § 106(3) is ambiguous and there is a reasonable interpretation of its provisions that aligns with the United States' treaty obligations. Because a careful review of the Copyright Act itself, legislative history, binding Supreme Court and Circuit precedent, and an extensive body of case law examining the Copyright Act reveals that § 106(3) does not contain a making-available right, concern for U.S. compliance with the WIPO treaties and the FTAs cannot override the clear congressional intent found in the statute itself. Therefore, Jury Instruction No. 15 was erroneous, and the judgment is vacated and a new trial is granted.

ANALYSIS

As to damages, the court "implored" Congress to amend the Copyright Act to address liability and damages in peer-to-peer network cases, noting that Thomas (D) allegedly infringed on the copyrights of 24 songs—the equivalent of approximately three CDs, costing less than $54, and yet the total damages awarded was $222,000—more than five hundred times the cost of buying 24 separate CDs and more than four thousand times the cost of three CDs. Although the court acknowledged that the Copyright Act was intended to permit statutory damages that are larger than the simple cost of the infringed works in order to make infringing a far less attractive alternative than legitimately purchasing the work, it concluded that "surely damages that are more than one hundred times the cost of the works would serve as a sufficient deterrent." On retrial, the jury again found Thomas (D) liable, and this time awarded $1.92 million to the recording companies (P). The judge in that case reduced the amount of the damages to $54,000, characterizing the original damages as "monstrous and shocking," and noting that the reduced damages were still "significant and harsh." *Capitol Records v. Thomas-Rassett*, 680 F. Supp. 2d 1045 (D. Minn. 2010).

Quicknotes

COPYRIGHT ACT Copyright Act of 1976 extends copyright protection to "original works of authorship fixed in any tangible medium of expression, now known or later developed, from which they can be perceived, reproduced, or otherwise communicated, either directly or with the aid of a machine or device." 17 U.S.C. § 102.

Continued on next page.

COPYRIGHT INFRINGEMENT A violation of one of the exclusive rights granted to an artist pursuant to Article I, Section 8, clause 8 of the United States Constitution over the reproduction, display, performance, distribution, and adaptation of his work for a period prescribed by statute.

DAMAGES Monetary compensation that may be awarded by the court to a party who has sustained injury or loss to his person, property or rights due to another party's unlawful act, omission or negligence.

SUA SPONTE An action taken by the court by its own motion and without the suggestion of one of the parties.

Bobbs-Merrill Company v. Straus

Copyright owner in novel (P) v. Retailer (D)

210 U.S. 339 (1908).

NATURE OF CASE: Lawsuit to restrain the sale of a copyrighted novel below a certain price.

FACT SUMMARY: The owner of the copyright in the novel "The Castaway" sought to enforce a notice appearing below the copyright notice that provided that the novel could not be sold for less than one dollar.

RULE OF LAW
Absent privity of contract, the sole right to vend granted to copyright holders does not create a right to impose limitations on the right of sale of future purchasers.

FACTS: Bobbs-Merrill Company (P) owned the copyright in a novel called "The Castaway." On the same page of the copyright notice and right below it, Bobbs-Merrill (P) included a notice that the book was not to be sold for less than one dollar. Isidor Straus and Nathan Straus (D), trading as R.H. Macy & Company, purchased copies of the book from a wholesale dealer for sale in their retail stores. Subsequently, Isidor Straus and Nathan Straus (D) sold copies of the book at retail for eighty-nine cents. Bobb-Merrill (P) sued to restrain the sale of "The Castaway" by Isidor Straus and Nathan Straus (D) at retail for less than one dollar.

ISSUE: Does the sole right to vend granted to a copyright holder allow the copyright holder to forever restrict the sale of a copyrighted work?

HOLDING AND DECISION: (Day, J.) No. The sole right to vend granted to a copyright holder pertains to his right to reproduce and sell his work. This right does not allow the copyright holder to impose a limitation on the sale of the work in perpetuity. Here, there was no privity of contract between Isidor Straus and Nathan Straus (D) on the one hand and Bobbs-Merrill Company (P) on the other hand. Once Bobbs-Merrill (P) sold the books to the wholesalers, it no longer could control the future sale. Once Isidor Straus and Nathan Straus (D) purchased the books from the wholesaler, they were free to sell it again without restriction.

ANALYSIS
A distinction must be drawn between a future purchaser's right to resell an authorized reproduction of a work and the right to actually reproduce the work. Although a future purchaser can resell the work without restriction, he is not authorized to publish a new edition of a work or otherwise reproduce it.

Quicknotes

COPYRIGHT Refers to the exclusive rights granted to an artist pursuant to Article I, section 8, clause 8 of the United States Constitution over the reproduction, display, performance, distribution, and adaptation of his work for a period prescribed by statute.

Quality King Distributors, Inc. v. L'anza Research International, Inc.

Manufacturer (P) v. Distributor (D)

523 U.S. 135 (1998).

NATURE OF CASE: Suit for copyright infringement.

FACT SUMMARY: L'anza Research International, Inc. (P), a manufacturer and distributor of hair-care products, brought a copyright infringement suit against Quality King Distributors, Inc. (D) for its allegedly unlawful importation of its products for resale to unauthorized retail outlets.

RULE OF LAW
The right of a copyright owner to prohibit the unauthorized importation of copies of its work is subject to the first sale doctrine of § 109(a).

FACTS: L'anza Research International, Inc. (L'anza) (P) was a California corporation in the business of manufacturing and selling shampoos, conditioners, and other hair-care products. L'anza (P) copyrighted the labels on its products. L'anza (P) sold its products to domestic distributors who agreed to resell within limited geographic areas only to authorized retailers. Internationally, L'anza (P) sold its products at 35% to 40% lower than it charged domestic distributors. In 1992 and 1993, L'anza's (P) distributor in the United Kingdom sold three shipments to a distributor in Malta. Those goods reentered the United States without L'anza's (P) permission and were sold by unauthorized retailers in California who had purchased them at a discount from Quality King Distributors, Inc. (Quality King) (D). L'anza (P) brought suit against Quality King (D) and others, alleging that the importation and distribution of the products violated L'anza's (P) exclusive rights under the Copyright Act. The district court rejected Quality King's (D) defense that its actions were protected under the first sale doctrine of section 109 and entered summary judgment in favor of L'anza (P). The court of appeals affirmed. The Supreme Court granted certiorari.

ISSUE: Is the right of a copyright owner to prohibit the unauthorized importation of copies of its work subject to the first sale doctrine of § 109(a)?

HOLDING AND DECISION: (Stevens, J.) Yes. The right of a copyright owner to prohibit the unauthorized importation of copies of its work is subject to the first sale doctrine of § 109(a). In *Bobbs-Merrill Co. v. Straus*, 210 U.S. 339 (1908), this Court held that the exclusive statutory right to "vend" a copyrighted work applied only to the first sale. This holding was codified by Congress in § 109 of the 1976 Act. That section provides that, notwithstanding § 106(3) (granting the copyright owner the exclusive right to distribute copies), the owner of a particular copy may sell or otherwise dispose of that copy without authorization of the copyright holder. The Court in *Bobbs-Merrill* distinguished between contract and statutory rights. Here L'anza (P) used its contracts with domestic distributors to limit their sales to authorized retail outlets. L'anza (P) cannot claim that unauthorized resales by such distributors infringes its exclusive right to distribution under the Act. Section 602 provides that the importation into the United States of copies or phonorecords of works acquired outside the country without the authorization of the copyright holder constitutes an infringement of the exclusive right of distribution of § 106. Under § 109, an owner is entitled to sell a particular copy of the copyrighted work without authorization of the copyright holder. Since § 602(a) provides that unauthorized importation is an infringement of an exclusive right under section 106, and since § 106 does not apply to resales by lawful owners, § 602(a) is inapplicable. Furthermore, the other provisions of the Act do not support the conclusion that Congress intended a violation of § 602 to be distinct from a violation of § 106. Reversed.

CONCURRENCE: (Ginsburg, J.) The Court addressed this case, involving an allegedly infringing product that made a "round-trip" journey from the United States to a point abroad and back again, but would not address cases involving allegedly infringing imported products manufactured abroad.

ANALYSIS

L'anza (P) argued that the provisions of § § 602(a) and 109 were superfluous, unless § 602(a) also applied to lawfully made copies because importation almost always constitutes a first sale. The Court rejected this argument on several bases. Moreover, it stated that this argument was based on the erroneous assumption that the two sections were equal in their scope. Section 602(a) is broader than § 109(a) because it encompasses works that are both subject to and not subject to the first sale doctrine. Thus, the Court concluded they were not superfluous.

Quicknotes

CERTIORARI A discretionary writ issued by a superior court to an inferior court in order to review the lower court's decisions; the Supreme Court's writ ordering such review.

COPYRIGHT ACT Copyright Act of 1976 extends copyright protection to "original works of authorship fixed in any

Continued on next page.

tangible medium of expression, now known or later developed, from which they can be perceived, reproduced, or otherwise communicated, either directly or with the aid of a machine or device." 17 U.S.C. § 102.

COPYRIGHT INFRINGEMENT A violation of one of the exclusive rights granted to an artist pursuant to Article I, section 8, clause 8 of the United States Constitution over the reproduction, display, performance, distribution, and adaptation of his work for a period prescribed by statute.

SUMMARY JUDGMENT Judgment rendered by a court in response to a motion by one of the parties, claiming that the lack of a question of material fact in respect to an issue warrants disposition of the issue without consideration by the jury.

Castle Rock Entertainment, Inc. v. Carol Publishing Group, Inc.

Copyright owner (P) v. Alleged infringer (D)

150 F.3d 132 (2d Cir. 1998).

NATURE OF CASE: Appeal from a summary judgment in favor of Castle Rock Entertainment, Inc. (P) and an order enjoining publication of allegedly infringing work.

FACT SUMMARY: Castle Rock Entertainment, Inc. (P), owner of the copyright in a television show, sued Carol Publishing Group, Inc., the publisher (D) of a trivia book based on the television show, for copyright and trademark infringement.

RULE OF LAW
A derivative work in a different medium can be substantially similar to the copyrighted work when the derivative work is based on original, protectable expression in the copyrighted work.

FACTS: Castle Rock Entertainment, Inc. (Castle Rock) (P) is the producer and copyright owner of each episode of the *Seinfeld* television series. Carol Publishing Group, Inc. (Carol Publishing) (D) published a book containing trivia questions and answers about the series. The source for every question and correct answer in the trivia book is the *Seinfeld* series, and the trivia book quotes from the series extensively. Castle Rock (P) filed an action alleging federal copyright and trademark infringement and state law unfair competition. The district court granted summary judgment to plaintiffs and enjoined the further publication of the trivia book. Carol Publishing (D) appealed.

ISSUE: Can a trivia book based on a television series be substantially similar to the protectable expression in the series when they are in different mediums?

HOLDING AND DECISION: (Walker, J.) Yes. The fact that they copy in a different medium or arrange the material in a different manner does not affect the substantial similarity test. Here, each question in the trivia book was based directly on original, protected expression in the television series. Because the characters and events tested in the trivia book spring from the *Seinfeld* authors' imaginations, the trivia book clearly copies copyrightable expression. Affirmed.

ANALYSIS

The defendants urged the court to consider other tests of similarity, arguing that the "substantial similarity" test is most often applied to more comparable works. The court denied the defendants' request to apply the following tests: (1) the "ordinary observer test," where the ordinary observer would regard the two works as the same in appeal or effect; (2) the "total concept and feel test," where the similarities of two works are judged as a whole; and (3) the "fragmented literal similarity test," which focuses on copying of direct quotations or close paraphrasing.

Quicknotes

COPYRIGHT Refers to the exclusive rights granted to an artist pursuant to Article I, section 8, clause 8 of the United States Constitution over the reproduction, display, performance, distribution, and adaptation of his work for a period prescribed by statute.

COPYRIGHT INFRINGEMENT A violation of one of the exclusive rights granted to an artist pursuant to Article I, section 8, clause 8 of the United States Constitution over the reproduction, display, performance, distribution, and adaptation of his work for a period prescribed by statute.

DERIVATIVE WORK A work of authorship that is based on a previous work.

ENJOIN The ordering of a party to cease the conduct of a specific activity.

SUMMARY JUDGMENT Judgment rendered by a court in response to a motion by one of the parties, claiming that the lack of a question of material fact in respect to an issue warrants disposition of the issue without consideration by the jury.

Warner Bros. Entertainment, Inc. v. RDR Books

Movie rights owner (P) v. Book publisher (D)

575 F. Supp. 2d 513 (S.D.N.Y. 2008).

NATURE OF CASE: Copyright infringement action asserting violations of the reproduction right and the right to produce derivative works.

FACT SUMMARY: J.K. Rowling (P), the author of the highly successful *Harry Potter* book series, and Warner Bros. Entertainment, Inc. (Warner Bros.) (P), which owned the exclusive film rights to the series, contended that RDR Books (D), a book publisher, infringed their reproduction right and the right to produce derivative works by seeking to publish "The Lexicon," "an A-to-Z guide to the creatures, characters, objects, events, and places that exist in the world of Harry Potter."

RULE OF LAW
(1) A prima facie copyright infringement case is established where a copyright owner shows that an alleged infringer has incorporated into the allegedly infringing work a quantitatively and qualitatively substantial portion of the original work.

(2) An allegedly infringing work that contains a substantial amount of material from an original work is not a derivative work where the allegedly infringing work gives the copyrighted material a purpose that differs from the purpose the material has in the original.

FACTS: J.K. Rowling (P) is the author of the immensely successful seven-book *Harry Potter* book series. Warner Bros. Entertainment, Inc. (Warner Bros.) (P) owns the exclusive film rights to the series. In addition to authoring the *Harry Potter* series, Rowling (P) has authored two companion books that are related to, and are derived from the series. Neither of these companion books is written in narrative form, but instead each chronicles and expands on the fictional facts that unfold in the *Harry Potter* series. Rowling (P) stated on a number of occasions that, in addition to the two companion books, she planned to publish a "Harry Potter encyclopedia." Vander Ark created and operated "The Harry Potter Lexicon" website, which was an online A-to-Z encyclopedia that collected and organized information from the Harry Potter books in one central source for fans to use for reference. The site contained descriptive indexed lists of spells, characters, creatures, and magical items from *Harry Potter* with hyperlinks to cross-referenced entries. The site was so comprehensive that even Rowling (P) and Warner Bros. (P) used it in their work in creating *Harry Potter* books and films. Eventually, RDR Books (D) entered discussions with Vander Ark for creating the first complete guide to the *Harry Potter* series that included information from the seventh and final *Harry Potter* novel. This guide was to be titled "The Lexicon" and was based on the encyclopedic portions of Vander Ark's website. The Lexicon is an A-to-Z guide to the creatures, characters, objects, events, and places that exist in the world of Harry Potter, and contains 2,437 entries that cull every item and character that appears in the *Harry Potter* works, no matter if it plays a significant or insignificant role in the story. Each entry, with the exception of the shortest ones, gathers and synthesizes pieces of information relating to its subject that appear scattered across the *Harry Potter* novels, the companion books, and published interviews of Rowling (P). The types of information contained in the entries include descriptions of the subject's attributes, role in the story, relationship to other characters or things, and events involving the subject. These snippets of information are generally followed by citations in parentheses that indicate where they were found within the corpus of the *Harry Potter* works, but the thoroughness of the Lexicon's citation, however, is not consistent, and some entries contain very few citations in relation to the amount material provided. On occasion, the Lexicon also provides commentary and background information from outside knowledge. In addition, the Lexicon contains a large amount of direct quotation or close paraphrasing of Rowling's (P) original language. While the Lexicon occasionally uses quotation marks to indicate Rowling's (P) language, it more often copies original language without quotation marks, often making it difficult to know which words are Rowling's (P) and which are Vander Ark's. Such close paraphrasing is not limited to the seven *Harry Potter* novels, but can be found in entries drawn from the companion books as well. Some of the Lexicon entries also contain summaries of certain scenes or key events in the *Harry Potter* series. Sometimes these plot elements are used to support an observation about a character's nature or development. Before RDR Books (D) could publish The Lexicon—which was in manuscript form—Rowling (P) and Warner Bros. (P) brought a copyright infringement action against it, asserting violations of the reproduction right and the right to produce derivative works.

ISSUE:
(1) Is a prima facie copyright infringement case established where a copyright owner shows that an alleged infringer has incorporated into the allegedly infringing work a quantitatively and qualitatively substantial portion of the original work?

(2) Is an allegedly infringing work that contains a substantial amount of material from an original work a derivative work where the allegedly infringing work gives the copyrighted material a purpose that differs from the purpose the material has in the original?

Continued on next page.

HOLDING AND DECISION: (Patterson, J.)

(1) Yes. A prima facie copyright infringement case is established where a copyright owner shows that an alleged infringer has incorporated into the allegedly infringing work a quantitatively and qualitatively substantial portion of the original work. Under the substantial similarity test, the appropriate inquiry is whether "the copying is quantitatively and qualitatively sufficient to support the legal conclusion that infringement (actionable copying) has occurred." Here, the quantitative amount of copying by the Lexicon from the *Harry Potter* series and the companion works is substantial. Such copying is in the form of paraphrasing, verbatim quotes, and appropriation of other protectible expression. Here, the quantum of copying is sufficient to support a finding of substantial similarity where the copied expression is entirely the product of the original author's imagination and creation. The qualitative copying is also sufficient to support a finding of substantial similarity given that the Lexicon draws its content from creative, original expression in the *Harry Potter* series and companion books. Notwithstanding that the invented facts that originate with the *Harry Potter* series and companion books are reproduced in the Lexicon in an order that is significantly different from that in the original, such a difference in arrangement does not preclude a finding of substantial similarity. Accordingly, Rowling (P) and Warner Bros. (P) have established a prima facie case of infringement.

(2) No. An allegedly infringing work that contains a substantial amount of material from an original work is not a derivative work where the allegedly infringing work gives the copyrighted material a purpose that differs from the purpose the material has in the original. A derivative work is a work based upon one or more preexisting works in which a work may be recast, transformed, or adapted. A work is not derivative where it is merely "based upon" the preexisting work(s). To be protected as a derivative work, the subsequent work must be "recast, transformed, or adapted" into another medium, mode, language, or revised version, while still representing the "original work of authorship." The argument by Rowling (P) and Warner Bros. (P), that a companion guide, such as the Lexicon, that contains a substantial amount of material from the underlying work is derivative, must be rejected. Here, because the Lexicon's use of plot elements is far from an "elaborate recounting" and does not follow the same plot structure as the *Harry Potter* novels, the suggestion that these portions of the Lexicon are "unauthorized abridgements" is unpersuasive. More significantly, the material in the Lexicon is not merely "transformed from one medium to another" for the purpose of retelling the Harry Potter story. Instead, the Lexicon gives the copyrighted material another purpose—to give the reader a ready understanding of individual elements in the elaborate world of Harry Potter that appear in voluminous and diverse sources. Therefore, the Lexicon no longer represents the original work, and it is not a derivative work. Judgment for RDR Books (D) on this issue.

ANALYSIS

The court ultimately rejected RDR Books' (D) fair use defense and permanently enjoined publication of the Lexicon, finding that the Lexicon "plundered" the underlying original works. However, in weighing the fair-use factors, the court found—as it did when it held that the Lexicon was not a derivative work—that the Lexicon was transformative. The court found that the best evidence of the Lexicon's transformative purpose was its demonstrated value as a reference source, and that its utility, as a reference guide to a multi-volume work of fantasy literature, demonstrated a productive use for a different purpose than the original works. The court said, "The Lexicon makes the elaborate imaginary world of Harry Potter searchable, item by item, and gives readers a complete picture of each item that cannot be gleaned by reading the voluminous series, since the material related to each item is scattered over thousands of pages of complex narrative and plot. The demand for and usefulness of this type of reference guide is evidenced by the publication of similar works." Thus, the Lexicon, or a similar work, would likely have passed copyright muster if it was constituted of less of the original work and the authors used more of their own words for each of the entries.

Quicknotes

COPYRIGHT INFRINGEMENT A violation of one of the exclusive rights granted to an artist pursuant to Article I, Section 8, clause 8 of the United States Constitution over the reproduction, display, performance, distribution, and adaptation of his work for a period prescribed by statute.

DERIVATIVE WORK A work of authorship that is based on a previous work.

FAIR USE An affirmative defense to a claim of copyright infringement providing an exception from the copyright owner's exclusive rights in a work for the purposes of criticism, comment, news reporting, teaching, scholarship or research; the determination of whether a use is fair is made on a case-by-case basis and requires the court to consider: (1) the purpose and character of the use; (2) the nature of the work; (3) the amount and substantiality of the portion used; and (4) the effect of the use on the potential market for, or value of, the work.

PRIMA FACIE CASE An action where the plaintiff introduces sufficient evidence to submit the issue to the judge or jury for determination.

Continued on next page.

CASENOTE LEGAL BRIEFS
Copyright

SUBSTANTIAL SIMILARITY In a copyright infringement action, the requirement that the plaintiff must show that the intended audience for the copyrighted and allegedly infringing works would find that the works were substantially similar.

Mirage Editions, Inc. v. Albuquerque A.R.T. Company

Copyright owner (P) v. Reproducer (D)

856 F.2d 1341 (9th Cir. 1988), cert denied, 489 U.S. 1018 (1989).

NATURE OF CASE: Appeal of order enjoining copyright infringement.

FACT SUMMARY: Albuquerque A.R.T. Company (D) engaged in the commercial activity of transferring copyrighted reprints of lithographs onto ceramic tiles, without the copyright holder's authorization.

RULE OF LAW
A person cannot commercially transfer copyrighted artworks onto other surfaces without authorization.

FACTS: Mirage Editions, Inc. (Mirage) (P) was the exclusive publisher of the works of the renowned artist Patrick Nagel, as well as the co-owner of the copyrights thereon. Mirage (P) published a collection of his works entitled *NAGEL: The Art of Patrick Nagel*. It came to Mirage's (P) attention that Albuquerque A.R.T. Company (D) was commercially engaged in the practice of transferring prints from the book onto ceramic tile. Mirage (P) sued for infringement. A district court issued an injunction, and Albuquerque A.R.T. (D) appealed.

ISSUE: May a person without authorization commercially transfer copyrighted artworks onto other surfaces?

HOLDING AND DECISION: (Brunetti, J.) No. A person cannot commercially transfer copyrighted artworks onto other surfaces without authorization. Under 17 U.S.C. § 106, the unauthorized derivative creation and distribution of copyrighted works is prohibited. A derivative work is broadly defined, at 17 U.S.C. § 101, "as any . . . form in which a work may be recast, transformed, or adapted." Here, the copyrighted prints were recast onto ceramic, so they were protected derivative works. Contrary to Albuquerque A.R.T.'s (D) assertions, the "first sale" doctrine does not help it. The doctrine permits a vendee of a copyrighted artwork to resell it without permission. However, the vendee is only allowed to resell it; he may not use it in the creation of a derivative work. Here, that is just what Albuquerque A.R.T. (D) has done, so the doctrine is unavailable to it. Affirmed.

ANALYSIS

The first sale doctrine is probably the most significant limitation on copyright distribution powers. The doctrine, codified at 17 U.S.C. § 109(a), permits free alienation of a legitimately purchased artwork. Without this rule, the secondary art market would be seriously endangered.

Quicknotes

COPYRIGHT INFRINGEMENT A violation of one of the exclusive rights granted to an artist pursuant to Article I, section 8, clause 8 of the United States Constitution over the reproduction, display, performance, distribution, and adaptation of his work for a period prescribed by statute.

INJUNCTION A court order requiring a person to do or prohibiting that person from doing a specific act.

Lee v. A.R.T. Company

Artist (P) v. Art retailer (D)

125 F.3d 580 (7th Cir. 1997).

NATURE OF CASE: Appeal from district court grant of summary judgment to defendant in a copyright infringement suit.

FACT SUMMARY: Lee (P) brought suit against A.R.T. Company (D), claiming that her exclusive right to make derivative works by mounting her art onto a ceramic tile and reselling the tiles was infringed.

RULE OF LAW
In order for a work of authorship to constitute a derivative work, it must possess a sufficient level of creativity.

FACTS: Lee (P) creates works of art that she sells through her firm Annie Lee & Friends. Deck the Walls, a chain of outlets, is a buyer of her works, which are registered with the Register of Copyrights. Deck the Walls sold some of Lee's (P) work to A.R.T. Company (D), which mounted the works on ceramic tiles and resold them. Lee (P) brought suit for monetary and injunctive relief, claiming these works were derivative works and could not be prepared without the permission of the copyright proprietor. The district court entered summary judgment for A.R.T. Company (D), and Lee (P) appealed.

ISSUE: In order for a work of authorship to constitute a derivative work, must it possess a sufficient level of creativity?

HOLDING AND DECISION: (Easterbrook, J.) Yes. In order for a work of authorship to constitute a derivative work, it must possess a sufficient level of creativity. A derivative work is a work "based on one or more preexisting works." 17 U.S.C. § 101. The district court concluded that the ceramic tile did not constitute an "original work of authorship" because it was no different than placing the picture in a frame or case. Courts have held that framing and other methods of mounting do not infringe the author's right to make derivative works. The Ninth Circuit has held that A.R.T. Company's (D) method of bonding the art to the tile with epoxy resin creates a derivative work. However, this court does not agree. The mounting process does not create a derivative work because the change to the work was not sufficiently original. Affirmed.

ANALYSIS

Lee (P) argued that a work may still be a derivative "despite the mechanical nature of the transformation." The court analyzed the present case, assuming that § 101 recognized non-original derivative works. Section 101 lists several examples of derivative works, including an art reproduction or "any other form in which a work may be recast, transformed or adapted." The court concluded that the mounting here did not constitute a transformation of Lee's (P) work since the work was not changed by the process.

Quicknotes

COPYRIGHT ACT SECTION 101 Section 101 of the Copyright Act of 1976, setting forth the definitions for purposes of the act.

COPYRIGHT INFRINGEMENT A violation of one of the exclusive rights granted to an artist pursuant to Article I, section 8, clause 8 of the United States Constitution over the reproduction, display, performance, distribution, and adaptation of his work for a period prescribed by statute.

DERIVATIVE WORK A work of authorship that is based on a previous work.

INJUNCTIVE RELIEF A court order issued as a remedy, requiring a person to do, or prohibiting that person from doing, a specific act.

SUMMARY JUDGMENT Judgment rendered by a court in response to a motion by one of the parties, claiming that the lack of a question of material fact in respect to an issue warrants disposition of the issue without consideration by the jury.

Lewis Galoob Toys, Inc. v. Nintendo of America, Inc.

Maker of video game enhancement device (D) v. Video game copyright holder (P)

964 F.2d 965 (9th Cir. 1992), cert. denied, 507 U.S. 985 (1993).

NATURE OF CASE: Appeal from a judgment finding no copyright infringement, dissolving a temporary injunction, and denying request for permanent injunction.

FACT SUMMARY: Nintendo of America, Inc. (Nintendo) (P) sought an order declaring that a video game enhancement device made by Lewis Galoob Toys, Inc. (Galoob) (D) infringed on Nintendo's (P) copyright in its video games and sought a permanent injunction enjoining Galoob (D) from marketing its device.

RULE OF LAW
A derivative work does not need to be fixed, as defined by the Copyright Act, to infringe on a valid copyright.

FACTS: Lewis Galoob Toys, Inc. (Galoob) (D) manufactured a device that hooked into a video game system and allowed players to alter video game features. Nintendo (P) claimed that the enhancement device infringed on its copyright in the underlying video games. The district court issued a judgment finding that Galoob's (D) device did not violate any Nintendo (P) copyrights, dissolving a temporary injunction, and denying Nintendo's (P) request for a permanent injunction enjoining Galoob (D) from marketing the enhancement device.

ISSUE: Does a product that temporarily enhances a video game infringe on the copyright in that video game?

HOLDING AND DECISION: (Farris, J.) No. No independent work is created, and it does not incorporate a portion of the copyrighted work in a concrete or permanent form. Here, the Galoob (D) device merely enhances the audiovisual display from Nintendo's (P) game. The device itself cannot duplicate any aspect of the Nintendo (P) game. The fact that there was a large market for Galoob's (D) device does not enter into the analysis and has no bearing on whether a work is an infringing derivative work. Affirmed.

ANALYSIS

A derivative work under the Copyright Act "is a work based upon one or more preexisting works, such as a translation, musical arrangement, dramatization, fictionalization, motion picture version, sound recording, art reproduction, abridgment, condensation, or any other form in which a work may be recast, transformed or adapted."

Quicknotes

COPYRIGHT ACT Copyright Act of 1976 extends copyright protection to "original works of authorship fixed in any tangible medium of expression, now known or later developed, from which they can be perceived, reproduced, or otherwise communicated, either directly or with the aid of a machine or device." 17 U.S.C. § 102.

COPYRIGHT INFRINGEMENT A violation of one of the exclusive rights granted to an artist pursuant to Article I, section 8, clause 8 of the United States Constitution over the reproduction, display, performance, distribution, and adaptation of his work for a period prescribed by statute.

DERIVATIVE WORK A work of authorship that is based on a previous work.

INJUNCTION A court order requiring a person to do or prohibiting that person from doing a specific act.

Micro Star v. FormGen Inc.

Software company (P) v. Software distributor (D)

154 F.3d 1107 (9th Cir. 1998).

NATURE OF CASE: Appeal from decision holding that a computer game product was not a derivative work.

FACT SUMMARY: FormGen Inc. (D) contends that its copyright is infringed by Micro Star's (P) unauthorized commercial exploitation of user-created game levels.

RULE OF LAW
The unauthorized commercial exploitation of copyrighted computer games, even highly complex games in which the user actually participates in manipulating the game levels, may constitute infringement.

FACTS: FormGen Inc. (D) made, distributed, and owns the rights to Duke Nukem 3D (D/N-3D), a very popular computer game. The basic game comes with twenty-nine levels, each with a different combination of scenery, aliens, and other challenges. The game also includes a "Build Editor," a utility that enables players to create their own levels. With FormGen's (D) encouragement, players frequently post levels they have created on the Internet where others can download them. Micro Star (P), a software distributor, downloaded 300 user-created levels, stamped them onto a CD, and then sold it commercially as Nuke It (N/I). Micro Star (P) filed suit in district court, seeking a declaratory judgment that N/I did not infringe on any of FormGen's (D) copyrights. FormGen (D) counterclaimed, seeking a preliminary injunction barring further production and distribution of N/I. The district court held that N/I was not a derivative work and therefore did not infringe FormGen's (D) copyright. FormGen (D) appealed.

ISSUE: May the unauthorized commercial exploitation of copyrighted computer games, even highly complex games in which the user actually participates in manipulating the game levels, constitute infringement?

HOLDING AND DECISION: (Kozinski, J.) Yes. The unauthorized commercial exploitation of copyrighted computer games, even highly complex games in which the user actually participates in manipulating the game levels, may constitute infringement. To succeed on the merits of its claim that N/I infringed FormGen's (D) copyright, FormGen (D) needed to show (1) ownership of the copyright D/N-3D and (2) copying of protected expression by Micro Star (P). The court focused on the latter issue, being satisfied that FormGen (D) had established its copyright ownership. FormGen (D) pointed out that a copyright holder enjoys the exclusive right to prepare derivative works based on D/N-3D. According to FormGen (D), the audiovisual displays generated when D/N-3D runs in conjunction with the N/I CD MAP files are derivative works that infringe this exclusivity. To qualify as a derivative work, a work must exist in concrete or permanent form and must substantially incorporate protected material from the preexisting work. This raised the question whether an exact description of an audiovisual display such as that described by MAP files counts as a permanent or concrete form. The court saw no reason it shouldn't. FormGen (D) also had to show that D/N-3D's and N/I's audiovisual displays were substantially similar in both ideas and expression. FormGen (D) would likely succeed in making this showing since the audiovisual displays generated when the player chooses the N/I levels comes entirely out of D/N-3D's source art library. The MAP files are also derivative works that incorporate D/N-3D's protected expression because, although MAP files do not contain art files themselves, the work that Micro Star (P) infringes is the D/N-3D story. A copyright owner holds the right to create sequels, and the stories told in the N/I MAP files are sequels, telling new tales of Duke's adventures. Micro Star's (P) use of FormGen's (D) protected expression is not protected by fair use. Lastly, FormGen (D) did not abandon its rights to protected expression, but warned players not to distribute user-created levels commercially and has actively enforced that limitation by bringing suits such as this one. Because FormGen (D) would likely succeed at trial, preliminary injunction was granted. Reversed and remanded.

ANALYSIS
This case involved appeals by both parties. The second appeal, brought by Micro Star (P), involved the packaging of N/I which included numerous "screen shots" of D/N-3D characters. The district court granted a preliminary injunction as to the screen shots, finding that N/I's packaging violated FormGen's (D) copyright by reproducing pictures of D/N-3D characters without a license. The court of appeals affirmed the decision.

Quicknotes

COPYRIGHT INFRINGEMENT A violation of one of the exclusive rights granted to an artist pursuant to Article I, section 8, clause 8 of the United States Constitution over the reproduction, display, performance, distribution, and adaptation of his work for a period prescribed by statute.

DECLARATORY JUDGMENT An adjudication by the courts which grants not relief but is binding over the legal status of the parties involved in the dispute.

Continued on next page.

DERIVATIVE WORK A work of authorship that is based on a previous work.

PRELIMINARY INJUNCTION An order issued by the court at the commencement of an action, requiring a party to refrain from conducting a specified activity that is the subject of the controversy, until the matter is determined.

Gilliam v. American Broadcasting Companies, Inc.

Comedian (P) v. Television broadcaster (D)

538 F.2d 14 (2d Cir. 1976).

NATURE OF CASE: Appeal of denial of injunction in copyright infringement action.

FACT SUMMARY: A comedy troupe contended that broadcasting edited versions of their comedy routines constituted copyright infringement.

RULE OF LAW
Unauthorized editing for rebroadcasting of a televised program constitutes copyright infringement.

FACTS: In the early 1970s, a controversial comedy troupe, Monty Python's Flying Circus, appeared in a self-titled series on the BBC, which consisted of numerous skits, sketches, and blackouts. Subsequent to this, American Broadcasting Companies (ABC) (D) obtained the rights to air several episodes. ABC (D) planned to air two 90-minute compilations of Python episodes. Unbeknownst to the troupe members, ABC (D) made substantial changes, editing out over 25% of the material for both commercial and editorial reasons. After the first telecast, Gilliam (P) and the other Python members sought an injunction against further broadcast, contending that the excisions constituted copyright infringement. The district court denied the injunction, and Gilliam (P) appealed.

ISSUE: Does unauthorized editing for rebroadcasting of a television program constitute copyright infringement?

HOLDING AND DECISION: (Lumbard, J.) Yes. Unauthorized editing of a television program for broadcasting constitutes copyright infringement. A recorded television program may be regarded as a work derived from its underlying script. The copyright holder of the script retains control over all uses of the script, even the recorded program itself. Consequently, to the extent that the scriptwriter has not parted with his copyright control, he had the copyright to the recorded version thereof. One who obtains permission to use a copyrighted script may not exceed the limits granted by the copyright holder. Where a licensee is granted permission to air a derivative work, this license does not automatically confer the right to edit the work. The ability of a copyright holder to control use of his work is paramount in copyright law, and the right to edit must be expressly granted. Here, ABC (D) was given permission to air certain Python material, but was not given permission to edit the material. Its doing so violated the copyright on the work. Further, such unauthorized editing constitutes mutilation of an original work, in violation of § 43(a) of the Lanham Act. [The court analyzed the traditional requisites for a preliminary injunction. It found that ABC's (D) actions had irreparably harmed Python's reputation, and that Gilliam (P) would likely succeed on the merits. It therefore ordered the district court to issue on injunction against further edited rebroadcasting.]

ANALYSIS

The Lanham Act was enacted to deal with trademarks. The Act is essentially a federal counterpart to state unfair competition laws, which prohibit the representation of a product as something it is not. It was applied here on the theory that ABC (D) was offering a "product" (the telecast) as a Python work, something it no longer was because of the editing.

Quicknotes

COPYRIGHT Refers to the exclusive rights granted to an artist pursuant to Article I, section 8, clause 8 of the United States Constitution over the reproduction, display, performance, distribution, and adaptation of his work for a period prescribed by statute.

COPYRIGHT INFRINGEMENT A violation of one of the exclusive rights granted to an artist pursuant to Article I, section 8, clause 8 of the United States Constitution over the reproduction, display, performance, distribution, and adaptation of his work for a period prescribed by statute.

DERIVATIVE WORK A work of authorship that is based on a previous work.

INJUNCTION A court order requiring a person to do or prohibiting that person from doing a specific act.

LANHAM ACT Name of the Trademark Act of 1946 which governs federal law regarding trademarks.

Lilley v. Stout

Photographer (P) v. Painter (D)

384 F. Supp. 2d 83 (D.D.C. 2005).

NATURE OF CASE: Action for infringement of the Visual Artist Rights Act of 1990 (VARA) and for copyright infringement.

FACT SUMMARY: Lilley (P), a photographer, contended that Stout (D), a painter, infringed Lilley's (P) rights under VARA and infringed his copyrights in photographs he had taken by using the photographs as the basis for one of Stout's (D) paintings and by using the photographs themselves in another work of art and claiming those works as her own.

RULE OF LAW
A photographic work is not a "work of visual art" as defined by the Visual Artist Rights Act of 1990 where the work is created for multiple purposes.

FACTS: Lilley (P), a photographer, and Stout (D), a painter, collaborated on works of art for several years, as well as having a personal relationship. At Stout's (D) request, Lilley (P) took photographs to be used as studies for paintings Stout (D) planned to create. Lilley (P) chose the subject of his photographs—a "red" room. After the two discussed which photographs would make good studies, Lilley (P) allowed Stout (D) to keep the photographic prints and negatives so that she could finalize her project. Stout (D) created one painting from the photographs and decided to use six of the photographs themselves as part of an artwork, entitled "Red Room at Five." The work initially did not include a colophon, "a notice that accompanies a work and provides information relating to the publication and authorship." After many requests, Lilley (P) received a colophon that stated: "Photographs by the artist and by Gary Lilley at the direction of the artist." Lilley (P) brought suit, claiming that the language of the colophon was an improper attribution of his "works of visual art" under VARA and that Stout's (D) selling both "Red Room at Five" and individual photographs taken by Lilley (P) as her own works infringed his copyrights in the photographs.

ISSUE: Is a photographic work a "work of visual art" as defined by VARA where the work is created for multiple purposes?

HOLDING AND DECISION: (Friedman, J.) No. A photographic work is not a "work of visual art" as defined by VARA where the work is created for multiple purposes. To determine whether Lilley (P) has a claim under VARA, it must first be determined whether the photographs at issue come within VARA's definition of "works of visual art." VARA defines a "work of visual art" with regard to photographic works as "a still photographic image produced for exhibition purposes only, existing in a single copy that is signed by the author, or in a limited edition of 200 copies or fewer that are signed and consecutively numbered by the author." The term "a still photographic image" is unambiguous and covers both photographic prints and negatives. Thus, it is indisputable that the photographic works at issue qualify as still photographic images. Therefore, the next step in the analysis is to determine whether they satisfy the remainder of the statute's definition. Stout (D) argues that because the photographs were taken for the purpose of serving as studies for her painting, they cannot have been "produced for exhibition purposes only." Lilley (P) claims he has averred sufficient facts to support an intent to exhibit the photographs. Given that a negative and a print are involved in the photographic process, and that both can be protected images, it is more useful to resolve the question of intent as of the time the work at issue is "produced." The reality is that a negative "produced" in one instant and a print "produced" in another may correspond to different intentions or purposes of the author. Lilley's (P) intent when he clicked the shutter of his camera and created the negatives is irrelevant to his claim. Instead, it is his probably different purpose in developing the negatives to produce the prints that raises the issue of whether they were "produced for exhibition purposes only." Because Lilley (P) admitted that the photographs were taken to serve as studies for Stout's (D) paintings, and because Lilley (P) and Stout (D) reviewed the frames to determine which images would make good studies, even if Lilley (P) intended to later exhibit the prints, the photographs were taken for multiple purposes, with the primary purpose being to assist Stout (D) in her artistic endeavors. Accordingly, because the discrete photographs at issue were not produced solely for exhibition purposes, Lilley's (P) photographic prints fail to satisfy the definition of "works of visual art" and Lilley (P) fails to state a claim under VARA. Judgment for Stout (D) as to this issue.

ANALYSIS

Congress enacted VARA to protect both the reputations of certain visual artists and the works of art they create. These protections are enumerated in the individual rights of "attribution" and "integrity," known collectively as "moral rights." The attribution right ensures that artists are correctly identified with the works of art they create, and that they are not identified with works created by others. The integrity right allows artists to protect their works against modifications and destructions that are prejudicial to their honors or reputations. Specifically, the rights of attribution

Continued on next page.

include the right to (a) claim authorship of a work he or she created, and (b) prevent the use of one's name as the author of a work that he or she did not create. See 17 U.S.C. § 106A(a)(1)-(2). The rights of integrity permit an author to (a) prevent any intentional distortion, mutilation, or other modification of his or her work, and (b) prevent any destruction of a work of recognized stature. Ownership of the copyright in a work is irrelevant to an author's standing to bring a VARA claim. Indeed, even if an author wishes to waive his or her rights under VARA, such a waiver can be effected only by a written instrument signed by the author that specifically identifies the work and the specific uses of that work. See 17 U.S.C. § 106A(e). Although the court determined that Lilley (P) failed to state a claim under VARA, it also ruled that he had made out a prima facie case of copyright infringement.

Quicknotes

COPYRIGHT INFRINGEMENT A violation of one of the exclusive rights granted to an artist pursuant to Article I, Section 8, clause 8 of the United States Constitution over the reproduction, display, performance, distribution, and adaptation of his work for a period prescribed by statute.

INFRINGEMENT Conduct in violation of a statute or contract that interferes with another's rights pursuant to law.

PRIMA FACIE CASE An action where the plaintiff introduces sufficient evidence to submit the issue to the judge or jury for determination.

Martin v. City of Indianapolis

Artist (P) v. Municipal government (D)

192 F.3d 608 (7th Cir. 1999).

NATURE OF CASE: Appeal from decision granting damages for statutory violation of the Visual Artists Rights Act of 1990 (VARA).

FACT SUMMARY: Martin (P) contends that his metal sculpture is a work of "recognized stature" worthy of protection under VARA.

RULE OF LAW
For the purposes of VARA protection, two elements must be satisfied for a work to be of "recognized stature." First, the work must have merit or intrinsic worth, and, second, the work must be recognized by art experts, members of the artistic community, or society.

FACTS: Martin (P) is an artist. He was employed as production coordinator for a metal contracting firm (the "Company"). It was in this position that he turned his artistic talents to metal sculpture fabrication. In 1984, Martin (P) received permission from the Indianapolis Metropolitan Development Commission to erect a large metal sculpture on land owned by John LaFollette, chairman of the Company. The resulting Project Agreement between the City of Indianapolis (D) and the Company granting a zoning variance to permit erection of the sculpture provided that the owner of the land and the owner of the sculpture would be notified in writing if the sculpture became incompatible with the existing land use. The sculpture, named "Symphony #1," was completed and erected in 1986. In 1992, the City (D) notified LaFollette of public hearings on the City's (D) proposed acquisition of various properties as part of an urban renewal plan. One of the properties to be acquired included the land that was home to Symphony #1. Martin (P) proposed that the Company would be willing to donate the sculpture to the City (D) if the sculpture was to be removed, provided that the City (D) would bear removal costs. The Mayor responded that he would refer Martin's (P) proposal to his staff to see what could be done. The City (D) thereafter purchased the land. Martin (P) again repeated his proposal and agreed to assist so Symphony #1 could be saved and moved without damage. The City (D) promised to contact Martin (P) in the event the sculpture was to be removed. Shortly thereafter, the City (D) demolished the sculpture without notice to Martin (P) or the Company. The district court granted summary judgment for Martin (P). City (D) appealed.

ISSUE: May any work of art qualify as one of "recognized stature" for VARA protection?

HOLDING AND DECISION: (Wood, J.) No. For the purposes of VARA protection, two elements must be satisfied for a work to be of "recognized stature." First, the work must have merit or intrinsic worth, and, second, it must be recognized by art experts, members of the artistic community, or society. Martin (P) offered no evidence of experts or others by deposition, affidavit, or interrogatories. However, Martin's (P) evidence of "stature" consisted of certain newspaper and magazine articles and various letters from an art gallery director and a letter of a newspaper editor, all in support of the sculpture. Although the City (D) objected that such proof was inadmissible hearsay, the court agreed with the assessment made by the district court. The statements offered by Martin (P) showed that the declarants said them, not that the statements were true. The statements contained within the exhibits show how art critics and the public viewed Martin's (P) work, particularly Symphony #1, and show that the sculpture was a matter worth reporting to the public. The statements were not hearsay because they were not being offered for the truth of the matters asserted therein. Furthermore, Martin (P) did not waive his VARA rights in a written waiver instrument. Therefore, Symphony #1 was protected by VARA as a work of "recognized stature," and Martin (P) was awarded appropriately. Affirmed.

CONCURRENCE AND DISSENT: (Manion, J.) The majority erred in granting summary judgment. The evidence presented by plaintiffs did not demonstrate that the Martin (P) sculpture was of "recognized stature." The plaintiffs presented no expert testimony as to this fact. This court needs to delineate a clearer definition of what constitutes "recognized stature" under VARA.

ANALYSIS

The Visual Artists Rights Act is an initial attempt to incorporate moral rights within federal copyright law. One interesting aspect of the Act is its limited scope; it protects only a narrow class of works of fine art. With respect to the right to prevent destruction, the Act covers only works of "recognized stature." This limitation is a radical departure in American copyright law and may force judges to make highly subjective aesthetic judgments.

Quicknotes

SUMMARY JUDGMENT Judgment rendered by a court in response to a motion by one of the parties, claiming that the lack of a question of material fact in respect to an issue warrants disposition of the issue without consideration by the jury.

Dastar Corp. v. Twentieth Century Fox Film Corp.

Video producer (D) v. Owner of book rights (P)

539 U.S. 23 (2003).

NATURE OF CASE: Appeal from affirmance of summary judgment in action for violation of § 43(a) of the Lanham Act.

FACT SUMMARY: Twentieth Century Fox Film Corporation (Fox) (P), owner of rights in a book entitled *Crusade in Europe*, sued Dastar Corp. (D), a producer of a video copy of a television series in the public domain which was based on the book. Fox (P) alleged that Dastar (D) marketed the video as its own product without giving credit to the original television series, and, therefore, falsely designated the origin of the video in violation of § 43(a) of the Lanham Act, codified at 15 U.S.C. § 1125(a).

RULE OF LAW
Section 43(a) of the Lanham Act does not prevent the unaccredited copying of an uncopyrighted work.

FACTS: General Dwight D. Eisenhower's World War II book, *Crusade in Europe*, was published by Doubleday, which registered the work's copyright and granted exclusive television rights to an affiliate of Twentieth Century Fox Film Corporation (Fox) (P). Fox (P), in turn, arranged for Time, Inc., to produce a *Crusade in Europe* television series based on the book, and Time assigned its copyright in the series to Fox (P). The series was first broadcast in 1949. In 1975, Doubleday renewed the book's copyright, but Fox (P) never renewed the copyright on the television series, which expired in 1977, leaving the series in the public domain. In 1988, Fox (P) reacquired the television rights in the book, including the exclusive right to distribute the *Crusade* television series on video and to sublicense others to do so. SFM Entertainment (P) and New Line Home Video, Inc. (P), acquired from Fox (P) the exclusive rights to manufacture and distribute *Crusade* on video. In 1995, Dastar Corp. (D) released a video set, *World War II Campaigns in Europe*, which it made from tapes of the original version of the *Crusade* television series and sold as its own product for substantially less than New Line's (P) video set. Fox (P), SFM (P), and New Line (P) brought an action alleging, inter alia, that Dastar's (D) sale of *Campaigns* without proper credit to the *Crusade* television series constituted "reverse passing off" in violation of § 43(a) of the Lanham Act. The district court granted summary judgment to Fox (P) and the other plaintiffs. The court of appeals affirmed in relevant part, holding, among other things, that because Dastar (D) copied substantially the entire *Crusade* series, labeled the resulting product with a different name, and marketed it without attribution to Fox (P), Dastar (D) had committed a "bodily appropriation" of Fox's (P) series, which was sufficient to establish the reverse passing off (the remedy for which was twice Dastar's (D) profits). The Supreme Court granted certiorari.

ISSUE: Does § 43(a) of the Lanham Act prevent the unaccredited copying of an uncopyrighted work?

HOLDING AND DECISION: (Scalia, J.) No. Section 43(a) of the Lanham Act does not prevent the unaccredited copying of an uncopyrighted work. Section 43(a) created a federal remedy against a person who used in commerce "a false designation of origin" of goods or services. The key issue thus depends on what the statute means by "origin." Fox's (P) claim would undoubtedly be sustained if Dastar (D) had bought some of New Line's (P) *Crusade* videotapes and merely repackaged them as its own. However, Dastar (D) has instead taken a creative work in the public domain, copied it, made modifications (arguably minor), and produced its very own series of videotapes. If "origin" refers only to the manufacturer or producer of the physical "good" that is made available to the public (here, the videotapes), Dastar (D) was the origin. If, however, "origin" includes the creator of the underlying work that Dastar (D) copied, then someone else [perhaps Fox (P)] was the origin of Dastar's (D) product. Because Dastar (D) was the "origin" of the physical products it sold as its own, Fox (P) cannot prevail on its Lanham Act claim. As dictionary definitions affirm, the most natural understanding of the "origin" of "goods"—the source of wares—is the producer of the tangible product sold in the marketplace, here Dastar's (D) *Campaigns* videotape. The phrase "origin of goods" in the Lanham Act is incapable of connoting the person or entity that originated the ideas that "goods" embody or contain. The consumer typically does not care about such origination, and § 43(a) should not be stretched to cover matters that are of no consequence to purchasers. Although purchasers do care about ideas or communications contained or embodied in a communicative product such as a video, giving the Lanham Act special application to such products would cause it to conflict with copyright law, which is precisely directed to that subject and which grants the public the right to copy without attribution once a copyright has expired. Recognizing a § 43(a) cause of action here would render superfluous the provisions of the Visual Artists Rights Act that grant an artistic work's author "the right ... to claim authorship of that work," 17 U.S.C. § 106A(a)(1)(A), but carefully limit and focus that right. It would also pose serious practical problems. Without a copyrighted work as the basepoint, the word "origin" has no discernable limits. Another practical difficulty of adopting a

Continued on next page.

special definition of "origin" for communicative products is that it places the manufacturers of those products in a difficult position. On the one hand, they would face Lanham Act liability for failing to credit the creator of a work on which their lawful copies are based; and on the other hand they could face Lanham Act liability for crediting the creator if that should be regarded as implying the creator's "sponsorship or approval" of the copy, 15 U.S.C. § 1125(a)(l)(A). In sum, "origin" refers to the producer of the tangible goods that are offered for sale, and not to the author of any idea, concept, or communication embodied in those goods. To hold otherwise would be akin to finding that § 43(a) created a species of perpetual patent and copyright, which Congress may not do. For merely saying it is the producer of the video, no Lanham Act liability attaches to Dastar (D). Reversed and remanded.

ANALYSIS

The Berne Convention for the Protection of Literary and Artistic Works requires member states to recognize the right of paternity. Such a right of attribution of authorship has been a feature of numerous legal systems (not including the U.S.) for many years and has not posed the kinds of problems postulated by Justice Scalia. It is arguable that requiring identification of a work's author once the work enters the public domain would not in any way interfere with the right to copy that work, and that, therefore, the kinds of "serious practical problems" anticipated by the Court would, in fact, never materialize. Nonetheless, as the Court points out, if Congress wishes to create such a right, it should do so as an addition to the law of copyright, not through the ambiguous use of "origin" in the Lanham Act.

Quicknotes

LANHAM ACT, § 43(A) Federal trademark infringement statute.

LANHAM ACT, § 1125 Imposes civil liability on any person who uses any trademark, false designation of origin, or false or misleading description of fact, that is likely to cause confusion or mistake or misrepresents the nature or origin of his or another's goods or services, to anyone likely to be damaged by that act.

Columbia Pictures Indus. v. Redd Horne, Inc.

Movie studio (P) v. Video store (D)

749 F.2d 154 (3d Cir. 1984).

NATURE OF CASE: Appeal of order enjoining copyright infringement and awarding damages.

FACT SUMMARY: Redd Horne, Inc. (D), a video rental outlet proprietor, also exhibited videos to the public without authorization.

RULE OF LAW
A video rental proprietor may not exhibit videos to the public without authorization.

FACTS: Redd Horne, Inc. (D) operated a videocassette rental outlet. In addition, it offered a service wherein patrons could reserve a small booth to watch videotapes in small groups. Redd Horne (D) did not obtain copyright holder authorization for this. Columbia Pictures Indus. (P) brought a copyright infringement suit. The district court issued an injunction and awarded damages, and Redd Horne (D) appealed.

ISSUE: May a video rental outlet proprietor exhibit videos to the public without authorization?

HOLDING AND DECISION: (Re, J.) No. A video rental outlet proprietor may not exhibit videos to the public without authorization. Section 106 of the Copyright Act prohibits, in the case of motion pictures and other audiovisual works, unauthorized public exhibition. A videocassette recording of a film may not be a motion picture per se, but it certainly falls within the definition of an audiovisual work. Here, the performance was clearly public, so Redd Horne (D) has violated § 106. The first sale doctrine, contrary to Redd Horne's (D) contentions, does not affect this conclusion. All that this doctrine does is permit a vendee to resell a work. All other copyrights are reserved. Here, the right to prevent public exhibition is one such right. Affirmed.

ANALYSIS

The rights of copyright holders are largely defined in § 106 of the Copyright Act, codified at 17 U.S.C. § 106. These include reproduction, preparation of derivative works, distribution of copies, exhibition, and display. Sometimes developments in technology make application of § 106 difficult, but courts usually do not find it hard to enforce the section.

Quicknotes

COPYRIGHT ACT Copyright Act of 1976 extends copyright protection to "original works of authorship fixed in any tangible medium of expression, now known or later developed, from which they can be perceived, reproduced, or otherwise communicated, either directly or with the aid of a machine or device." 17 U.S.C. § 102.

COPYRIGHT INFRINGEMENT A violation of one of the exclusive rights granted to an artist pursuant to Article I, section 8, clause 8 of the United States Constitution over the reproduction, display, performance, distribution, and adaptation of his work for a period prescribed by statute.

ENJOIN The ordering of a party to cease the conduct of a specific activity.

INJUNCTION A court order requiring a person to do or prohibiting that person from doing a specific act.

Cartoon Network LP v. CSC Holdings, Inc.

Copyright holder (P) v. Cable company (D)

536 F.3d 121 (2d Cir. 2008), cert. denied, 129 S. Ct. 2890 (2009).

NATURE OF CASE: Appeal from summary judgment for plaintiff in declaratory and injunctive action for copyright infringement asserting claims for infringement of the rights of reproduction and public performance.

FACT SUMMARY: Cablevision (D), a cable company that had developed a remote storage digital video recorder system (RS-DVR) that would permit its customers to receive playback of programs offered with the customers' cable subscriptions, contended that the RS-DVR system did not infringe the exclusive rights of reproduction and public performance of content providers (P) in the movies and television programs offered for playback.

RULE OF LAW
A cable operator does not violate the public performance rights of the copyright owner of a motion picture or other audiovisual work by transmitting the work to a single customer who has pre-selected the work for playback.

FACTS: Cablevision (D), a cable company, developed a remote storage digital video recorder system (RS-DVR) that would permit its customers to receive playback of programs offered with the customers' cable subscriptions. The system worked by enabling customers to record cable programming on central hard drives housed and maintained by Cablevision (D) at a location other than the customers' televisions. Absent RS-DVR, cable companies such as Cablevision (D) generally transmit in real time a single data stream of programs provided by various content providers (P) that hold the copyrights on movies and television programs. With RS-DVR, that data stream is split into two streams: the first is routed immediately to customers as before, and the second stream flows into a device called the Broadband Media Router (BMR), which buffers the data stream, reformats it, and sends it to the "Arroyo Server," which consists of two data buffers and a number of high-capacity hard disks. The entire stream of data moves to the first buffer (the "primary ingest buffer"), at which point the server automatically inquires as to whether any customers want to record any of that programming. If a customer has requested a particular program, the data for that program move from the primary buffer into a secondary buffer, and then onto a portion of one of the hard disks allocated to that customer. As new data flow into the primary buffer, they overwrite a corresponding quantity of data already on the buffer. The primary ingest buffer holds no more than 0.1 seconds of each channel's programming at any moment, so that every tenth of a second, the data residing on this buffer are automatically erased and replaced. The data buffer in the BMR holds no more than 1.2 seconds of programming at any time. The customer, however, is involved in this complex system only to the extent of pre-selecting a program for recording by using a remote control, or similarly selecting a program while it is ongoing. A customer cannot, however, record the earlier portion of a program once it has begun. To begin playback, the customer selects the show from an on-screen list of previously recorded programs, which sends a signal, via cable, to the Arroyo Server to initiate playback. Customers can select for playback only those programs to which they subscribe, and Cablevision (D) has the ability to limit the channels that have the RS-DVR option. The content providers (P) brought suit, claiming that the RS-DVR infringed their copyright. Specifically, they first claimed that by briefly storing data in the primary ingest buffer and other data buffers integral to the function of the RS-DVR, Cablevision (D) would make copies of protected works and thereby directly infringe the content providers' (P) exclusive right of reproduction. Second, they claimed that by copying programs onto the Arroyo Server hard disks (the "playback copies"), Cablevision (D) would again directly infringe the reproduction right. And third, they claimed that by transmitting the data from the Arroyo Server hard disks to its RS-DVR customers in response to a playback request, Cablevision (D) would directly infringe their exclusive right of public performance. Agreeing with all three arguments, the district court awarded summary declaratory judgment to plaintiffs. The court of appeals granted review. [As to the first claim, the appellate court reversed, holding that because the data were not held in the buffers for more than a transitory duration, the copies were not "fixed," so there was no violation of the reproduction right. As to the second claim, the court also reversed, holding that the copies were not made by Cablevision (D), but were made by its customers, thus holding that Cablevision (D) was not directly liable, but leaving open the question of whether Cablevision (D) might be secondarily liable.]

ISSUE: Does a cable operator violate the public performance rights of the copyright owner of a motion picture or other audiovisual work by transmitting the work to a single customer who has pre-selected the work for playback?

HOLDING AND DECISION: (Walker, J.) No. A cable operator does not violate the public performance rights of the copyright owner of a motion picture or other audiovisual work by transmitting the work to a single customer who has pre-selected the work for playback. A copyright owner has the exclusive right, in the case of motion pictures and other audiovisual works, to perform

Continued on next page.

the copyrighted work publicly. The Copyright Act provides that a performance is "public" if it is made in a public place or before a large number of persons other than in a familial setting, or if it is transmitted to a public place or to the public, whether the members of the public capable of receiving the performance or display receive it in the same place or in separate places and at the same time or at different times. Here, the transmission of copyrighted works is at issue, implicating the Act's "transmit clause," rather than direct public performance of a work. While it is undisputed that when a RS-DVR playback occurs a transmission is involved, it is not clear whether that transmission is a "performance" or whether it is being made "to the public." The transmit clause does, however, make relevant a consideration of who is capable of receiving the transmission. Here, Cablevision (D) correctly argues that only one subscriber is capable of receiving any given RS-DVR transmission. That is because each RS-DVR transmission is made by an individual subscriber using a single unique copy of a work that can be decoded exclusively by that subscriber's cable box. The district court incorrectly found that the RS-DVR playbacks constituted public performances because "Cablevision would transmit the same program to members of the public, who may receive the performance at different times, depending on whether they view the program in real time or at a later time as an RS-DVR playback." The district court thus suggested that, in considering whether a transmission is "to the public," the potential audience of the underlying work whose content is being transmitted is considered, rather than the potential audience of a particular transmission of that work. This analysis is unsupported by the language of the transmit clause, which speaks of people capable of receiving a particular "transmission" or "performance," and not of the potential audience of a particular "work." Applying the district court's approach would render the "to the public" language surplusage, since the potential audience for every copyrighted audiovisual work is the general public, and any transmission of such a work would constitute a public performance. If the transmit clause did not contemplate the existence of non-public, private transmissions, there would have been no need for Congress to have used the qualifier "public." It is also inconsistent with the transmit clause to consider the potential audience of an upstream transmission by a third party when determining whether a defendant's own subsequent transmission of a performance is "to the public," because such an approach not only obviates any possibility of a purely private transmission, but also creates results that Congress did not intend—such as rendering a customer who records a program and later transmits the recording to a television liable for publicly performing the work simply because some other party (e.g., a cable company) had once transmitted the same underlying performance to the public. Instead, the correct analysis focuses on the potential audience of a given transmission by an alleged infringer to determine whether that transmission is "to the public." With RS-DVR, that potential audience is a single subscriber who receives a single, unique copy of the requested work. Moreover, the use of a distinct copy affects the transmit clause inquiry because the use of a unique copy may limit the potential audience of a transmission and is therefore relevant to whether that transmission is made "to the public." Given that each RS-DVR transmission is made to a given subscriber using a distinct copy made by that subscriber, such a transmission is not "to the public," and the public performance right is not violated. Summary judgment for the content providers (P) is reversed and granted to Cablevision (D).

ANALYSIS

Transmitting a performance and receiving a transmission are both recognized to be legal performances of the work, under the multiple performance doctrine, which was first posited by Justice Louis Brandeis in 1931, and later adopted by the definition of performance in the Copyright Act. The court in this case left open the question of whether the customer or Cablevision (D) (or both) would be "performing" the RS-DVR copy, but did note that its conclusion that the customer, not Cablevision (D), "does" the copying did not dictate a parallel conclusion that the customer, and not Cablevision (D), "performs" the copyrighted work, since the definitions that delineate the contours of the reproduction and public performance rights vary in significant ways. While only the customer or Cablevision (D) could have been found to be a direct infringer of the reproduction right (with the other perhaps being secondarily liable), either of these parties, or both, could have been found liable for infringing the performance right had the court determined that the performance was made "to the public."

Quicknotes

COPYRIGHT ACT Copyright Act of 1976 extends copyright protection to "original works of authorship fixed in any tangible medium of expression, now known or later developed, from which they can be perceived, reproduced, or otherwise communicated, either directly or with the aid of a machine or device." 17 U.S.C. § 102.

COPYRIGHT INFRINGEMENT A violation of one of the exclusive rights granted to an artist pursuant to Article I, Section 8, clause 8 of the United States Constitution over the reproduction, display, performance, distribution, and adaptation of his work for a period prescribed by statute.

SUMMARY JUDGMENT Judgment rendered by a court in response to a motion made by one of the parties, claiming that the lack of a question of material fact in respect to an issue warrants disposition of the issue without consideration by the jury.

Perfect 10, Inc. v. Amazon.com, Inc.

Web porn publisher (P) v. Internet company (D)

508 F.3d 1146 (9th Cir. 2007).

NATURE OF CASE: Appeal from preliminary injunction in copyright infringement action.

FACT SUMMARY: Google, Inc. (D) claimed that even if its transmission of thumbnail images of Perfect 10, Inc.'s (P) copyrighted nude images, or its in-line linking to or framing of full-size images that infringed Perfect 10's (P) copyright in the images constituted infringement of Perfect 10's (P) display or distribution rights, its use nevertheless constituted a fair use.

RULE OF LAW
(1) A computer owner that stores an image as electronic information and serves that electronic information directly to a user displays the electronic information in violation of a copyright holder's exclusive display right in the image.
(2) A computer owner that in-line links to or frames a full-size image does not infringe the distribution right of the image's copyright owner when the image is displayed on a user's computer screen.
(3) A search engine's owner's appropriation of a copyrighted image for use as an indexed thumbnail picture is a protected "fair use" under the copyright law where the balance of the statutory fair use factors favors the search engine owner.

FACTS: Perfect 10, Inc. (P) markets and sells copyrighted images of nude models, and operates a subscription website on the Internet whereby subscribers pay a monthly fee to view Perfect 10 (P) images in a "members' area" of the site. Subscribers must use a password to log into the members' area. Perfect 10 (P) has also licensed reduced-size copyrighted images for download and use on cell phones. Google, Inc. (D) operates a search engine, a software program that automatically accesses thousands of websites (collections of web pages) on the Internet and indexes them within a database stored on Google's (D) computers. When a Google (D) user accesses the Google (D) website and types in a search query, Google's (D) software searches its database for websites responsive to that search query. Google (D) then sends relevant information from its index of websites to the user's computer. Google's (D) search engines can provide results in the form of text, images, or videos. The Google (D) search engine that provides responses in the form of images is called "Google Image Search." Google Image Search identifies text in its database responsive to the query and then communicates to users the images associated with the relevant text. Google's (D) software cannot recognize and index the images themselves. Google Image Search provides search results as a web page of small images called "thumbnails," which are stored in Google's (D) servers. The thumbnail images are reduced, lower-resolution versions of full-sized images stored on third-party computers. When a user clicks on a thumbnail image, Google (D)'s software directs the user's browser to create on the user's computer screen a small rectangular box that contains the Google (D) thumbnail and a larger box that contains the full-size image, which the user's computer has been instructed to access from the third-party site that houses that image. Google (D) does not store the images that fill this larger box and does not communicate the images to the user. The two boxes together appear to be coming from the same source, since they are in the same frame, but actually come from two sources—Google (D) and the third-party website. The process by which the web page directs a user's browser to incorporate content from different computers into a single window is referred to as "in-line linking." The term "framing" refers to the process by which information from one computer appears to frame and annotate the in-line linked content from another computer. Google (D) also stores web page content in its cache, which ultimately means that Google's (D) cache copy can provide a user's browser with valid directions to an infringing image even though the updated web page no longer includes that infringing image. In addition to its search engine operations, Google (D) generates revenue through a business program called "AdSense." Under this program, a website owner can register with Google (D) to become an AdSense "partner." The owner then places HTML instructions on its web pages that signal Google's (D) server to place advertising on the web pages that is relevant to the web pages' content. Google's (D) computer program selects the advertising automatically by means of an algorithm, and the AdSense participants share the revenues that flow from such advertising with Google (D). Some website publishers pirated Perfect 10's (P) images and Google's (D) search engine automatically indexed the web pages containing the pirated images and provided thumbnail versions of the images in response to user inquiries. Perfect 10 (P) repeatedly sent Google (D) that its thumbnail images and in-line linking to the full-size images infringed Perfect 10's (P) copyright and when Google (D) continued its search engine practices, Perfect 10 (P) filed a copyright infringement action against Google (D), and sought a preliminary injunction to prevent Google (D) from infringing Perfect 10's (P) copyright in its images and linking to websites that

Continued on next page.

provide full-size infringing versions of Perfect 10's (P) photographs. The district court granted the preliminary injunction, finding harm to the derivative market for Perfect 10's (P) reduced-size images. The court also ruled that Google's (D) search engine likely infringed Perfect 10's (P) display right with respect to the infringing thumbnails, but that Perfect 10 (P) was not likely to prevail on its claim that Google (D) violated either Perfect 10's (P) display or distribution right with respect to its full-size infringing images. In reaching these conclusions, the district court used what it called a "server test," reasoning that a computer owner that stores an image as electronic information and serves that electronic information directly to the user is displaying the electronic information in violation of a copyright holder's exclusive display right. Conversely, the court reasoned that the owner of a computer that does not store and serve the electronic information to a user is not displaying that information, even if such owner in-line links to or frames the electronic information. The district court also reasoned that distribution requires an "actual dissemination" of a copy, and since Google (D) did not communicate the full-size images to the user's computer, Google (D) did not distribute these images. Google (D) raised the affirmative defense that its use was a fair use, but the district court rejected this defense. The court of appeals granted review.

ISSUE:

(1) Does a computer owner that stores an image as electronic information and serves that electronic information directly to a user display the electronic information in violation of a copyright holder's exclusive display right in the image?

(2) Does a computer owner that in-line links to or frames a full-size image infringe the distribution right of the image's copyright owner when the image is displayed on a user's computer screen?

(3) Is a search engine's owner's appropriation of a copyrighted image for use as an indexed thumbnail picture a protected "fair use" under the copyright law where the balance of the statutory fair use factors favors the search engine owner?

HOLDING AND DECISION: (Ikuta, J.)

(1) Yes. A computer owner that stores an image as electronic information and serves that electronic information directly to a user displays the electronic information in violation of a copyright holder's exclusive display right in the image. The district court's reasoning and "server test" comport with the language in the Copyright Act, and, therefore, its ruling is correct with respect to Perfect 10's (P) display rights. Based on the plain language of the statute, a person displays a photographic image by using a computer to fill a computer screen with a copy of the photographic image fixed in the computer's memory. Google's (D) computers store thumbnail versions of Perfect 10's (P) copyrighted images and communicate copies of those thumbnails to Google's (D) users. Therefore, Perfect 10 (P) has made a prima facie case that Google's (D) communication of its stored thumbnail images directly infringes Perfect 10's (P) display right. Conversely, Google's (D) computers do not store the full-size photographic images, but merely in-line links to, and frames, those images. Therefore, Google (D) does not have a copy of the images for purposes of the Copyright Act, i.e., it does not have any "material objects . . . in which a work is fixed . . . and from which the work can be perceived, reproduced, or otherwise communicated" and thus Google (D) cannot communicate a copy as defined under 17 U.S.C. § 101. While Google (D) may facilitate access to infringing copies, such assistance only implicates contributory liability—not direct liability—for copyright infringement. Even if such in-line linking and framing may cause some computer users to believe they are viewing a single Google (D) web page, the Copyright Act, unlike the Trademark Act, does not protect a copyright holder against acts that cause consumer confusion. Finally, the same analysis is applicable to Google's (D) cache.

(2) No. A computer owner that in-line links to or frames a full-size image does not infringe the distribution right of the image's copyright owner when the image is displayed on a user's computer screen. Again, the district court's ruling is consistent with the Copyright Act's language. Under § 106(3), a copyright owner has the exclusive right "to distribute copies. . . . "Copies" means "material objects . . . in which a work is fixed," and the Supreme Court has indicated that in the electronic context, copies may be distributed electronically. Because the full-size images are not on Google's (D) computers, it cannot "distribute" them. It is the third-party website publisher's computer that distributes copies of the images by transmitting the photographic image electronically to the user's computer. Moreover, Perfect 10's (P) argument that merely making the images "available" constitutes distribution is unsupported. A "deemed distribution" rule that is applicable in other contexts is inapplicable to Google (D) because Google (D) does not own a collection of Perfect 10's (P) full-size images and does not communicate these images to the computers of people using Google's (D) search engine; it only indexes the images. Google (D) therefore cannot be deemed to distribute copies of these images.

(3) Yes. A search engine's owner's appropriation of a copyrighted image for use as an indexed thumbnail picture is a protected "fair use" under the copyright law where the balance of the statutory fair use factors favors the search engine owner. Although Perfect 10 (P) would likely prevail in its prima facie case that Google's (D) thumbnail images infringe its display rights, Perfect 10

Continued on next page.

(P) has the burden of showing a likelihood that it will prevail against Google's (D) affirmative fair use defense. The first fair use factor, 17 U.S.C. § 107(1), requires a court to consider "the purpose and character of the use, including whether such use is of a commercial nature or is for nonprofit educational purposes." A "transformative work" is one that alters the original work "with new expression, meaning, or message." Here, Google's (D) use of thumbnails is highly transformative. Google's (D) search engine provides social benefit by incorporating an original work into a new work that serves as an electronic reference tool, thereby providing an entirely new use for the original work. The district court concluded that because Google's (D) use of the thumbnails could supersede Perfect 10's (P) cell phone download use and because the use was commercial because Google's (D) thumbnails "lead users to sites that directly benefit Google's bottom line" through the AdSense program, this fair use factor weighed "slightly" in favor of Perfect 10 (P). The district court's conclusion as to this factor is erroneous because the superseding use was nonexistent insofar as the district court did not find that any downloads for mobile phone use had taken place, and because there was no evidence that AdSense websites containing infringing images significantly contributed to Google's (D) bottom line. Accordingly, the significantly transformative nature of Google's (D) search engine, particularly in light of its public benefit, outweighs Google's (D) superseding and commercial uses of the thumbnails in this case. A weighing of these considerations must promote flexibility and account for the rule that "the more transformative the new work, the less will be the significance of other factors, like commercialism, that may weigh against a finding of fair use." The second fair use factor is "the nature of the copyrighted work," 17 U.S.C. § 107(2). Perfect 10's (P) images are "creative in nature" and thus "closer to the core of intended copyright protection than are more fact-based works." However, because the photos appeared on the Internet before Google (D) used thumbnail versions in its search engine results, this factor weighs only slightly in favor of Perfect 10 (P). The third fair use factor, 17 U.S.C. § 107(3), asks whether the amount and substantiality of the portion used in relation to the copyrighted work as a whole are reasonable in relation to the purpose of the copying. Here, this factor is neutral and does not weigh in favor of either party because Google's (D) use of the entire photographic image was reasonable in light of the purpose of a search engine and since using less than the entire image would be less helpful to a computer user. The fourth fair use factor is "the effect of the use upon the potential market for or value of the copyrighted work." The district court here correctly held that Google's (D) use of thumbnails did not hurt Perfect 10's (P) market for full-size images. Perfect 10 (P) argues that the district court erred because the likelihood of market harm may be presumed if the intended use of an image is for commercial gain. However, this presumption does not arise when a work is transformative because "market substitution is at least less certain, and market harm may not be so readily inferred." As already discussed, Google's (D) thumbnail images were highly transformative, and there was no evidence of market harm to Perfect 10's (P) full-size images. Accordingly, the district court did not err as to this ruling. The district court did err, however, in determining that Google's (D) thumbnails would harm the market for reduced-size images, since Perfect 10 (P) adduced no evidence that actual sales of such images had been made for cell phone use. Any potential harm to Perfect 10's (P) market remains hypothetical, and, therefore, this factor favors neither party. Weighing the fair use factors leads to the conclusion that Google's (D) use was a fair use, especially in light of the public utility served by its search engine and the transformative nature of its use. Perfect 10 (P) is unlikely to be able to overcome Google's (D) fair use defense. Accordingly, the preliminary injunction regarding Google's (D) use of thumbnail images is vacated. Reversed as to this issue.

ANALYSIS

Although finding that Google (D) was not liable for its copyright infringement since its use was a fair use, the court in this case nevertheless ruled that Google (D) could be contributorily liable for copyright infringement since an actor may be contributorily liable for intentionally encouraging direct infringement if the actor knowingly takes steps that are substantially certain to result in such direct infringement. Here, the court found that Google (D) substantially assisted websites to distribute their infringing copies to a worldwide market and assisted a worldwide audience of users to access infringing materials. The court said it could not discount the effect of such a service on copyright owners, even though Google's (D) assistance is available to all websites, not just infringing ones. The court concluded that Google (D) could be held contributorily liable if it had knowledge that infringing Perfect 10 (P) images were available using its search engine, could take simple measures to prevent further damage to Perfect 10's (P) copyrighted works, and failed to take such steps. The court remanded so the district court could make factual findings necessary to resolve this issue.

Quicknotes

COPYRIGHT Refers to the exclusive rights granted to an artist pursuant to Article I, section 8, clause 8 of the United States Constitution over the reproduction, display, performance, distribution, and adaptation of his work for a period prescribed by statute.

Continued on next page.

COPYRIGHT INFRINGEMENT A violation of one of the exclusive rights granted to an artist pursuant to Article I, section 8, clause 8 of the United States Constitution over the reproduction, display, performance, distribution, and adaptation of his work for a period prescribed by statute.

FAIR USE An affirmative defense to a claim of copyright infringement providing an exception from the copyright owner's exclusive rights in a work for the purposes of criticism, comment, news reporting, teaching, scholarship or research; the determination of whether a use is fair is made on a case-by-case basis and requires the court to consider: (1) the purpose and character of the use; (2) the nature of the work; (3) the amount and substantiality of the portion used; and (4) the effect of the use on the potential market for, or value of, the work.

PRELIMINARY INJUNCTION A judicial mandate issued to require or restrain a party from certain conduct; used to preserve a trial's subject matter or to prevent threatened injury.

Newton v. Diamond

Copyright owner (P) v. Alleged infringer (D)

388 F.3d 1189 (9th Cir. 2004).

NATURE OF CASE: Appeal from a defense summary judgment in a music copyright infringement lawsuit.

FACT SUMMARY: When James Newton (P) sued the Beastie Boys (D) for infringement when they used some short portions of his copyrighted music in their own song, the Beastie Boys (D) argued that such use was de minimis hence not actionable.

RULE OF LAW
The de minimis use of a copyrighted musical composition does not constitute infringement.

FACTS: James Newton (P) composed the song "Choir," a piece for flute and voice based on African-American gospel music. Subsequently, the rock group Beastie Boys (D) used portions of "Choir" in their own song "Pass the Mic." The portions used consisted of a "looped" six second portion as a background element in their song. While it was unclear whether the sample was altered or manipulated, the sound engineer stated that alterations of tone, pitch, and rhythm are commonplace. Newton (P) sued the Beastie Boys (D), alleging infringement of his copyright in the underlying composition. The district court granted summary judgment in favor of the Beastie Boys (D) on the grounds, inter alia, that the latter's use of the work was de minimis and therefore not actionable. Newton (P) appealed.

ISSUE: Does the de minimis use of a copyrighted musical composition constitute infringement?

HOLDING AND DECISION: (Schroeder, J.) No. The de minimis use of a copyrighted musical composition does not constitute infringement. On the facts of the record, no reasonable juror could find the sampled portion of the composition to be a quantitatively or qualitatively significant portion of the Beastie Boys' (D) composition as a whole. Quantitatively, the three-note sequence at issue appears only once in Newton's (P) composition. When played, the segment lasts six seconds and is roughly only two percent of the four-and-a-half minute "Choir" sound recording licensed by the Beastie Boys (D). The Beastie Boys' (D) expert concluded that the compositional elements of the sampled section do not represent the heart or the hook of the "Choir" composition, but rather are "simple, minimal, and insignificant." The two works are substantially dissimilar in concept and feel, that is, in their overall thrust and meaning. Put another way, to say that a use is de minimis because no audience would recognize the appropriation is thus to say that the use is not sufficiently significant. Affirmed.

DISSENT: (Graber, J.) The instant composition, even standing alone, is distinctive enough for a fact-finder reasonably to conclude that an average audience would recognize the appropriation of the sampled segment and that Beastie Boys' (D) use was therefore not de minimis. Even passages with relatively few notes, as here, may be qualitatively significant.

ANALYSIS

The principle that trivial copying does not constitute actionable infringement has long been a part of copyright law.

Quicknotes

COPYRIGHT Refers to the exclusive rights granted to an artist pursuant to Article I, section 8, clause 8 of the United States Constitution over the reproduction, display, performance, distribution, and adaptation of his work for a period prescribed by statute.

COPYRIGHT INFRINGEMENT A violation of one of the exclusive rights granted to an artist pursuant to Article I, section 8, clause 8 of the United States Constitution over the reproduction, display, performance, distribution, and adaptation of his work for a period prescribed by statute.

DE MINIMIS Insignificant; trivial; not of sufficient significance to resort to legal action.

INTER ALIA Among other things.

SUMMARY JUDGMENT Judgment rendered by a court in response to a motion by one of the parties, claiming that the lack of a question of material fact in respect to an issue warrants disposition of the issue without consideration by the jury.

Bridgeport Music, Inc. v. Dimension Films

Copyright owner (P) v. Alleged infringer (D)

410 F.3d 792 (6th Cir. 2005).

NATURE OF CASE: Appeal from a summary judgment in favor of a defendant in a music copyright infringement lawsuit.

FACT SUMMARY: When Bridgeport Music, Inc. (P) sued Dimension Films (D) for copyright infringement of a portion of a musical composition, Bridgeport (P) argued that since Dimension (D) did not dispute that it sampled Bridgeport's (P) copyrighted recording, Dimension (D) could not assert a substantial similarity or de minimis defense.

RULE OF LAW
When an alleged infringer does not dispute that it sampled a copyrighted sound recording, a substantial similarity or de minimis argument may not be used.

FACTS: The musical copyright and sound recording copyright to the song "Get Off Your Ass and Jam" by George Clinton, Jr. are owned by Bridgeport Music, Inc. (P). Dimension Films (D) released a film which used a three-note combination solo guitar "riff" lasting four seconds which was taken from the "Get Off" song. The riff was copied, the pitch lowered, and the fragment "looped" and extended to 16 beats. It was then repeated in the film in five places for approximately seven seconds each time. Bridgeport (P) sued Dimension (D) for copyright infringement. The district court found for Dimension (D), and Bridgeport (P) appealed.

ISSUE: When an alleged infringer does not dispute that it sampled a copyrighted sound recording, may a substantial similarity or de minimis argument be used?

HOLDING AND DECISION: (Guy, J.) No. When an alleged infringer does not dispute that it sampled a copyrighted sound recording, a substantial similarity or de minimis argument may not be used. Under the Copyright Statute, a sound recording owner has the exclusive right to "sample" his own recording. The clear rule of get a license or do not sample does not stifle creativity in any significant way. If an artist wants to incorporate a "riff" from another work in his or her recording, he is free to do so as long as he pays for that right. Furthermore, the market will control the license price and keep it within bounds. Sampling is never accidental. It is not like the case of a composer who has a melody in his head, perhaps not even realizing that the reason he hears this melody is that it is the work of another which he has heard before. Here, the portion of the song at issue is an arpeggiated chord—that is, three notes that, if struck together comprise a chord but instead are played one at a time in very quick succession that is repeated several times at the opening of the purported infringing song. The rapidity of the notes and the way they are played produce a high-pitched whirling sound that captures the listener's attention and creates anticipation of what is to follow. When you sample a sound recording, as here, you know you are taking another's work product. Reversed and remanded.

ANALYSIS

As the *Bridgeport Music* decision points out, the incidence of "live and let live" has been relatively high, which explains why so many instances of sampling go unprotested and why so many sampling controversies have been settled.

Quicknotes

COPYRIGHT INFRINGEMENT A violation of one of the exclusive rights granted to an artist pursuant to Article I, section 8, clause 8 of the United States Constitution over the reproduction, display, performance, distribution, and adaptation of his work for a period prescribed by statute.

DE MINIMIS Insignificant; trivial; not of sufficient significance to resort to legal action.

SUMMARY JUDGMENT Judgment rendered by a court in response to a motion by one of the parties, claiming that the lack of a question of material fact in respect to an issue warrants disposition of the issue without consideration by the jury.

Arista Records, LLC v. Launch Media, Inc.

Sound recording copyright holder (P) v. Radio webcaster (D)

578 F.3d 148 (2d Cir. 2009), cert. denied, 130 S. Ct. 1290 (2010).

NATURE OF CASE: Appeal from judgment in action for infringement of sound recording copyrights.

FACT SUMMARY: Sound recording copyright holders (collectively "BMG") (P) contended that Launch Media, Inc. (Launch) (D), which operated an internet radio webcasting service called LAUNCHcast, infringed their sound recording copyrights because LAUNCHcast was an "interactive service" within the meaning of 17 U.S.C. § 114(j)(7) since it "specially created" programs for users within the meaning of § 114(j)(7).

RULE OF LAW
An internet radio webcasting service does not "specially create" programs for users within the meaning of 17 U.S.C. § 114(j)(7) where the user does not have sufficient control over the interactive service to be able to predict the songs the user will hear.

FACTS: Launch Media, Inc. (Launch) (D) operated an internet radio webcasting service called LAUNCHcast. The service enables a user to create personalized radio "stations" that play songs that are within a particular genre or similar to a particular artist or song the user selects. The user does this by selecting artists whose music the user prefers and by rating music genres the user enjoys. The user also specifies a percentage of new music, i.e., songs the user has not previously rated, that the user would like to incorporate into the user's station (the "unrated quota") of no less than 20%. The use also indicates whether the user permits playing songs with profane lyrics. Once LAUNCHcast begins playing music based on the user's musical preferences, the user rates the songs, artists, or albums LAUNCHcast plays on a scale from zero to 100, with 100 being the best rating. Through the use of hyperlinks, the user can see the history of past songs played; can purchase music that has been played; or can share the station with other users, who become the user's DJs. While a song is playing, the user has the ability to pause the song, skip the song, or delete the song from the station by rating the song zero. Notably, the user may not go back to restart the song that is playing, or repeat any of the previously played songs in the playlist. Whenever the user logs into LAUNCHcast and selects a station, LAUNCHcast generates a playlist of 50 songs based on several variables, but the user does not know which songs have been selected. LAUNCHcast creates the playlist through a complex selection process, involving a "hashtable" of around 4,000 songs to which are added 1,000 of the most popular songs—songs most highly rated by all LAUNCHcast users—in the bandwidth specified by the user, provided those songs are not already on the hashtable. More songs are added to the hashtable based on LAUNCHcast's algorithms until there are around 10,000 songs on the hashtable. The playlist of 50 songs is drawn from the hashtable, again based on a set of rules, and the ordering of the playlist songs is random. Sound recording copyright holders (collectively "BMG") (P) brought suit, contending that Launch (D) had infringed their sound recording copyrights because LAUNCHcast was an "interactive service" within the meaning of 17 U.S.C. § 114(j)(7) since it "specially created" programs for users within the meaning of § 114(j)(7). The district court rendered judgment, and the court of appeals granted review. [The procedural posture of the case is not set forth in the casebook extract.]

ISSUE: Does an internet radio webcasting service "specially create" programs for users within the meaning of 17 U.S.C. § 114(j)(7) where the user does not have sufficient control over the interactive service to be able to predict the songs the user will hear?

HOLDING AND DECISION: (Wesley, J.) No. An internet radio webcasting service does not "specially create" programs for users within the meaning of 17 U.S.C. § 114(j)(7) where the user does not have sufficient control over the interactive service to be able to predict the songs the user will hear. Under 17 U.S.C. § 114(j)(7), an "interactive service" "is one that enables a member of the public to receive a transmission of a program specially created for the recipient, or on request, a transmission of a particular sound recording, whether or not as part of a program, which is selected by or on behalf of the recipient." The statute itself offers little guidance as to the meaning of "specially created," so that this operative phrase must be determined from Congress' intent in enacting the statute in 1998. That intent was to prevent the diminution in record sales through outright piracy of music or new digital media that offered listeners the ability to select music in such a way that they would forego purchasing records. BMG (P) argues that any service that reflects user input is specially created for and by the user and therefore qualifies as an interactive service, whereas Launch (D) argues that a service is not interactive simply because it offers the consumer some degree of influence over the programming offered by the webcaster. Thus, the issue is whether LAUNCHcast is an "interactive service" as a matter of law. LAUNCHcast is interactive under the statute if a user can either (1) request—and have played—a particular sound recording, or (2) receive a

Continued on next page.

transmission of a program "specially created" for the user. Here, it is clear that auser cannot request and expect to hear a particular song on demand; therefore, LAUNCHcast does not meet the first definition of interactive. The issue therefore becomes whether the second definition of interactive is met. Based on Congress' purpose in enacting § 114, it must be determined whether LAUNCHcast leads to a diminution in record sales. If a user has sufficient control over the interactive service such that she can predict the songs she will hear, much as she would if she owned the music herself and could play each song at will, she would have no need to purchase the music she wishes to hear. A key part of this analysis must therefore be whether an interactive service provides a degree of predictability—based on choices made by the user—that approximates the predictability the music listener seeks when purchasing music. Here, based on the way LAUNCHcast functions, it is clear that users are not provided sufficient control such that playlists are so predictable that users will choose to listen to the webcast in lieu of purchasing music, thereby diminishing record sales. The way the hashtable is created ensures that the user has almost no ability to choose, let alone predict, which specific songs will be pooled in anticipation for selection to the playlist. Although the user has control over the genre of songs to be played for 5,000 songs, this degree of control is no different from a traditional radio listener expressing a preference for one type of music station over another type. LAUNCHcast also generates the playlist with safeguards to prevent the user from limiting the number of songs in the list eligible for play by selecting a narrow genre, and even the ways in which songs are rated include variables beyond the user's control. And, as a last step, LAUNCHcast randomly orders the songs in the playlist, and the user does not even view the playlist or have the ability to select songs therefrom. Thus, a user cannot listen to the playlist of another user and anticipate the songs to be played from that playlist, even if the user has selected the same preferences and rated all songs, artists, and albums identically as the other user. The only thing a user can predict with certainty and can control is that by rating a song at zero the user will not hear that song on that station again. This ability not to listen to a particular song is not a copyright violation. For these reasons, as a matter of law, LAUNCHcast does not fall within the scope of the definition of an interactive service created for individual users. Judgment for Launch (D) as to this issue.

▶ ANALYSIS

The consequence of this decision of first impression is not that Launch (D) will not have to pay anything to BMG (P), but that it will only have to pay a statutory licensing fee set by the Copyright Royalty Board rather than negotiate individual licensing fees for each of the songs it provides on LAUNCHcast. BMG (P), as a sound recording copyright holder, has no copyright in the general performance of a sound recording, but does have the exclusive right "to perform the copyrighted [sound recording] publicly by means of a digital audio transmission," 17 U.S.C. § 106(6). Thus, BMG (P) has a right to demand that those who perform—i.e., play or broadcast—its copyrighted sound recording pay an individual licensing fee to BMG (P) if the performance of the sound recording occurs through an "interactive service." If the performance of the sound recording does not occur through an interactive service, then the performer is only liable for the statutory licensing fee.

Quicknotes

COPYRIGHT INFRINGEMENT A violation of one of the exclusive rights granted to an artist pursuant to Article I, Section 8, clause 8 of the United States Constitution over the reproduction, display, performance, distribution, and adaptation of his work for a period prescribed by statute.

CHAPTER 6

Different Types of Infringement

Quick Reference Rules of Law

	PAGE
1. **Direct Infringement.** The operator of a bulletin board service and an Internet access provider cannot be held liable for copyright infringement as direct infringers when a third-party user uploads infringing copyrighted works onto a website bulletin board. (Religious Technology Center v. Netcom On-Line Communication Services, Inc.)	106
2. **Contributory Infringement.** (1) One may be vicariously liable for copyright infringement if he has the right and ability to supervise the infringing activity and also has a direct financial interest in such activities. (2) One who, with knowledge of the infringing activity, induces, causes, or materially contributes to the infringing conduct of another may be held liable as a contributory infringer. (Fonovisa, Inc. v. Cherry Auction, Inc.)	108
3. **Contributory Infringement.** (1) A search engine's owner may be contributorily liable for copyright infringement by third parties where it has knowledge that infringing copies are available using its search engine, can take simple measures to prevent further damage to copyrighted works, and fails to take such steps. (2) A search engine's owner is not vicariously liable for copyright infringement by third-party websites where it does not have the right or ability to stop or limit the directly infringing conduct of such websites. (Perfect 10, Inc. v. Amazon.com, Inc.)	109
4. **Contributory Infringement.** (1) The owner of a credit card payment system is not liable for contributory copyright infringement where the owner has knowledge of copyright infringement by websites but nevertheless continues to process and profit from purchases made at those websites. (2) The owner of a credit card payment system is not liable for vicarious copyright infringement where the owner does not have the right and ability to supervise the infringing conduct. (Perfect 10, Inc. v. Visa International Service Association)	112
5. **Device Manufacturers and Liability for Inducing Infringement.** One who distributes a device to promote its use to infringe copyright, as shown by affirmative steps to foster infringement, is liable for the resulting acts of infringement by third parties. (Metro-Goldwyn-Mayer Studios Inc. v. Grokster, Ltd.)	114
6. **Criminal Infringement.** Liability for criminal copyright infringement requires a showing that the infringement was a "voluntary, intentional violation of a known legal duty." (United States v. Moran)	116
7. **Criminal Infringement.** In the Copyright Act, Congress specified the criminal penalties for copyright infringement, and these specific penalties should not be supplemented without congressional action. (United States v. LaMacchia)	117

Religious Technology Center v. Netcom On-Line Communication Services, Inc.

Copyright holders (P) v. Bulletin board operator (D) and Internet access provider (D)

907 F. Supp. 1361 (N.D. Cal. 1995).

NATURE OF CASE: Copyright infringement suit against copyright infringer, bulletin board operator, and Internet access provider.

FACT SUMMARY: Religious Technology Center (RTC) (P), a copyright holder, sued Klemesrud (D), a computer bulletin board service operator, and Netcom On-Line Communication Services, Inc. (Netcom) (D), an Internet access provider, for failing to stop postings by Erlich (D) on a bulletin board website that RTC (P) claimed violated its copyright.

RULE OF LAW
The operator of a bulletin board service and an Internet access provider cannot be held liable for copyright infringement as direct infringers when a third-party user uploads infringing copyrighted works onto a website bulletin board.

FACTS: Religious Technology Center (RTC) (P) held copyrights in the unpublished and published works of L. Ron Hubbard, the late founder of the Church of Scientology. Erlich (D), a former minister of the church, posted portions of the copyrighted work on the Internet to Usenet (a.r.s.) through a computer bulletin board service (BBS) website operated by Klemesrud (D), who gained connection to the Internet through Netcom On-Line Communication Services, Inc. (Netcom) (D), an Internet service provider. After failing to stop Erlich (D) from posting the copyrighted work to the bulletin board, RTC (P) asked Klemesrud (D) and Netcom (D) to keep Erlich (D) off the system. Both denied the request, and RTC (P) sued them both, along with Erlich (D) for copyright infringement. It was undisputed that when Erlich (D) posted his allegedly infringing messages to a.r.s., temporary copies of his postings were made on Klemesrud's (D), Netcom's (D) and Usenet computers. Usenet servers maintained postings from newsgroups for a short period of time—eleven days for Netcom's (D) system and three days for Klemesrud's (D) system. One issue was whether Klemesrud (D) and Netcom (D) could be held liable as direct infringers.

ISSUE: Can the operator of a bulletin board service and an Internet access provider be held liable for copyright infringement as direct infringers when a third-party user uploads infringing copyrighted works onto a website bulletin board?

HOLDING AND DECISION: (Whyte, J.) No. The operator of a bulletin board service and an Internet access provider cannot be held liable for copyright infringement as direct infringers when a third-party user uploads infringing copyrighted works onto a website bulletin board. Even though the infringing copies were left on Klemesrud's (D) and Netcom's (D) computers for at most 11 days, they were sufficiently "fixed" to constitute recognizable copies. This raises the question of whether possessors of computers are liable for incidental copies automatically made on their computers using their software as part of a process initiated by a third party. Here, the incidental copying was necessary to Netcom's (D) system of transmitting information to and from the Internet. Netcom's (D) system, which automatically and uniformly creates temporary copies of all data sent through it, is not unlike a copying machine. Although some of the people using the machine may directly infringe copyrights, courts analyze the machine owner's liability under the rubric of contributory infringement, not direct infringement. To hold otherwise would lead to unreasonable liability. In the cyberspace context, such liability could extend to every single Usenet server in the worldwide link of computers transmitting Erlich's (D) message to every other computer; there is no need to construe the Copyright Act to make all of these parties infringers. Although copyright is a strict liability statute, there should still be some element of volition or causation—which is lacking where a defendant's system is merely used to create a copy by a third party. Judgment for Klemesrud (D) and Netcom (D) on this issue.

ANALYSIS

Copyright is a strict liability statute. A claim for direct infringement does not require any showing of intent or any particular state of mind. However, the distinction may be made between violations of a copyright owner's right to publicly distribute and display copies and violations of the owner's reproduction rights. Here, the court held that the storage on a BBS operator's system of infringing copies and retransmission to other servers is not a direct infringement by the BBS operator of the exclusive right to reproduce the work where such copies are uploaded by an infringing user. Other courts faced with a similar situation concluded that such storage could, however, constitute direct infringement of the public distribution and display rights.

Quicknotes

COPYRIGHT Refers to the exclusive rights granted to an artist pursuant to Article I, section 8, clause 8 of the United States Constitution over the reproduction, display,

Continued on next page.

performance, distribution, and adaptation of his work for a period prescribed by statute.

COPYRIGHT INFRINGEMENT A violation of one of the exclusive rights granted to an artist pursuant to Article I, section 8, clause 8 of the United States Constitution over the reproduction, display, performance, distribution, and adaptation of his work for a period prescribed by statute.

# Fonovisa, Inc. v. Cherry Auction, Inc.

Recording company (P) v. Swap meet organizer (D)

76 F.3d 259 (9th Cir. 1996).

NATURE OF CASE: Appeal from dismissal of copyright and trademark enforcement action.

FACT SUMMARY: Fonovisa, Inc. (P) sued Cherry Auction, Inc. (D), the operators of a swap meet where third-party vendors routinely sold counterfeit recordings that infringed on Fonovisa's (P) copyrights and trademarks.

RULE OF LAW
(1) One may be vicariously liable for copyright infringement if he has the right and ability to supervise the infringing activity and also has a direct financial interest in such activities.
(2) One who, with knowledge of the infringing activity, induces, causes, or materially contributes to the infringing conduct of another may be held liable as a contributory infringer.

FACTS: Cherry Auction, Inc. (D) operated a swap meet in Fresno, California. Cherry Auction (D) collected a daily rental fee from each vendor and supplied parking and advertising. It also retained the right to exclude vendors for patent and trademark infringement. Nevertheless, it permitted vendors to openly sell counterfeit recordings of Latin music copyrighted by Fonovisa, Inc. (P). It also refused to assist an ongoing sheriff's investigation into the sale of counterfeit products. Fonovisa (P) sued Cherry Auction (D) for contributory copyright infringement, vicarious copyright infringement, and contributory trademark infringement. Concluding that Cherry Auction (D) neither supervised nor profited from the vendors' sales, the district court dismissed the suit. Fonovisa (P) appealed.

ISSUE:
(1) May one be vicariously liable for copyright infringement if he has the right and ability to supervise the infringing activity and also has a direct financial interest in such activities?
(2) May one who, with knowledge of the infringing activity, induces, causes, or materially contributes to the infringing conduct of another be held liable as a contributory infringer?

HOLDING AND DECISION: (Schroeder, J.)
(1) Yes. One may be vicariously liable for copyright infringement if he has the right and ability to supervise the infringing activity and also has a direct financial interest in such activities. As the promoter and organizer of the swap meet in question, Cherry Auction (D) had sufficient control over the direct infringers, the vendors, to police their activities. It also received substantial financial benefits from the infringing sales via daily rental fees, admission fees, concession stand sales, and parking fees. Thus, Fonovisa (P) has alleged both control and direct financial benefit sufficient to state a claim for vicarious copyright infringement.
(2) Yes. One who, with knowledge of the infringing activity, induces, causes or materially contributes to the infringing conduct of another may be held liable as a contributory infringer. In this case, Cherry Auction (D) protected the infringers' identities when it refused to share basic information about them with the local sheriff. Moreover, providing the site and facilities for known infringing activity is sufficient to establish contributory liability. Also, since Cherry Auction (D) clearly disregarded its vendors' blatant trademark infringements, Fonovisa (P) has also stated a claim for contributory trademark infringement. Reversed and remanded.

ANALYSIS

The standard for contributory trademark infringement was set forth in *Inwood Laboratories, Inc. v. Ives Laboratories*, 456 U.S. 844 (1982). To be liable, the defendant must (1) intentionally induce another to infringe on a trademark or (2) continue to supply a product knowing that the recipient is using the product to engage in trademark infringement. The defendant in *Inwood* distributed drugs to a pharmacist, knowing that the pharmacist was mislabeling the drugs with a protected trademark rather than using the generic label.

Quicknotes

COPYRIGHT Refers to the exclusive rights granted to an artist pursuant to Article I, section 8, clause 8 of the United States Constitution over the reproduction, display, performance, distribution, and adaptation of his work for a period prescribed by statute.

COPYRIGHT INFRINGEMENT A violation of one of the exclusive rights granted to an artist pursuant to Article I, section 8, clause 8 of the United States Constitution over the reproduction, display, performance, distribution, and adaptation of his work for a period prescribed by statute.

Perfect 10, Inc. v. Amazon.com, Inc.

Web porn publisher (P) v. Internet company (D)

508 F.3d 1146 (9th Cir. 2007).

NATURE OF CASE: Appeal from preliminary injunction in copyright infringement action.

FACT SUMMARY: Perfect 10, Inc. (P) contended that Google, Inc. (D) was secondarily liable—contributorily and vicariously—for third-party websites' reproducing, displaying, and distributing unauthorized copies of Perfect 10's (P) nude images on the Internet.

RULE OF LAW
(1) A search engine's owner may be contributorily liable for copyright infringement by third parties where it has knowledge that infringing copies are available using its search engine, can take simple measures to prevent further damage to copyrighted works, and fails to take such steps.

(2) A search engine's owner is not vicariously liable for copyright infringement by third-party websites where it does not have the right or ability to stop or limit the directly infringing conduct of such websites.

FACTS: Perfect 10, Inc. (P) markets and sells copyrighted images of nude models, and operates a subscription website on the Internet whereby subscribers pay a monthly fee to view Perfect 10 (P) images in a "members' area" of the site. Subscribers must use a password to log into the members' area. Perfect 10 (P) has also licensed reduced-size copyrighted images for download and use on cell phones. Google, Inc. (D) operates a search engine, a software program that automatically accesses thousands of websites (collections of web pages) on the Internet and indexes them within a database stored on Google's (D) computers. When a Google (D) user accesses the Google (D) website and types in a search query, Google's (D) software searches its database for websites responsive to that search query. Google (D) then sends relevant information from its index of websites to the user's computer. Google's (D) search engines can provide results in the form of text, images, or videos. The Google (D) search engine that provides responses in the form of images is called "Google Image Search." Google Image Search identifies text in its database responsive to the query and then communicates to users the images associated with the relevant text. Google's (D) software cannot recognize and index the images themselves. Google Image Search provides search results as a web page of small images called "thumbnails," which are stored in Google's (D) servers. The thumbnail images are reduced, lower-resolution versions of full-sized images stored on third-party computers. When a user clicks on a thumbnail image, Google (D)'s software directs the user's browser to create on the user's computer screen a small rectangular box that contains the Google (D) thumbnail and a larger box that contains the full-size image, which the user's computer has been instructed to access from the third-party site that houses that image. Google (D) does not store the images that fill this larger box and does not communicate the images to the user. The two boxes together appear to be coming from the same source, since they are in the same frame, but actually come from two sources—Google (D) and the third-party website. The process by which the web page directs a user's browser to incorporate content from different computers into a single window is referred to as "in-line linking." The term "framing" refers to the process by which information from one computer appears to frame and annotate the in-line linked content from another computer. Google (D) also stores web page content in its cache, which ultimately means that Google's (D) cache copy can provide a user's browser with valid directions to an infringing image even though the updated web page no longer includes that infringing image. In addition to its search engine operations, Google (D) generates revenue through a business program called "AdSense." Under this program, a website owner can register with Google (D) to become an AdSense "partner." The owner then places HTML instructions on its web pages that signal Google's (D) server to place advertising on the web pages that is relevant to the web pages' content. Google's (D) computer program selects the advertising automatically by means of an algorithm, and the AdSense participants share the revenues that flow from such advertising with Google (D). Some website publishers pirated Perfect 10's (P) images and Google's (D) search engine automatically indexed the web pages containing the pirated images and provided thumbnail versions of the images in response to user inquiries. Perfect 10 (P) repeatedly sent Google (D) notices that its thumbnail images and in-line linking to the full-size images infringed Perfect 10's (P) copyright, and, when Google (D) continued its search engine practices, Perfect 10 (P) filed a copyright infringement action against Google (D), and sought a preliminary injunction to prevent Google (D) from infringing Perfect 10's (P) copyright in its images and linking to websites that provided full-size infringing versions of Perfect 10's (P) photographs. Perfect 10 (P) also sought to hold Google (D) contributorily and vicariously liable for infringement by third-party websites. The district court granted the preliminary injunction, finding harm to the derivative market for Perfect 10's (P) reduced-size images. The district court held that Google (D) could not be contributorily liable, because, even assuming Google (D) had

Continued on next page.

actual knowledge of infringing material available on its system, Google (D) did not materially contribute to infringing conduct because it did not undertake any substantial promotional or advertising efforts to encourage visits to infringing websites, nor provide a significant revenue stream to the infringing websites. The district court also held that Google (D) could not be vicariously liable because Perfect 10 (P) failed to show that Google (D) had the right or ability to make third-party websites stop their direct infringement. The court of appeals granted review.

ISSUE:

(1) May a search engine's owner be contributorily liable for copyright infringement by third parties where it has knowledge that infringing copies are available using its search engine, can take simple measures to prevent further damage to copyrighted works, and fails to take such steps?

(2) A search engine's owner is not vicariously liable for copyright infringement by third-party websites where it does not have the right or ability to stop or limit the directly infringing conduct of such websites?

HOLDING AND DECISION: (Ikuta, J.)

(1) Yes. A search engine's owner may be contributorily liable for copyright infringement by third parties where it has knowledge that infringing copies are available using its search engine, can take simple measures to prevent further damage to copyrighted works, and fails to take such steps. In the cyberspace context, case law has held that a service provider's knowing failure to prevent infringing actions can be the basis for imposing contributory liability, and that intent can be imputed under such circumstances. This ruling provides copyright holders a meaningful way to protect their rights, since it may be impossible to enforce rights in the protected work effectively against all direct infringers, and the only practical alternative is to go against the distributor of the copying device for secondary liability. Here, the district court erroneously held that even assuming Google (D) had actual knowledge of infringing material available on its system, Google (D) did not materially contribute to infringing conduct because it did not undertake any substantial promotional or advertising efforts to encourage visits to infringing websites, nor provide a significant revenue stream to the infringing websites. Google (D) substantially assists websites to distribute their infringing copies to a worldwide market and assists a worldwide audience of users to access infringing materials. The impact of Google's (D) service on copyright holders cannot be discounted, even though Google's (D) assistance is available to all websites, not just infringing ones. Accordingly, Google (D) can be held contributorily liable if it had knowledge that infringing Perfect 10 (P) images were available using its search engine, could take simple measures to prevent further damage to Perfect 10's (P) copyrighted works, and failed to take such steps. However, the factual issues of the adequacy of Perfect 10's (P) notices to Google (D), and Google's (D) response thereto, must be resolved on remand. Reversed and remanded as to this issue.

(2) No A search engine's owner is not vicariously liable for copyright infringement by third-party websites where it does not have the right or ability to stop or limit the directly infringing conduct of such websites. To establish vicarious liability, a plaintiff must establish that the defendant exercised control over the direct infringer by having both the legal right and practical ability to stop the direct the infringer's conduct. Here, the district court correctly concluded that Perfect 10 (P) failed to establish such control. Google (D) did not have contracts with third-party websites that empowered it to stop or limit those websites from reproducing, displaying, and distributing infringing copies of Perfect 10's (P) images on the Internet. Although Google (D) had the right to terminate an AdSense partnership, such a right did not give Google (D) the right to stop direct infringement by third-party websites since an infringing third-party website could continue infringing conduct after its participation in the AdSense program ended. Moreover, Google (D) lacks the practical ability to police infringing conduct because its software lacks the ability to analyze every image on the Internet, compare each image to all the other copyrighted images that exist in the world and determine whether a certain image on the web infringes someone's copyright. For these reasons, Perfect 10 (P) failed to show a likelihood of success on its vicarious liability theory. Affirmed as to this issue.

▶ ANALYSIS

Perfect 10 (P) argued in connection with its vicarious liability claim that Google (D) could manage its own operations to avoid indexing websites with infringing content and linking to third-party infringing sites. The court found that this was a claim of contributory liability, not vicarious liability, explaining that although the lines between direct infringement, contributory infringement, and vicarious liability are not clearly drawn, in general, contributory liability is based on the defendant's failure to stop its own actions which facilitate third-party infringement, while vicarious liability is based on the defendant's failure to cause a third party to stop its directly infringing activities. Here, the court viewed Google's (D) failure to change its operations to avoid assisting websites to distribute their infringing content as possibly constituting contributory liability, but not vicarious liability.

Quicknotes

COPYRIGHT Refers to the exclusive rights granted to an artist pursuant to Article I, section 8, clause 8 of the

Continued on next page.

United States Constitution over the reproduction, display, performance, distribution, and adaptation of his work for a period prescribed by statute.

COPYRIGHT INFRINGEMENT A violation of one of the exclusive rights granted to an artist pursuant to Article I, section 8, clause 8 of the United States Constitution over the reproduction, display, performance, distribution, and adaptation of his work for a period prescribed by statute.

FAIR USE An affirmative defense to a claim of copyright infringement providing an exception from the copyright owner's exclusive rights in a work for the purposes of criticism, comment, news reporting, teaching, scholarship or research; the determination of whether a use is fair is made on a case-by-case basis and requires the court to consider: (1) the purpose and character of the use; (2) the nature of the work; (3) the amount and substantiality of the portion used; and (4) the effect of the use on the potential market for, or value of, the work.

PRELIMINARY INJUNCTION A judicial mandate issued to require or restrain a party from certain conduct; used to preserve a trial's subject matter or to prevent threatened injury.

Perfect 10, Inc. v. Visa International Service Association

Porn publisher (P) v. Credit card company (D)

494 F.3d 788 (9th Cir. 2007), cert. denied, 128 S.Ct. 2871 (2008).

NATURE OF CASE: Appeal from dismissal of action for secondary liability under the copyright laws.

FACT SUMMARY: Perfect 10, Inc. (P) sued several credit card companies and affiliated banks (collectively "Defendants") (D) for secondary liability under the copyright laws because Defendants (D) continued to process credit card payments to websites that infringed Perfect 10's (P) intellectual property rights after being notified by Perfect 10 (P) of infringement by those websites.

RULE OF LAW
(1) The owner of a credit card payment system is not liable for contributory copyright infringement where the owner has knowledge of copyright infringement by websites but nevertheless continues to process and profit from purchases made at those websites.
(2) The owner of a credit card payment system is not liable for vicarious copyright infringement where the owner does not have the right and ability to supervise the infringing conduct.

FACTS: Perfect 10, Inc. (P) is a publisher, in hard copy and on the web, of copyrighted photographs of nude women. Allegedly, numerous websites based in several countries stole its proprietary images, altered them, and illegally offered them for sale online. Perfect 10 (P) repeatedly notified several credit card companies and affiliated banks (collectively "Defendants") (D) that process credit card payments to the allegedly infringing websites of the alleged copyright infringement, but the Defendants (D) took no action in response to the notices. Perfect 10 (P) then brought suit against the Defendants (D), who collect fees for their services in these transactions, for secondary—contributory and vicarious—liability under the copyright laws. The district court dismissed for failure to state a claim, and the court of appeals granted review.

ISSUE:
(1) Is the owner of a credit card payment system liable for contributory copyright infringement where the owner has knowledge of copyright infringement by websites but nevertheless continues to process and profit from purchases made at those websites?
(2) Is the owner of a credit card payment system liable for vicarious copyright infringement where the owner does not have the right and ability to supervise the infringing conduct?

HOLDING AND DECISION: (Smith, Jr., J.)
(1) No. The owner of a credit card payment system is not liable for contributory copyright infringement where the owner has knowledge of copyright infringement by websites but nevertheless continues to process and profit from purchases made at those websites. A defendant is a contributory infringer if it (1) has knowledge of a third party's infringing activity, and (2) "induces, causes, or materially contributes to the infringing conduct." To prevail, Perfect 10 (P) must show that the Defendants (D) induced, caused, or materially contributed to the infringement. Here, the Defendants (D) cannot be said to materially contribute to the infringement because they have no direct connection to that infringement. It is not alleged that any infringing material passes over Defendants' (D) payment networks or through their payment processing systems, or that Defendants' (D) systems are used to alter or display the infringing images, or to locate them. The infringement here rests on reproduction, alteration, display and distribution, which can occur without payment. While the Defendants (D) make it easier for infringement to be profitable, which may encourage further infringement, payment via a credit card is not essential to the infringing activity and does not assist in the location of infringing material, as other funding methods, such as advertising revenue, are available. Because Defendants (D) do not induce or materially contribute to the infringing activity, Perfect 10's (P) contributory copyright infringement claim fails, and there is no need to address Defendants' (D) knowledge of the infringing activity. Affirmed as to this issue.
(2) No. The owner of a credit card payment system is not liable for vicarious copyright infringement where the owner does not have the right and ability to supervise the infringing conduct. A defendant is a vicarious infringer if it has (1) the right and ability to supervise the infringing conduct and (2) a direct financial interest in the infringing activity. Here, the Defendants (D) do not have the right and ability to control the infringing activity. Although the Defendants (D) could have stopped processing credit card payments to the infringing websites, based on Defendants' (D) rules and regulations prohibiting certain illegal activities, this ability does not rise to the level of "right and ability to control." Stated differently, the mere ability to withdraw a financial "carrot" does not create the "stick" of "right and ability to control" that vicarious infringement requires. Because Defendants (D) do not have the right and ability to control the alleged infringing conduct, Perfect 10 (P) does not have a viable claim of vicarious liability. Accordingly, the issue of direct financial interest need not be reached. Affirmed as to this issue.

Continued on next page.

DISSENT: (Kozinski, J.) Because Perfect 10's (P) allegations must be accepted as true on a motion to dismiss, Perfect 10 (P) has easily made out a claim of secondary liability, since it must be accepted that Defendants (D) knowingly provide a financial bridge between buyers and sellers of pirated works. As to contributory infringement, caselaw provides that the Defendants (D) are liable if they "had knowledge that infringing Perfect 10 (P) images were available using [their payment systems], could take simple measures to prevent further damage to Perfect 10's (P) copyrighted works, and failed to take such steps." Even if the Defendants' (D) conduct is one or two steps removed from the infringing conduct, the materiality of their contribution to that activity turns on how significantly the activity helps infringement, not on how it is characterized. Here, Defendants' (D) participation is not just an economic incentive for infringement; it's an essential step in the infringement process. Thus, Defendants (D) are providing very significant help to the direct infringers. Also, the majority correctly recognizes that assisting the location of infringing material constitutes contributory infringement, but they incorrectly distinguish locating infringing images more central to infringement than paying for them. If infringing images can't be found, there can be no infringement; but if infringing images can't be paid for, there can be no infringement either—both locating and paying for infringing images is central to infringement. Finally, the majority's assertion that infringement could continue because other funding mechanisms may exist is inconsistent with prior caselaw, which has not suggested that the existence of other means of infringement is a relevant consideration. As to vicarious liability, contrary to the majority's position, the Defendants (D) do, as a contractual matter, have the right and ability to stop or limit the infringing activity, but have refused to exercise that right. If merchants remove infringing material in response to Defendants' (D) demands, infringement will stop or be limited. If merchants do not comply, the Defendants (D) can remove them from the credit card network, thus also stopping or limiting. Merely because the infringers can find other ways of doing business is irrelevant; the issue is whether Defendants' (D) exercise of their rights would make direct infringement more difficult and thereby diminish the scale of infringing activity. In a commercial environment, taking away payment processing makes it extremely difficult for the infringers to distribute the infringing works; thus, the Defendants (D) effectively control distribution of the infringing material.

ANALYSIS

The dissent's claims that payment processing is "an essential step in the infringement process," that "Defendants (D) are directly involved in every infringing transaction where payment is made by credit card," and that the "credit cards, in fact, control distribution of the infringing material" suggests that the dissent believes that the Defendants (D) are directly infringing when they process these payments, rather than being secondarily liable. The argument to that, however, is that payment is not part of the actual process of infringing "reproduction, alteration, display and distribution" rights.

Quicknotes

COPYRIGHT INFRINGEMENT A violation of one of the exclusive rights granted to an artist pursuant to Article I, Section 8, clause 8 of the United States Constitution over the reproduction, display, performance, distribution, and adaptation of his work for a period prescribed by statute.

COPYRIGHT LAW Refers to the exclusive rights granted to an artist pursuant to Article I, section 8, clause 8 of the United States Constitution over the reproduction, display, performance, distribution, and adaptation of his work for a period prescribed by statute.

MOTION TO DISMISS Motion to terminate an action based on the adequacy of the pleadings, improper service or venue, etc.

SECONDARY LIABILITY Liability that does not arise except upon the default in performance by the party directly liable for the obligation.

Metro-Goldwyn-Mayer Studios Inc. v. Grokster, Ltd.

Copyright owners (P) v. Distributor of software (D)

545 U.S. 913 (2005).

NATURE OF CASE: Appeal from a summary judgment in favor of a defendant in a copyright infringement lawsuit.

FACT SUMMARY: When Grokster, Ltd. (D) freely distributed software by which any computer user could easily and without payment download copyrighted music, Metro-Goldwin-Mayer Studios Inc. (MGM) (P) and other movie studios, recording companies, songwriters, and music publishers sued Grokster, Ltd. (D) for their users' infringements.

RULE OF LAW
One who distributes a device to promote its use to infringe copyright, as shown by affirmative steps to foster infringement, is liable for the resulting acts of infringement by third parties.

FACTS: Grokster, Ltd. (D) distributes software, free of charge, by which users of computers can share electronic files through so-called peer-to-peer networks by which the users' computers communicate with others directly, not through central servers. Grokster (D) uses no servers to intercept the content of the search requests or to mediate the file transfers conducted by users of the software, there being no central point through which the substance of the communications passes in either direction. Nearly 90% of the files available for download on Grokster's (D) system were copyrighted works. Over 100 million copies of the software in question have been downloaded, and billions of files are shared across the networks each month. Copyright infringement by users of the software is conceded by Grokster (D). Grokster (D) received no direct revenue from the copyright infringement itself, but rather from the sale of advertising on its website. A group of copyright holders ("MGM," for short) (P) sued Grokster (D) for copyright infringement. The district court, although holding that those who used the Grokster (D) software to download copyrighted material were indeed infringers (a point not here contested), the court, nonetheless, granted summary judgment in favor of Grokster (D) as to any infringement liability from distribution of their software on the grounds that such distribution did not provide the distributors with actual knowledge of specific acts of infringement. The court of appeals affirmed, and MGM (P) appealed.

ISSUE: Is one who distributes a device to promote its use to infringe copyright, as shown by affirmative steps to foster infringement, liable for the resulting acts of infringement by third parties?

HOLDING AND DECISION: (Souter, J.) Yes. One who distributes a device to promote its use to infringe copyright, as shown by affirmative steps to foster infringement, is liable for the resulting acts of infringement by third parties. When a widely shared service or product, as here, is used to commit infringement, it may be impossible to enforce rights in the protected works effectively against all direct infringers. One infringes contributorily by intentionally inducing or encouraging direct infringement, and infringes vicariously by profiting from direct infringement by declining to exercise a right to stop or limit it. Although the Copyright Act does not expressly render anyone liable for infringement committed by another, these doctrines of secondary liability emerged from common law principles and are well established in the law. In the instant case, where an article, such as Grokster's (D) software program at issue, is "good for nothing else" but infringement, there is no injustice in presuming or imputing an intent to infringe. Here, there is no question but that Grokster (D) widely advertised the infringing use of its software, and indeed encouraged its infringing use, and even instructed potential users on how to engage in its infringing use by downloading copyrighted music. Grokster (D) even went so far as to distribute an electronic newsletter containing links to articles promoting its software's ability to access copyrighted popular music. "The unlawful objective is unmistakable." Reversed and remanded.

CONCURRENCE: (Ginsburg, J.) There is in the instant case at least a genuine issue as to the liability of Grokster (D), not only for actively inducing infringement, but also, or alternatively, based on the distribution of its software products, for contributory copyright infringement.

CONCURRENCE: (Breyer, J.) The rule of secondary liability for the resulting acts of infringement by third parties allows those who develop new products that are capable of substantial noninfringing uses to know, at the beginning, that distribution of their product will not yield massive monetary liability. At the same time, it helps deter them from distributing products that have no other real function than—or that are specially intended for—copyright infringement. The rule, furthermore, is forward-looking in that it does not confine its scope to a static snapshot of a product's current uses (thereby threatening technologies that have underdeveloped future markets).

ANALYSIS

As noted by the Supreme Court in its *MGM* decision, the mere knowledge of infringing potential of a particular device or product, or of actual infringing uses, would not be enough to subject a distributor to liability. The inducement rule, instead, premises liability on purposeful, culpable expression and conduct, hence does nothing to

Continued on next page.

compromise legitimate commerce or discourage innovation having a lawful premise.

Quicknotes

CONTRIBUTORY INFRINGEMENT The intentional assisting of another in the unlawful appropriation of a patented work.

COPYRIGHT ACT Copyright Act of 1976 extends copyright protection to "original works of authorship fixed in any tangible medium of expression, now known or later developed, from which they can be perceived, reproduced, or otherwise communicated, either directly or with the aid of a machine or device." 17 U.S.C. § 102.

COPYRIGHT INFRINGEMENT A violation of one of the exclusive rights granted to an artist pursuant to Article I, section 8, clause 8 of the United States Constitution over the reproduction, display, performance, distribution, and adaptation of his work for a period prescribed by statute.

SUMMARY JUDGMENT Judgment rendered by a court in response to a motion by one of the parties, claiming that the lack of a question of material fact in respect to an issue warrants disposition of the issue without consideration by the jury.

United States v. Moran

United States (P) v. Owner of movie rental business (D)

757 F. Supp. 1046 (D. Neb. 1991).

NATURE OF CASE: Criminal copyright infringement action.

FACT SUMMARY: The Federal Bureau of Investigation (the FBI) confiscated from the owner of a video rental store extra copies he had produced of copyrighted films.

RULE OF LAW
Liability for criminal copyright infringement requires a showing that the infringement was a "voluntary, intentional violation of a known legal duty."

FACTS: Moran (D) owned a movie rental business at which agents of the FBI (P), executing a court-ordered search warrant, seized unauthorized copies of copyrighted films that Moran (D) had produced. Moran (D) testified that he had made the copies to "insure" his authorized versions after a number of them had been vandalized by customers. Moran (D) also testified that he believed that "insuring" was legal. The facts revealed that Moran (D) made only one copy of each authorized version in his possession and that he never attempted to rent out both the authorized version and the copy at the same time.

ISSUE: Does the word "willfully" as used in the provision of the Copyright Act providing for criminal copyright infringement necessitate a showing of intent to infringe?

HOLDING AND DECISION: (Kopf, Magistrate J.) Yes. The term "willfully" under 17 U.S.C. § 506(a) means that infringement was a "voluntary, intentional violation of a known legal duty." In the civil context, a distinction is drawn between infringement that is committed willfully and innocent infringement. The same distinction should be applied in the criminal context. Here, the test was whether Moran (D) truly believed that he could legally make one copy of each authorized version he had purchased. The Government (P) here failed to prove beyond a reasonable doubt that Moran (D) acted willfully. Therefore, defendant is not guilty.

ANALYSIS

Over time, criminal sanctions for copyright infringement have increased, including stiffer penalties and more active enforcement. At the same time, there has also been a lowering of standards for the conduct that will be considered criminal.

Quicknotes

COPYRIGHT Refers to the exclusive rights granted to an artist pursuant to Article I, section 8, clause 8 of the United States Constitution over the reproduction, display, performance, distribution, and adaptation of his work for a period prescribed by statute.

COPYRIGHT INFRINGEMENT A violation of one of the exclusive rights granted to an artist pursuant to Article I, section 8, clause 8 of the United States Constitution over the reproduction, display, performance, distribution, and adaptation of his work for a period prescribed by statute.

United States v. LaMacchia

United States (P) v. Computer hacker (D)

871 F. Supp. 535 (D. Mass. 1994).

NATURE OF CASE: Motion to dismiss indictment for wire fraud.

FACT SUMMARY: The defendant was indicted under a wire fraud statute for setting up and maintaining a bulletin board website that allowed the uploading and downloading of copyrighted computer software and games.

RULE OF LAW
In the Copyright Act, Congress specified the criminal penalties for copyright infringement, and these specific penalties should not be supplemented without congressional action.

FACTS: LaMacchia (D), a student at the Massachusetts Institute of Technology, created an electronic bulletin board from which users could upload and download copyrighted software applications and computer games. LaMacchia (D) was indicted and charged with violating a wire fraud statute, alleging that he had caused software companies the loss of millions of dollars. The charge did not allege that LaMacchia (D) derived any personal benefit from the bulletin board. LaMacchia (D) moved to dismiss the wire fraud charge, arguing that the government (P) could not use a wire fraud statute to enforce copyright.

ISSUE: Can the government (P) use penalties not specified in the Copyright Act to enforce copyright?

HOLDING AND DECISION: (Stearns, J.) No. As determined by the Supreme Court's decision in *Dowling v. United States*, 473 U.S. 207 (1985), Congress was careful to set forth specific criminal penalties for copyright infringement. Those penalties should not be supplemented without congressional action. Here, subjecting defendant to criminal penalty under the wire fraud statue would circumvent the intent of Congress to limit the penalties for copyright infringement. LaMacchia's (D) motion to dismiss was allowed.

ANALYSIS

Congress responded to the *LaMacchia* court's decision by enacting the No Electronic Theft (NET) Act. Among other things, NET Act added a new provision for criminal liability under which an infringer is held criminally liable when his infringement involves the willful "reproduction or distribution, including by electronic means, during any 180-day period, of one or more copies of phonorecords of one or more copyrighted works with a total retail value of more than $1,000."

Quicknotes

COPYRIGHT Refers to the exclusive rights granted to an artist pursuant to Article I, section 8, clause 8 of the United States Constitution over the reproduction, display, performance, distribution, and adaptation of his work for a period prescribed by statute.

COPYRIGHT ACT Copyright Act of 1976 extends copyright protection to "original works of authorship fixed in any tangible medium of expression, now known or later developed, from which they can be perceived, reproduced, or otherwise communicated, either directly or with the aid of a machine or device." 17 U.S.C. § 102.

COPYRIGHT INFRINGEMENT A violation of one of the exclusive rights granted to an artist pursuant to Article I, section 8, clause 8 of the United States Constitution over the reproduction, display, performance, distribution, and adaptation of his work for a period prescribed by statute.

INDICTMENT A formal written accusation made by the prosecution to the grand jury under oath, charging an individual with a criminal offense.

MOTION TO DISMISS Motion to terminate a trial based on the adequacy of the pleadings.

CHAPTER 7

Fair Use

Quick Reference Rules of Law

	PAGE
1. **Cultural Interchange.** Publication of portions of a work soon to be published is not fair use. (Harper & Row, Publishers, Inc. v. Nation Enterprises)	120
2. **Cultural Interchange.** The commercial purpose of a work is only one element of the inquiry into the work's purpose and character for fair use purposes. (Campbell v. Acuff-Rose Music, Inc.)	121
3. **Cultural Interchange.** One factor of an analysis of fair use is whether the new work has a transformative purpose, that is, whether it adds something new, with a further purpose, to the original work. (Castle Rock Entertainment, Inc. v. Carol Publishing Group, Inc.)	122
4. **Cultural Interchange.** The reproduction of photographs for a good-faith newsworthy purpose constitutes fair use. (Núñez v. Caribbean International News Corp. [El Vocero de Puerto Rico])	123
5. **Cultural Interchange.** A book publisher's appropriation of copyrighted poster and ticket images in a biographical book in reduced-size format is a protected "fair use" under the copyright law where the balance of the statutory fair use factors favors the publisher. (Bill Graham Archives v. Dorling Kindersley Ltd.)	124
6. **Technical Interchange.** Disassembly of a copyrighted object code is a fair use of the material if it is the only means of access to uncopyrighted elements of the code and there is a legitimate reason for seeking such access. (Sega Enterprises Ltd. v. Accolade, Inc.)	127
7. **Technical Interchange.** Intermediate infringement of copyrighted materials where the final product does not contain infringing material is likely to be viewed as fair use. (Sony Computer Entertainment, Inc. v. Connectix Corp.)	128
8. **Technical Interchange.** A search engine's owner's appropriation of a copyrighted image for use as an indexed thumbnail picture is a protected "fair use" under the copyright law where the balance of the statutory fair use factors favors the search engine owner. (Perfect 10, Inc. v. Amazon, Inc.)	129
9. **Market Failure or "Productive Consumption"?** The marketing of videocassette recorders does not infringe on the copyrights of recorded works. (Sony Corporation of America v. Universal City Studios, Inc.)	131
10. **Market Failure or "Productive Consumption"?** The retransmission by a service of original works and the free distribution of those works to users of the service does not constitute fair use. (A&M Records, Inc. v. Napster, Inc.)	132
11. **Market Failure or "Productive Consumption"?** The practice of circulating copies of scientific journals so that employees may copy articles contained therein does not constitute a fair use. (American Geophysical Union v. Texaco, Inc.)	133

Harper & Row, Publishers, Inc. v. Nation Enterprises

Book publisher (P) v. Magazine (D)

471 U.S. 539 (1985).

NATURE OF CASE: Review of reversal of award of damages for copyright infringement.

FACT SUMMARY: Nation Enterprises (D) contended that its use of quotes from a yet-unpublished set of memoirs constituted fair use.

RULE OF LAW
Publication of portions of a work soon to be published is not fair use.

FACTS: Harper & Row, Publishers, Inc. (P) obtained the rights to publish President Ford's memoirs, *A Time to Heal*. *Time* magazine contracted for the rights to preview the work immediately prior to publication. Prior to the publication of the article by *Time* magazine, Nation Enterprises (D), publisher of *The Nation* magazine, obtained a copy of the Ford manuscript. *The Nation* published an article that quoted the manuscript regarding the Nixon pardon. *Time* then declined to run the article it had planned and canceled its contract with Harper (P). Harper (P) sued Nation Enterprises (D) for copyright infringement. The district court awarded damages for infringement. The Second Circuit reversed, holding Nation Enterprises' (D) use to be a "fair use" under 17 U.S.C. § 107. The Supreme Court granted certiorari.

ISSUE: Is publication of portions of a work soon to be published a fair use?

HOLDING AND DECISION: (O'Connor, J.) No. Publication of portions of a work soon to be published is not a fair use. The notion behind the fair use doctrine is that one using a copyrighted work should not have to obtain a copyright holder's permission to use the copyrighted work in a situation where a reasonable copyright holder would in fact grant permission. Section 107 of the Copyright Act, which codified the doctrine, expressly noted in its legislative history that it was not intended to modify the common law. In terms of reasonableness, it is not reasonable to expect a copyright holder to allow another person to "scoop" it by publishing his material ahead of time. With respect to § 107's language, the section lists four factors to be considered in applying the doctrine. The two factors most salient here are purpose of the use and effect on the market. Normally, a fair use will not be one of economic competition with the copyright holder, which is precisely what prior publication of a copyrighted work is. Further, the effect on the market of such a use is illustrated by what happened here: it greatly lessens the market value of the copyrighted work. The conclusion therefore presents itself that, in almost all cases, prior publication of a work awaiting publication will not be a fair use. Such was the case here. Reversed.

DISSENT: (Brennan, J.) The Court errs in holding that *The Nation*'s quotation of 300 words from the unpublished 200,000-word manuscript of President Gerald R. Ford infringed the copyright of the manuscript. The Court threatens the creative process and the free flow of ideas under the First Amendment while concurrently constricting the fair use doctrine. This was not the intent of the Congress when it established legislation protecting the economic interests of copyright holders.

ANALYSIS

"Fair use" is a well-established common law doctrine. It was recognized by the Supreme Court as early as 1841. In *Folsom v. Marsh*, 9 F. Cas. 342 (1841), Justice Story permitted use of quotes by a reviewer as a "fair use." Use of quotes in criticism of a work has remained a major application of the doctrine.

Quicknotes

CERTIORARI A discretionary writ issued by a superior court to an inferior court in order to review the lower court's decisions; the Supreme Court's writ ordering such review.

COPYRIGHT ACT Copyright Act of 1976 extends copyright protection to "original works of authorship fixed in any tangible medium of expression, now known or later developed, from which they can be perceived, reproduced, or otherwise communicated, either directly or with the aid of a machine or device." 17 U.S.C. § 102.

COPYRIGHT INFRINGEMENT A violation of one of the exclusive rights granted to an artist pursuant to Article I, section 8, clause 8 of the United States Constitution over the reproduction, display, performance, distribution, and adaptation of his work for a period prescribed by statute.

FAIR USE An affirmative defense to a claim of copyright infringement providing an exception from the copyright owner's exclusive rights in a work for the purposes of criticism, comment, news reporting, teaching, scholarship or research; the determination of whether a use is fair is made on a case-by-case basis and requires the court to consider: (1) the purpose and character of the use; (2) the nature of the work; (3) the amount and substantiality of the portion used; and (4) the effect of the use on the potential market for, or value of, the work.

Campbell v. Acuff-Rose Music, Inc.

Recording artist (D) v. Music publisher (P)

510 U.S. 569 (1994).

NATURE OF CASE: Review of reversal of summary judgment for the defense in copyright infringement action.

FACT SUMMARY: 2 Live Crew (D) contended that its parody of Roy Orbison's song, "Oh, Pretty Woman," was a fair use within the meaning of the Copyright Act of 1976, but the appellate court concluded that the commercial nature of the parody rendered it presumptively unfair.

RULE OF LAW
The commercial purpose of a work is only one element of the inquiry into the work's purpose and character for fair use purposes.

FACTS: 2 Live Crew (D) recorded a rap parody of the Roy Orbison hit "Oh, Pretty Woman." Acuff-Rose Music, Inc. (P), the copyright holder of the original song, sued 2 Live Crew (D) for copyright infringement. The district court granted summary judgment for 2 Live Crew (D), having concluded that its song made fair use of Orbison's original. The appeals court reversed and remanded. It concluded that every commercial use is presumptively unfair and that the blatantly commercial purpose of 2 Live Crew's (D) version prevented it from constituting fair use. 2 Live Crew (D) appealed.

ISSUE: Is the commercial purpose of a work the determining element of the inquiry into the work's purpose and character for fair use purposes?

HOLDING AND DECISION: (Souter, J.) No. The commercial purpose of a work is only one element of the inquiry into the work's purpose and character for fair use purposes. The other elements to be considered are the nature of the copyrighted work, the amount and substantiality of the portion used in relation to the copyrighted work as a whole, and the effect of the use upon the potential market for the copyrighted work. In this case, it was error for the court of appeals to conclude that the commercial nature of 2 Live Crew's (D) parody rendered it presumptively unfair. No such evidentiary presumption exists for either the first factor—the character and purpose of the use—or the fourth factor—market harm. The court also erred in holding that 2 Live Crew (D) had copied excessively from the Orbison original, considering the satiric purpose of their version. Reversed and remanded to evaluate the amount taken from the original, its transformative elements, and potential for market harm.

ANALYSIS

Dictionaries define "parody" as a literary or artistic work that imitates the characteristic style of an author or a work for comic effect or ridicule. Copyright law recognizes that a parodist must use some elements of a prior author's composition in order to create a new one that comments on that author's work. Parody needs to mimic an original to make its point, but it may or may not be fair use depending on whether it could be perceived as commenting on, or criticizing, the original.

Quicknotes

COPYRIGHT ACT Copyright Act of 1976 extends copyright protection to "original works of authorship fixed in any tangible medium of expression, now known or later developed, from which they can be perceived, reproduced, or otherwise communicated, either directly or with the aid of a machine or device." 17 U.S.C. § 102.

COPYRIGHT INFRINGEMENT A violation of one of the exclusive rights granted to an artist pursuant to Article I, section 8, clause 8 of the United States Constitution over the reproduction, display, performance, distribution, and adaptation of his work for a period prescribed by statute.

FAIR USE An affirmative defense to a claim of copyright infringement providing an exception from the copyright owner's exclusive rights in a work for the purposes of criticism, comment, news reporting, teaching, scholarship or research; the determination of whether a use is fair is made on a case-by-case basis and requires the court to consider: (1) the purpose and character of the use; (2) the nature of the work; (3) the amount and substantiality of the portion used; and (4) the effect of the use on the potential market for, or value of, the work.

SUMMARY JUDGMENT Judgment rendered by a court in response to a motion by one of the parties, claiming that the lack of a question of material fact in respect to an issue warrants disposition of the issue without consideration by the jury.

Castle Rock Entertainment, Inc. v. Carol Publishing Group, Inc.

Copyright owner (P) v. Alleged infringer (D)

150 F.3d 132 (2d Cir. 1998).

NATURE OF CASE: Appeal from summary judgment in favor of Castle Rock (P) and order enjoining publication of allegedly infringing work.

FACT SUMMARY: The holder of the copyright in a television show (P) sued the publisher of a trivia book (D) based on that television show for copyright and trademark infringement.

RULE OF LAW
One factor of an analysis of fair use is whether the new work has a transformative purpose, that is, whether it adds something new, with a further purpose, to the original work.

FACTS: Castle Rock Entertainment (Castle Rock) (P) is the producer and copyright owner of each episode of the "Seinfeld" television series. Carol Publishing Group, Inc. (Carol Publishing) (D) published a book containing trivia questions and answers about the series. The source for every question and correct answer in the trivia book is the "Seinfeld" series, and the trivia book quotes extensively from series episodes. Castle Rock (P) filed an action alleging federal copyright and trademark infringement and state law unfair competition. The district court granted summary judgment to plaintiffs and enjoined the further publication of the trivia book. Carol Publishing (D) appealed.

ISSUE: Is a quiz book based on a television series considered a fair use of the series when it cannot be said to have a transformative purpose or to add something new to the original work?

HOLDING AND DECISION: (Walker, Jr., J.) No. Although the analysis of whether a work is considered a fair use is a multi-factored analysis, of significant importance is whether the new work adds something new to the original work. Here, the quiz book cannot be said to add something new. It contains no analysis and so minimally alters the original expression from the series that it shows an utter lack of a transformative purpose. This lack of a transformative purpose overshadows the other factors of the analysis. Although the second factor is important here, the fact that the series is fictional, the first factor has more bearing in this case. An analysis of the third factor, the portion of the original work used, shows that the quiz book takes a significant portion directly from the series. An analysis of the fourth factor, effect on the market or value of the original, shows that the quiz book substitutes for the derivative market that the copyright holder could have developed. Therefore, the quiz book cannot be said to be a fair use of the television series. Affirmed.

ANALYSIS

It is interesting to note that when considering the fourth factor, the effect on the market or value of the original, the court here found that the quiz book could substitute for a derivative market that the copyright holder could have developed, even though the copyright holder had not shown any interest in exploiting that market.

Quicknotes

COPYRIGHT INFRINGEMENT A violation of one of the exclusive rights granted to an artist pursuant to Article I, section 8, clause 8 of the United States Constitution over the reproduction, display, performance, distribution, and adaptation of his work for a period prescribed by statute.

ENJOIN The ordering of a party to cease the conduct of a specific activity.

FAIR USE An affirmative defense to a claim of copyright infringement providing an exception from the copyright owner's exclusive rights in a work for the purposes of criticism, comment, news reporting, teaching, scholarship or research; the determination of whether a use is fair is made on a case-by-case basis and requires the court to consider: (1) the purpose and character of the use; (2) the nature of the work; (3) the amount and substantiality of the portion used; and (4) the effect of the use on the potential market for, or value of, the work.

SUMMARY JUDGMENT Judgment rendered by a court in response to a motion by one of the parties, claiming that the lack of a question of material fact in respect to an issue warrants disposition of the issue without consideration by the jury.

Núñez v. Caribbean International News Corp. (El Vocero de Puerto Rico)

Photographer (P) v. News organization (D)

235 F.3d 18 (1st Cir. 2000).

NATURE OF CASE: Appeal from a copyright infringement claim involving modeling photographs.

FACT SUMMARY: The district court dismissed the copyright infringement claim with prejudice, finding fair use.

RULE OF LAW
The reproduction of photographs for a good-faith newsworthy purpose constitutes fair use.

FACTS: Núñez (P), a professional photographer, took several photographs of Joyce Giraud, Miss Universe Puerto Rico 1997, for use in Giraud's modeling portfolio. Núñez (P) then distributed the photos, including one in which the beauty queen was nearly naked, to various members of the Puerto Rico modeling community. Controversy arose over the appropriateness of these photographs, particularly the one in which Giraud appeared nearly nude. A local television station displayed Núñez's (P) photographs on screen and asked random citizens whether they believed the photos were "pornographic," and Giraud's fitness to retain the Miss Universe Puerto Rico crown was questioned. *El Vocero de Puerto Rico* (D) later obtained several of the photographs and published three of them over the course of a week, along with several articles about the controversy. Núñez (P) filed this action, claiming that the reprint of his photographs in *El Vocero* (D) violated the Copyright Act of 1976. The district court dismissed Núñez's (P) complaint with prejudice, and Núñez (P) appealed.

ISSUE: Does *El Vocero*'s (D) unauthorized use of Núñez's (P) photographs in reporting a story constitute fair use?

HOLDING AND DECISION: (Torruella, J.) Yes. Caribbean International News Corp. ("Caribbean") (D) sought both to "inform" and to "gain commercially" with its publication of Núñez's (P) photographs. Commercial use weighs heavily against a finding of fair use if it constitutes more than mere reproduction for profitable use, and *El Vocero* (D), by using Núñez's (P) photograph as a marketing tool, went beyond mere reproduction for profitable use. Nevertheless, *El Vocero*'s (D) use was fair use, because it was done in good faith and was meant to be informative. It would have been difficult to report the story without reprinting the photograph. In addition, publication in *El Vocero* (D) did not destroy the market for the sale of these photos to other newspapers reporting the controversy because Núñez (P) never attempted to make such sales, supposing he could have under his contract with Giraud. Further, publication of Núñez's (P) photographs in *El Vocero* (D) only increased demand for the photographs in other contexts. Affirmed.

ANALYSIS

The reasoning in *Núñez* (P) suggests some limitations on the newsworthiness allowance under fair use. The result may have differed, for example, if the photos had been obtained illegally or had been reproduced in bad faith.

Quicknotes

COPYRIGHT ACT Copyright Act of 1976 extends copyright protection to "original works of authorship fixed in any tangible medium of expression, now known or later developed, from which they can be perceived, reproduced, or otherwise communicated, either directly or with the aid of a machine or device." 17 U.S.C. § 102.

COPYRIGHT INFRINGEMENT A violation of one of the exclusive rights granted to an artist pursuant to Article I, section 8, clause 8 of the United States Constitution over the reproduction, display, performance, distribution, and adaptation of his work for a period prescribed by statute.

FAIR USE An affirmative defense to a claim of copyright infringement providing an exception from the copyright owner's exclusive rights in a work for the purposes of criticism, comment, news reporting, teaching, scholarship or research; the determination of whether a use is fair is made on a case-by-case basis and requires the court to consider: (1) the purpose and character of the use; (2) the nature of the work; (3) the amount and substantiality of the portion used; and (4) the effect of the use on the potential market for, or value of, the work.

Bill Graham Archives v. Dorling Kindersley Ltd.

Copyright owner (P) v. Book publisher (D)

448 F.3d 605 (2d Cir. 2006).

NATURE OF CASE: Appeal from dismissal on summary judgment of copyright infringement action.

FACT SUMMARY: Bill Graham Archives, LLC (P), which owned the copyright in images on Grateful Dead event posters and tickets, contended that Dorling Kindersley Ltd. (D) infringed its copyright by publishing seven of the images in reduced size in a book on the history of the Grateful Dead.

RULE OF LAW
A book publisher's appropriation of copyrighted poster and ticket images in a biographical book in reduced-size format is a protected "fair use" under the copyright law where the balance of the statutory fair use factors favors the publisher.

FACTS: Bill Graham Archives, LLC (BGA) (P) owned the copyright in seven Grateful Dead (a rock band) event posters and ticket images that Dorling Kindersley Ltd. (DK) (D), in collaboration with Grateful Dead Productions, sought to reprint in reduced-size in a book titled Grateful Dead: The Illustrated Trip (Illustrated Trip), which was intended as a cultural history of the band. Illustrated Trip contains over 2000 images representing dates in the Grateful Dead's history, in chronological order with a timeline, with explanatory text. A typical page of the book features a collage of images, text, and graphic art designed to simultaneously capture the eye and inform the reader. DK (D) initially sought permission from BGA (P) to reprint the images, but, after it could not secure such permission, published the book with the images without a license or grant of permission. The images are displayed in significantly reduced form and are accompanied by captions describing the concerts they represent. When DK (D) refused to meet BGA's (P) post-publication license fee demands, BGA (P) filed suit for copyright infringement. The district court dismissed the action on summary judgment, and the court of appeals granted review.

ISSUE: Is a book publisher's appropriation of copyrighted poster and ticket images in a biographical book in reduced-size format a protected "fair use" under the copyright law where the balance of the statutory fair use factors favors the publisher?

HOLDING AND DECISION: (Restani, J.) Yes. A book publisher's appropriation of copyrighted poster and ticket images in a biographical book in reduced-size format is a protected "fair use" under the copyright law where the balance of the statutory fair use factors favors the publisher. Under 17 U.S.C. § 107(1), the first factor is "the purpose and character of the use, including whether such use is of a commercial nature or is for nonprofit educational purposes." Most important is whether the nature of the work is "transformative," i.e., "whether the new work merely supersede[s] the objects of the original creation, or instead adds something new, with a further purpose or different character, altering the first with new expression, meaning, or message." BGA (P) argues that as a matter of law merely placing poster images along a timeline is not a transformative use, contrary to the district court's finding. BGA's (P) argument must be rejected because here, Illustrated Trip is a biographical work documenting and commemorating the band's 30-year history, and courts have frequently afforded fair use protection to the use of copyrighted material in biographies, recognizing such works as forms of historic scholarship, criticism, and comment that require incorporation of original source material for optimum treatment of their subject. Moreover, DK's (D) purpose in using the images at issue is plainly different from the original purpose for which they were created. Originally, the images fulfilled the dual purposes of artistic expression and promotion, as the posters were distributed to generate public interest in the Grateful Dead and to convey information to a large number people about the band's forthcoming concerts. In contrast, DK (D) used each of BGA's (P) images as historical artifacts to document and represent the actual occurrence of Grateful Dead concerts featured on Illustrated Trip's timeline. The images, in some instances, help the reader's understanding of the biographical text by marking important concerts. In sum, DK's (D) use of the disputed images is transformative both when accompanied by referencing commentary and when standing alone. This conclusion is strengthened by the manner in which they significantly reduced the size of the reproductions, which permits readers to recognize the historical significance of the posters, but is inadequate to offer more than a glimpse of their expressive value. The expressive value of the original images was further minimized by combining them with a timeline, textual material, and original graphical artwork to create a collage that ensures that the images at issue are employed only to enrich the presentation of the cultural history of the Grateful Dead, not to exploit copyrighted artwork for commercial gain. Yet another factor that supports the conclusion that the use was transformative is that the images constitute an inconsequential (less than one-fifth of one percent) portion of the book. Also, no BGA (P) image takes up more than one-eighth of a page in a book or is given more prominence than any other image on the page. Finally, the commercial nature of the use also supports a finding that the use was transformative, since the book does

Continued on next page.

not exploit the use of BGA's (P) images as such for commercial gain, i.e., they are not used in commercial advertising or in any other way to promote the sale of the book, and their use is merely incidental to the commercial biographical value of the book. The first factor weighs in favor of DK (D). The second fair use factor, under 17 U.S.C. § 107(2), is "the nature of the copyrighted work." In assessing this factor, the court considers "the protection of the reasonable expectations of one who engages in the kinds of creation/authorship that the copyright seeks to encourage." Here, the images are creative artworks, which are traditionally the core of intended copyright protection. The district court found this factor weighed in favor of BGA (P), but limited the weight it gave to it because the posters were published extensively. The district court was correct that creative works of art are the kind of works that weigh in favor of the copyright holder. However, the second fair use factor may be of limited usefulness where the creative work of art is being used for a transformative purpose, as here, where the images were used for their historical, rather than creative, qualities. The third fair use factor, under 17 U.S.C. § 107(3), is "the amount and substantiality of the portion used in relation to the copyrighted work as a whole." Although each image was reproduced in its entirety, courts have held that such copying does not necessarily weigh against fair use because copying the entirety of a work is sometimes necessary to make a fair use of the image. Because this reasoning is sound, the third-factor inquiry must take into account that "the extent of permissible copying varies with the purpose and character of the use." Applying this reasoning here, even though the copyrighted images are copied in their entirety, the visual impact of their artistic expression is significantly limited because of their reduced size. Therefore, such use by DK (D) was tailored to further its transformative purpose by ensuring the reader's recognition of the images as historical artifacts of Grateful Dead concert events. Accordingly, the third fair use factor does not weigh against fair use. Finally, the fourth fair use factor, under 17 U.S.C. § 107(4), is "the effect of the use upon the potential market for or value of the copyrighted work." Here, it is undisputed that DK's (D) use of the images did not impact BGA's (P) primary market for the sale of the poster images. Instead, the inquiry is whether DK's (D) use impacted BGA's (P) potential to develop a derivative market—in this case, the market for licensing BGA's (P) images for use in books. Although BGA (P) lost royalty revenues from DK (D), and it is indisputable that, as a general matter, a copyright holder is entitled to demand a royalty for licensing others to use its copyrighted work, and that the impact on potential licensing revenues is a proper subject for consideration in assessing the fourth factor, if the secondary user's failure to pay royalties was automatically held to constitute market harm, the fourth fair use factor would always favor the copyright holder. By definition, every fair use involves some loss of royalty revenue because the secondary user has not paid royalties. Therefore, it cannot be said that BGA (P) suffered market harm merely because DK (D) did not obtain and pay for a license to use the images.

Instead, the inquiry focuses on the impact on potential licensing revenues for "traditional, reasonable, or likely to be developed markets." Even though DK (D) paid other copyright owners to reproduce their copyrighted works, and even though BGA (P) licensed its images to others and was willing to license images to DK (D) [but for a fee that was unacceptable to DK (D)], neither of these arguments shows impairment to a traditional, as opposed to a transformative market. The market at issue is the transformative one of using the images for their historical significance, and because copyright owners may not preempt exploitation of transformative, fair use, markets, BGA (P) did not suffer market harm due to the loss of license fees. The balance of the fair use factors weighs in DK's (D) favor, so its use was a fair use and did not infringe BGA's (P) copyrights. Affirmed.

ANALYSIS

The fair use doctrine was first codified in the Copyright Act of 1976, which describes the four non-exclusive factors that must be considered in determining fair use. The ultimate test of fair use, however, has been said to be whether the copyright law's goal of "promoting the Progress of Science and useful Arts," would be better served by allowing the use than by preventing it. Thus, by concluding that the fair use factors favored DK's (D) use is essentially a conclusion that progress of the arts was better served by permitting such use.

Quicknotes

COPYRIGHT Refers to the exclusive rights granted to an artist pursuant to Article I, section 8, clause 8 of the United States Constitution over the reproduction, display, performance, distribution, and adaptation of his work for a period prescribed by statute.

COPYRIGHT ACT Copyright Act of 1976 extends copyright protection to "original works of authorship fixed in any tangible medium of expression, now known or later developed, from which they can be perceived, reproduced, or otherwise communicated, either directly or with the aid of a machine or device." 17 U.S.C. § 102.

COPYRIGHT INFRINGEMENT A violation of one of the exclusive rights granted to an artist pursuant to Article I, section 8, clause 8 of the United States Constitution over the reproduction, display, performance, distribution, and adaptation of his work for a period prescribed by statute.

FAIR USE An affirmative defense to a claim of copyright infringement providing an exception from the copyright owner's exclusive rights in a work for the purposes of criticism, comment, news reporting, teaching, scholarship or research; the determination of whether a use is fair is made on a case-by-case basis and requires the court to consider: (1) the purpose and character of the use;

Continued on next page.

(2) the nature of the work; (3) the amount and substantiality of the portion used; and (4) the effect of the use on the potential market for, or value of, the work.

SUMMARY JUDGMENT Judgment rendered by a court in response to a motion by one of the parties, claiming that the lack of a question of material fact in respect to an issue warrants disposition of the issue without consideration by the jury.

Sega Enterprises Ltd. v. Accolade, Inc.

Video game maker (P) v. Game maker (D)

977 F.2d 1510 (9th Cir. 1992).

NATURE OF CASE: Appeal from preliminary injunction issued in a copyright infringement case.

FACT SUMMARY: Accolade, Inc. (D) copied and then disassembled Sega Enterprises Ltd.'s (Sega's) (P) video game programs in order to discover the requirements for compatibility with Sega's (P) console.

RULE OF LAW
Disassembly of a copyrighted object code is a fair use of the material if it is the only means of access to uncopyrighted elements of the code and there is a legitimate reason for seeking such access.

FACTS: Sega Enterprises Ltd.(Sega) (P) and Accolade, Inc. (D) manufactured and marketed video game cartridges. In order to render its own games compatible with Sega's (P) console, Accolade (D) "reverse engineered" Sega's (P) video game programs to discover the requirements for compatibility with the console. To do this, it first copied Sega's (P) copyrighted code in its entirety, then disassembled it to see how it worked. Accolade (D) then created its own games for use with Sega's (P) console, but did not copy Sega's (P) programs or use any of its codes. Sega (P) sued for copyright infringement. The district court granted Sega's (P) motion for a preliminary injunction preventing Accolade (D) from further disassembly of Sega's (P) object codes. Accolade (D) appealed.

ISSUE: Is disassembly of a copyrighted object code a fair use of the material if it is the only means of access to uncopyrighted elements of the code and there is a legitimate reason for seeking such access?

HOLDING AND DECISION: (Reinhardt, J.) Yes. Disassembly of a copyrighted object code is a fair use of the material if it is the only means of access to uncopyrighted elements of the code and there is a legitimate reason for seeking such access. Section 107 of the Copyright Act of 1976 lists four factors to be considered in determining whether a particular use is a fair one: (1) the purpose and character of the use; (2) the nature of the copyrighted work; (3) the amount and substantiality of the portion used in relation to the copyrighted work as a whole; and (4) the effect of the use upon the market for the copyrighted work. In this case, Accolade (D) sought only to become a legitimate competitor in the field of Sega (P) compatible video games. Therefore, it had a legitimate, nonexploitative purpose for copying Sega's (P) code. Secondly, Sega's (P) video game programs must be afforded a lower degree of protection than more traditional literary works because they contain unprotected aspects that cannot be examined without copying. Thirdly, the fact that Accolade (D) disassembled entire programs written by Sega (P) should receive little weight. Finally, Accolade's (D) copying may have affected the market, but not significantly, since consumers tend to buy many video games rather than just one. Accordingly, Accolade (D) has the better case on the fair use issue. Reversed.

ANALYSIS

An issue similar to reverse engineering was raised in *Triad Systems Corp. v. Southeastern Express Co.*, 64 F.3d 1330 (9th Cir. 1995). In that case, Southeastern copied Triad's software into Triad's computer as part of an attempt to service the computer. The Ninth Circuit concluded that such copying was not fair use because it was neither creative nor transformative and did not provide the marketplace with new creative works. Instead, the copies made by Southeastern undoubtedly diminished the value of Triad's copyright.

Quicknotes

COPYRIGHT ACT Copyright Act of 1976 extends copyright protection to "original works of authorship fixed in any tangible medium of expression, now known or later developed, from which they can be perceived, reproduced, or otherwise communicated, either directly or with the aid of a machine or device." 17 U.S.C. § 102.

COPYRIGHT INFRINGEMENT A violation of one of the exclusive rights granted to an artist pursuant to Article I, section 8, clause 8 of the United States Constitution over the reproduction, display, performance, distribution, and adaptation of his work for a period prescribed by statute.

FAIR USE An affirmative defense to a claim of copyright infringement providing an exception from the copyright owner's exclusive rights in a work for the purposes of criticism, comment, news reporting, teaching, scholarship or research; the determination of whether a use is fair is made on a case-by-case basis and requires the court to consider: (1) the purpose and character of the use; (2) the nature of the work; (3) the amount and substantiality of the portion used; and (4) the effect of the use on the potential market for, or value of, the work.

PRELIMINARY INJUNCTION An order issued by the court at the commencement of an action, requiring a party to refrain from conducting a specified activity that is the subject of the controversy, until the matter is determined.

Sony Computer Entertainment, Inc. v. Connectix Corp.

Computer entertainment firm (P) v. Computer software firm (D)

203 F.3d 596 (9th Cir.), cert denied, 531 U.S. 871 (2000).

NATURE OF CASE: Appeal from a copyright infringement claim involving reverse engineering of a basic input-output system (BIOS).

FACT SUMMARY: The district court granted an injunction in favor of Sony Computer Entertainment, Inc. (Sony) (P), finding that Connectix Corp.'s (D) reverse-engineering process infringed upon Sony's (P) copyrights.

RULE OF LAW
Intermediate infringement of copyrighted materials where the final product does not contain infringing material is likely to be viewed as fair use.

FACTS: Sony Computer Entertainment, Inc. (Sony) (P) markets and produces the Sony PlayStation console, a small computer with hand controls that connects to a television and plays games that are inserted into the PlayStation on compact discs (CDs). Sony (P) owns the copyright on the basic input-output system, or BIOS, the software that operates its PlayStation. In July, 1998, Connectix Corp. (D) began developing a Virtual Game Station for Macintosh that "emulates" the functioning of the PlayStation console. Connectix (D) engineers purchased a PlayStation and extracted the Sony (P) BIOS from a chip inside the console. They then copied the Sony (P) BIOS into the RAM of their computers and observed the functioning of the Sony (P) BIOS in conjunction with the Virtual Game Station hardware-emulation software as that software was being developed by Connectix (D). After developing the hardware-emulation software, Connectix (D) engineers used the Sony (P) BIOS to "debug" it. In doing so, they repeatedly copied and disassembled discrete portions of the Sony (P) BIOS. During development of the Virtual Game Station, Connectix (D) contacted Sony (P) for "technical assistance." Sony (P) declined. Connectix (D) completed the Virtual Game Station for Macintosh in late December 1998 or early January 1999, and marketed the completed product as a "PlayStation emulator." Sony (P) sued Connectix (D), claiming that when Connectix (D) reverse engineered Sony's (P) code during the course of creating the Virtual Game Station, it infringed upon Sony's (P) copyrights. The district court granted Sony (P) an injunction, and Connectix (D) appealed.

ISSUE: Where the product created from the intermediate commercial use of copyrighted materials is transformative in nature, does it constitute fair use?

HOLDING AND DECISION: (Canby, J.) Yes. Sony's (P) BIOS is far removed from the core of intended copyright protection because it contains unprotected aspects that cannot be examined without copying. This case involves an intermediate infringement, where the final product itself does not contain infringing material. In such cases, the fact that Connectix (D) copied the entire BIOS multiple times carries little weight. What is important is that the character of Connectix's (D) product is that of a wholly new product, despite its similarities to the uses and functions of the Sony PlayStation. As such, it is less likely to cause a substantially adverse effect on the potential market for the Sony PlayStation. Reversed.

ANALYSIS

The *Sony* decision suggests that software protection under copyright laws turns on whether the use is intermediate and the end result is transformative.

Quicknotes

COPYRIGHT Refers to the exclusive rights granted to an artist pursuant to Article I, section 8, clause 8 of the United States Constitution over the reproduction, display, performance, distribution, and adaptation of his work for a period prescribed by statute.

COPYRIGHT INFRINGEMENT A violation of one of the exclusive rights granted to an artist pursuant to Article I, section 8, clause 8 of the United States Constitution over the reproduction, display, performance, distribution, and adaptation of his work for a period prescribed by statute.

INJUNCTION A court order requiring a person to do or prohibiting that person from doing a specific act.

Perfect 10, Inc. v. Amazon, Inc.

Web porn publisher (P) v. Internet company (D)

508 F.3d 1146 (9th Cir. 2007).

NATURE OF CASE: Appeal from preliminary injunction in copyright infringement action.

FACT SUMMARY: Google, Inc. (D) claimed that even if its transmission of thumbnail images of Perfect 10, Inc.'s (P) copyrighted nude images, or its in-line linking to or framing of full-size images that infringed Perfect 10's (P) copyright in the images constituted infringement of Perfect 10's (P) display or distribution rights, its use nevertheless constituted a fair use.

RULE OF LAW
A search engine's owner's appropriation of a copyrighted image for use as an indexed thumbnail picture is a protected "fair use" under the copyright law where the balance of the statutory fair use factors favors the search engine owner.

FACTS: Perfect 10, Inc. (P) markets and sells copyrighted images of nude models, and operates a subscription website on the Internet whereby subscribers pay a monthly fee to view Perfect 10 (P) images in a "members' area" of the site. Subscribers must use a password to log into the members' area. Perfect 10 (P) has also licensed reduced-size copyrighted images for download and use on cell phones. Google, Inc. (D) operates a search engine, a software program that automatically accesses thousands of websites (collections of web pages) on the Internet and indexes them within a database stored on Google's (D) computers. When a Google (D) user accesses the Google (D) website and types in a search query, Google's (D) software searches its database for websites responsive to that search query. Google (D) then sends relevant information from its index of websites to the user's computer. Google's (D) search engines can provide results in the form of text, images, or videos. The Google (D) search engine that provides responses in the form of images is called "Google Image Search." Google Image Search identifies text in its database responsive to the query and then communicates to users the images associated with the relevant text. Google's (D) software cannot recognize and index the images themselves. Google Image Search provides search results as a web page of small images called "thumbnails," which are stored in Google's (D) servers. The thumbnail images are reduced, lower-resolution versions of full-sized images stored on third-party computers. When a user clicks on a thumbnail image, Google (D)'s software directs the user's browser to create on the user's computer screen a small rectangular box that contains the Google (D) thumbnail and a larger box that contains the full-size image, which the user's computer has been instructed to access from the third-party site that houses that image. Google (D) does not store the images that fill this larger box and does not communicate the images to the user. The two boxes together appear to be coming from the same source, since they are in the same frame, but actually come from two sources—Google (D) and the third-party website. The process by which the web page directs a user's browser to incorporate content from different computers into a single window is referred to as "in-line linking." The term "framing" refers to the process by which information from one computer appears to frame and annotate the in-line linked content from another computer. Google (D) also stores web page content in its cache, which ultimately means that Google's (D) cache copy can provide a user's browser with valid directions to an infringing image even though the updated web page no longer includes that infringing image. In addition to its search engine operations, Google (D) generates revenue through a business program called "AdSense." Under this program, a website owner can register with Google (D) to become an AdSense "partner." The owner then places HTML instructions on its web pages that signal Google's (D) server to place advertising on the web pages that is relevant to the web pages' content. Google's (D) computer program selects the advertising automatically by means of an algorithm, and the AdSense participants share the revenues that flow from such advertising with Google (D). Some website publishers pirated Perfect 10's (P) images and Google's (D) search engine automatically indexed the web pages containing the pirated images and provided thumbnail versions of the images in response to user inquiries. Perfect 10 (P) repeatedly sent Google (D) notices that its thumbnail images and in-line linking to the full-size images infringed Perfect 10's (P) copyright and when Google (D) continued its search engine practices, Perfect 10 (P) filed a copyright infringement action against Google (D), and sought a preliminary injunction to prevent Google (D) from infringing Perfect 10's (P) copyright in its images and linking to websites that provide full-size infringing versions of Perfect 10's (P) photographs. Google (D) raised the affirmative defense that its use was a fair use, but the district court rejected this defense, finding that the first, second and fourth fair use factors weighed slightly in Perfect 10's (P) favor, and that the third factor was neutral. The district court granted the preliminary injunction, finding harm to the derivative market for Perfect 10's (P) reduced-size images. The court of appeals granted review.

ISSUE: Is a search engine's owner's appropriation of a copyrighted image for use as an indexed thumbnail picture a protected "fair use" under the copyright law where the balance of the statutory fair use factors favors the search engine owner?

Continued on next page.

HOLDING AND DECISION: (Ikuta, J.) Yes. A search engine's owner's appropriation of a copyrighted image for use as an indexed thumbnail picture is a protected "fair use" under the copyright law where the balance of the statutory fair use factors favors the search engine owner. The first fair use factor [17 U.S.C. § 107(1)] requires a court to consider "the purpose and character of the use." A "transformative work" is one that alters the original work "with new expression, meaning, or message." Here, Google's (D) use of thumbnails is highly transformative. Google's (D) search engine provides social benefit by incorporating an original work into a new work that serves as an electronic reference tool, thereby providing an entirely new use for the original work. Even though the entire original work is taken, it serves an entirely different function than the original, and therefore the use is transformative. The district court concluded that because Google's (D) use of the thumbnails could supersede Perfect 10's (P) cell phone download use and because the use was commercial because Google's (D) thumbnails "lead users to sites that directly benefit Google's bottom line" through the AdSense program, this fair use factor weighed "slightly" in favor of Perfect 10 (P). The district court's conclusion as to this factor is erroneous because the superseding use was nonexistent insofar as the district court did not find that any downloads for mobile phone use had taken place, and because there was no evidence that AdSense websites containing infringing images significantly contributed to Google's (D) bottom line. Accordingly, the significantly transformative nature of Google's (D) search engine, particularly in light of its public benefit, heavily outweighs Google's (D) superseding and commercial uses of the thumbnails in this case. The second fair use factor is "the nature of the copyrighted work" [17 U.S.C. § 107(2)]. Perfect 10's (P) images are "creative in nature" and thus "closer to the core of intended copyright protection than are more fact-based works." However, because the photos appeared on the Internet before Google (D) used thumbnail versions in its search engine results, this factor weighs only slightly in favor of Perfect 10 (P). The third fair use factor asks whether the amount and substantiality of the portion used in relation to the copyrighted work as a whole are reasonable in relation to the purpose of the copying [17 U.S.C. § 107(3)]. Here, this factor is neutral and does not weigh in favor of either party because Google's (D) use of the entire photographic image was reasonable in light of the purpose of a search engine and since using less than the entire image would be less helpful to a computer user. The fourth fair use factor is "the effect of the use upon the potential market for or value of the copyrighted work." The district court here correctly held that Google's (D) use of thumbnails did not hurt Perfect 10's (P) market for full-size images. Perfect 10 (P) argues that the district court erred because the likelihood of market harm may be presumed if the intended use of an image is for commercial gain. However, this presumption does not arise when a work is transformative because "market substitution is at least less certain, and market harm may not be so readily inferred." As already discussed, Google's (D) thumbnail images were highly transformative, and there was no evidence of market harm to Perfect 10's (P) full-size images. Accordingly, the district court did not err as to this ruling. The district court did err, however, in determining that Google's (D) thumbnails would harm the market for reduced-size images, since Perfect 10 (P) adduced no evidence that actual sales of such images had been made for cell phone use. Any potential harm to Perfect 10's (P) market remains hypothetical, and, therefore, this factor favors neither party. Weighing the fair use factors leads to the conclusion that Google's (D) use was a fair use, especially in light of the public utility served by its search engine and the transformative nature of its use. Perfect 10 (P) is unlikely to be able to overcome Google's (D) fair use defense. Accordingly, the preliminary injunction regarding Google's (D) use of thumbnail images is vacated. Reversed as to this issue.

ANALYSIS

The courts have articulated the principle that the fair use factors must be analyzed flexibly in light of new circumstances, especially during periods of rapid technological change. Accordingly, the Supreme Court has directed that "the more transformative the new work, the less will be the significance of other factors, like commercialism, that may weigh against a finding of fair use." *Campbell v. Acuff-Rose Music, Inc.*, 510 U.S. 569 at 579 (1994).

Quicknotes

COPYRIGHT Refers to the exclusive rights granted to an artist pursuant to Article I, section 8, clause 8 of the United States Constitution over the reproduction, display, performance, distribution, and adaptation of his work for a period prescribed by statute.

COPYRIGHT INFRINGEMENT A violation of one of the exclusive rights granted to an artist pursuant to Article I, section 8, clause 8 of the United States Constitution over the reproduction, display, performance, distribution, and adaptation of his work for a period prescribed by statute.

FAIR USE An affirmative defense to a claim of copyright infringement providing an exception from the copyright owner's exclusive rights in a work for the purposes of criticism, comment, news reporting, teaching, scholarship or research; the determination of whether a use is fair is made on a case-by-case basis and requires the court to consider: (1) the purpose and character of the use; (2) the nature of the work; (3) the amount and substantiality of the portion used; and (4) the effect of the use on the potential market for, or value of, the work.

PRELIMINARY INJUNCTION A judicial mandate issued to require or restrain a party from certain conduct; used to preserve a trial's subject matter or to prevent threatened injury.

Sony Corporation of America v. Universal City Studios, Inc.

VCR manufacturer (D) v. Movie studio (P)

464 U.S. 417 (1984).

NATURE OF CASE: Review of order reversing dismissal of copyright infringement action.

FACT SUMMARY: Universal City Studios (P) contended that Sony Corporation of America (D) contributed to copyright infringement by marketing videocassette recorders.

RULE OF LAW
The marketing of videocassette recorders does not infringe on the copyrights of recorded works.

FACTS: In the 1970s, Sony Corporation of America (Sony) (D) began marketing the Betamax videocassette recorder, which allowed home recording of televised programs. Several holders of copyrights on televised programs brought an action seeking injunctive relief and damages for copyright infringement. The district court found that most copyright holders of televised programs did not object to home recording and that home recording did not impair the value of the copyrights of those who did. The district court held Sony (D) not to be in violation of copyright laws. The Ninth Circuit reversed. The Supreme Court granted certiorari.

ISSUE: Does the marketing of videocassette recorders infringe on the copyrights of recorded works?

HOLDING AND DECISION: (Stevens, J.) No. The marketing of videocassette recorders does not infringe on the copyrights of recorded works. Such marketing could not directly infringe on copyrights. Rather, the contention is that, by marketing recording devices, Sony (D) contributes to infringement. However, if the act complained of has a substantial noninfringing dimension, the fact that it facilitates some infringement will not establish contributory infringement. Here, it was established at trial that most uses of the Betamax are for "time-shifting" rather than permanent storage, and that most copyright holders of televised works had no objection to such use. Further, even as to those holders who did object, no showing of any actual damages was made. In light of these facts, it is impossible not to conclude that the marketing of videocassette recorders offered substantial noninfringing uses thereof. Therefore, no infringement has occurred. Reversed.

DISSENT: (Blackmun, J.) The majority erred in holding that the making of a videotape recording for home viewing is a productive use of a copyrighted work, susceptible to application of the fair use doctrine under the Copyright Act. In doing so, the majority stretched the fair use doctrine beyond its intended domain, depriving authors of control over their works and their incentive to create.

ANALYSIS

Unauthorized time-shifting may be considered an example of the "fair use" doctrine, which is codified at 17 U.S.C. § 107. This equitable doctrine allows a court to sanction an unauthorized use of a copyrighted work. Generally speaking, the use must be noncommercial to be within the ambit of § 107. Such was the case here.

Quicknotes

CERTIORARI A discretionary writ issued by a superior court to an inferior court in order to review the lower court's decisions; the Supreme Court's writ ordering such review.

COPYRIGHT Refers to the exclusive rights granted to an artist pursuant to Article I, section 8, clause 8 of the United States Constitution over the reproduction, display, performance, distribution, and adaptation of his work for a period prescribed by statute.

COPYRIGHT INFRINGEMENT A violation of one of the exclusive rights granted to an artist pursuant to Article I, section 8, clause 8 of the United States Constitution over the reproduction, display, performance, distribution, and adaptation of his work for a period prescribed by statute.

FAIR USE An affirmative defense to a claim of copyright infringement providing an exception from the copyright owner's exclusive rights in a work for the purposes of criticism, comment, news reporting, teaching, scholarship or research; the determination of whether a use is fair is made on a case-by-case basis and requires the court to consider: (1) the purpose and character of the use; (2) the nature of the work; (3) the amount and substantiality of the portion used; and (4) the effect of the use on the potential market for, or value of, the work.

A&M Records, Inc. v. Napster, Inc.

Record company (P) v. Internet music site (D)

239 F.3d 1004 (9th Cir. 2001).

NATURE OF CASE: Appeal from preliminary injunction.

FACT SUMMARY: The district court granted a preliminary injunction, finding that Napster, Inc. (D) users are not fair users.

RULE OF LAW
The retransmission by a service of original works and the free distribution of those works to users of the service does not constitute fair use.

FACTS: Napster, Inc. (D), a small Internet start-up, makes its MusicShare software freely available for Internet users to download. Users who obtain Napster's (D) software can then share MP3 music files with others logged into the Napster system. Napster (D) allows direct exchange without payment of the MP3 files stored by its users. When Napster (D) users log on, they are automatically connected to a Napster-operated server, which reads the list of names of MP3 files that the user has elected to make available. Through a directory and index of all such lists, users who are logged on can locate and download any stored piece of music, simply by entering the name of the song and the name of the recording artist on the MusicShare search page and clicking the "Find It" button. Napster (D) had a policy making compliance with all copyright laws one of the "terms of use" of its service, but parties differ as to when and how effectively this policy was instituted. A&M Records, Inc. (P) filed suit alleging contributory and vicarious federal copyright infringement and related state law violations by Napster (D). The district court found that Napster (D) users are not fair users, and Napster (D) appealed.

ISSUE: Does the retransmission of copyrighted works over an Internet server and the free distribution of such works to users constitute fair use?

HOLDING AND DECISION: (Beezer, J.) No. Napster (D) merely retransmits original works in a different medium and thus has not transformed a copyrighted work. Even though the copies are not offered for sale, Napster's (D) repeated and exploitative copying of copyrighted works constitutes commercial use because the infringing copies were made to save the expense of purchasing authorized copies and were traded for other copyrighted works. In addition, the file transfer of protected works on Napster's (D) site constituted wholesale copying, further militating against a finding of fair use. Finally, Napster's (D) site harms the recording companies' market by reducing audio CD sales among college students and by raising barriers to the ability of the recording studios to enter successfully into the market for the digital downloading of music.

ANALYSIS

The court concluded in *Napster* that the preliminary injunction was too broad in that it placed the entire burden on Napster (D) to police the system for infringement. In line with the standards for contributory infringement and vicarious liability, the court thus remanded with instructions to place on plaintiffs the burden to notify Napster (D) of copyrighted works or files containing such works available on the Napster (D) system.

Quicknotes

CONTRIBUTORY INFRINGEMENT The intentional assisting of another in the unlawful appropriation of a patented work.

COPYRIGHT Refers to the exclusive rights granted to an artist pursuant to Article I, section 8, clause 8 of the United States Constitution over the reproduction, display, performance, distribution, and adaptation of his work for a period prescribed by statute.

COPYRIGHT INFRINGEMENT A violation of one of the exclusive rights granted to an artist pursuant to Article I, section 8, clause 8 of the United States Constitution over the reproduction, display, performance, distribution, and adaptation of his work for a period prescribed by statute.

FAIR USE An affirmative defense to a claim of copyright infringement providing an exception from the copyright owner's exclusive rights in a work for the purposes of criticism, comment, news reporting, teaching, scholarship or research; the determination of whether a use is fair is made on a case-by-case basis and requires the court to consider: (1) the purpose and character of the use; (2) the nature of the work; (3) the amount and substantiality of the portion used; and (4) the effect of the use on the potential market for, or value of, the work.

PRELIMINARY INJUNCTION An order issued by the court at the commencement of an action, requiring a party to refrain from conducting a specified activity that is the subject of the controversy, until the matter is determined.

American Geophysical Union v. Texaco, Inc.

Publisher (P) v. Alleged infringer (D)

60 F.3d 913 (2d Cir. 1995).

NATURE OF CASE: Interlocutory appeal in a class action suit for copyright infringement.

FACT SUMMARY: Publishers (P) of various scientific journals brought a class action against Texaco, Inc. (D) based on its practice of circulating one copy of their journals and encouraging their research employees to make copies of the articles therein for their personal, archival use.

RULE OF LAW
The practice of circulating copies of scientific journals so that employees may copy articles contained therein does not constitute a fair use.

FACTS: American Geophysical Union (P) and 82 other publishers (P) brought a class action suit against Texaco, Inc. (D) claiming that its unauthorized copying of articles from their journals constituted copyright infringement. Texaco (D) asserted the affirmative defense of fair use. Texaco (D) employs 400 to 500 researchers nationwide for the purpose of developing new products and technology. Texaco (D) subscribes to many scientific and technical journals, maintaining a large library. The parties stipulated that one scientist, Chickering, would be selected as the representative of the entire group. The library circulated the journals and encouraged the researchers to make copies for their own use and return the original copy to the library. Chickering had eight particular copies of such articles in his files.

ISSUE: Does the practice of circulating copies of scientific journals so that employees may copy articles contained therein constitute a fair use?

HOLDING AND DECISION: (Newman, J.) No. The practice of circulating copies of scientific journals so that employees may copy articles contained therein does not constitute a fair use. The first factor in the fair use analysis is the "nature and character of the use, including whether such use is of a commercial nature or for nonprofit educational purposes." Here the library circulated the one copy and invited the researchers to make copies of it for their own use. Chickering testified that the copies in his files were made for his own convenience and for future use and that he did not even use five of the copies. This type of photocopying may be characterized as archival and is done to avoid payment for additional subscriptions. The requirement that the court consider whether the purpose of the work is commercial or non-profit requires the court to find against fair use when the infringer directly and exclusively obtains financial rewards as a result of the copying. The courts are also willing to find a secondary use fair if the use benefits the public interest. While Texaco's (D) copying may not rise to the level of commercial exploitation, due to the for-profit nature of Texaco's (D) business it cannot be said that it did not derive some economic benefit as a result of the copying. Where the secondary use is merely a reproduction of the original, there is little justification or a finding of fair use. The second fair use factor, "the nature of the copyrighted work," weighs in Texaco's (D) favor since the works were factual rather than fictional. The third factor is "the amount and substantiality of the portion used." For purpose of this case the work consists of each journal article, not the issue of the journal from which it was copied. Thus, Texaco (D) copied the entire works. This factor weighs in favor of the publishers. Fourth, the court must consider "the effect of the use upon the potential market for or value of the copyrighted work." The focus of the analysis is on the potential market for the individual articles. The evidence in respect to this factor did not favor either side in respect to sales of additional journals subscriptions, back issues, and back volumes. However, the district court also concluded that the photocopying affected the value of the publishers' copyrights. Since the publishers (P) were able to demonstrate substantial economic harm to the value of the copyrights as a result of the copying, this factor weighed in favor of the publishers (P). Since three of the four factors in the fair use analysis weighed in favor of the publishers, the district court was correct in concluding that Texaco's (D) photocopying did not constitute fair use. Affirmed.

DISSENT: (Jacobs, J.) Here, the only harm to any market would be to the supposed market in photocopy licenses. However, the Copyright Clearance Center Inc. (CCC) scheme is neither traditional nor reasonable, and its development into a "real market" would be subject to substantial impediments. In short, there is no normal market in photocopy licenses and no real consensus among publishers that there ought to be one. CCC has itself admitted that the mechanism for the negotiation of a photocopy license fee is often not even in place.

ANALYSIS
Generally a copyright owner has the exclusive right to authorize specified uses of his work and may demand a royalty for licensing others to utilize the work. The effect of the infringement on such revenues may be considered in determining the harm to the potential market for the work.

Continued on next page.

The courts have recognized, however, that in respect to such effects on licensing revenues, the court may only consider those markets that either already exist or are likely to develop.

Quicknotes

CLASS ACTION SUIT A suit commenced by a representative on behalf of an ascertainable group that is too large to appear in court, who shares a commonality of interests and who will benefit from a successful result.

COPYRIGHT INFRINGEMENT A violation of one of the exclusive rights granted to an artist pursuant to Article I, section 8, clause 8 of the United States Constitution over the reproduction, display, performance, distribution, and adaptation of his work for a period prescribed by statute.

FAIR USE An affirmative defense to a claim of copyright infringement providing an exception from the copyright owner's exclusive rights in a work for the purposes of criticism, comment, news reporting, teaching, scholarship or research; the determination of whether a use is fair is made on a case-by-case basis and requires the court to consider: (1) the purpose and character of the use; (2) the nature of the work; (3) the amount and substantiality of the portion used; and (4) the effect of the use on the potential market for, or value of, the work.

INTERLOCUTORY APPEAL The appeal of an issue that does not resolve the disposition of the case, but is essential to a determination of the parties' legal rights.

CHAPTER 8

Copyright and Contract

Quick Reference Rules of Law

	PAGE

1. **Modes of Transfer: Implied Licenses.** A non-exclusive license for the use of computer software will be implied where a putative licensee has requested the creator to create the software; the creator creates the requested software and delivers it to the putative licensee; and the creator intends that the putative licensee use, retain, and modify the software. (Asset Marketing Systems, Inc. v. Gagnon) — *136*

2. **Modes of Transfer: The Revision "Privilege" for Collective Works.** Electronic and CD-ROM databases containing individual articles from multiple editions of periodicals are not reproduced and distributed as part of revisions of individual periodical issues from which the articles were taken, hence publishers of periodicals may not relicense individual articles to databases under the Copyright Act section governing collective works, absent a transfer of copyright from authors of the individual articles. (New York Times Company v. Tasini) — *138*

3. **New Uses and Old Language.** Where the language of a license is broad enough to include a new use, the license will cover that new medium, unless specifically excluded by the grantor. (Boosey & Hawkes Music Publishers, Ltd. v. The Walt Disney Company) — *140*

4. **New Uses and Old Language.** A publisher's exclusive license to print, publish, and sell an author's work "in book form," does not extend to ebooks. (Random House v. Rosetta Books, LLC) — *141*

5. **New Licensing Models and the Contract/License Distinction.** A transfer of a copy of software is properly characterized as a sale, rather than as a license, where the transfer agreement permits the transferee to retain the copy indefinitely and does not permit the transferor to regain possession of the transferred copy. (Vernor v. Autodesk, Inc.) — *142*

6. **New Licensing Models and the Contract/License Distinction.** Where an open source license contains restrictions on a user's right to modify and distribute the licensed work in furtherance of the economic and other goals of the open source project, and those restrictions are stated to be conditions and the language of the license supports the interpretation that the restrictions are conditions, those restrictions are copyright conditions, rather than covenants to the license. (Jacobsen v. Katzer) — *144*

7. **Misuse.** A copyright holder's licensing agreement does not misuse the holder's copyright where the agreement is not likely to interfere with creative expression to such a degree that it affects in any significant way the policy interest in increasing the public store of creative activity or any other copyright policy. (Video Pipeline, Inc. v. Buena Vista Home Entertainment, Inc.) — *146*

8. **Misuse.** An antitrust violation may constitute copyright misuse. (In re Napster, Inc. Copyright Litigation) — *148*

Asset Marketing Systems, Inc. v. Gagnon

Corporation (D) v. Independent contractor (P)

542 F.3d 748 (9th Cir. 2008), cert. denied, 129 S.Ct. 2442 (2009).

NATURE OF CASE: Appeal from summary judgment involving a copyright claim.

FACT SUMMARY: Gagnon (P), an independent contractor who had been hired by Asset Marketing Systems, Inc. (AMS) (D) to write six computer programs for it, contended that AMS (D) infringed his copyrights in the programs by continuing to use and modify them without his consent. AMS (D) defended by asserting, inter alia, an implied license to use the programs.

RULE OF LAW
A non-exclusive license for the use of computer software will be implied where a putative licensee has requested the creator to create the software; the creator creates the requested software and delivers it to the putative licensee; and the creator intends that the putative licensee use, retain, and modify the software.

FACTS: Asset Marketing Systems, Inc. (AMS) (D) hired Gagnon (P) as an independent contractor to write computer software for AMS (D). Over the course of four years, AMS (D) paid Gagnon (P) over $2 million, $250,000 of which was for custom software development and computer classes. Gagnon (P) developed six computer programs for AMS (D). Gagnon (P) never expressly granted AMS (D) a license to the software. The parties did, however, enter, or consider entering, several contracts. The first was a Technical Services Agreement (TSA), which provided that Gagnon's (P) services would include "Custom Application Programming—Consultant will provide Contractor with specific add-on products to enhance Contractor's current in-house database application." AMS (D) claimed that two years later, Gagnon (P) signed a Vendor Nondisclosure Agreement (NDA), which would have given AMS (D) ownership of all intellectual property developed for AMS (D) by Gagnon (P), but he claimed that the document was a forgery and that his signature could not be authenticated. A year after that, Gagnon (P) proposed that AMS (D) sign an Outside Vendor Agreement (OVA) that included a proprietary rights clause that any intellectual property created by Gagnon (P) for AMS (D) would be Gagnon's (P) property to which AMS (D) would have a nonexclusive license. AMS (D) countered with a redlined version of this clause, whereby AMS (D) would own the intellectual property unless otherwise agreed. Neither version was executed. Before the parties' relationship ended, Gagnon (P) wrote to AMS (D), indicating that it had always been his position that AMS (D) would be entitled to unlimited software licensing as long as he had a business relationship with AMS (D). After the parties formally terminated their relationship, Gagnon (P) sent AMS (D) a letter demanding payment for the continued use of the computer programs he had created and for him to not disclose the programs to AMS's (D) competitors, and AMS (D) countered with a letter demanding that Gagnon (P) provide all source code and copies of the software to AMS (D), and asserting that AMS (D) owned the copyright in the programs. Gagnon (P) followed up with a cease and desist letter asserting that AMS's (D) use of the programs was unauthorized, and AMS (D) responded by asserting that Gagnon (P) could not unilaterally stop AMS (D) from continuing to use and update the programs because it had an irrevocable license to use, copy, and modify the programs based on the course of conduct of the parties. Suit was brought, and Gagnon (P) claimed that AMS (D) infringed his copyright in the programs because AMS (D) used them without obtaining a license or permission from Gagnon (P). AMS (D) defended by asserting, inter alia, an implied license to use the programs. [The procedural posture of the case is not set forth in the casebook extract.]

ISSUE: Will a non-exclusive license for the use of computer software be implied where a putative licensee has requested the creator to create the software; the creator creates the requested software and delivers it to the putative licensee; and the creator intends that the putative licensee use, retain, and modify the software?

HOLDING AND DECISION: (Smith, J.) Yes. A non-exclusive license for the use of computer software will be implied where a putative licensee has requested the creator to create the software; the creator creates the requested software and delivers it to the putative licensee; and the creator intends that the putative licensee use, retain, and modify the software. Whereas exclusive licenses must be in writing, non-exclusive licenses may be implied. Such licenses have previously been implied in the context of movie footage and architectural drawings using a similar three-pronged test, where the third prong has differed to reflect the protected right at issue. Here, that prong asks whether Gagnon (P) intended that AMS (D) use, retain, and modify the programs. As to the first prong of the test, AMS (D) requested Gagnon (P) to create the programs. He did not create the programs on his own initiative and market them to AMS (D), but created them, and subsequently modified them, in response to AMS's (D) requests. Therefore, the first prong of the test is satisfied. As to the second prong, Gagnon (P) created the software for AMS (D) and delivered it. Gagnon (P) conceded that the programs were created specifically for AMS (D), which paid for the work.

Continued on next page.

Additionally, Gagnon (P) delivered them when he installed them onto the AMS (D) computers and stored the source code on-site at AMS (D). Even if AMS (D) could not locate the source code on its computers after the parties' relationship terminated, Gagnon's (P) conduct manifested an objective intent to give AMS (D) an unlimited license at the time of creation, so that when he stored the source code at AMS (D), the code was delivered. Thus, the second prong is satisfied. Finally, with respect to the third prong, the question of intent is an objective one, i.e., whether at the time of the creation and delivery of the software Gagnon (P) manifested an intent that AMS (D) use, retain, and modify the programs, as gleaned from the parties' course of conduct. Several factors are appropriately used to determine such objective intent. One factor is whether the parties were engaged in a short-term discrete transaction as opposed to an ongoing relationship. Here the parties had an ongoing service relationship that indicates neither an intent to grant nor deny a license without Gagnon's (P) future involvement. A second factor is whether the creator utilized written contracts providing that copyrighted materials could only be used with the creator's future involvement or express permission. Here, nothing in the TSA indicated Gagnon's (P) understanding or intent that continued use of the programs would be prohibited after the TSA terminated. Because AMS (D) paid Gagnon (P) for his work, and because custom software is far less valuable without the ability to modify it, it "defies logic" that AMS (D) could not have used the programs without further payment pursuant to a separate licensing arrangement that was never mentioned in the TSA. The OVA also did not evidence any intent by Gagnon (P) to limit AMS's (D) use of the programs. Under the unexecuted OVA, Gagnon (P) claimed copyright in the intellectual property he created while working for AMS (D), but also granted AMS (D) a non-exclusive, unlimited license in the software. Moreover, a licensing agreement was not discussed until the parties ended their relationship; Gagnon (P) delivered the software without any caveats or limitations on AMS's (D) use of the programs. The parties' conduct evidenced Gagnon's (P) intent at the time of creation and delivery of the software to grant AMS (D) an unlimited, non-exclusive license to the software. Accordingly, such a license is implied, and, because AMS (D) paid consideration for it, the license is irrevocable, since otherwise it would be illusory. Judgment for AMS (D) as to this issue.

ANALYSIS

The court notes that though delivery of a copy of software does not compel the conclusion that Gagnon (P) granted AMS (D) a license, it is a relevant factor that the court may consider. Thus, while delivery of a tangible copy in which the copyrighted expression is fixed is not dispositive of intent, it is a factor that may be relied upon in determining that an implied license has been granted. Presumably, such delivery is not dispositive of intent because copyright ownership is distinct from ownership of the underlying object in which the copyrightable expression is fixed. See 17 U.S.C. § 202.

Quicknotes

CEASE AND DESIST ORDER An order from a court or administrative agency prohibiting a person or business from continuing a particular course of conduct.

INTELLECTUAL PROPERTY A body of law pertaining to the ownership of rights in intangible products of the human intellect.

INTER ALIA Among other things.

SUMMARY JUDGMENT Judgment rendered by a court in response to a motion made by one of the parties, claiming that the lack of a question of material fact in respect to an issue warrants disposition of the issue without consideration by the jury.

New York Times Company v. Tasini

Publisher (D) v. Author (P)

533 U.S. 483 (2001).

NATURE OF CASE: Appeal from summary judgment in favor of authors in their Copyright Act infringement suit against publishers.

FACT SUMMARY: Tasini and other freelance authors (P) of articles previously published in periodicals brought a copyright infringement action against the *New York Times* (D) and other publishers and owners of electronic databases after the articles were made available on such databases without the authors' consent.

RULE OF LAW
Electronic and CD-ROM databases containing individual articles from multiple editions of periodicals are not reproduced and distributed as part of revisions of individual periodical issues from which the articles were taken, hence publishers of periodicals may not relicense individual articles to databases under the Copyright Act section governing collective works, absent a transfer of copyright from authors of the individual articles.

FACTS: Tasini and other freelance authors (P) of articles previously published in periodicals brought a copyright infringement action against the *New York Times* (D) and other publishers and owners of electronic databases after the authors' articles were made available on such databases, arguing that electronic and CD-ROM databases containing individual articles from multiple editions of periodicals were not reproduced and distributed "as part of" "revisions" of individual periodical issues from which articles were taken, hence the publishers of the periodicals should not be permitted to relicense the individual articles to databases under the Copyright Act section governing collective works, absent transfer of copyright. The federal district court entered summary judgment for the *New York Times* (D), and the court of appeals reversed and entered summary judgment in favor of the authors. The *New York Times* (D) appealed.

ISSUE: May publishers of periodicals relicense individual articles to electronic and CD-ROM databases under the Copyright Act section governing collective works, absent a transfer of copyright from the authors of the individual articles?

HOLDING AND DECISION: (Ginsburg, J.) No. Section 201(c) of the Copyright Act (Act) does not authorize the copying at issue here. The publishers are not sheltered by the Act because the databases reproduce and distribute articles standing alone and not in context, not "as part of that particular collective work" to which the author contributed, "as part of . . . any revision" thereof, or "as part of . . . any later collective work in the same series." Where, as here, a freelance author has contributed an article to a collective work, copyright in the contribution vests initially in its author, under the Act. Copyright in the collective work vests in the collective author (here, the Print Publisher) and extends only to the creative material contributed by that author, not to "the preexisting material employed in the work." Congress enacted the provisions of the 1976 revision of the Copyright Act at issue to address the unfair situation under prior law, whereby authors risked losing their rights when they placed an article in a collective work. Essentially, Section 201(c) of the Act adjusts a publisher's copyright in its collective work to accommodate a freelancer's copyright in his or her contribution. If there is demand for a freelance article standing alone or in a new collection, the Act allows the freelancer to benefit from that demand; after authorizing initial publication, the freelancer may also sell the article to others. It would scarcely preserve the author's copyright in a contribution as contemplated by Congress if a print publisher, without the author's permission, could reproduce or distribute discrete copies of the contribution in isolation or within new collective works. The publishers' warning that a ruling for the authors will have "devastating" consequences, punching gaping holes in the electronic record of history, is unavailing since it hardly follows from this decision that an injunction against the inclusion of these articles in the databases (much less all freelance articles in any databases) must issue. Affirmed.

DISSENT: (Stevens, J.) Dividing the collective work (a single edition of the *New York Times*) into individual article ASCII files can be considered a "revision" of that day's *New York Times* as long as each article refers to the original collective work and as long as the rest of the collective work is readily accessible to the reader of the individual file at the same time the reader is accessing the individual file.

ANALYSIS

The Court explained that in determining whether articles have been reproduced and distributed "as part of" a "revision," the Court focuses on the articles as presented to, and perceptible by, a database user. Here, the three databases presented articles to users clear of the context provided either by the original periodical editions or by any revision of those editions. The databases first prompt users to search the universe of their contents: thousands

Continued on next page.

or millions of files containing individual articles from thousands of collective works (i.e., editions), either in one series (the *New York Times*) or in scores of series (the sundry titles in NEXIS). When the user conducts a search, each article appears as a separate item within the search result. In NEXIS and *New York Times*, an article appears to a user without the graphics, formatting, or other articles with which it was initially published.

Quicknotes

COPYRIGHT Refers to the exclusive rights granted to an artist pursuant to Article I, section 8, clause 8 of the United States Constitution over the reproduction, display, performance, distribution, and adaptation of his work for a period prescribed by statute.

COPYRIGHT ACT Copyright Act of 1976 extends copyright protection to "original works of authorship fixed in any tangible medium of expression, now known or later developed, from which they can be perceived, reproduced, or otherwise communicated, either directly or with the aid of a machine or device." 17 U.S.C. § 102.

COPYRIGHT INFRINGEMENT A violation of one of the exclusive rights granted to an artist pursuant to Article I, section 8, clause 8 of the United States Constitution over the reproduction, display, performance, distribution, and adaptation of his work for a period prescribed by statute.

INJUNCTION A court order requiring a person to do or prohibiting that person from doing a specific act.

SUMMARY JUDGMENT Judgment rendered by a court in response to a motion by one of the parties, claiming that the lack of a question of material fact in respect to an issue warrants disposition of the issue without consideration by the jury.

Boosey & Hawkes Music Publishers, Ltd. v. The Walt Disney Company

Assignee of copyright in musical work (P) v. Alleged infringer (D)

145 F.3d 481 (2d Cir. 1998).

NATURE OF CASE: Action seeking an interpretation of a license agreement and damages for copyright infringement.

FACT SUMMARY: Boosey & Hawkes Music Publishers, Ltd. (P), the assignee of copyrights for Igor Stravinsky's "The Rite of Spring," sought a declaration that a 1939 agreement granting The Walt Disney Company (D) the right to use "The Rite of Spring" in its movie "Fantasia" did not include the grant of rights to Disney (D) to use the work in video format.

RULE OF LAW
Where the language of a license is broad enough to include a new use, the license will cover that new medium, unless specifically excluded by the grantor.

FACTS: In 1938, The Walt Disney Company (D) sought permission to use Stravinsky's "The Rite of Spring" in a motion picture. In 1939, the parties executed a licensing agreement that allowed Disney (D) to use the work in one motion picture. The motion picture, "Fantasia," was released in 1940 and featured animated scenes set, in part, to "The Rite of Spring," although the composition was shortened and otherwise edited. Since 1940, "Fantasia" has been re-released at least seven times, all under the 1939 license, and parts of "Fantasia" have been shown on television. Boosey & Hawkes Music Publishers, Inc. (Boosey) (P), the assignee of the copyright, has never objected to any of these distributions. In 1991, Disney (D) released "Fantasia" in video format for sale in the United States and foreign countries. Boosey (P) brought this action claiming that the 1939 license did not include the use of "The Rite of Spring" in video format.

ISSUE: Does a license to exploit a copyrighted work extend to new marketing channels made possible through technological advancements?

HOLDING AND DECISION: (Leval, J.) Yes. Where the language of a license is broad enough to include a new use, the license will cover that new medium unless specifically excluded by the grantor. The license should be viewed according to ordinary contract principles. Where a contract is more reasonably read to convey one meaning, the party that argues a different meaning bears the burden of negotiating for language that would express an agreed upon limitation. Here, the plain reading of the contract and the term "motion picture" would include a motion picture distributed in video format. To exclude additional usage, Stravinsky would need to take responsibility for adding the proper language to the license.

ANALYSIS
The court discusses two lines of reasoning with regard to new uses not specifically included in a license agreement. The first approach would deem the phrase "motion picture" to mean only what that phrase was understood to mean at the time of licensing agreement; it would not, therefore, include new, unanticipated technology. The second approach, that favored in this case, would include within the term "motion picture" any new technology the nature of which would reasonably fall within the scope of the medium for which the license was originally granted.

Quicknotes

COPYRIGHT Refers to the exclusive rights granted to an artist pursuant to Article I, section 8, clause 8 of the United States Constitution over the reproduction, display, performance, distribution, and adaptation of his work for a period prescribed by statute.

COPYRIGHT INFRINGEMENT A violation of one of the exclusive rights granted to an artist pursuant to Article I, section 8, clause 8 of the United States Constitution over the reproduction, display, performance, distribution, and adaptation of his work for a period prescribed by statute.

Random House v. Rosetta Books, LLC

Publishing company (P) v. Alleged copyright infringer (D)

150 F. Supp. 2d 613 (S.D.N.Y. 2001), aff'd 283 F.3d 490 (2d Cir. 2002).

NATURE OF CASE: Suit for copyright infringement and injunctive relief.

FACT SUMMARY: When Rosetta Books, LLC (D) created ebooks (for the internet) of authors who had previously given exclusive licenses to Random House (P) to print, publish, and sell their works "in book form," Random House (P) sought to enjoin Rosetta's (D) ebooks on the grounds that ebooks constituted "in book form."

RULE OF LAW
A publisher's exclusive license to print, publish, and sell an author's work "in book form," does not extend to ebooks.

FACTS: In the 1960s and 1970s, several distinguished authors granted to Random House (P) the exclusive licenses to print, publish, and sell their works "in book form." In 2001, Rosetta Books, LLC (D) launched its ebook business and contracted with those same authors to license to it the right to publish those same books in digital form as ebooks for the internet. Ebooks are digital books that one can read on the computer screen or an electronic device. They are created by converting digitalized text into a format readable by computer software. Random House (P) brought suit in federal district court against Rosetta Books (D) for copyright infringement and injunctive relief.

ISSUE: Does a publisher's exclusive license to print, publish, and sell an author's work "in book form," extend to ebooks?

HOLDING AND DECISION: (Stein, J.) No. A publisher's exclusive license to print, publish, and sell an author's work "in book form," does not extend to ebooks. Not only does the language of the contract itself clearly lead to the conclusion that Random House (P) does not own the right to publish the works as ebooks, but also a reasonable person cognizant of the customs, practices, usages, and terminology as generally understood in the particular trade or business, would conclude that the grant language does not include ebooks. Here, the so-called "new use" of the authors' materials—electronic digital signals sent over the internet—is in a separate medium from the original use: printed words on paper. The need for a software program to interact with the data in order to make it usable, also distinguishes analog formats from digital formats. Even Random House's (P) own expert testified that the media are distinct because information stored digitally can be manipulated in ways that analog information cannot. Here, the policy rationale of encouraging development in new technology is well served by finding that the licensors (the authors) retain these "new use" rights to their works. In the twenty first century, it cannot be said that licensees such as book publishers and movie producers are ipso facto more likely to make advances in digital technology than start-up companies. Relief denied.

ANALYSIS

As made clear in the *Random House* decision, the contractual phrase, "To print, publish, and sell the work in book form," is understood in the publishing industry to be a "limited" grant. Furthermore, the publishing industry generally interprets the phrase "in book form" as granting the publisher the exclusive right to publish a hardcover trade book in English for distribution in North America.

Quicknotes

COPYRIGHT INFRINGEMENT A violation of one of the exclusive rights granted to an artist pursuant to Article I, section 8, clause 8 of the United States Constitution over the reproduction, display, performance, distribution, and adaptation of his work for a period prescribed by statute.

ENJOIN The ordering of a party to cease the conduct of a specific activity.

INJUNCTIVE RELIEF A court order issued as a remedy, requiring a person to do, or prohibiting that person from doing, a specific act.

IPSO FACTO By the fact itself.

Vernor v. Autodesk, Inc.

eBay reseller (P) v. Software company (D)

2009 WL 3187613 (W.D. Wash. Sept. 30, 2009).

NATURE OF CASE: Action for declaratory judgment as to copyright infringement.

FACT SUMMARY: Vernor (P), who was stopped by Autodesk, Inc. (D) from making further sales of Autodesk's (D) "AutoCAD packages" on eBay, contended that, as the owner of the AutoCAD packages, he had not infringed Autodesk's (D) copyrights in the AutoCAD software by making previous sales of the packages, and would not infringe the copyrights through future sales, since he was protected by the first sale doctrine of § 109 of the Copyright Act and the reproduction exception of § 117.

RULE OF LAW
A transfer of a copy of software is properly characterized as a sale, rather than as a license, where the transfer agreement permits the transferee to retain the copy indefinitely and does not permit the transferor to regain possession of the transferred copy.

FACTS: Vernor (P), who makes his living by selling merchandise on eBay, obtained software packages known as "AutoCAD packages" that had been developed by Autodesk, Inc. (D). Each AutoCAD package was comprised of a box that contained a jewel case containing a compact disk encoded with Autodesk's (D) copyrighted AutoCAD software and a license agreement. The jewel case was sealed with a sticker advising that, among other things, "[t]his software is subject to the license agreement that appears during the installation process or is included in the package." Vernor (P) attempted to sell the AutoCAD packages on eBay in 2005 and 2007. When Autodesk (D) discovered his attempted sales in 2005, it invoked the "takedown" provisions of the Digital Millennium Copyright Act (DMCA) and delayed Vernor's (P) sales. In 2007, Autodesk's (D) similar deployment of the takedown provisions not only delayed his sales, but also resulted in eBay's barring him from selling anything for a month. Vernor (P) had bought the AutoCAD packages he attempted to sell in 2007 from Cardwell/Thomas Associates (CTA) as part of CTA's sale of office equipment. In 2002, CTA had agreed, when it upgraded its AutoCAD software—which it had obtained in 1999—to destroy the AutoCAD packages it had sold to Vernor (P), and Autodesk (D) subsequently obtained a consent judgment against CTA in which CTA agreed that it had breached its promise to destroy the AutoCAD packages, and that it had transferred those packages to Vernor (P) in violation of Autodesk's (D) copyright. However, in 1999, CTA had only agreed to adhere to Autodesk's (D) software license. This license, which governed the use and disposition of the software, included, among other things, a provision that indicated that "[t]itle and copyrights to the Software and accompanying materials and any copies made by you remain with Autodesk." Although the license required the transferee to destroy the software upon an upgrade, it did not give Autodesk (D) the right to regain possession of the software. Vernor (P) brought suit seeking a declaratory judgment that his successful sales of the AutoCAD packages, and any potential future sales of the packages, did not and would not violate Autodesk's (D) copyright in the AutoCAD software. Vernor (P) asserted that he was the owner of the AutoCAD packages and therefore was protected by the first sale doctrine of § 109 of the Copyright Act and the reproduction exception of § 117. Autodesk (D) argued that it still owned the packages and that Vernor (P) was liable for direct and contributory copyright infringement.

ISSUE: Is a transfer of a copy of software properly characterized as a sale, rather than as a license, where the transfer agreement permits the transferee to retain the copy indefinitely and does not permit the transferor to regain possession of the transferred copy?

HOLDING AND DECISION: (Jones, J.) Yes. A transfer of a copy of software is properly characterized as a sale, rather than as a license, where the transfer agreement permits the transferee to retain the copy indefinitely and does not permit the transferor to regain possession of the transferred copy. The dispute here can be resolved by determining whether the software license accompanying the AutoCAD package copies CTA acquired in 1999 effected a sale or a mere license. If it effected a sale, then CTA transferred ownership to Vernor (P), who can claim protection under the first sale doctrine of § 109 and the reproduction exception of § 117. If the license effected a mere license, then Autodesk (D) is the owner of the copies, and Vernor (P) will be liable for copyright infringement. To be clear, it is undisputable that Autodesk (D) licensed the software itself; the issue is about the copies containing the software—which can either be sold or licensed. The court of appeals precedent in this area is conflicting. In one case involving the transfer of film prints, *United States v. Wise*, 550 F.2d 1180, (9th Cir. 1977), the court held that a transfer agreement effected a sale, notwithstanding that it purported to retain title in the transferor, and notwithstanding restrictions that prevented the sale, lease, license, or loan of the print and eliminated all uses of the film except for the transferee's in-home display, where the agreement permitted the transferee to retain the copy indefinitely and did not permit the transferor to regain

Continued on next page.

possession of the transferred copy. On the other hand, the court of appeals subsequently was more deferential to a transfer agreement's characterization of itself as a license in a trio of cases [*MAI Sys. Corp. v. Peak Computer, Inc.*, 991 F.2d 511 (9th Cir. 1993); *Triad Sys. Corp. v. Southeastern Express Co.*, 64 F.3d 1330 (9th Cir. 1995); and *Wall Data Inc. v. Los Angeles County Sheriff's Dep't*, 447 F.3d 769 (9th Cir. 2006)] involving software licenses. Applying *Wise* leads to the conclusion that the transfer of AutoCAD copies via the license was a transfer of ownership, because even though it severely restricted the use and disposition of the copies by CTA and purported to retain title in Autodesk (D), it did not grant Autodesk (D) the right to regain possession of the copies. Autodesk's (D) decision to let its licensees retain possession of the software forever, and its failure to regain possession of the copies, cannot be characterized as something other than a transfer of ownership, despite numerous restrictions on that ownership. Under the trio of cases that came 25 years after *Wise*, the court of appeals concluded that a licensee who obtains a software copy with a license that "makes it clear that she or he is granting only a license to the copy of the software" and "imposes significant restrictions on the purchaser's ability to redistribute or transfer that copy" is "not an owner" of the copy. Thus, if the trio's precedent was followed, Autodesk (D) would prevail. However, the precedent of *Wise* and that of the trio is in irreconcilable—and unavoidable—conflict. When faced with such a situation, the court must follow the older precedent, which in this case is *Wise*. Even though *Wise* construed the statutory predecessor to § 109, it is unlikely, based on rules of statutory construction, that the term "owner" in the prior statute differs in meaning from its meaning in the current Act. However, the lack of legislation addressing computer licensing raises several policy considerations. For example, Autodesk (D) argues that this court's interpretation of "owner" will harm consumers and software producers alike by raising software prices that result from increased piracy that results from software resale. Vernor (P), on the other hand, contends that Autodesk's (D) preferred interpretation of "owner" would give copyright holders the ability to destroy secondary markets for their works by the simply declaring transfers of copies of their works to be "licenses" rather than sales. Autodesk's (D) argument does not account for reduced resale prices, and also is unconvincing because its premise that resale causes increased piracy is faulty. The degree of piracy depends on the number of pirates, who presumably are just as happy to pirate copies sold by software developers as copies sold be resellers. Vernor's (P) argument is similarly unconvincing. In any event, the decision rendered here is based on legal precedent, rather than policy judgment, which is best left to Congress. Judgment for Vernor (P).

▶ ANALYSIS

Although the interpretation of "owner" in the Copyright Act no doubt has important consequences for software producers and consumers, it is unlikely that this decision will have far-reaching consequences, given that courts across the nation have issued rulings that adopt and reject the equivalent of the parties' positions here. Some courts favor the copyright holder, whereas others favor the consumer. As the court intimates in its brief discussion of policy considerations, given the "cacophony" of opinions throughout the various jurisdictions, and because this is an area fraught with conflicting policy considerations, there is a need for Congress to address this issue head-on through legislation.

Quicknotes

COPYRIGHT ACT Copyright Act of 1976 extends copyright protection to "original works of authorship fixed in any tangible medium of expression, now known or later developed, from which they can be perceived, reproduced, or otherwise communicated, either directly or with the aid of a machine or device." 17 U.S.C. § 102.

COPYRIGHT INFRINGEMENT A violation of one of the exclusive rights granted to an artist pursuant to Article I, Section 8, clause 8 of the United States Constitution over the reproduction, display, performance, distribution, and adaptation of his work for a period prescribed by statute.

DECLARATORY JUDGMENT A judgment of the court establishing the rights of the parties.

Jacobsen v. Katzer

Open source software licensor (P) v. Commercial competitor (D)

535 F.3d 1373 (Fed. Cir. 2008).

NATURE OF CASE: Appeal from denial of preliminary injunction in action for copyright infringement and breach of contract.

FACT SUMMARY: Jacobsen (P), the manager of an open source software group called Java Model Railroad Interface (JMRI), contended that Katzer and Kamind Associates, Inc. [collectively "Katzer/Kamind" (D)] infringed Jacobsen's (P) copyright in the open source computer programming code by breaching the open source license, titled the Artistic License, by using some of the code in software developed by Katzer/Kamind (D) without adhering to the Artistic License's conditions.

RULE OF LAW
Where an open source license contains restrictions on a user's right to modify and distribute the licensed work in furtherance of the economic and other goals of the open source project, and those restrictions are stated to be conditions and the language of the license supports the interpretation that the restrictions are conditions, those restrictions are copyright conditions, rather than covenants to the license.

FACTS: Jacobsen (P) managed an open source software group called Java Model Railroad Interface (JMRI), which created a computer programming application called DecoderPro, which allows model railroad enthusiasts to use their computers to program the decoder chips that control model trains. Katzer and Kamind Associates, Inc. [collectively "Katzer/Kamind" (D)] offered a competing software product, Decoder Commander. During the development of Decoder Commander, Katzer/Kamind (D) downloaded and used portions of the DecoderPro software as part of Decoder Commander. While DecoderPro files were available for download from SourceForge and for use by the public free of charge, the downloadable files contained copyright notices and were governed by an Artistic License, which was contained in a COPYING file. The Artistic License granted users the right to copy, modify, and distribute the software, but placed conditions on such use. Katzer/Kamind (D) did not comply with the Artistic License's conditions because the Decoder Commander software did not include (1) the authors' names, (2) JMRI copyright notices, (3) references to the COPYING file, (4) an identification of SourceForge or JMRI as the original source of the definition files, and (5) a description of how the files or computer code, and the file names, had been changed from the original source code and original file names, without reference to the original JMRI files or information on where to get the Standard Version. In addition, if a downloader did not assent to the conditions stated in the COPYING file, he was instructed to "make other arrangements with the Copyright Holder." Katzer/Kamind (D) did not make any such "other arrangements." Jacobsen (P), who owned the copyrights in DecoderPro, brought suit for copyright infringement and breach of contract, and moved for a preliminary injunction. The district court ruled that Katzer/Kamind's (D) alleged violation of the conditions of the license may have constituted a breach of the nonexclusive license, but did not create liability for copyright infringement where it would not otherwise exist, so that Jacobsen (P) only had a cause of action for breach of contract. The court of appeals granted review.

ISSUE: Where an open source license contains restrictions on a user's right to modify and distribute the licensed work in furtherance of the economic and other goals of the open source project, and those restrictions are stated to be conditions and the language of the license supports the interpretation that the restrictions are conditions, are those restrictions copyright conditions, rather than covenants to the license?

HOLDING AND DECISION: (Hochberg, J.) Yes. Where an open source license contains restrictions on a user's right to modify and distribute the licensed work in furtherance of the economic and other goals of the open source project, and those restrictions are stated to be conditions and the language of the license supports the interpretation that the restrictions are conditions, those restrictions are copyright conditions, rather than covenants to the license. Jacobsen (P) has made out a prima facie case of copyright infringement, but Katzer/Kamind (D) argues that they cannot be liable for copyright infringement because they had a license to use the material. The key issue thus is whether the terms of the Artistic License are conditions of, or merely covenants to, the copyright license. A copyright owner who grants a nonexclusive license to use his copyrighted material waives his right to sue the licensee for copyright infringement and can sue only for breach of contract. However, if a license is limited in scope and the licensee acts outside the scope, the licensor can bring an action for copyright infringement. If the terms of the Artistic License are both covenants and conditions, they limit the scope of the license and are governed by copyright law, but, if they are merely covenants, they are governed by contract law. Here, the Artistic License on its face states that it creates conditions, and uses the phrase "provided

Continued on next page.

that," which under state law indicates a condition. Moreover, the conditions in the Artistic License are crucial to enable the copyright holder to retain the ability to benefit from the work of downstream users. By requiring that users who modify or distribute the copyrighted material retain the reference to the original source files, the Artistic License has the effect of alerting downstream users of the "upstream" open source project, who may then join as collaborators. The district court erroneously interpreted the Artistic License to permit a user to modify the material "in any way" because it did not account for the License's clear express restrictions on a downloader's rights to modify and distribute the work that were necessary to accomplish the objectives of the open source licensing collaboration. A copyright holder who engages in open sources licensing and chooses to exact consideration in the form of compliance with requirements of disclosure and explanation of changes, rather than money, is entitled to a remedy for infringement just as if he had sought a licensing fee. However, because in such situations a calculation of damages is inherently speculative, these types of license restrictions might well be rendered meaningless absent the copyright holder's ability to enforce them through injunctive relief. Thus, because the clear language of the Artistic License created conditions to protect the economic rights at issue, by requiring attribution and modification transparency that would serve to drive traffic to the open source incubation page and to inform downstream users of the project as well as to permit the copyright holder to learn about the uses for his software and gain others' knowledge that could be used to advance future software releases, the terms of the Artistic License are enforceable copyright conditions. Vacated and remanded for a determination as to whether Jacobsen (P) is entitled to an injunction.

ANALYSIS

Public licenses, often referred to as "open source" licenses, are used by artists, authors, educators, software developers, and scientists who wish to create collaborative projects and to dedicate certain works to the public. Several types of public licenses have been designed to provide creators of copyrighted materials a means to protect and control their copyrights. Creative Commons, one of the amici curiae in this case, provides free copyright licenses to allow parties to dedicate their works to the public or to license certain uses of their works while keeping some rights reserved. In exchange and in consideration for this collaborative work, the copyright holder permits users to copy, modify and distribute the software code subject to conditions that serve to protect downstream users and to keep the code accessible. By requiring that users copy and restate the license and attribution information, a copyright holder can ensure that recipients of the redistributed computer code know the identity of the owner as well as the scope of the license granted by the original owner. The Artistic License in this case also required that changes to the computer code be tracked so that downstream users would know what part of the computer code was the original code created by the copyright holder and what part had been newly added or altered by another collaborator. Additionally, the lack of money changing hands in open source licensing does not mean that there is no economic consideration, however. There are substantial benefits, including economic benefits, to the creation and distribution of copyrighted works under public licenses that range far beyond traditional license royalties. These include generating market share for programs, increasing reputation and name recognition, and rapid improvements to a product.

Quicknotes

BREACH OF CONTRACT Unlawful failure by a party to perform its obligations pursuant to contract.

COPYRIGHT INFRINGEMENT A violation of one of the exclusive rights granted to an artist pursuant to Article I, Section 8, clause 8 of the United States Constitution over the reproduction, display, performance, distribution, and adaptation of his work for a period prescribed by statute.

DAMAGES Monetary compensation that may be awarded by the court to a party who has sustained injury or loss to his person, property or rights due to another party's unlawful act, omission or negligence.

INJUNCTIVE RELIEF A court order issued as a remedy, requiring a person to do, or prohibiting that person from doing, a specific act.

PRELIMINARY INJUNCTION A judicial mandate issued to require or restrain a party from certain conduct; used to preserve a trial's subject matter or to prevent threatened injury.

PRIMA FACIE CASE An action where the plaintiff introduces sufficient evidence to submit the issue to the judge or jury for determination.

Video Pipeline, Inc. v. Buena Vista Home Entertainment, Inc.

Movie trailer distributor (P) v. Movie production company (D)

342 F.3d 191, 203 (3d Cir. 2003), *cert. denied*, 540 U.S. 1178 (2004).

NATURE OF CASE: Appeal from grant of preliminary injunction in action seeking declaratory judgment of copyright non-infringement.

FACT SUMMARY: Video Pipeline, Inc. (P), a distributor of movie trailers, contended that Disney's (D) licensing agreements misused Disney's (D) copyright in its films because the agreements suppressed criticism of Disney (D), its films, and the film industry.

RULE OF LAW
A copyright holder's licensing agreement does not misuse the holder's copyright where the agreement is not likely to interfere with creative expression to such a degree that it affects in any significant way the policy interest in increasing the public store of creative activity or any other copyright policy.

FACTS: Video Pipeline, Inc. (P) distributed movie trailers to home video retailers, and obtained the trailers from movie production companies under license. Video Pipeline (P) moved its business to the Internet, where it included in its online database trailers it received under license from Disney (D), a movie production company. Because Disney's (D) License Agreement did not permit this use, Disney (D) requested that Video Pipeline (P) remove the trailers from the database, and Video Pipeline (P) complied with that request. Video Pipeline (P) then filed suit seeking a declaratory judgment that its online use of the trailers did not violate copyright law, and Disney (D) terminated the License Agreement. Video Pipeline (P) decided to replace some of the removed Disney (D) trailers by copying approximately two minutes from each of at least 62 Disney (D) movies to create its own "clip previews" of the movies. The district court granted Disney's (D) request for a preliminary injunction prohibiting Video Pipeline (P) from using the clip previews, and also ruled that Video Pipeline's (P) use was not a fair use. Video Pipeline (P) also contended that certain Disney (D) licensing agreements with other online movie trailer distributors constituted misuse of Disney's (D) copyrights because the agreements, which licensed trailers for websites, suppressed criticism by requiring licensees to agree to not criticize Disney (D), the entertainment industry, the licensed film, or anyone connected to Disney (D) or the film. The district court held that Video Pipeline (P) likely would not succeed on this copyright misuse defense. The court of appeals granted review.

ISSUE: Does a copyright holder's licensing agreement misuse the holder's copyright where the agreement is not likely to interfere with creative expression to such a degree that it affects in any significant way the policy interest in increasing the public store of creative activity or any other copyright policy?

HOLDING AND DECISION: (Ambro, J.) No. A copyright holder's licensing agreement does not misuse the holder's copyright where the agreement is not likely to interfere with creative expression to such a degree that it affects in any significant way the policy interest in increasing the public store of creative activity or any other copyright policy. The well-established patent misuse doctrine has been applied by some courts in the copyright area, but usually such application is made where the copyright holder uses its copyright for anticompetitive purposes. However, the doctrine will be applied wherever a holder uses its copyright to thwart copyright policy, such as where a copyright is used to prevent the progress of the arts and sciences. In other words, it is possible that a copyright holder could leverage its copyright to restrain the creative expression of another without engaging in anticompetitive behavior or implicating the fair use and idea/expression doctrines. Although Disney's (D) licensing agreements do seek to restrict expression, i.e., criticism, they are not likely to interfere with creative expression to such a degree that they will affect in any significant way the policy interest in increasing the public store of creative activity. A licensee is still free to express criticism on websites not connected with the trailers, and viewers are still able to obtain criticism from sources other than the licensees. In fact, not permitting Disney (D) to control the environment in which trailers for its movies will be displayed likely will lead to Disney's (D) refusal to license trailers at all, thus depriving the public of expression. Accordingly, while the copyright misuse doctrine may be a viable defense in other circumstances, it is inapplicable here because, on this record, Disney's (D) licensing agreements do not interfere significantly with copyright policy (while holding to the contrary might, in fact, do so). Affirmed.

ANALYSIS

The misuse doctrine extends from the equitable principle that courts may appropriately withhold their aid where the plaintiff is using the right asserted contrary to the public interest. Misuse, however, is not cause to invalidate the copyright or patent, but instead precludes its enforcement during the period of misuse. To defend on misuse grounds, the alleged infringer need not be subject to the purported misuse, just as Video Pipeline (P) here was not subject to

Continued on next page.

the licensing agreements it adduced to argue that Disney (D) was engaging in misuse.

Quicknotes

DECLARATORY JUDGMENT A judgment of the court establishing the rights of the parties.

FAIR USE An affirmative defense to a claim of copyright infringement providing an exception from the copyright owner's exclusive rights in a work for the purposes of criticism, comment, news reporting, teaching, scholarship or research.

PRELIMINARY INJUNCTION A judicial mandate issued to require or restrain a party from certain conduct; used to preserve a trial's subject matter or to prevent threatened injury.

In re Napster, Inc. Copyright Litigation

Discovery determinations

191 F. Supp. 2d 1087 (N.D. Cal. 2002).

NATURE OF CASE: Discovery request.

FACT SUMMARY: When Napster (D) was sued by MusicNet (P) for possible violation of a joint venture agreement between the two, Napster (D) sought discovery to obtain evidence to establish that MusicNet's (P) actions constituted antitrust violations so as to give rise to the defense of copyright misuse.

RULE OF LAW
An antitrust violation may constitute copyright misuse.

FACTS: MusicNet (P), which was a combination of several music companies, entered into a series of joint ventures with Napster (D) to provide platforms for the digital distribution of music. The agreement allowed Napster (D) access to all of the copyrighted music licensed to MusicNet (P). The agreement explicitly limited Napster's (D) ability to obtain individual licenses from any of the individual recording companies. MusicNet (P) sued Napster (D) for alleged violation of the agreement. Napster (D) argued that the court should allow for discovery on its claim that MusicNet's (P) entry into the digital distribution market runs afoul of antitrust laws and gives rise to the defense of copyright misuse.

ISSUE: May an antitrust violation constitute copyright misuse?

HOLDING AND DECISION: (Patel, J.) Yes. An antitrust violation may constitute copyright misuse. To establish that the alleged antitrust violations of MusicNet (P) actually constitute federal copyright violations, Napster (D) must, however, establish a nexus between the alleged anti-competitive actions of MusicNet (P) and the latter's power over the copyrighted material. Napster (D) must be permitted to have further discovery in its attempt to gather evidence to support its contentions that the licensing clauses in its agreement with MusicNet (P) is unduly restrictive and violates antitrust, and that MusicNet's (P) practices as they enter the digital market, are so anti-competitive as to give rise to a misuse defense on the grounds of antitrust violation. The critical issue is that the agreement binds Napster (D) to obtain licenses from MusicNet (P) and not its competitors. Napster (D), therefore, appears to be caught in the position where its only options were to sign the agreement to gain access to the catalogs of the major record companies and thereby incur these restrictions or to refuse to sign the agreement and have virtually no access to most commercially available music. MusicNet (P) cannot hide behind the shell of a joint venture to protect themselves from a misuse claim. Even on the undeveloped record before the court, "these joint ventures look bad, sound bad and smell bad." MusicNet (P) contends that it should not matter for the purposes of copyright misuse if they engage in price-fixing because the behavior is unrelated to the manner in which MusicNet (P) uses its copyright monopoly. However, there is no doubt that price-fixing carries antitrust and public policy considerations that may be relevant to misuse. On the record, Napster (D) has demonstrated a sufficient nexus to allow for further discovery on this issue, and its motion is accordingly granted.

ANALYSIS

As the court indicates in *In re Napster Copyright Litigation*, the burden of proof rests with the party who asserts that an antitrust violation is giving rise to a defense of copyright misuse.

Quicknotes

ANTITRUST Body of federal law prohibiting business conduct that constitutes a restraint on trade.

BURDEN OF PROOF The duty of a party to introduce evidence to support a fact that is in dispute in an action.

COPYRIGHT Refers to the exclusive rights granted to an artist pursuant to Article I, section 8, clause 8 of the United States Constitution over the reproduction, display, performance, distribution, and adaptation of his work for a period prescribed by statute.

DISCOVERY Pretrial procedure during which one party makes certain information available to the other.

JOINT VENTURE Venture undertaken based on an express or implied agreement between the members, common purpose and interest, and an equal power of control.

MONOPOLY A privilege or right conferred upon an individual or entity granting it the exclusive power to manufacture, sell and distribute a particular service or commodity; a market condition in which one or a few companies control the sale of a product or service thereby restraining competition in respect to that article or service.

CHAPTER 9

Technological Protections

Quick Reference Rules of Law

		PAGE
1.	**The Digital Millennium Copyright Act (DMCA) and Circumvention of Technological Protections.** Linking to a site containing circumvention technology is actionable under the DMCA only if the link is made (a) with the knowledge that the offending material is on the linked-to site, (b) with knowledge that such circumvention technology may not lawfully be offered, and (c) with the purpose of creating or maintaining a link through which to disseminate that technology. (Universal City Studios, Inc. v. Reimerdes)	150
2.	**Access and Interoperable Products.** Under the Anticircumvention Provision of the DMCA (17 U.S.C. § 1201), circumvention is not infringement. (Chamberlain Group, Inc. v. Skylink Tech., Inc.)	152
3.	**Access and Interoperable Products.** An authentication sequence code does not necessarily control "access" to a copyrighted computer program within the meaning of the Anticircumvention Provision of the DMCA. (Lexmark International, Inc. v. Static Control Components, Inc.)	154
4.	**Protection for Copyright Management Information.** For purposes of § 1202 of the DMCA, a logo and a hyperlink are not "copyright management information" (CMI) where there is no evidence that an automated system would use the logo or hyperlink to manage or protect copyrights. (IQ Group, Ltd. v. Wiesner Publishing, LLC)	156
5.	**Protection for Copyright Management Information.** Making copies of photographs available on a website without the relevant copyright management information is actionable under the DMCA only if the person who displays such images knows or should know that this will lead to infringement of the photographer's copyright. (Kelly v. Arriba Soft Corp.)	158

Universal City Studios, Inc. v. Reimerdes

Motion picture studios (P) v. Computer hackers (D)

111 F. Supp. 2d 294 (S.D.N.Y. 2000), aff'd sub nom. *Universal City Studios, Inc. v. Corley*, 273 F.3d 429 (2d Cir. 2001).

NATURE OF CASE: Action under the Digital Millennium Copyright Act (DCMA) to enjoin defendants' actions.

FACT SUMMARY: Computer hackers developed a computer program that circumvents the encryption system designed to prevent the copying of motion pictures on digital versatile disks (DVDs).

RULE OF LAW
Linking to a site containing circumvention technology is actionable under the DMCA only if the link is made (a) with the knowledge that the offending material is on the linked-to site, (b) with knowledge that such circumvention technology may not lawfully be offered, and (c) with the purpose of creating or maintaining a link through which to disseminate that technology.

FACTS: Plaintiffs distribute many of their motion pictures for home use on digital versatile disks (DVDs), which contain copies of the motion pictures in digital form. They protect these motion pictures from copying by using an encryption system called CSS. In September 1999, Jon Johansen, a 15-year-old Norwegian boy, and two persons using pseudonyms whom he had met online, reverse engineered a licensed DVD player and discovered the CSS encryption algorithm and keys. Johansen then used this information to devise DeCSS, a program allowing playback of encrypted DVDs on non-compliant computers and the copying of decrypted files to computer hard drives, which he posted on his website. Further, Johansen announced the code on an Internet mailing list. The movie studios (P) discovered the availability of DeCSS in October 1999 and proceeded to send a number of cease and desist letters to various websites posting DeCSS, some of which responded by removing it. In January 2000, the plaintiffs brought this action under the DMCA. Defendants removed DeCSS from their site but, as a self-proclaimed act of "electronic civil disobedience," they linked their site to a large number of others that continued to make DeCSS available. Defendants contend that their actions do not violate DMCA and, in the alternative, that the DMCA, as applied to computer programs or code, violates the First Amendment.

ISSUE: Do posting a system for decrypting motion picture DVDs or linking to other sites that post such systems violate the DMCA?

HOLDING AND DECISION: (Kaplan, J.) Yes. The DMCA aims at preventing traffic in any technology that has only a limited commercially significant purpose or use other than to circumvent a technological measure that effectively controls access to a work protected under the Copyright Act. In this case, Johansen's DeCSS was created solely for the purpose of decrypting CSS, and that is all that it does. Defendants' use of DeCSS on their websites did not fall under one of the exceptions to the DMCA because they did not post it to achieve interoperability, as defined by the statute, and the posting did not contribute to "good faith research" or "security testing." The fair use defense does not apply to claims under the DMCA. Further, the defendants, by urging others to disseminate DeCSS and to inform defendants of such dissemination so that defendants could link their site to these mirror sites, engaged in the functional equivalent of transferring the DeCSS code, in violation of the DMCA. In itself, however, linking to a site containing unlawful circumvention technology does not incur liability or risk injunction, unless those responsible for the link clearly knew the site contained offending material, knew that such circumvention technology cannot lawfully be offered, and created or maintained the link in order to disseminate that technology. Appropriate injunction and declaratory relief issued.

ANALYSIS

The appeal of *Reimerdes* focused on the defendants' constitutional challenges to Section 1201(a)(2) of the DMCA. The appeals court agreed that instructions in computer code qualify as speech protected under the First Amendment and that the regulation imposed by 1201(a)(2) is content-neutral and permissible.

Quicknotes

CEASE AND DESIST ORDER An order from a court or administrative agency prohibiting a person or business from continuing a particular course of conduct.

ENJOIN The ordering of a party to cease the conduct of a specific activity.

FAIR USE An affirmative defense to a claim of copyright infringement providing an exception from the copyright owner's exclusive rights in a work for the purposes of criticism, comment, news reporting, teaching, scholarship or research; the determination of whether a use is fair is made on a case-by-case basis and requires the court to consider: (1) the purpose and character of the use; (2) the nature of the work; (3) the amount and substantiality of

Continued on next page.

the portion used; and (4) the effect of the use on the potential market for, of value of, the work.

FIRST AMENDMENT Prohibits Congress from enacting any law respecting an establishment of religion, prohibiting the free exercise of religion, abridging freedom of speech or the press, the right of peaceful assembly and the right to petition for a redress of grievances.

Chamberlain Group, Inc. v. Skylink Tech., Inc.

Owner of copyrighted computer program (P) v. Alleged trafficker in circumvention devices (D)

381 F.3d 1178 (Fed. Cir. 2004), *cert. denied*, 544 U.S. 923 (2005).

NATURE OF CASE: Appeal from a summary judgment in favor of a defendant in a suit for violation of the Anticircumvention Provision of the Digital Millennium Copyright Act (DMCA).

FACT SUMMARY: When Chamberlain Group, Inc. (Chamberlain) (P) argued that Skylink Tech., Inc. (D) was in violation of the anticircumvention provision of the DMCA, the latter argued that Chamberlain's (P) unconditional sale of its product implied authorization.

RULE OF LAW
Under the Anticircumvention Provision of the DMCA (17 U.S.C. § 1201), circumvention is not infringement.

FACTS: Chamberlain Group, Inc. (Chamberlain) (P) developed an automatic garage door opener system (GDO) incorporating a copyrighted "rolling code" computer program that constantly changes the transmitter signal needed to open the garage door. Skylink Tech., Inc.'s (Skylink's) (D) "Model 39" transmitter, which did not incorporate rolling code, nevertheless allowed users to operate Chamberlain's (P) GDO by allowing unauthorized users to circumvent the security inherent in rolling codes. Chamberlain (P) brought suit against Skylink (D), not alleging copyright infringement, but alleging that because Chamberlain's (P) opener and transmitter both incorporate computer programs "protected by copyright" and because rolling codes are a "technical measure" that "controls access" to those programs, that therefore Skylink (D) was prima facie liable for violating 17 U.S.C. § 1201 (prohibiting trafficking in circumvention devices). The district court granted Skylink's (D) motion for summary judgment on the grounds, inter alia, that Chamberlain's (P) unconditional sale of its GDO implied authorization.

ISSUE: Under the Anticircumvention Provision of the DMCA (17 U.S.C. § 1201), is circumvention infringement?

HOLDING AND DECISION: (Gajarsa, J.) No. Under the Anticircumvention Provision of the DMCA (17 U.S.C. § 1201), circumvention is not infringement. Chamberlain (P) is misguided in its argument that all uses of products containing copyrighted software to which a technological measure controlled access are now per se illegal under the DMCA unless the manufacturer provided consumers with explicit authorization. To the contrary, the DMCA does not empower manufacturers to prohibit consumers from using embedded software products in conjunction with competing products. The anticircumvention provisions convey no additional property rights to manufacturers in and of themselves. They simply provide property owners with new ways to secure their property. Like all property owners taking legitimate steps to protect their property, however, copyright owners relying on the anticircumventions provisions remain bound by all other relevant bodies of law. The DMCA did not "fundamentally alter" the legal landscape governing the reasonable expectations of consumers or competitors or the manner in which courts analyze industry practices, nor render the pre-DMCA history of the GDO irrelevant. The DMCA's structure, legislative history, and context within the Copyright Act all support the conclusion that Chamberlain's (P) warranty conditions and website postings cannot render users of Skylink's (D) "Model 39" product as "unauthorized" users for the purposes of establishing trafficking liability under the DMCA. Affirmed.

ANALYSIS

As noted in the *Chamberlain* decision, Chamberlain's (P) proposed construction of the DMCA ignored the significant differences between defendants whose accused products enable copying and those, like Skylink (D), whose accused products enable only legitimate uses of copyrighted software. As the court further explained, to allow copyright owners to use technological measures to block all access to their copyrighted works, would in fact create two distinct copyright regimes, and such was not the congressional purpose of the DMCA.

Quicknotes

COPYRIGHT Refers to the exclusive rights granted to an artist pursuant to Article I, section 8, clause 8 of the United States Constitution over the reproduction, display, performance, distribution, and adaptation of his work for a period prescribed by statute.

COPYRIGHT INFRINGEMENT A violation of one of the exclusive rights granted to an artist pursuant to Article I, section 8, clause 8 of the United States Constitution over the reproduction, display, performance, distribution, and adaptation of his work for a period prescribed by statute.

INTER ALIA Among other things.

PRIMA FACIE An action in which the plaintiff introduces sufficient evidence to submit an issue to the judge or jury for determination.

Continued on next page.

SUMMARY JUDGMENT Judgment rendered by a court in response to a motion by one of the parties, claiming that the lack of a question of material fact in respect to an issue warrants disposition of the issue without consideration by the jury.

Lexmark International, Inc. v. Static Control Components, Inc.

Owner of copyrighted computer program (P) v. Alleged trafficker in circumvention devices (D)

387 F.3d 522 (6th Cir. 2005).

NATURE OF CASE: Appeal from a preliminary injunction in favor of the owner of a copyrighted computer program.

FACT SUMMARY: When Static Control Components (SCC) (D) made a chip that incorporated Lexmark International, Inc.'s (P) authentication code thus enabling non-Lexmark printer cartridges to be used in Lexmark (P) printers, Lexmark (P) sued SCC (D) for violation of the Anticircumvention Provision of the Digital Millennium Copyright Act (DMCA).

RULE OF LAW
An authentication sequence code does not necessarily control "access" to a copyrighted computer program within the meaning of the Anticircumvention Provision of the DMCA.

FACTS: Lexmark International, Inc. (Lexmark) (P) created toner loading programs for its laser and inkjet printers, which control a variety of its printer functions. Lexmark (P) also uses an "authentication sequence" that performs a "secret handshake" between each Lexmark (P) printer and a microchip on each Lexmark (P) toner cartridge. If the "handshake" is not properly performed, the printer will not operate, blocking consumers from using toner cartridges that Lexmark (P) has not authorized. Static Control Components (SCC) (D) makes a wide range of technology products, including microchips that it sells to third-party companies for use in remanufactured toner cartridges. SCC's (D) chips contain an unauthorized copy of Lexmark's (P) toner loading program and authentication sequence to make its product compatible with the Lexmark (P) printers but at a lower cost. Lexmark (P) sued SCC (D), alleging that the latter's chip violated the Anticircumvention Provision of the DMCA by selling a product that circumvents "access controls" on the printer engine program.

ISSUE: Does an authentication sequence code necessarily control "access" to a copyrighted computer program within the meaning of the Anticircumvention Provision of the DMCA?

HOLDING AND DECISION: (Sutton, J.) No. An authentication sequence code does not necessarily control "access" to a copyrighted computer program within the meaning of the Anticircumvention Provision of the DMCA. In the instant case, it is not Lexmark's (P) authentication sequence that controls access to its printer engine program. It is the purchase of a Lexmark (P) printer that allows "access" to the program. Anyone who buys a Lexmark (P) printer may read the literal code of that printer directly from the printer memory, with or without the benefit of the authentication sequence, and the data from the program may be translated into readable source code after which copies may be freely distributed. In other words, no security device protects access to the printer engine program code; accordingly, no security device must be circumvented to obtain access to the program code. While it is true that the authentication sequence may well block one form of access to make use of the printer engine program, it does not block another relevant form of access, namely, the ability to obtain a copy of the work or to make use of the literal elements of the program. Furthermore, the Digital Millennium Copyright Act not only requires an offending technological measure to "control access," but also requires the measure to control that access "effectively." Thus, it seems clear that the provision does not naturally extend to a technological measure, such as here, that merely restricts one form of access but leaves another route wide open. Reversed.

CONCURRENCE: (Merritt, J.) It should be made clear that companies like Lexmark (P) cannot use the DMCA in conjunction with copyright law to create monopolies of manufactured goods for themselves just by tweaking the facts of the case. To adopt Lexmark's (P) reading of the DMCA would mean that manufacturers could potentially create monopolies for replacement parts merely by using similar, but more creative, lock-out codes.

ANALYSIS

As the *Lexmark* decision makes clear, in the essential setting where the DMCA applies, the copyright protection operates on two planes: in the literal code governing the work and in the visual or audio manifestation generated by the code's execution. In the *Lexmark* case, the copyrightable expression in the printer engine program, by contrast, operated on only one plane: in the literal elements of the program, its source and object code.

Quicknotes

COPYRIGHT Refers to the exclusive rights granted to an artist pursuant to Article I, section 8, clause 8 of the United States Constitution over the reproduction, display, performance, distribution, and adaptation of his work for a period prescribed by statute.

Continued on next page.

PRELIMINARY INJUNCTION An order issued by the court at the commencement of an action, requiring a party to refrain from conducting a specified activity that is the subject of the controversy, until the matter is determined.

IQ Group, Ltd. v. Wiesner Publishing, LLC

Online advertising company (P) v. Advertising distributor (D)

409 F. Supp. 2d 587 (D.N.J. 2006).

NATURE OF CASE: Motion for summary judgment in action for infringement of § 1202 of the Digital Millennium Copyright Act (DMCA).

FACT SUMMARY: IQ Group, Ltd. (IQ) (P), an online advertising company that had prepared online ads for two insurance companies, claimed that Wiesner Publishing, LLC (Wiesner) (D) and the insurance companies violated § 1202 of the DMCA when Wiesner (D) distributed the ads that IQ (P) had prepared but removed IQ's (P) logo and a hyperlink to IQ's (P) website.

RULE OF LAW
For purposes of § 1202 of the DMCA, a logo and a hyperlink are not "copyright management information" (CMI) where there is no evidence that an automated system would use the logo or hyperlink to manage or protect copyrights.

FACTS: IQ Group, Ltd. (IQ) (P), an online advertising company, prepared online ads for two insurance companies. The ads contained IQ's (P) logo and a hyperlink to copyright information on its website. Subsequently, the insurance companies hired Wiesner Publishing, LLC (Wiesner) (D) to distribute the ads. Wiesner (D) used the identical ads, but removed IQ's (P) logo and the hyperlink to its website. IQ (P) brought suit, claiming that Wiesner (D) and the insurance companies violated § 1202 of the DMCA by removing the logo and hyperlink. Wiesner (D) moved for summary judgment.

ISSUE: For purposes of § 1202 of the DMCA, are a logo and a hyperlink "copyright management information" where there is no evidence that an automated system would use the logo or hyperlink to manage or protect copyrights?

HOLDING AND DECISION: (Greenaway, J.) No. For purposes of § 1202 of the DMCA, a logo and a hyperlink are not "copyright management information" (CMI) where there is no evidence that an automated system would use the logo or hyperlink to manage or protect copyrights. Section 1202(c) defines "copyright management information" in eight categories. IQ (P) contends that the logo falls into several of these categories: category 2 ("the name of, and other identifying information about, the author of a work"), category 3 ("the name of, and other identifying information about, the copyright owner of the work"), and category 7 ("identifying numbers or symbols referring to such information or links to such information"). IQ (P) also contends that the hyperlink falls into categories 3 and 7, and that the linked website falls within category 6 ("terms and conditions for use of the work"). A broad reading of the section would render IQ's (P) argument plausible. However, to do so would be to blur the lines between trademark and copyright—which the United States Supreme Court has cautioned against—as it would allow a trademark or service mark to invoke DMCA provisions meant to protect copyrights. Broadly read, copyright management information (CMI) could encompass a logo that is on a digital communication, since the logo can convey information that indicates the source of the communication. However, the legislative history requires a narrower reading of the statute. Professor Julie Cohen [one of the co-authors of the casebook] argues that the DMCA directly protects not copyrights themselves, but technological measures that protect copyrights in digital technology. Under this view, CMI is limited to components of such technological measures, which can control access to works, such that the technology attached to the work itself defines and protects the legal rights of the copyright owner. The legislative history supports this position. The DMCA brought United States copyright law into compliance with international treaties of the World Intellectual Property Organization (WIPO), under which technical measures such as CMI are components of automated copyright protection systems. Additionally, the rationale of § 1202, which was drafted before the WIPO treaties, is to facilitate systems that track and monitor uses of copyrighted works as well as license rights and indicate attribution, creation and ownership interests by protecting the information embedded in digital versions of a work that indicates authorship and ownership as well as authorized uses of the work. CMI was thus understood to be information about authorship, ownership, and permitted uses of a work that is included in digital versions of the work so as to implement "rights management functions" of "rights management systems" that are electronic and automated within the environment of a computer network. This seems to be Congress's view, based on the view of the drafting committee (the Working Group on Intellectual Property Rights). Accordingly, CMI is distinguished from traditional management of copyrights as conducted by people who control access to, and reproduction of, copyrighted works. Such traditional management is covered by the Copyright Act. Applying this narrowed view of CMI here, there was no evidence presented the logo and hyperlink on the ads at issue functioned as a component of an automated copyright protection or management system. Therefore, as a matter of law, they are not CMI. Summary judgment is granted to Wiesner (D).

Continued on next page.

ANALYSIS

This was the first reported case to address the definition of CMI. Although the ads at issue were sent via email, and thus likely copied and distributed as part of an automated process within a computer network environment, the court found that this did not bring the information removal within § 1202. IQ (P) did not allege that the logo or the hyperlink were intended to function as a component of an automated copyright protection or management system, and the court concluded that, to the extent that they functioned to protect copyright at all, they functioned to inform people who would make copyright management decisions—a function which, according to the court, is protected by the Copyright Act.

Quicknotes

COPYRIGHT Refers to the exclusive rights granted to an artist pursuant to Article I, Section 8, clause 8 of the United States Constitution over the reproduction, display, performance, distribution, and adaptation of his work for a period prescribed by statute.

COPYRIGHT ACT Copyright Act of 1976 extends copyright protection to "original works of authorship fixed in any tangible medium of expression, now known or later developed, from which they can be perceived, reproduced, or otherwise communicated, either directly or with the aid of a machine or device." 17 U.S.C. § 102.

COPYRIGHT INFRINGEMENT A violation of one of the exclusive rights granted to an artist pursuant to Article I, Section 8, clause 8 of the United States Constitution over the reproduction, display, performance, distribution, and adaptation of his work for a period prescribed by statute.

SUMMARY JUDGMENT Judgment rendered by a court in response to a motion made by one of the parties, claiming that the lack of a question of material fact in respect to an issue warrants disposition of the issue without consideration by the jury.

TRADEMARK Any word, name, symbol, device or combination thereof that is either currently utilized, or which a person has a bona fide intent to utilize, in commerce in order to distinguish his goods from those of another.

Kelly v. Arriba Soft Corp.

Photographer (P) v. Website (D)

77 F. Supp. 2d 1116 (C.D. Cal. 1999), *aff'd in part and rev'd in part on other grounds*, 336 F.3d 811 (9th Cir. 2003).

NATURE OF CASE: Claim alleging copyright infringement and violation of the Digital Millennium Copyright Act (DMCA).

FACT SUMMARY: The defendant's website indexed several of the photographer's images without the relevant copyright management information.

RULE OF LAW
Making copies of photographs available on a website without the relevant copyright management information is actionable under the DMCA only if the person who displays such images knows or should know that this will lead to infringement of the photographer's copyright.

FACTS: Defendant owns Arriba Vista Image Searcher, a visual search engine, which works by maintaining an indexed database of approximately two million thumbnail images obtained using a "crawler." Kelly (P), a photographer specializing in photographs of California gold rush country and in images related to the works of Laura Ingalls Wilder, maintains two websites containing such images. In January 1999, defendant's crawler indexed thirty-five of Kelly's (P) images, making thumbnails of them available to its users. Defendant removed these images on receipt of a notice of copyright infringement. In April, Kelly (P) filed this action alleging violation of his copyrights in these images and alleging defendant violated the DMCA by removing or altering the copyright management information associated with the images.

ISSUE: Does the re-posting of photographs without the relevant copyright management information constitute a violation of the DMCA?

HOLDING AND DECISION: (Taylor, J.) No. Making copies of photographs available on a website without the relevant copyright management information is actionable under the DMCA only if the person who displays such images knows or should know that this will lead to infringement of the photographer's copyright. The copyright management information does not appear in Kelly's (P) images and thus was not included in the indexed thumbnail images. Kelly (P) must demonstrate that the defendant knew or should have known that making Kelly's (P) images available to users without the relevant copyright management information would lead to infringement of Kelly's (P) copyrights. When users enlarged the photographs, they were provided with the name of the website where the photos originated and with a link to that site. Kelly's (P) site presumably supplied the copyright management information. Defendant warns its users that restrictions may apply to the use of images in its index and instructs them not to copy or use images without first checking with the originating websites. Thus, defendant did not have reasonable grounds to know that it would cause users to infringe on Kelly's (P) copyrights. Kelly's (P) images are vulnerable to copyright infringement simply because they are displayed on websites. Judgment for the defendant.

ANALYSIS

Under § 1202 of the DMCA, a plaintiff must demonstrate that an alleged violator had "reasonable grounds to know" that its actions would lead to copyright infringement.

Quicknotes

COPYRIGHT Refers to the exclusive rights granted to an artist pursuant to Article I, section 8, clause 8 of the United States Constitution over the reproduction, display, performance, distribution, and adaptation of his work for a period prescribed by statute.

COPYRIGHT INFRINGEMENT A violation of one of the exclusive rights granted to an artist pursuant to Article I, section 8, clause 8 of the United States Constitution over the reproduction, display, performance, distribution, and adaptation of his work for a period prescribed by statute.

CHAPTER 10

State Law Theories of Protection

Quick Reference Rules of Law

		PAGE

1. **Federal Intellectual Property Preemption.** A state's unfair competition law cannot impose liability for, or prohibit, the copying of an article that is unprotectable under either federal patent or copyright laws. (Sears, Roebuck & Co. v. Stiffel Co.) — 160

2. **Federal Intellectual Property Preemption.** Inasmuch as Congress has left unattended the area of federal protection or nonprotection of recordings against acts of piracy thereupon, a state remains free to adopt and enforce a law making the pirating of such recordings a criminal offense. (Goldstein v. California) — 161

3. **Federal Intellectual Property Preemption.** Federal law does not preempt state trade secret law. (Kewanee Oil Co. v. Bicron Corp.) — 162

4. **Federal Intellectual Property Preemption.** States may not prohibit the duplication of unpatented or unpatentable articles. (Bonito Boats, Inc. v. Thunder Craft Boats, Inc.) — 163

5. **Express Preemption under the 1976 Act.** Where state law claims do not allege any qualitatively different conduct on the part of the infringing party, they are preempted by the Copyright Act. (Harper & Row, Publishers, Inc. v. Nation Enterprises) — 164

6. **Express Preemption under the 1976 Act.** If other elements are required, in addition to or instead of, the acts of reproduction, performance, distribution or display, in order to constitute a state-created cause of action, then the right does not lie within the general scope of copyright, and there is no preemption. (Video Pipeline, Inc. v. Buena Vista Home Entertainment, Inc.) — 165

7. **The Right of Publicity.** Baseball players do not have a state law right of publicity in their televised performances. (Baltimore Orioles, Inc. v. Major League Baseball Players Association) — 167

8. **The Right of Publicity.** State law claims asserting rights to privacy and publicity are not preempted under the Copyright Act. (Brown v. Ames) — 168

9. **The Right of Publicity.** A person's right of publicity may be usurped even if the offending use did not incorporate that person's likeness. (White v. Samsung Electronics America, Inc.) — 169

10. **Misappropriation.** A party engages in unfair competition when it interferes without authorization in the other party's normal business operations in order to divert a portion of profits for its own benefit. (International News Service v. Associated Press) — 170

11. **Misappropriation.** A "hot news" misappropriation claim may survive preemption for material within the realm of copyright law. (National Basketball Association v. Motorola, Inc.) — 171

12. **Contract.** The Copyright Act does not preempt a prohibition on reverse engineering contained in a shrinkwrap license. (Bowers v. Baystate Technologies, Inc.) — 172

Sears, Roebuck & Co. v. Stiffel Co.

Retailer (D) v. Lamp designer (P)

376 U.S. 225 (1964).

NATURE OF CASE: Action seeking damages for unfair competition.

FACT SUMMARY: Although Stiffel Co. (P) had obtained design and mechanical patents on a "pole lamp" it placed on the market, Sears, Roebuck & Co. (D) thereafter began to sell its own version at a much cheaper price.

RULE OF LAW
A state's unfair competition law cannot impose liability for, or prohibit, the copying of an article that is unprotectable under either federal patent or copyright laws.

FACTS: Having designed a pole lamp that it marketed, Stiffel Co. (P) obtained both design and mechanical patents thereon. In a short time, Sears, Roebuck & Co. (Sears) (D) came out with the same lamp, but it sold at a much cheaper price. As a result, Stiffel (P) brought an action seeking damages for unfair competition, but the court held that the patents Stiffel (P) had secured were invalid for want of invention. It nonetheless recognized that the lamps were substantially identical and, noting that customers might be confused, the court held that Sears (D) had engaged in unfair competition by marketing the confusingly similar lamps. From that decision, Sears (D) appealed, the court of appeals affirmed, and the Supreme Court granted certiorari.

ISSUE: If a particular article is one which neither the federal patent or copyright laws protect, can a state's unfair competition law impose liability for or prohibit the copying the article?

HOLDING AND DECISION: (Black, J.) No. Just as a state can not directly encroach upon federal patent or copyright law, it may not use its own laws on unfair competition or any other subject to protect an article which is left unprotected under the aforementioned federal laws. These federal systems of protection have occupied the field, and state law in those areas is preempted by the applicable federal scheme. Thus, where, as in this case, a state's unfair competition law clashes with the objectives of federal patent or copyright law, in providing a uniform system of protection while also preserving free competition where it is deemed appropriate, it must yield under the doctrine of preemption. Since Stiffel (P) was unable to obtain protection under the federal copyright or patent laws, its article was among those the federal scheme desired to leave unprotected, and the state cannot enter into the picture and extend protection. Reversed.

ANALYSIS

The preemption doctrine, on which this case was decided, flows from the Supremacy Clause in Article IV of the Constitution, which makes federally enacted laws the supreme law of the land. The result is that when Congress passes laws that "occupy" a particular field, that action serves to "preempt" states from taking individual action in that area. It is an important concept in dealing with patents and copyrights, for a national system of protection could easily be thwarted and would be all but useless were inventors and authors uncertain whether their federal rights were effectively altered depending upon which state they were in. This type of uncertainty would have a damaging effect on the generation of new ideas and new products, which really depends on a nationwide standard of protection.

Quicknotes

CERTIORARI A discretionary writ issued by a superior court to an inferior court in order to review the lower court's decisions; the Supreme Court's writ ordering such review.

COPYRIGHT Refers to the exclusive rights granted to an artist pursuant to Article I, section 8, clause 8 of the United States Constitution over the reproduction, display, performance, distribution, and adaptation of his work for a period prescribed by statute.

ENCROACHMENT The unlawful intrusion onto another's property.

PATENT A limited monopoly conferred on the invention or discovery of any new or useful machine or process that is novel and nonobvious.

PREEMPTION Judicial preference recognizing the procedure of federal legislation over state legislation of the same subject matter.

UNFAIR COMPETITION Any dishonest or fraudulent rivalry in trade and commerce, particularly imitation and counterfeiting.

Goldstein v. California

State (P) v. Copier of sound recordings (D)

412 U.S. 546 (1972).

NATURE OF CASE: Review of a criminal conviction for "pirating" recordings produced by others.

FACT SUMMARY: Goldstein (D) was convicted under a California (P) criminal statute that forbade copying performances off of commercially sold recordings without the permission of the owner of the master tape or record.

RULE OF LAW
Inasmuch as Congress has left unattended the area of federal protection or nonprotection of recordings against acts of piracy thereupon, a state remains free to adopt and enforce a law making the pirating of such recordings a criminal offense.

FACTS: Sound recordings had not been given specific federal copyright protection when Goldstein (D) was convicted under a California (P) law prohibiting the pirating of commercially sold records or tapes. Contending that this criminal statute was an unconstitutional exercise of state power, insofar as it sought to provide protection to a work uncopyrightable under federal law, Goldstein (D) appealed.

ISSUE: Can a state make the pirating of commercially sold records or tapes a crime if Congress has left the question of federal copyright protection of such recordings unattended?

HOLDING AND DECISION: (Burger, C.J.) Yes. Where Congress has left unattended the question of providing protection to a certain category of work, such as records and tapes, states are free to implement their own laws making it a crime to engage in the pirating of such works. The preemption doctrine would prohibit state laws only insofar as they clash with federal copyright laws. In those areas where Congress has not chosen to exercise its rights to provide protection or not provide it but has left the area unattended, the Constitution allows the states to act. An overview of the legislative history of the actions of Congress indicates that Congress never decided whether sound recordings should be protected or should remain free. In such an absence of federal occupation of the field, any state was free to legislate. This is precisely what California (P) did. It passed a law designed to ensure the continued production of new recordings and thereby stabilize what is a large industry in California (P). The premise that this is an impermissible grant of a state copyright of unlimited duration cannot be accepted. There is no unyielding national interest that would require an inference that state power to grant such copyrights has been relinquished to exclusive federal control. The effect of a state-provided protection is limited by the borders of the granting state. Thus, even a perpetual protection would only have a narrowly circumscribed tendency to inhibit progress in the arts and sciences. There being no further basis on which to challenge this statute, the conviction was proper and the judgment below is affirmed.

DISSENT: (Douglas, J.) "Cases like *Sears* were surcharged with 'unfair competition' and the present one with 'pirated recordings.' But free access to products on the market is the consumer interest protected by the failure of Congress to extend patents or copyrights into various areas."

ANALYSIS

Sears and *Compco* would seem to indicate a contrary result. Those cases seemed to indicate that congressional silence evidenced a desire to forego protection in favor of free competition in the subject area. That would not seem to be the actual case, however, since Congress has acted to protect recordings "fixed" before February 15, 1972.

Quicknotes

COPYRIGHT Refers to the exclusive rights granted to an artist pursuant to Article I, section 8, clause 8 of the United States Constitution over the reproduction, display, performance, distribution, and adaptation of his work for a period prescribed by statute.

PREEMPTION Judicial preference recognizing the procedure of federal legislation over state legislation of the same subject matter.

Kewanee Oil Co. v. Bicron Corp.

Crystal manufacturer (P) v. Competitor (D)

416 U.S. 470 (1974).

NATURE OF CASE: Review of order dissolving injunction against disclosure of trade secrets.

FACT SUMMARY: Bicron Corp. (D) contended that federal patent law preempted Ohio trade secret law.

RULE OF LAW
Federal law does not preempt state trade secret law.

FACTS: [Facts not stated in casebook excerpt.]

ISSUE: Does federal patent law preempt state trade secret law?

HOLDING AND DECISION: (Burger, C.J.) No. Federal patent law does not preempt state trade secret law. It is well established that states are free to regulate the area of intellectual property, provided that such regulations do not conflict with applicable federal law. In the area of federal patent law and its state law equivalent, trade secret protection, Congress has not explicitly mandated preemption. Therefore, preemption will be found only if state trade secret law interferes with the policies underlying patent law. The purpose of patent law is to promote invention, as is the purpose of trade secret law. Since their goals do not conflict, the question becomes whether the two laws conflict in operation. As an initial matter, trade secret law is broader than patent law; many things which may be trade secrets are not patentable. Clearly there is no conflict in this context, as trade secret law takes nothing from patent law. In cases where a certain trade secret is also patentable, the potential for conflict is greater. Nonetheless, this Court believes the conflict to be minimal. Granted, patent law mandates disclosure of the patent process, while trade secrets involve nondisclosure. Nonetheless, the advantages of a patent on a product or process are so great that, as a matter of practicality, one possessing a patentable product or process will almost always opt for the patent. The only likely result of declaring trade secret law preempted would be to encourage frivolous patent applications and to promote extensive intracompany secrecy, neither of which is socially desirable. For these reasons, patent law does not preempt state trade secret law. Reversed.

CONCURRENCE: (Marshall, J.) While the Court is incorrect in assuming that inventors will almost always opt for a patent over trade secret protection, nothing indicates that Congress intended to coerce inventors to go the route of patents rather than trade secrets.

DISSENT: (Douglas, J.) Congress in the patent laws has declared that every article not covered by a valid patent is within the public domain. State trade secret law undercuts this intent.

ANALYSIS

A patent application requires disclosure of the essential features of a product. If a product is patented, this information becomes public. While an inventor can be somewhat selective about the information provided to the patent office, sufficient information must be provided to make the product "work." For this reason, a patent almost always makes the keeping of a trade secret impossible.

Quicknotes

INJUNCTION A court order requiring a person to do or prohibiting that person from doing a specific act.

INTELLECTUAL PROPERTY A body of law pertaining to the ownership of rights in intangible products of the human intellect.

PATENT A limited monopoly conferred on the invention or discovery of any new or useful machine or process that is novel and nonobvious.

PREEMPTION Judicial preference recognizing the procedure of federal legislation over state legislation of the same subject matter.

TRADE SECRETS A secret formula used in the manufacture of a particular product that is not known to the general public.

Bonito Boats, Inc. v. Thunder Craft Boats, Inc.

Boat designer (P) v. Manufacturer (D)

489 U.S. 141 (1989).

NATURE OF CASE: Review of order voiding state law prohibiting duplication of boat hulls.

FACT SUMMARY: Thunder Craft Boats, Inc. (D) contended that Florida's law prohibiting the duplication of unpatented boat hulls violated federal patent laws.

RULE OF LAW
States may not prohibit the duplication of unpatented or unpatentable articles.

FACTS: Florida enacted a law prohibiting the duplication of molded boat hulls. Bonito Boats, Inc. (Bonito) (P), which had designed a certain type of boat hull mold and had commercially exploited it, brought an action against Thunder Craft Boats, Inc. (Thunder Craft) (D). Bonito (P) alleged that Thunder Craft (D) had copied the design of its hull. The design was not patented. The trial court held the Florida law to be preempted by federal patent law and declared the law invalid. The appellate and Florida Supreme Courts affirmed, and the Supreme Court granted certiorari.

ISSUE: May states prohibit the duplication of unpatented or unpatentable articles?

HOLDING AND DECISION: (O'Connor, J.) No. States may not prohibit the duplication of unpatented or unpatentable articles. Federal patent law reflects a very careful balance between healthy competition and rewarding innovation. A person who meets the requirements of novelty, usefulness, and nonobviousness will be rewarded with a temporary monopoly; all other utilitarian articles may be exploited by the public. Federal patent laws, in order to determine what is protected, must also determine what is not protected. The balance struck in patent laws requires that all nonpatented, publicly known designs be freely traded. If states were free to grant de facto monopolies to unpatented or unpatentable articles, the balance struck in federal patent laws would be upset. Here, the Florida law is a good illustration. Bonito (P) did not apply for a patent. Consequently, federal patent law would permit any competitor to use its design. The Florida law prevents this. Consequently, the Florida law acts to upset the fine balance created in patent law. Since the law is inconsistent with federal law, it must fail. Affirmed.

ANALYSIS

This case should not be taken to mean that there is no place for state laws in the law of intellectual property. State unfair competition laws have coexisted with federal law in this area for quite some time, with little evidence of incompatibility. In the instant case, the Court indicated it had no inclination to strike down state trade secret or unfair competition laws.

Quicknotes

CERTIORARI A discretionary writ issued by a superior court to an inferior court in order to review the lower court's decisions; the Supreme Court's writ ordering such review.

MONOPOLY A privilege or right conferred upon an individual or entity granting it the exclusive power to manufacture, sell and distribute a particular service or commodity; a market condition in which one or a few companies control the sale of a product or service thereby restraining competition in respect to that article or service.

PATENT A limited monopoly conferred on the invention or discovery of any new or useful machine or process that is novel and nonobvious.

PREEMPTION Judicial preference recognizing the procedure of federal legislation over state legislation of the same subject matter.

Harper & Row, Publishers, Inc. v. Nation Enterprises

Publisher (P) v. News magazine (D)

723 F.2d 195 (2d Cir. 1983), *rev'd on other grounds*, 471 U.S. 539 (1985).

NATURE OF CASE: Copyright infringement action.

FACT SUMMARY: News magazine published excerpts from an unpublished manuscript.

RULE OF LAW
Where state law claims do not allege any qualitatively different conduct on the part of the infringing party, they are preempted by the Copyright Act.

FACTS: Gerald R. Ford contracted with Harper & Row, Publishers, Inc. (P) and Reader's Digest in February 1977 to publish his as yet unwritten memoirs. The memoirs were to contain material concerning the Watergate crisis, Mr. Ford's pardon of former president Nixon, and Mr. Ford's reflections on this period, its personalities, and its morality. The agreement gave Harper & Row (P) the right to publish the Ford memoirs in book form and the exclusive right to license prepublication excerpts, known as "first serial rights." In 1979, as Ford's memoirs were nearing completion, Harper & Row (P) negotiated a prepublication agreement with *Time*, a weekly news magazine. *Time* agreed to pay $25,000, $12,500 in advance and an additional $12,500 at publication, in exchange for the right to excerpt 7,500 words from Ford's account of the Nixon pardon. The issue featuring the excerpts was to be released one week before shipment of the full book to bookstores. Exclusivity was an important consideration for the agreement, and Harper & Row (P) instituted procedures designed to maintain the confidentiality of the manuscript. Two to three weeks before the scheduled release of the *Time* article, an unidentified person brought the manuscript to Victor Navasky, the editor of *The Nation*. Navasky hastily pulled together a news article featuring quotes, paraphrases, and facts drawn exclusively from the manuscript. The 2,250-word article was released on April 3, 1979. Harper & Row (P) brought this action alleging copyright infringement, conversion, and tortious interference with contractual relations.

ISSUE: Are plaintiff's conversion and tortious interference with contractual relations claims preempted by the Copyright Act?

HOLDING AND DECISION: (Kaufman, J.) Yes. Plaintiffs based the factual elements of their conversion claim on the unlawful possession of the physical property of the Ford manuscript. As such, they based their claim in unauthorized publication, and sought to uphold a right that was coextensive with the exclusive right protected by the Copyright Act. In the alternative, plaintiffs based their conversion claim in the possession of the papers themselves. This took the claim outside the exclusive ambit of the Copyright Act, but the claim failed on its own accord. Conversion requires dominion and control over the chattels involved. In this case, one of a number of copies of a manuscript was removed for a short period of time. The tortious interference with contractual relations claim is preempted by the Copyright Act, because the alleged right (right of the author and his licensed publishers to exercise and enjoy the right of pre-book publication serialization rights) is the same as the exclusive right under the Act of preparing derivative works based on the copyrighted work.

ANALYSIS

Section 301 is designed to separate those state law claims that are fundamentally about copying from those that are fundamentally about something else.

Quicknotes

CONVERSION The act of depriving an owner of his property without permission or justification.

COPYRIGHT ACT Copyright Act of 1976 extends copyright protection to "original works of authorship fixed in any tangible medium of expression, now known or later developed, from which they can be perceived, reproduced, or otherwise communicated, either directly or with the aid of a machine or device." 17 U.S.C. § 102.

COPYRIGHT INFRINGEMENT A violation of one of the exclusive rights granted to an artist pursuant to Article I, section 8, clause 8 of the United States Constitution over the reproduction, display, performance, distribution, and adaptation of his work for a period prescribed by statute.

DERIVATIVE WORK A work of authorship that is based on a previous work.

PREEMPTION Judicial preference recognizing the procedure of federal legislation over state legislation of the same subject matter.

TORTIOUS INTERFERENCE WITH CONTRACTUAL RELATIONSHIP An intentional tort whereby a defendant intentionally elicits the breach of a valid contract resulting in damages.

Video Pipeline, Inc. v. Buena Vista Home Entertainment, Inc.

Distributor of video previews (P) v. Copyright owner (D)

210 F. Supp. 2d 552 (D.N.J. 2002).

NATURE OF CASE: Motion to dismiss state law claims on preemption grounds.

FACT SUMMARY: When Buena Vista Home Entertainment (BVHE) (D) counterclaimed against Video Pipeline, Inc. (P) for copyright infringement and violation of various state law rights, Video Pipeline (P) argued that the counterclaims were preempted by the federal Copyright Act.

RULE OF LAW
If other elements are required, in addition to or instead of, the acts of reproduction, performance, distribution or display, in order to constitute a state-created cause of action, then the right does not lie within the general scope of copyright, and there is no preemption.

FACTS: Buena Vista Home Entertainment (BVHE) (D) manufactures and distributes videos of movies to which it owns the copyright. Video Pipeline, Inc. (P) puts together previews of videos which it markets to home video distributors. Video Pipeline (P) and BVHE (D) made an agreement authorizing Video Pipeline (P) to exhibit copyrighted promotional previews supplied by BVHE (D). When Video Pipeline (P) began streaming these previews via the internet to on-line customers of its video retailers, BVHE (D) rescinded the agreement, demanding return of the previews. Video Pipeline (P) sued BVHE (D) to obtain a declaratory judgment that the internet streaming did not infringe BVHE's (D) copyrights or violate any of BVHE's (D) other rights. BVHE (D) counterclaimed for copyright infringement and violation of various state law rights. Video Pipeline (P) moved to dismiss the state law claims on preemption grounds.

ISSUE: If other elements are required, in addition to or instead of, the acts of reproduction, performance, distribution or display, in order to constitute a state-created cause of action, then does the right lie outside the general scope of copyright so that there is no preemption?

HOLDING AND DECISION: (Simandle, J.) Yes. If other elements are required, in addition to or instead of, the acts of reproduction, performance, distribution or display, in order to constitute a state-created cause of action, then the right does not lie within the general scope of copyright, and there is no preemption. Here, BVHE (D) essentially maintains that Video Pipeline (P) "passed off" its clip previews, which contain BVHE's (D) trademarks, as having been created and produced by BVHE (D). Unfair competition claims involving "passing off" are generally not preempted by federal copyright law. As BVHE (D) correctly contends, passing off claims are not preempted primarily because such claims include the *extra* element of deception or misrepresentation which is not an element of a copyright claim. Thus, BVHE's (D) counterclaim specifically asserting that Video Pipeline (P) engaged in "passing off" under state law unfair competition can be construed to encompass the allegation that Video Pipeline (P) is distributing its own products, here clip previews, and representing to the public that they are those of BVHE (D). This necessarily involves the "extra element" of misrepresentation or deception which is not an element for copyright infringement. As such, the "passing off" claim is an actionable claim not preempted by the federal Copyright Act. So too, BVHE (D) is correct in its assertion that its conversion and replevin claims for the return of its video clips are not preempted because these claims involve "rights to tangible property" not equivalent to the exclusive rights protected by copyright law. This viewpoint, furthermore, is soundly supported by Professor Nimmer [1 Nimmer on Copyright § 1.01[B][1][i], at 1-41 (2001)]. Video Pipeline's (P) motion to dismiss on the grounds of federal preemption is accordingly denied.

ANALYSIS

As set forth in the Copyright Act, a state common law or statutory claim is preempted if: (1) the particular work in question is copyrightable under the Act; and (2) the state law seeks to vindicate "legal or equitable rights that are equivalent" to one of the bundle of exclusive rights already protected by federal copyright. The *Video Pipeline* decision makes clear that a proper preemption analysis, therefore, encompasses both a subject matter requirement and an "equivalency" requirement.

Quicknotes

ACTIONABLE Unlawful activity from which a cause of action may arise.

COPYRIGHT ACT Copyright Act of 1976 extends copyright protection to "original works of authorship fixed in any tangible medium of expression, now known or later developed, from which they can be perceived, reproduced, or otherwise communicated, either directly or with the aid of a machine or device." 17 U.S.C. § 102.

COPYRIGHT INFRINGEMENT A violation of one of the exclusive rights granted to an artist pursuant to Article I,

Continued on next page.

section 8, clause 8 of the United States Constitution over the reproduction, display, performance, distribution, and adaptation of his work for a period prescribed by statute.

COUNTERCLAIM An independent cause of action brought by a defendant to a lawsuit in order to oppose or deduct from the plaintiff's claim.

DECLARATORY JUDGMENT An adjudication by the courts which grants not relief but is binding over the legal status of the parties involved in the dispute.

MOTION TO DISMISS Motion to terminate a trial based on the adequacy of the pleadings.

PREEMPTION Judicial preference recognizing the procedure of federal legislation over state legislation of the same subject matter.

UNFAIR COMPETITION Any dishonest or fraudulent rivalry in trade and commerce, particularly imitation and counterfeiting.

Baltimore Orioles, Inc. v. Major League Baseball Players Association

Major league baseball club (D) v. Major league players association (P)

805 F.2d 663 (7th Cir. 1986), cert. denied, 480 U.S. 941 (1987).

NATURE OF CASE: Appeal from a right of publicity claim.

FACT SUMMARY: The trial court determined that telecasts were copyrightable and that baseball clubs, rather than the players, owned the copyrights in the telecasts.

RULE OF LAW
Baseball players do not have a state law right of publicity in their televised performances.

FACTS: The Major League Baseball Players Association (Players Association) (P) claimed that they have the exclusive rights to the televised performances of players during major league baseball games. The ball clubs (D) own the copyrights in the telecasts of major league baseball games, of which players' televised performances are a part. The Players Association (P) brought this action on behalf of its members, alleging that the televised performances infringed the players' rights of publicity. The district court entered judgment for the defendant, and the baseball players appealed.

ISSUE: Does the Copyright Act preempt the right of publicity claims?

DECISION AND HOLDING: (Eschbach, J.) Yes. The ball clubs' (D) copyright in the telecasts of major league baseball games preempts the players' rights of publicity in their game-time performances. A two-prong test for preemption exists under § 301: (1) the work in which the right is asserted must be fixed in tangible form and come within the subject matter of copyright, as specified in § 102, and (2) the right must be equivalent to any of the rights specified in § 106. The telecasts are fixed in tangible form because they are recorded simultaneously with their transmission and are audiovisual works, which come within the subject matter of copyright. Players' performances are part of these telecasts and, as such, are fixed in tangible form and come within the subject matter of copyright, as specified in § 102. Further, a right in a work conferred by state law is equivalent to a right to perform a telecast of that work if the state law right is infringed merely by broadcasting the work. Here, the players' state law right of publicity is violated merely by the broadcasting of baseball games. Thus, the state law right that players assert in this case meets the two-prong test for preemption by federal copyright law.

ANALYSIS
To be "fixed" in tangible form, a work must be recorded "by or under the authority of the author." Thus, if the author does not tape or otherwise record her performance, she may still assert a state law right of publicity in her performance if a television station tapes and broadcasts her performance.

Quicknotes

COPYRIGHT Refers to the exclusive rights granted to an artist pursuant to Article I, section 8, clause 8 of the United States Constitution over the reproduction, display, performance, distribution, and adaptation of his work for a period prescribed by statute.

COPYRIGHT ACT Copyright Act of 1976 extends copyright protection to "original works of authorship fixed in any tangible medium of expression, now known or later developed, from which they can be perceived, reproduced, or otherwise communicated, either directly or with the aid of a machine or device." 17 U.S.C. § 102.

COPYRIGHT ACT SECTION 102 Section 102 of the Copyright Act of 1976 extends copyright protection to "original works of authorship fixed in any tangible medium of expression, now known or later developed, from which they can be perceived, reproduced, or otherwise communicated, either directly or with the aid of a machine or device." 17 U.S.C. section 102. The statute sets forth the categories included in the term "works of authorship," and denies copyright protection to ideas or procedures.

INFRINGEMENT Conduct in violation of statue or that interferes with another's rights pursuant to law.

PREEMPTION Judicial preference recognizing the procedure of federal legislation over state legislation of the same subject matter.

RIGHT OF PUBLICITY The right of a person to control the commercial exploitation of his name or likeness.

Brown v. Ames

Blues musicians, songwriters, producers, or heirs of such (P) v. Music producer (D)

201 F.3d 654 (5th Cir. 2000).

NATURE OF CASE: Appeal from a state law misappropriation claim.

FACT SUMMARY: The district court determined that appellees' state law claims of misappropriation are not preempted by the Copyright Act.

RULE OF LAW
State law claims asserting rights to privacy and publicity are not preempted under the Copyright Act.

FACTS: During 1990, Ames (D), d/b/a Home Cooking Records, licensed to Collectibles master recordings for commercial exploitation that included performances by appellees. This license agreement also purportedly gave Collectibles the right to use the names, photographs, likenesses, and biographical material of all those whose performances were on the master recordings. Using the master recordings, Collectibles manufactured and distributed CDs as well as music catalogs with the likenesses of the performers on or in them. In 1994, appellees brought this suit for copyright infringement, for violations of the Lanham Act, and for misappropriation of name and likeness under Texas state law. At trial, the jury found that Ames (D) and Collectibles had misappropriated the names and likenesses of the appellees and had infringed copyrights held by some of the appellees. Ames (D) and Collectibles appealed, asserting that the Copyright Act preempts appellees' state-law misappropriation claim.

ISSUE: Does the Copyright Act preempt a state-law claim for misappropriation?

HOLDING AND DECISION: (Jones, J.) No. The right protected by the tort of misappropriation does not fall within the subject matter of copyright. The tort of misappropriation protects a person's persona. A persona is not a writing of an author within the meaning of copyright. Thus, the misappropriation claim does not fit the parameters of § 301 preemption. The claim of misappropriation does not conflict with the purposes of copyright protection. In fact, Congress, in drafting § 301, was aware of state law rights of privacy and publicity and indicated its intention that such state law actions remain. Thus conflict preemption is inappropriate here. Although one court's controversial decision, that of *Baltimore Orioles v. Major League Baseball Players Ass'n*, 805 F.2d 663 (7th Cir. 1986), held that performances in a baseball game were within the subject matter of copyright because the videotape of the game fixed the players' performances in tangible form, the case has been heavily criticized for holding the game to be a protectable work simply because the performance was recorded on videotape that was itself copyrightable. In any event, *Baltimore Orioles* is distinguishable because the instant performers did not give permission to market their recordings or photographs. A name or likeness is not copyrightable simply because they are placed on CD's and tapes or in catalogs that have copyrightable subject matter recorded on them. Affirmed.

ANALYSIS

As the *Brown* decision indicates, the States remain free to promote originality and creativity in their own domains. The case for federal preemption is particularly weak where Congress has indicated its awareness of the operation of state law in a field of federal interest and has nonetheless decided to stand by both concepts and to tolerate whatever tension there is between them.

Quicknotes

COPYRIGHT ACT Copyright Act of 1976 extends copyright protection to "original works of authorship fixed in any tangible medium of expression, now known or later developed, from which they can be perceived, reproduced, or otherwise communicated, either directly or with the aid of a machine or device." 17 U.S.C. § 102.

COPYRIGHT INFRINGEMENT A violation of one of the exclusive rights granted to an artist pursuant to Article I, section 8, clause 8 of the United States Constitution over the reproduction, display, performance, distribution, and adaptation of his work for a period prescribed by statute.

LANHAM ACT Name of the Trademark Act of 1946 which governs federal law regarding trademarks.

MISAPPROPRIATION The unlawful use of another's property or funds.

PREEMPTION Judicial preference recognizing the procedure of federal legislation over state legislation of the same subject matter.

TORT A legal wrong resulting in a breach of duty, which is intentionally or purposefully committed by the wrongdoer.

White v. Samsung Electronics America, Inc.

TV star (P) v. Electronics manufacturer (D)

989 F.2d 1512 (9th Cir. 1993) (en banc).

NATURE OF CASE: Denial of motion for rehearing en banc.

FACT SUMMARY: Vanna White (P), a well-known television personality, contended that an advertisement by Samsung Electronics America, Inc. (D) had usurped her right of publicity, even though her likeness had not been incorporated in the advertisement.

RULE OF LAW
A person's right of publicity may be usurped even if the offending use did not incorporate that person's likeness.

FACTS: Samsung Electronics America, Inc. (Samsung) (D) ran an advertisement showing a robot dressed in a wig, gown, and jewelry in a manner reminiscent of Vanna White (P) of the television game show *Wheel of Fortune*. The advertisement included the caption "Longest running game show," indicating that Samsung (D) would outlast White's (P) run on *Wheel of Fortune*. White (P) sued, alleging violations of state statutory and common law right to publicity and the federal Lanham Act. The district court dismissed, and White (P) appealed.

ISSUE: May a person's right to publicity be usurped even if the offending use did not incorporate that person's likeness?

HOLDING AND DECISION: (Holding and decision not stated in casebook excerpt.)

DISSENT: (Kozinski, J.) The majority erred in holding that the right of publicity extends beyond name and likeness to any "appropriation" of one's identity, to anything that evokes one's personality. The majority's holding squashed creativity and robbed the public of the right to create and enjoy parodies of celebrities. Beyond simply misinterpreting California state law, however, the majority's decision directly contradicted the federal Copyright Act. Copyright law provides the right to make "fair use" parodies. Additionally, by broadly interpreting California right to publicity law, the majority gave California far too much control over artists in other states. In doing so, they violated the dormant clause of the Copyright Act that maintains that state intellectual property laws can stand only as long as they don't prejudice the interests of other States.

▶ ANALYSIS

A similar and better-known case was *Midler v. Ford Motor Co.*, 849 F.2d 460 (9th Cir. 1988). There, Ford had unsuccessfully attempted to persuade entertainer Bette Midler to release the rights to her version of the song "Do You Want to Dance" to be used in an advertisement. Ford then hired a Midler "sound-alike" to record the song, which Ford then incorporated into an advertisement. Midler successfully argued that her right of publicity had been violated.

Quicknotes

COPYRIGHT ACT Copyright Act of 1976 extends copyright protection to "original works of authorship fixed in any tangible medium of expression, now known or later developed, from which they can be perceived, reproduced, or otherwise communicated, either directly or with the aid of a machine or device." 17 U.S.C. § 102.

EN BANC The hearing of a matter by all the judges of the court, rather than only the necessary quorum.

FAIR USE An affirmative defense to a claim of copyright infringement providing an exception from the copyright owner's exclusive rights in a work for the purposes of criticism, comment, news reporting, teaching, scholarship or research; the determination of whether a use is fair is made on a case-by-case basis and requires the court to consider: (1) the purpose and character of the use; (2) the nature of the work; (3) the amount and substantiality of the portion used; and (4) the effect of the use on the potential market for, or value of, the work.

LANHAM ACT Name of the Trademark Act of 1946 which governs federal law regarding trademarks.

International News Service v. Associated Press

News service (D) v. News service (P)

248 U.S. 215 (1918).

NATURE OF CASE: Action for unfair competition in trade.

FACT SUMMARY: Associated Press (AP) (P) brought suit against International News Service (INS) (D) for "pirating" its dispatches published by AP-member newspapers and distributing them.

RULE OF LAW
A party engages in unfair competition when it interferes without authorization in the other party's normal business operations in order to divert a portion of profits for its own benefit.

FACTS: Associated Press (AP) (P) and International News Service (INS) (D) were competing organizations in the business of gathering and disseminating news for publication in the United States. AP (P) brought suit against INS (D) for "pirating" dispatches published by AP (P) and distributing them to INS (D) papers. The district court enjoined INS (D) from obtaining the news reports. The court of appeals broadened the injunction. INS (D) appealed.

ISSUE: Does a party engage in unfair competition when it interferes without authorization in the other party's normal business operations in order to divert a portion of profits for its own benefit?

HOLDING AND DECISION: (Pitney, J.) Yes. A party engages in unfair competition when it interferes without authorization in the other party's normal business operations in order to divert a portion of profits for its own benefit. INS (D), by its very act, admits it is taking material that has been acquired by AP (P) as the result of organization and the expenditure of labor, skill, money, and which is salable by AP (P) for money, and that INS (D) in appropriating it and selling it as its own is endeavoring to reap where it has not sown, and by disposing of it to newspapers that are competitors of AP's (P) members is appropriating to itself the harvest of those who have sown it. This process amounts to an unauthorized interference with the normal operation of AP's (P) business precisely at the point where the profit is to be reaped. The transaction speaks for itself. News matter, however little susceptible of ownership or dominion in the absolute sense, is stock in trade, to be gathered at the cost of enterprise, organization, skill, labor and money, and to be distributed and sold to those who will pay money for it, as for any other merchandise. As between news gatherers, therefore, the news must be regarded as quasi-property, irrespective of the rights of either, as against the public.

DISSENT: (Holmes, J.) When an uncopyrightable work is published there is no right to protection from it being copied.

DISSENT: (Brandeis, J.) Knowledge and ideas, after their voluntary communication to others, become free for common use. The only exceptions are communications which involve creation, invention, or discovery. Creation of a new private right in this regard may cause serious injury to the general public unless the boundaries of such new right are definitely established and wisely guarded. This, however, would be a legislative matter.

ANALYSIS

As the Supreme Court points out in the *INS* decision, INS's (D) contention that the news is abandoned to the public for all purposes when published in the first newspaper by the AP (P), is untenable. Abandonment is a question of intent, and the entire organization of the AP (P) negated such a purpose because the cost of the service would be prohibitive if the reward were so limited. The Court reasoned that permitting indiscriminate publication by anybody for profit in competition with the original news gatherer would render publication so little profitable as in effect to cut off the service.

Quicknotes

INJUNCTION A court order requiring a person to do or prohibiting that person from doing a specific act.

QUASI-CONTRACT An implied contract created by law to prevent unjust enrichment.

UNFAIR COMPETITION Any dishonest or fraudulent rivalry in trade and commerce, particularly imitation and counterfeiting.

National Basketball Association v. Motorola, Inc.

Professional sports association (P) v. Manufacturer of paging device (D)

105 F.3d 841 (2d Cir. 1997).

NATURE OF CASE: Appeal from a claim asserting copyright infringement and misappropriation.

FACT SUMMARY: The district court dismissed the National Basketball Association's (NBA) (P) federal claims for relief but granted a permanent injunction on the NBA's (P) state-law misappropriation claim.

RULE OF LAW
A "hot news" misappropriation claim may survive preemption for material within the realm of copyright law.

FACTS: In January 1996, Motorola, Inc. (D) made available to the public the SportsTrax paging device to supply users with information on sporting events. SportsTrax relies on a "data feed" supplied by Sports Team Analysis and Tracking Systems (STATS) reporters who watch the games on television or listen to them on the radio. The reporters, using personal computers, track score changes during NBA games, as well as successful and missed shots, fouls, and clock updates. The information is relayed by modem to the STATS host computer, where it is compiled, analyzed, and formatted for retransmission to SportsTrax users via a common carrier and hence by satellite to various local FM radio networks, which in turn emit the signal received by the individual SportsTrax pagers. The National Basketball Association's (NBA) (P) brought a number of claims against Motorola (D) and SportsTrax, including a copyright infringement claim and a state law misappropriation claim. The district court below dismissed the NBA's (P) federal claims for relief, but granted a permanent injunction on the NBA's (P) misappropriation claim.

ISSUE: Can a "hot news" misappropriation claim survive preemption for actions concerning material within the realm of copyright?

HOLDING AND DECISION: (Winter, J.) Only a narrow "hot news" misappropriation claim survives preemption for actions concerning material within the realm of copyright. The additional elements that allow a "hot news" claim to survive preemption are (1) the time-sensitive value of factual information; (2) free riding by a defendant; and (3) the threat to the very existence of the product or service provided by the plaintiff. In this case, Motorola (D) and SportsTrax are engaged in the collection of facts about NBA (P) games, the transmission of these facts on a network, the assembly of these facts by a specific service, and the transmission of the facts to pagers or an on-line server. In this way, Motorola (D) and SportsTrax expend their own resources, rather than free-ride on the NBA's (P) product, Gamestats. They are thus not engaged in unlawful misappropriation under the "hot news" test.

ANALYSIS

In another part of this decision, *National Basketball Association v. Motorola* rejects a partial preemption rule.

Quicknotes

COPYRIGHT Refers to the exclusive rights granted to an artist pursuant to Article I, section 8, clause 8 of the United States Constitution over the reproduction, display, performance, distribution, and adaptation of his work for a period prescribed by statute.

COPYRIGHT INFRINGEMENT A violation of one of the exclusive rights granted to an artist pursuant to Article I, section 8, clause 8 of the United States Constitution over the reproduction, display, performance, distribution, and adaptation of his work for a period prescribed by statute.

COPYRIGHT LAW Copyright Act of 1976 extends copyright protection to "original works of authorship fixed in any tangible medium of expression, now known or later developed, from which they can be perceived, reproduced, or otherwise communicated, either directly or with the aid of a machine or device." 17 U.S.C. § 102.

INJUNCTION A court order requiring a person to do or prohibiting that person from doing a specific act.

MISAPPROPRIATION The unlawful use of another's property or funds.

PREEMPTION Judicial preference recognizing the procedure of federal legislation over state legislation of the same subject matter.

Bowers v. Baystate Technologies, Inc.

Patent holder (P) v. Software developer (D) [Party designations on counterclaim]

320 F.3d 1317 (Fed. Cir.), cert. denied, 539 U.S. 928 (2003).

NATURE OF CASE: Appeal from judgment for counterclaim plaintiff on claim of breach of contract.

FACT SUMMARY: Baystate Technologies, Inc. (D), which a jury had found had violated a shrinkwrap license prohibiting reverse engineering of patented software offered by Bowers (P), contended that the Copyright Act preempted the prohibition on reverse engineering.

RULE OF LAW
The Copyright Act does not preempt a prohibition on reverse engineering contained in a shrinkwrap license.

FACTS: Bowers (P) offered patented software with a shrinkwrap license that prohibited reverse engineering. Baystate Technologies, Inc. (Baystate) (D) brought a declaratory judgment action of non-infringement, invalidity, or unenforceability of the Bowers (P) patent, and Bowers (P) counterclaimed for copyright infringement and breach of contract based on Baystate's (D) reverse engineering of the Bowers (P) software. A jury found for Bowers (P), as counterclaim plaintiff, on both claims. The court of appeals granted review.

ISSUE: Does the Copyright Act preempt a prohibition on reverse engineering contained in a shrinkwrap license?

HOLDING AND DECISION: (Rader, J.) No. The Copyright Act does not preempt a prohibition on reverse engineering contained in a shrinkwrap license. Courts respect freedom of contract and do not lightly set aside freely-entered agreements, and most courts that have faced this issue have ruled that the Copyright Act does not preempt contractual constraints on copying. Preemption is precluded where a state cause of action requires an extra element, beyond mere copying, preparation of derivative works, performance, distribution or display. Because a state law contract claim has additional elements of proof beyond those in a copyright claim, Bowers' (P) contract claim is not preempted. It should also be noted that such a holding is not inconsistent with precedent that provides that reverse engineering is a copyright fair use, or with the Digital Millennium Copyright Act, which expressly provides that reverse engineering is not copyright infringement. Finally, while the Fifth Circuit has held a state law prohibiting all copying of a computer program is preempted by the federal Copyright Act, *Vault Corp. v. Quaid Software, Ltd.*, 847 F.2d 255 (5th Cir. 1988), the precedent followed by this court would not extend this concept to include private contractual agreements supported by mutual assent and consideration. Because the record supports that Baystate (D) reverse engineered Bowers' (P) software, and because Bowers' (P) license clearly prohibited such conduct, the jury's finding that Baystate (D) breached the license agreement must be upheld. Affirmed.

CONCURRENCE AND DISSENT: (Dyk, J.) The majority's approach eviscerates the fair use defense and copyright policy. The test for preemption by copyright law should be whether the state law "substantially impedes the public use of the otherwise unprotected" material. The "equivalent in substance" test used by the majority to determine whether a state law is preempted by the Copyright Act provides that a state law action is equivalent in substance to a copyright infringement claim and thus preempted by the Copyright Act where the additional element merely concerns the extent to which authors and their licensees can prohibit unauthorized copying by third parties. Because a state is not free to eliminate the fair use defense, a state law that allows a copyright holder to simply label its products so as to eliminate a fair use defense would "substantially impede" the public's right to fair use and allow the copyright holder, through state law, to protect material that is unprotectible under the Copyright Act as a fair use. Although the majority correctly concludes that a state may permit parties to freely negotiate away the fair use defense or to agree not to engage in uses of copyrighted material that are permitted by the copyright law—the free negotiation being the extra element required by the equivalence in substance test—a shrinkwrap license does not constitute such free negotiation. Instead, a shrinkwrap license is a contract of adhesion, since the only choice offered to the purchaser is to avoid making the purchase in the first place. Thus, state law permits the copyright holder to eliminate the fair use defense—or any other protection in the Copyright Act for that matter—in every instance at its option. Finally, the majority misreads the *Vault* case. There, the Fifth Circuit held that the specific provision of state law that authorized contracts prohibiting reverse engineering, decompilation, or disassembly of computer programs was preempted by federal law because it conflicted with a portion of the Copyright Act and because it "'touched upon an area' of federal copyright law." However, from a preemption standpoint, there is no distinction between a state law that explicitly validates a contract that restricts reverse engineering (*Vault*) and general common law that permits such a restriction (as here). On the contrary, the preemption clause of the Copyright Act makes clear that it covers "any such right or equivalent right in any such work under the common law or statutes of any State."

Continued on next page.

ANALYSIS

The court did not reach Bowers' (P) copyright claim because the district court had omitted from the final damage award what it found were duplicative copyright damages, finding that the breach of contract damages arose from the same copying and included the same lost sales that formed the basis for the copyright damages. Because the court affirmed the district court's omission of the copyright damages, it did not need to reach the merits of Bowers' (P) copyright infringement claim. However, even if it had, presumably it would have ruled that Baystate's (D) conduct was a fair use exception to copyright infringement, based on its explanation that its holding on the preemption issue left untouched *Atari Games Corp. v. Nintendo of Am., Inc.*, 975 F.2d 832, (Fed. Cir. 1992), which provides that reverse engineering is a copyright fair use.

Quicknotes

BREACH OF CONTRACT Unlawful failure by a party to perform its obligations pursuant to contract.

COPYRIGHT ACT Copyright Act of 1976 extends copyright protection to "original works of authorship fixed in any tangible medium of expression, now known or later developed, from which they can be perceived, reproduced, or otherwise communicated, either directly or with the aid of a machine or device." 17 U.S.C. § 102.

COPYRIGHT INFRINGEMENT A violation of one of the exclusive rights granted to an artist pursuant to Article I, Section 8, clause 8 of the United States Constitution over the reproduction, display, performance, distribution, and adaptation of his work for a period prescribed by statute.

COUNTERCLAIM An independent cause of action brought by a defendant to a lawsuit in order to oppose or deduct from the plaintiff's claim.

DAMAGES Monetary compensation that may be awarded by the court to a party who has sustained injury or loss to his person, property or rights due to another party's unlawful act, omission or negligence.

DECLARATORY JUDGMENT A judgment of the court establishing the rights of the parties.

FAIR USE An affirmative defense to a claim of copyright infringement providing an exception from the copyright owner's exclusive rights in a work for the purposes of criticism, comment, news reporting, teaching, scholarship or research; the determination of whether a use is fair is made on a case-by-case basis and requires the court to consider: (1) the purpose and character of the use; (2) the nature of the work; (3) the amount and substantiality of the portion used; and (4) the effect of the use on the potential market for, or value of, the work.

CHAPTER 11

The Copyright Infringement Lawsuit

Quick Reference Rules of Law

	PAGE

1. **Proper Court.** When a complaint alleges a claim or seeks a remedy provided by the Copyright Act, federal jurisdiction is properly invoked. (Bassett v. Mashantucket Pequot Tribe) — 177

2. **The Registration Requirement and Filing Too Early.** A copyright holder's failure to comply with the registration requirement of § 411(a) of the Copyright Act does not restrict a federal court's subject-matter jurisdiction over infringement claims involving unregistered works. (Reed Elsevier, Inc. v. Muchnick) — 178

3. **Filing Too Late.** In the case of continuing copyright infringements, an action may be brought for all acts that accrued within the three years preceding the filing of the suit. (Roley v. New World Pictures, Ltd.) — 180

4. **Proper Plaintiffs (Standing): Copyright Infringement.** An exclusive license in a particular market is sufficient to confer standing as long as the license is memorialized in a writing signed by the owner of the copyright. (Eden Toys, Inc. v. Florelee Undergarment Co.) — 181

5. **Proper Plaintiffs (Standing): Declaratory Judgment Actions.** An actual controversy exists in copyright litigation when there exists a "reasonable apprehension" of litigation and when the declaratory plaintiff actually has produced or is prepared to produce an infringing product. (Bryan Ashley International, Inc. v. Shelby Williams Industries, Inc.) — 182

6. **Proper Defendants.** The Copyright Remedy Clarification Act is an improper exercise of congressional legislative power. (Chavez v. Arte Publico Press) — 183

7. **Jury Trial.** The Seventh Amendment provides a right to a jury trial when the copyright owner elects to recover statutory damages. (Feltner v. Columbia Pictures Television, Inc.) — 184

8. **International Issues.** The interests of the parties in copyright property are determined by the law of the state with the most significant relationship to the property and the parties. (Itar-Tass Russian News Agency v. Russian Kurier, Inc.) — 185

9. **International Issues.** The holder of a foreign copyright who sues for infringement in the United States courts is entitled to the same remedies as is a holder of a United States copyright. (Bridgeman Art Library, Ltd. v. Corel Corp.) — 186

10. **Civil Remedies: Injunctions.** In the special circumstances in which great public injury would be worked by an injunction, the courts might instead award damages or a continuing royalty. (Abend v. MCA, Inc.) — 187

11. **Civil Remedies: Injunctions.** The future sale or lease of an infringing copy will not be enjoined where the copy is manifested in a permanent building or structure and the balance of hardships and the public interest weigh against such an injunction. (Christopher Phelps & Associates, LLC v. Galloway) — 188

CHAPTER 11

12. **Civil Remedies: Injunctions.** (1) In determining whether to grant a permanent copyright injunction, irreparable harm may not be presumed where liability has been established. (2) For purposes of determining whether a permanent copyright injunction should issue, irreparable harm is demonstrated either where the defendant has induced and would continue to induce far more infringement than it could ever possibly redress with damages or where the defendant's inducement of infringement renders copyrights particularly vulnerable to continuing infringement on an enormous scale. (Metro-Goldwyn-Mayer Studios, Inc. v. Grokster, Ltd.) — 190

13. **Civil Remedies: Injunctions.** The focus of injunctive relief is on the defendants before the court. (Universal City Studios, Inc. v. Reimerdes) — 192

14. **Civil Remedies: Damages and Profits.** In apportioning damages under Section 504(a) of the Copyright Act, the goal is to award damages proportionate to the contribution of the copyright owner and no more. (Frank Music Corp. v. Metro-Goldwyn-Mayer Inc.) — 193

15. **Civil Remedies: Damages and Profits.** A court may resolve, as a matter of law, that a copyright infringer's revenues are not attributable to infringement where there is no conceivable connection between the infringement and a given revenue stream or where, despite the existence of a conceivable link, the plaintiff has failed to offer anything more than mere speculation as to the existence of a causal connection between the infringement and the claimed revenues. (Bouchat v. Baltimore Ravens Football Club, Inc.) — 194

16. **Civil Remedies: Damages and Profits.** The Copyright Act does not apply extraterritorially except where an act of infringement is completed entirely within the United States and such infringing act enabled further exploitation abroad. (Los Angeles News Service v. Reuters Television International, Ltd.) — 197

17. **Civil Remedies: Statutory Damages.** (1) Copyright infringement is "willful" where as a matter of law the infringer recklessly disregards the copyright holder's property rights and its reliance on a fair-use defense is objectively unreasonable. (2) A court does not abuse its discretion in awarding statutory copyright damages where the court recognizes that it has discretion and the record does not support a finding that the court failed to exercise this discretion. (3) Statutory copyright damages awarded in a civil action cannot violate the Constitution's Eighth Amendment as an excessive fine where the government neither prosecutes the action nor participates in the award. (4) A statutory copyright damages award does not violate due process where it is not so severe and oppressive as to be wholly disproportioned to the offense and obviously unreasonable. (Zomba Enterprises, Inc. v. Panorama Records, Inc.) — 198

18. **Civil Remedies: Attorneys' Fees.** An award of attorneys' fees to a prevailing defendant that has furthered the underlying purposes of the Copyright Act rests in the sound discretion of the district courts, and such discretion is not limited by a requirement of culpability on the part of the losing party. (Fantasy, Inc. v. Fogerty) — 201

19. **Civil Remedies: Attorneys' Fees.** A court does not abuse its discretion in denying a request for attorney's fees for successfully defending a copyright infringement claim where the court has based its decision on factors such as frivolousness, motivation, and objective reasonableness. (Positive Black Talk Inc. v. Cash Money Records Inc.) — 202

Bassett v. Mashantucket Pequot Tribe

Film and television producer (P) v. Indian tribe (D)

204 F.3d 343 (2d Cir. 2000).

NATURE OF CASE: Appeal from the grant of a motion to dismiss a claim asserting breach of contract and copyright infringement.

FACT SUMMARY: The district court granted defendant's motion to dismiss for lack of subject matter jurisdiction.

RULE OF LAW
When a complaint alleges a claim or seeks a remedy provided by the Copyright Act, federal jurisdiction is properly invoked.

FACTS: Debra Bassett (P) operates Bassett Productions (P), a business that produces films and television programs. In October 1994, Bassett (P) met with representatives of the Mashantucket Pequot Tribe (Tribe) (D) to discuss the possibility of producing a film about the 1636-1638 Pequot War. In August 1995, Bassett Productions (P) entered into a letter agreement (Letter Agreement) with the Tribe (D) for the development and production of the film. The Letter Agreement defined Bassett Productions (P) as the producer of the film and the Tribe (D) as the owner. It also stipulated that "at such time" that the Tribe (D) approved the final draft of the screenplay, Bassett Productions (P) would have the exclusive rights to produce the film for exhibition at the Pequot Museum. Some time prior to October 30, 1995, Bassett (P) delivered a script for the proposed film to the Tribe (D). On October 30, 1995, the Tribe (D) sent notice to Bassett (P), terminating the Letter Agreement. Following the termination of the Letter Agreement, the Tribe (D) continued to pursue the development and production of a film on the 1636-1638 Pequot War for exhibition at the Museum. In October 1996, filming was completed on a film set to screen at the museum in the "near future" as part of a tourist attraction. Bassett (P) commenced this suit in September 1996, seeking an injunction and other copyright remedies. The district court dismissed Bassett's (P) suit on the defendant's motion for lack of subject matter jurisdiction, and Bassett (P) appealed.

ISSUE: How should § 1338 jurisdiction be analyzed in hybrid copyright and contract cases?

HOLDING AND DECISION: (Leval, J.) The two part *T.B. Harms* test should be applied. In this way, a suit arises under the Copyright Act if the complaint is for a remedy expressly granted by the Act or the complaint asserts a claim requiring construction of the Act. In this case, Bassett's (P) claim alleges defendants violated the Copyright Act and seeks an injunctive remedy expressly granted by the Act. Thus, Bassett's (P) action falls within the jurisdictional grant of § 1338. Reversed.

ANALYSIS
Pursuant to supplemental jurisdiction under § 1367, a federal court may assert subject matter jurisdiction over additional claims that are so related to claims in the action within original jurisdiction that they form part of the same case or controversy.

Quicknotes

BREACH OF CONTRACT Unlawful failure by a party to perform its obligations pursuant to contract.

COPYRIGHT ACT Copyright Act of 1976 extends copyright protection to "original works of authorship fixed in any tangible medium of expression, now known or later developed, from which they can be perceived, reproduced, or otherwise communicated, either directly or with the aid of a machine or device." 17 U.S.C. § 102.

COPYRIGHT INFRINGEMENT A violation of one of the exclusive rights granted to an artist pursuant to Article I, section 8, clause 8 of the United States Constitution over the reproduction, display, performance, distribution, and adaptation of his work for a period prescribed by statute.

INJUNCTION A court order requiring a person to do or prohibiting that person from doing a specific act.

MOTION TO DISMISS Motion to terminate a trial based on the adequacy of the pleadings.

REMEDY Compensation for violation of a right or injuries sustained.

Reed Elsevier, Inc. v. Muchnick

Online publisher (D) v. Freelance author (P)

___U.S.___, 130 S. Ct. 1237 (2010).

NATURE OF CASE: Appeal from reversal of approval of settlement of class action for copyright infringement.

FACT SUMMARY: Over the objections of freelance authors (P), the district court approved the settlement of a copyright infringement class action between publishers (D) and authors (P) relating to both registered and unregistered works. The court of appeals sua sponte raised the question whether § 411(a) of the Copyright Act deprives federal courts of subject-matter jurisdiction over infringement claims involving unregistered copyrights, concluding that the district court lacked jurisdiction to certify the class or approve the settlement.

RULE OF LAW
A copyright holder's failure to comply with the registration requirement of § 411(a) of the Copyright Act does not restrict a federal court's subject-matter jurisdiction over infringement claims involving unregistered works.

FACTS: Authors (P) separately brought suit against online and print publishers (D) for copyright infringement. The suits were consolidated into a class action, with the consolidated complaint alleging that the named plaintiffs each owned at least one copyright, typically in a freelance article written for a newspaper or a magazine, that they had registered in accordance with § 411(a) of the Copyright Act. The class, however, included both authors who had registered their copyrighted works and authors who had not. Over the objections of freelance authors (P), the district court approved the certification of the class and the settlement of the class action, and entered final judgment. On appeal, the court of appeals sua sponte raised the question whether § 411(a) deprives federal courts of subject-matter jurisdiction over infringement claims involving unregistered copyrights, concluding that the district court lacked jurisdiction to certify the class or approve the settlement. The court of appeals accordingly reversed, and the Supreme Court granted certiorari.

ISSUE: Does a copyright holder's failure to comply with the registration requirement of § 411(a) of the Copyright Act restrict a federal court's subject-matter jurisdiction over infringement claims involving unregistered works?

HOLDING AND DECISION: (Thomas, J.) No. A copyright holder's failure to comply with the registration requirement of § 411(a) of the Copyright Act does not restrict a federal court's subject-matter jurisdiction over infringement claims involving unregistered works. Because the distinction between jurisdictional conditions and claim-processing rules can be confusing in practice, federal courts and litigants should use the term "jurisdictional" only when it is apposite. A statutory requirement is considered jurisdictional if Congress has clearly stated that the requirement count as jurisdictional; a condition not ranked as such should be treated as nonjurisdictional in character. Therefore, it must be determined whether § 411(a) "clearly states" that its registration requirement is jurisdictional. The answer is that it does not. Although § 411(a)'s last sentence contains the word "jurisdiction," that sentence speaks to a court's adjudicatory authority to determine a copyright claim's registrability and says nothing about whether a federal court has subject-matter jurisdiction to adjudicate claims for infringement of unregistered works. Moreover, § 411(a)'s registration requirement is located in a provision separate from those granting federal courts subject-matter jurisdiction over those respective claims, and no other factor suggests that the registration requirement can be read to "speak in jurisdictional terms or refer in any way to the jurisdiction of the district courts." Section 411(a) contains several exceptions that permit courts to adjudicate infringement claims involving unregistered works, and it would be unusual to ascribe jurisdictional significance to a condition subject to these sorts of exceptions. Threshold requirements that claimants must complete, or exhaust, before filing a lawsuit have also been held to be nonjurisdictional, and the registration requirement is such a threshold requirement, since it imposes a precondition to filing a claim that is not clearly labeled jurisdictional, is not located in a jurisdiction-granting provision, and admits of congressionally authorized exceptions. This result is not changed by looking to the Court's precedent in *Bowles v. Russell*, 551 U.S. 205 (2007). *Bowles* does not stand for the proposition that where Congress did not explicitly label a statutory condition as jurisdictional, a court nevertheless should treat it as such if that is how the condition consistently has been interpreted and if Congress has not disturbed that interpretation. Instead, *Bowles* stands for the proposition that context, including the Court's interpretation of similar provisions in many years past, is relevant to whether a statute ranks a requirement as jurisdictional. The treatment of § 411(a)'s registration requirement as jurisdictional over the years is one factor of the context that must be considered, but it is not a dispositive factor. The other factors, already discussed, lead to the conclusion that the registration requirement is more akin to a nonjurisdictional precondition. Accordingly, § 411(a)'s

Continued on next page.

registration requirement is nonjurisdictional, notwithstanding its prior jurisdictional treatment. Reversed.

ANALYSIS

Section 411(a) expressly allows courts to adjudicate infringement claims involving unregistered works in three circumstances: where the work is not a U.S. work, where the infringement claim concerns rights of attribution and integrity under § 106A, or where the holder attempted to register the work and registration was refused. Separately, § 411(c) permits courts to adjudicate infringement actions over certain kinds of unregistered works where the author "declare[s] an intention to secure copyright in the work" and "makes registration for the work, if required by subsection (a), within three months after [the work's] first transmission." 17 U.S.C. §§ 411(c)(1)-(2).

Quicknotes

CERTIORARI A discretionary writ issued by a superior court to an inferior court in order to review the lower court's decisions; the Supreme Court's writ ordering such review.

CLASS ACTION A suit commenced by a representative on behalf of an ascertainable group that is too large to appear in court, who shares a commonality of interests and who will benefit from a successful result.

COPYRIGHT ACT Copyright Act of 1976 extends copyright protection to "original works of authorship fixed in any tangible medium of expression, now known or later developed, from which they can be perceived, reproduced, or otherwise communicated, either directly or with the aid of a machine or device." 17 U.S.C. § 102.

COPYRIGHT INFRINGEMENT A violation of one of the exclusive rights granted to an artist pursuant to Article I, Section 8, clause 8 of the United States Constitution over the reproduction, display, performance, distribution, and adaptation of his work for a period prescribed by statute.

SUA SPONTE An action taken by the court by its own motion and without the suggestion of one of the parties.

Roley v. New World Pictures, Ltd.
Screen writer (P) v. Film financier (D)

19 F.3d 479 (9th Cir. 1994).

NATURE OF CASE: Claim of copyright infringement.

FACT SUMMARY: The district court dismissed an infringement claim as barred by the three-year statute of limitations mandated by the Copyright Act.

RULE OF LAW
In the case of continuing copyright infringements, an action may be brought for all acts that accrued within the three years preceding the filing of the suit.

FACTS: Some time before 1972, Roley (P) wrote a screenplay originally entitled "A Little Visit Home." He later renamed the screenplay "Sleep Tight, Little Sister." In 1985, Roley (P) gave defendant Coblenz, a friend and successful film producer, the original copy of his work to produce as a screenplay. Coblenz declined the project. In August 1987, Coblenz invited Roley (P) to a screening of his new movie "Sister, Sister," financed by New World Entertainment Limited. After viewing the film, Roley (P) concluded that it was a production of his screenplay "Sleep Tight, Little Sister." Coblenz denied this claim, advising Roley (P) that the film was based upon a 1970s screenplay by Ginny Cerrella entitled "Louisiana Swamp Murders." Roley (P) retained counsel in pursuing a copyright infringement action. In late 1987 and early 1988, New World's insurance carrier, Fireman's Fund, rejected Roley's (P) claim, advising him that it found no similarity between the two works and, in any event, the screenplay for the film was written independently of Coblenz. The film opened unsuccessfully and was withdrawn from distribution. It was subsequently shown on television in 1988 and 1992. Roley (P) filed his complaint against Coblenz and New World in February 1991. In June 1992, both Coblenz and New World filed motions for summary judgment, arguing that Roley's (P) copyright infringement claims were barred by the three-year statute of limitations.

ISSUE: When does a copyright infringement action accrue?

HOLDING AND DECISION: (Tang, J.) The Copyright Act bars recovery on any claim for damages that accrued more than three years before commencement of the suit. Roley (P) filed this copyright infringement claim in February 7, 1991. Thus, the statute bars recovery of any damages that accrued prior to February 7, 1988. Roley's (P) action accrued in August 1987, when he attended the screening of "Sister, Sister." Because Roley (P) failed to produce any evidence that appellees engaged in actionable conduct after February 7, 1988, the district court's summary judgments were affirmed.

ANALYSIS

Once a defendant establishes a statute of limitations defense, the plaintiff may then be able to show reasons for tolling the statute. Under the Copyright Act, tolling must be predicated upon an equitable ground recognized under federal law.

Quicknotes

ACTIONABLE Unlawful activity from which a cause of action may arise.

COPYRIGHT ACT Copyright Act of 1976 extends copyright protection to "original works of authorship fixed in any tangible medium of expression, now known or later developed, from which they can be perceived, reproduced, or otherwise communicated, either directly or with the aid of a machine or device." 17 U.S.C. § 102.

COPYRIGHT INFRINGEMENT A violation of one of the exclusive rights granted to an artist pursuant to Article I, section 8, clause 8 of the United States Constitution over the reproduction, display, performance, distribution, and adaptation of his work for a period prescribed by statute.

STATUTE OF LIMITATIONS A law prescribing the period in which a legal action may be commenced.

SUMMARY JUDGMENT Judgment rendered by a court in response to a motion by one of the parties, claiming that the lack of a question of material fact in respect to an issue warrants disposition of the issue without consideration by the jury.

Eden Toys, Inc. v. Florelee Undergarment Co.

Toy manufacturer (P) v. Undergarment manufacturer (D)

697 F.2d 27 (2d Cir. 1982).

NATURE OF CASE: Suit for copyright infringement by exclusive licensee.

FACT SUMMARY: The district court found that a nightshirt manufactured by an undergarment manufacturer featured a character largely identical to a character drawn by a toy manufacturer.

RULE OF LAW
An exclusive license in a particular market is sufficient to confer standing as long as the license is memorialized in a writing signed by the owner of the copyright.

FACTS: Paddington and Company, Limited (Paddington), a British corporation, holds all rights to Paddington Bear children's books and all characters therein. In 1975, Paddington entered into an agreement with Eden Toys, Inc. (P), an American corporation, granting Eden Toys (P) exclusive North American rights to produce and sell, and to sublicense the production and sale of, a number of Paddington products. This agreement was amended in 1980 to grant Eden Toys (P) the exclusive North American rights to produce and sublicense all Paddington products except books, tapes and records, stage plays, motion pictures, and radio and television productions. Between 1975 and 1977, Ivor Wood, the illustrator for the Paddington books, drew a series of sketches for the use of Eden Toys (P) and its sublicensees. Using the Wood sketches as a point of departure, the C.R. Gibson Company, pursuant to a sublicense from Eden Toys (P), produced a design for gift wrap that included seven drawings of Paddington Bear. In November 1979, Eden Toys (P) discovered that Florelee Undergarment Co. (D) was selling a nightshirt featuring a print of a bear found by the district court to be "identical in all respects" to one of the Eden/Gibson drawings of Paddington Bear. Eden Toys (P) commenced this copyright infringement suit as the exclusive North American licensee of Paddington products. Eden Toys (P) admitted that adult clothing was not clearly among the licensed products listed in the 1975 agreement between Eden Toys (P) and Paddington, but it contended that it had been operating under an informal understanding with Paddington, later formalized in 1980, giving Eden Toys (P) the exclusive North American right to produce any Paddington Bear product except books, records, and a few other items not relevant in this case.

ISSUE: When will something short of an assignment of the copyright be sufficient to confer standing?

HOLDING AND DECISION: (Mansfield, J.) To maintain a copyright infringement claim, a non-owner of the copyright must allege that they have an exclusive license in the market being infringed. For valid exclusive licenses, the statute of frauds provision of the Copyright Act requires an instrument of conveyance, or a note or memorandum of transfer signed by the owner of the rights conveyed. If Eden Toys (P) could not assert such an exclusive license, it could not maintain this copyright infringement suit in its own name. Paddington had, however, granted Eden Toys (P) an informal exclusive license in the market in which Florelee (D) sold—adult clothing—an informal license later confirmed in a writing signed by Paddington. Thus, Eden Toys (P) could sue in its own name, without joining Paddington, for infringement of any Paddington-owned copyrights in that market.

ANALYSIS
Although exclusive licensees have standing to maintain a copyright infringement action, agents do not. *Plunkett v. Doyle,* 2001 Copr. L. Dec. § 28,237 (S.D.N.Y. 2001), stands for the proposition that a literary rights manager who holds the rights to manage, negotiate, license, and otherwise cause and permit exploitation of copyrighted works lacks standing under the Copyright Act because she is neither an owner nor an exclusive licensee of the works.

Quicknotes

COPYRIGHT Refers to the exclusive rights granted to an artist pursuant to Article I, section 8, clause 8 of the United States Constitution over the reproduction, display, performance, distribution, and adaptation of his work for a period prescribed by statute.

COPYRIGHT ACT Copyright Act of 1976 extends copyright protection to "original works of authorship fixed in any tangible medium of expression, now known or later developed, from which they can be perceived, reproduced, or otherwise communicated, either directly or with the aid of a machine or device." 17 U.S.C. § 102.

COPYRIGHT INFRINGEMENT A violation of one of the exclusive rights granted to an artist pursuant to Article I, section 8, clause 8 of the United States Constitution over the reproduction, display, performance, distribution, and adaptation of his work for a period prescribed by statute.

Bryan Ashley International, Inc. v. Shelby Williams Industries, Inc.

Furniture seller (P) v. Furniture seller (D)

932 F. Supp. 290 (S.D. Fla. 1996).

NATURE OF CASE: Action seeking a declaratory judgment.

FACT SUMMARY: Plaintiff seeks declaratory judgment that its activities do not infringe defendant's copyright.

RULE OF LAW
An actual controversy exists in copyright litigation when there exists a "reasonable apprehension" of litigation and when the declaratory plaintiff actually has produced or is prepared to produce an infringing product.

FACTS: Bryan Ashley International, Inc. (Bryan Ashley) (P) and Shelby Williams Industries, Inc. (Shelby) (D) sell furniture, including rattan and wicker items. On September 5, 1995, Shelby's (D) counsel sent a letter warning Bryan Ashley (P) of its alleged misappropriation of Shelby's (D) intellectual property and demanding that Bryan Ashley (P) cease and desist from the alleged misappropriation or risk disgorgement of profits improperly gained as well as reimbursement to defendant for attorneys' fees incurred. In response, Bryan Ashley (P) filed this declaratory judgment action, seeking a declaration that it had not violated the Copyright Act. Shelby (D) contended that no actual controversy existed and moved for partial judgment on the pleadings.

ISSUE: Does an actual controversy exist when the purported copyright owner has not asserted a claim of copyright infringement?

HOLDING AND DECISION: (Highsmith, J.) Yes. An actual controversy can exist when the purported copyright owner has not asserted a claim of copyright infringement under two circumstances: (1) when there is a threat or other action by the copyright owner that creates a reasonable apprehension on the part of the declaratory plaintiff that it will face an infringement suit; and (2) when the accused infringer or declaratory plaintiff actually has produced or is prepared to produce an allegedly infringing product. In this case, the letter from Shelby's (D) counsel amounted to an action creating a "reasonable apprehension" of litigation, satisfying the first requirement, and the continued sale of the potentially infringing products satisfied the second requirement. Thus, Bryan Ashley (P) sufficiently demonstrated that an actual controversy existed in this case.

ANALYSIS

The *Bryan Ashley* case illustrates that sending a cease-and-desist letter may have serious consequences for control over the forum in which the ensuing litigation may occur.

Quicknotes

CEASE AND DESIST ORDER An order from a court or administrative agency prohibiting a person or business from continuing a particular course of conduct.

COPYRIGHT Refers to the exclusive rights granted to an artist pursuant to Article I, section 8, clause 8 of the United States Constitution over the reproduction, display, performance, distribution, and adaptation of his work for a period prescribed by statute.

COPYRIGHT ACT Copyright Act of 1976 extends copyright protection to "original works of authorship fixed in any tangible medium of expression, now known or later developed, from which they can be perceived, reproduced, or otherwise communicated, either directly or with the aid of a machine or device." 17 U.S.C. § 102.

COPYRIGHT INFRINGEMENT A violation of one of the exclusive rights granted to an artist pursuant to Article I, section 8, clause 8 of the United States Constitution over the reproduction, display, performance, distribution, and adaptation of his work for a period prescribed by statute.

DECLARATORY JUDGMENT An adjudication by the courts which grants not relief but is binding over the legal status of the parties involved in the dispute.

INTELLECTUAL PROPERTY A body of law pertaining to the ownership of rights in intangible products of the human intellect.

MISAPPROPRIATION The unlawful use of another's property or funds.

Chavez v. Arte Publico Press

Author (P) v. Publisher (D)

204 F.3d 601 (5th Cir. 2000).

NATURE OF CASE: Copyright infringement claim.

FACT SUMMARY: Copyright infringement claimant alleges that a state university is constitutionally subject to suit under the Copyright Remedy Clarification Act (CRCA).

RULE OF LAW
The CRCA is an improper exercise of congressional legislative power.

FACTS: Plaintiff Chavez sued the Arte Publico Press (D) of the University of Houston, alleging that the university infringed her copyright by continuing to publish her book without her consent. The University of Houston countered that it enjoyed immunity from an unconsented-to suit in federal court under the Eleventh Amendment and that, therefore, Chavez's (P) suit should be dismissed.

ISSUE: Did Congress have authority to abrogate state sovereign immunity in the CRCA?

HOLDING AND DECISION: (Jones, J.) No. Congress may abrogate the states' sovereign immunity when acting to enforce constitutional rights pursuant to section 5 of the Fourteenth Amendment. The three-part test to be applied in this determination involves an examination of (1) the nature of the injury to be remedied, (2) Congress's consideration of the adequacy of state remedies to redress the injury, and (3) the coverage of the legislation. The CRCA's legislative history identifies no pattern of copyright infringement by the states and barely considered the availability of state remedies for infringement, and Congress did nothing to confine the reach of CRCA by limiting the remedy to certain types of infringement or providing for suits only against states with questionable remedies or a high incidence of infringement. Thus, the CRCA failed the three-part test for constitutional abrogations of sovereign immunity. Case dismissed.

ANALYSIS

If states can infringe the rights of copyright owners, the United States may be in violation of its international treaty obligations.

Quicknotes

COPYRIGHT INFRINGEMENT A violation of one of the exclusive rights granted to an artist pursuant to Article I, section 8, clause 8 of the United States Constitution over the reproduction, display, performance, distribution, and adaptation of his work for a period prescribed by statute.

FOURTEENTH AMENDMENT Declares that no state shall make or enforce any law which shall abridge the privileges and immunities of citizens of the United States.

REMEDY Compensation for violation of a right or injuries sustained.

SOVEREIGN IMMUNITY Immunity of government from suit without its consent.

Feltner v. Columbia Pictures Television, Inc.

Television station owner (D) v. Television broadcaster (P)

523 U.S. 340 (1998).

NATURE OF CASE: Copyright infringement action alleging unauthorized broadcasting of television programs.

FACT SUMMARY: The District Court denied Columbia Pictures Television, Inc.'s (P) request for a jury trial on statutory damages, and the court of appeals affirmed.

RULE OF LAW
The Seventh Amendment provides a right to a jury trial when the copyright owner elects to recover statutory damages.

FACTS: Petitioner Feltner (D) owns Krypton International Corporation (Krypton). In 1990, Krypton acquired three television stations in the southeastern United States. Columbia Pictures Television, Inc. (Columbia) (P) licensed several television series to these stations, including "Who's the Boss," "Silver Spoons," "Hart to Hart," and "T.J. Hooker." After the stations became delinquent in making their royalty payments to Columbia (P), Krypton and Columbia (P) entered into negotiations to restructure the stations' debt. These discussions were unavailing, and Columbia (P) terminated the stations' license agreements in October 1991. Despite Columbia's (P) termination, the stations continued broadcasting the programs. Columbia (P) sued Feltner (D), Krypton, the stations, various Krypton subsidiaries, and certain Krypton officers, alleging copyright infringement arising from the stations' unauthorized broadcasting of the programs.

ISSUE: Does the Seventh Amendment provide a right to a jury trial on the issue of statutory damages under the Copyright Act?

HOLDING AND DECISION: (Thomas, J.) Yes. The Seventh Amendment applies not only to common-law causes of action, but also to actions brought to enforce statutory rights analogous to those common-law causes of action ordinarily decided in English law courts, as opposed to those customarily heard by courts of equity or admiralty, in the late eighteenth century. Prior to the adoption of the Seventh Amendment, the common law and statutes in both England and the United States granted copyright owners causes of action for infringement. Such copyright suits were tried in courts of law, before juries. The Court recognized the "general rule" that monetary relief is legal and that an award of statutory damages may serve purposes traditionally associated with legal relief, such as compensation and punishment.

ANALYSIS

Typically, plaintiffs in infringement actions will seek both damages and injunctive relief. In such actions, all damage claims are triable to a jury.

Quicknotes

CAUSE OF ACTION A fact or set of facts the occurrence of which entitle a party to seek judicial relief.

COPYRIGHT ACT Copyright Act of 1976 extends copyright protection to "original works of authorship fixed in any tangible medium of expression, now known or later developed, from which they can be perceived, reproduced, or otherwise communicated, either directly or with the aid of a machine or device." 17 U.S.C. § 102.

COPYRIGHT INFRINGEMENT A violation of one of the exclusive rights granted to an artist pursuant to Article I, section 8, clause 8 of the United States Constitution over the reproduction, display, performance, distribution, and adaptation of his work for a period prescribed by statute.

INJUNCTIVE RELIEF A court order issued as a remedy, requiring a person to do, or prohibiting that person from doing, a specific act.

ROYALTY Payment to the owner of property for the use or sale of such property either as a percentage of profits or per unit sold.

SEVENTH AMENDMENT Provides that no fact tried by a jury shall be otherwise re-examined in any court of the United States, other than according to the rules of the common law.

Itar-Tass Russian News Agency v. Russian Kurier, Inc.

Russian newspaper agency (P) v. Publisher (D)

153 F.3d 82 (2d Cir. 1998).

NATURE OF CASE: Appeal from a decision granting relief for copyright infringements.

FACT SUMMARY: Russian Kurier, Inc. (D) copied approximately 500 articles from Itar-Tass Russian News Agency's (P) publications without permission.

RULE OF LAW
The interests of the parties in copyright property are determined by the law of the state with the most significant relationship to the property and the parties.

FACTS: Kurier (D) is a Russian language weekly newspaper circulating in New York City. Itar-Tass Russian News Agency (Itar-Tass) (P) is a Russian newswire service and news gathering company based in Moscow. Kurier (D) copied about 500 articles that first appeared in Itar's (P) publications and distributions. The copied material, though extensive, was a small percentage of the total number of articles published in Kurier (D). The district court enjoined Kurier (D) from copying articles that have appeared or will appear in Itar's (P) publications, and it awarded Itar (P) substantial damages for copyright infringement. Kurier (D) appealed.

ISSUE: Are the interests of the parties in copyright property determined by the law of the state with the most significant relationship to the property and parties?

HOLDING AND DECISION: (Newman, J.) Yes. The interests of the parties in copyright property are determined by the law of the state with the most significant relationship to the property and the parties. Since the works at issue were created by Russian nationals and first published in Russia, Russian law is the appropriate source of law to determine issues of ownership rights. Selection of Russian law to determine copyright ownership is, however, subject to one procedural qualification. Under United States law, an owner (including one determined according to foreign law) may sue for infringement in a United States court only if it meets the standing test of 17 U.S.C. § 501(b), which accords standing only to the legal or beneficial owner of an exclusive right. On infringement issues, the governing conflicts principle is usually the place of the tort, which in this case is clearly the United States. Therefore, United States law still applies to the infringement issues. The division of issues between ownership and infringement issues will not always be easily made. If the issue is the relatively straightforward one of which of two contending parties owns a copyright, the issue is unquestionably an ownership issue, and the law of the country with the closet relationship to the work will apply to settle the ownership issue. But in some cases, including this one, the issue is not simply who owns the copyright but also what is the nature of the ownership interest. Yet as a court considers the nature of an ownership interest, there is some risk that it will readily shift the inquiry over to the issue of whether an alleged copy has infringed the asserted copyright. Whether a copy infringes depends in part on the scope of the interest of the copyright owner. Though the issues are related, the nature of a copyright interest is an issue distinct from the issue of whether the copyright has been infringed. This case is one that requires consideration not simply of who owns an interest, but as to the newspapers, the nature of the interest that is owned. As Itar-Tass (P) is within the scope of Article 14 of the Russian Copyright Law and enjoys the benefit of the Russian version of the work-for-hire doctrine, Itar-Tass (P) is entitled to injunctive relief to prevent unauthorized copying of its articles and to damages for such copying. Affirmed.

ANALYSIS

The place of a work's first publication is an important factor in determining what national law applies to issues of copyright ownership under the rule set out here. But this case should not be misunderstood to hold that copyright ownership issues will always be governed by the law of the country where the works were first published. In some cases, ownership will be appropriately determined by the law of a state which has the most significant relationship to the property and the parties.

Quicknotes

COPYRIGHT Refers to the exclusive rights granted to an artist pursuant to Article I, section 8, clause 8 of the United States Constitution over the reproduction, display, performance, distribution, and adaptation of his work for a period prescribed by statute.

COPYRIGHT INFRINGEMENT A violation of one of the exclusive rights granted to an artist pursuant to Article I, section 8, clause 8 of the United States Constitution over the reproduction, display, performance, distribution, and adaptation of his work for a period prescribed by statute.

INJUNCTIVE RELIEF A court order issued as a remedy, requiring a person to do, or prohibiting that person from doing, a specific act.

Bridgeman Art Library, Ltd. v. Corel Corp.

Copyright holder (P) v. Competitor (D)

36 F. Supp. 2d 191 (S.D.N.Y. 1999).

NATURE OF CASE: Appeal from summary judgment entered in favor of alleged infringer.

FACT SUMMARY: The Bridgeman Art Library, Ltd. (P) brought a claim for copyright infringement against Corel Corp. (D).

RULE OF LAW
The holder of a foreign copyright who sues for infringement in the United States courts is entitled to the same remedies as is a holder of a United States copyright.

FACTS: Bridgeman Art Library, Ltd. (Bridgeman) (P) had the rights to market reproductions of art in the public domain owned by museums and other collectors. Bridgeman (P) reproduced identical copies of the works in transparencies and digital files and distributed them in CD-ROM format. Corel Corp. (D) also marketed software, including reproductions of artwork in the public domain. Bridgeman (P) commenced an action against Corel (D) for copyright infringement. The district court entered summary judgment in favor of Corel (D).

ISSUE: Does the Berne Convention require application of foreign law in determining the existence of a valid copyright?

HOLDING AND DECISION: (Kaplan, J.) No. The sole source of copyright protection in the United States is the Copyright Act. Although under the Berne Convention, United States courts will extend certain copyright protections to foreign copyright holders, those protections cannot exceed what is allowed in the Copyright Act. Here, Bridgeman (P) sought to enforce a British copyright in foreign works that are not original. Under the Copyright Act there is no protection for works that are not original, and thus the copyright cannot be enforced in a United States court.

ANALYSIS

Article 5 of the Berne Convention provides that "[a]uthors shall enjoy, in respect of works for which they are protected under this Convention, in countries of the Union other than the country of origin, the rights which their respective laws do now or may hereafter grant to their nationals, as well as the rights specially granted by this convention," and that "the extent of protection, as well as the means of redress of the country where protection is claimed."

Quicknotes

COPYRIGHT Refers to the exclusive rights granted to an artist pursuant to Article I, section 8, clause 8 of the United States Constitution over the reproduction, display, performance, distribution, and adaptation of his work for a period prescribed by statute.

COPYRIGHT ACT Copyright Act of 1976 extends copyright protection to "original works of authorship fixed in any tangible medium of expression, now known or later developed, from which they can be perceived, reproduced, or otherwise communicated, either directly or with the aid of a machine or device." 17 U.S.C. § 102.

COPYRIGHT INFRINGEMENT A violation of one of the exclusive rights granted to an artist pursuant to Article I, section 8, clause 8 of the United States Constitution over the reproduction, display, performance, distribution, and adaptation of his work for a period prescribed by statute.

REMEDY Compensation for violation of a right or injuries sustained.

SUMMARY JUDGMENT Judgment rendered by a court in response to a motion by one of the parties, claiming that the lack of a question of material fact in respect to an issue warrants disposition of the issue without consideration by the jury.

Abend v. MCA, Inc.

Screenplay writer (P) v. Film producer (D)

863 F.2d 1465 (9th Cir. 1988).

NATURE OF CASE: Copyright infringement action seeking injunctive relief.

FACT SUMMARY: The owner of the rights to the underlying story behind a motion picture sought to enjoin the owners of the derivative motion picture from further exhibition of the movie.

RULE OF LAW
In the special circumstances in which great public injury would be worked by an injunction, the courts might instead award damages or a continuing royalty.

FACTS: Cornell Woolrich wrote the story "It Had to Be Murder," which was first published in February 1942. In 1945, Woolrich agreed to assign the rights to make motion picture versions of six of his stories, including "It Had to Be Murder," to B.G. De Sylva Productions. He also agreed to renew the copyrights in the stories at the appropriate time and to assign the same motion picture rights to De Sylva Productions for the 28-year renewal term. In 1953, Jimmy Stewart and Alfred Hitchcock's production company, Patron, Inc., obtained the motion picture rights in "It Had to Be Murder" from De Sylva's successors in interest. In 1954, Patron, along with Paramount Pictures, produced and distributed "Rear Window," the motion picture version of Woolrich's story. Woolrich died in 1968 without surviving spouse or child before he could obtain for Patron, as promised, the rights in the renewal term. Woolrich left his property to a trust administered by his executor, Chase Manhattan Bank. Chase Manhattan assigned the renewal rights to Abend (P) for $650 plus 10% of all proceeds from exploitation of the story. "Rear Window" was broadcast on the ABC television network in 1971. Abend (P) notified Stewart and Hitchcock that he owned the renewal rights in the copyright and that their distribution of the motion picture without his permission infringed his copyright in the story. Hitchcock and Stewart nevertheless entered into a second license with ABC to rebroadcast the motion picture. In 1974, Abend (P) commenced this suit alleging copyright infringement.

ISSUE: Would money damages in lieu of injunctive relief weaken the economic incentives created by copyright law?

HOLDING AND DECISION: (Pregerson, J.) No. Where great public injury would be worked by an injunction, the courts might in such special circumstances award damages or a continuing royalty instead. In this case, the success of "Rear Window" had much to do with the performances of Grace Kelly and James Stewart, the directing of Alfred Hitchcock, and the substantial money and effort expended by Patron. An injunction would work a great injustice for the owners of the film and would prevent them from enjoying legitimate profits derived from exploitation of the "new matter" comprising the derivative work, which is given express copyright protection by § 7 of the 1909 Act. The injunction would also deprive the public for many years to come of the opportunity to view a classic film. The district court is deemed capable of calculating damages caused to the fair market value of plaintiff's story by the re-release of the film.

ANALYSIS

Some suggest that the court's decision in *Abend* effectively created a compulsory license. A compulsory license scheme is described as a liability regime. Congress has instituted compulsory licenses in certain areas of the Copyright Act.

Quicknotes

COPYRIGHT Refers to the exclusive rights granted to an artist pursuant to Article I, section 8, clause 8 of the United States Constitution over the reproduction, display, performance, distribution, and adaptation of his work for a period prescribed by statute.

COPYRIGHT ACT Copyright Act of 1976 extends copyright protection to "original works of authorship fixed in any tangible medium of expression, now known or later developed, from which they can be perceived, reproduced, or otherwise communicated, either directly or with the aid of a machine or device." 17 U.S.C. § 102.

COPYRIGHT INFRINGEMENT A violation of one of the exclusive rights granted to an artist pursuant to Article I, section 8, clause 8 of the United States Constitution over the reproduction, display, performance, distribution, and adaptation of his work for a period prescribed by statute.

DERIVATIVE WORK A work of authorship that is based on a previous work.

ENJOIN The ordering of a party to cease the conduct of a specific activity.

INJUNCTION A court order requiring a person to do or prohibiting that person from doing a specific act.

INJUNCTIVE RELIEF A court order issued as a remedy, requiring a person to do, or prohibiting that person from doing, a specific act.

Christopher Phelps & Associates, LLC v. Galloway

Architectural firm (P) v. Homeowner (D)

492 F.3d 532 (4th Cir. 2007).

NATURE OF CASE: Appeal from denial of injunction in copyright infringement action.

FACT SUMMARY: Christopher Phelps & Associates, LLC (Phelps & Associates) (P) contended that it was entitled to permanently enjoin Galloway's (D) future sale or lease of a house that he built using Phelps & Associates' (P) copyrighted architectural plans without permission.

RULE OF LAW
The future sale or lease of an infringing copy will not be enjoined where the copy is manifested in a permanent building or structure and the balance of hardships and the public interest weigh against such an injunction.

FACTS: After Galloway (D) began construction of a house using architectural plans designed and copyrighted by Christopher Phelps & Associates, LLC (Phelps & Associates) (P), without permission, Phelps & Associates (P) sued Galloway (D) for copyright infringement and sought damages, disgorgement of profits, and injunctive relief. A jury found that Galloway (D) infringed Phelps & Associates' (P) copyright and awarded it $20,000 in damages. The district court declined to enter an injunction, finding that the jury verdict had made Phelps & Associates (P) "whole." Phelps & Associates (P) appealed, seeking entry of an injunction prohibiting the future lease or sale of the infringing house and mandating the destruction or return of the infringing plans. The court of appeals granted review.

ISSUE: Will the future sale or lease of an infringing copy be enjoined where the copy is manifested in a permanent building or structure and the balance of hardships and the public interest weigh against such an injunction?

HOLDING AND DECISION: (Niemeyer, J.) No. The future sale or lease of an infringing copy will not be enjoined where the copy is manifested in a permanent building or structure and the balance of hardships and the public interest weigh against such an injunction. Whether to grant an injunction rests in the court's equitable discretion, and, ordinarily, a party will be entitled to an injunction where it has demonstrated that: (1) it has suffered an irreparable injury; (2) remedies available at law are inadequate to compensate for that injury; (3) considering the balance of hardships between the plaintiff and defendant, a remedy in equity is warranted; and (4) the public interest would not be disserved by a permanent injunction. Here, Phelps & Associates (P) has demonstrated the first two factors, but not the third and fourth. The first factor is satisfied because irreparable injury often derives from the nature of copyright violations, which deprive the copyright holder of intangible exclusive rights. The second factor is satisfied because damages at law will not remedy the continuing existence of Phelps & Associates' (P) design in the Galloway (D) house. Moreover, while the calculation of future damages and profits for each future sale might be possible, any such effort would entail a substantial amount of speculation that renders the effort difficult or impossible at this point. As to the third and fourth factors, Phelps & Associates (P) has already been compensated for the copying and use of its design. A sale of the house would not be a second copy or manifestation of the design, but merely a transfer of the structure in which the design was first copied. An injunction against sale would benefit Phelps & Associates' (P) legitimate interests only slightly because the infringing house would retain the same form and location, remaining a permanent nuisance to the copyright regardless of whether there is an injunction. An injunction against sale would neither undo the prior infringement, nor diminish the chances of future copying. At the same time, a permanent injunction would impose a draconian burden on Galloway (D), effectively creating a lis pendens on the house and subjecting him to contempt proceedings simply for selling his own property. Additionally, a building such as the house at issue has a predominantly functional character, which is why injunctions are not routinely issued against substantially completed houses whose designs violate architectural copyrights, especially where the houses are inhabited. The inhabitant's interest in remaining in the house, with the same rights as other homeowners to alienate his property, is substantial and, in this case, trumps Phelps & Associates' (P) interests in any injunction prohibiting a lease or sale of the house. Another reason the third and fourth factors are not satisfied is that an injunction against sale of the house would be overbroad, as it would encumber a great deal of property unrelated to the infringement, thus essentially rendering the injunction punitive in nature. Such an injunction also would undermine an ancient reluctance by the courts to restrain the alienability of real property. Finally, the ultimate discretion to grant the requested injunctive relief rests with the district court, and there has been no evidence presented that it abused its discretion. Phelps & Associates' (P) argument that denial of the injunction is tantamount to a judicially-created license must be rejected because remedies under the Copyright Act are much broader than a mere license. An infringer risks not only having to pay damages and

Continued on next page.

disgorging profits, but also risks destruction of the infringing copy. While granting an injunction to destroy an infringing article might be usual with respect to personal property, refusing to order destruction or the inalienability of property is also consistent with the Copyright Act's remedial scheme. Affirmed as to this issue. [Remanded for consideration of whether destruction of the plans should be ordered.]

ANALYSIS

American copyright law, pre-Berne Convention, denied protection to constructed architectural works altogether, as they were considered "useful articles." For that reason, such structures remained unprotected by United States copyright law from passage of the current Copyright Act until enactment of an amendment, the Architectural Works Copyright Protection Act of 1990 (Act). Prior to this legislation, copyright protection for the work of design professionals was afforded only to drawings and specifications. Thus, the author of the design had no copyright remedy if a duplicate structure was constructed from the original drawings and specifications or from the building itself, provided the drawings and specifications were themselves not copied. Although under the Act a copyright holder has the exclusive right to prepare derivative works from the original, the right to make or distribute copies and the right to publish the work, infringement of which exclusive rights theoretically entitles the owner to injunctive relief to stop the infringement and to monetary damages, this case demonstrates that courts will continue to exercise their discretion in whether to issue injunctions under the Act.

Quicknotes

COPYRIGHT ACT Copyright Act of 1976 extends copyright protection to "original works of authorship fixed in any tangible medium of expression, now known or later developed, from which they can be perceived, reproduced, or otherwise communicated, either directly or with the aid of a machine or device." 17 U.S.C. § 102.

COPYRIGHT INFRINGEMENT A violation of one of the exclusive rights granted to an artist pursuant to Article I, Section 8, clause 8 of the United States Constitution over the reproduction, display, performance, distribution, and adaptation of his work for a period prescribed by statute.

DAMAGES Monetary compensation that may be awarded by the court to a party who has sustained injury or loss to his person, property or rights due to another party's unlawful act, omission or negligence.

INJUNCTION A court order requiring a person to do, or prohibiting that person from doing, a specific act.

INJUNCTIVE RELIEF A court order issued as a remedy, requiring a person to do, or prohibiting that person from doing, a specific act.

LIS PENDENS A pending action.

Metro-Goldwyn-Mayer Studios, Inc. v. Grokster, Ltd.

Copyright owners (P) v. Software distributor (D)

518 F. Supp. 2d 1197 (N.D. Cal. 2007).

NATURE OF CASE: Motion for permanent injunction in copyright infringement action on remand from U.S. Supreme Court.

FACT SUMMARY: When Grokster, Ltd. (D) and StreamCast Networks, Inc. (D) freely distributed software by which any computer user could easily and without payment download copyrighted music, Metro-Goldwin-Mayer Studios Inc. (MGM) (P) and other movie studios, recording companies, songwriters, and music publishers sued Grokster (D) and StreamCast (D) for their users' infringements and sought to permanently enjoin such infringements.

RULE OF LAW
(1) In determining whether to grant a permanent copyright injunction, irreparable harm may not be presumed where liability has been established.

(2) For purposes of determining whether a permanent copyright injunction should issue, irreparable harm is demonstrated either where the defendant has induced and would continue to induce far more infringement than it could ever possibly redress with damages or where the defendant's inducement of infringement renders copyrights particularly vulnerable to continuing infringement on an enormous scale.

FACTS: Grokster, Ltd. (D) and StreamCast Networks, Inc. (D) distributed software, free of charge, by which users of computers could share electronic files through so-called peer-to-peer networks by which the users' computers communicated with others directly, not through central servers. Grokster (D) and StreamCast (D) used no servers to intercept the content of the search requests or to mediate the file transfers conducted by users of the software, there being no central point through which the substance of the communications passes in either direction. Nearly 90% of the files available for download on Grokster's (D) and StreamCast's (D) system were copyrighted works. Over 100 million copies of the software in question were downloaded, and billions of files were shared across the networks each month. Copyright infringement by users of the software was conceded by Grokster (D) and StreamCast (D). Grokster (D) and StreamCast (D) received no direct revenue from the copyright infringement itself, but rather from the sale of advertising on its website. Also, StreamCast (D) gave away software with the goal of capturing email addresses of users so it could promote its software interface, which would be used to induce copyright infringement. A group of copyright holders ("MGM," for short) (P) sued Grokster (D) and StreamCast (D) for copyright infringement. The district court, although holding that those who used the Grokster (D) and StreamCast (D) software to download copyrighted material were indeed infringers (a point not here contested), the court, nonetheless, granted summary judgment in favor of Grokster (D) and StreamCast (D) as to any infringement liability from distribution of their software on the grounds that such distribution did not provide the distributors with actual knowledge of specific acts of infringement. The court of appeals affirmed, but the U.S. Supreme Court reversed, finding that Grokster (D) and StreamCast (D) could be liable on a theory of inducing copyright infringement. The Court remanded the case to the district court, which found Grokster (D) and StreamCast (D) liable for inducing copyright infringement, and MGM (P) moved for a permanent injunction against Grokster (D) and StreamCast (D).

ISSUE:
(1) In determining whether to grant a permanent copyright injunction, may irreparable harm be presumed where liability has been established?

(2) For purposes of determining whether a permanent copyright injunction should issue, is irreparable harm demonstrated either where the defendant has induced and would continue to induce far more infringement than it could ever possibly redress with damages or where the defendant's inducement of infringement renders copyrights particularly vulnerable to continuing infringement on an enormous scale?

HOLDING AND DECISION: (Wilson, J.)
(1) No. In determining whether to grant a permanent copyright injunction, irreparable harm may not be presumed where liability has been established. The appropriate test after *eBay Inc. v. MercExchange, L.L.C.*, 547 U.S. 388 (2006) for determining whether a permanent copyright injunction should be granted is the traditional four-part test, not a two-part test that asks only if there has been past infringement and whether there is a likelihood of future infringements. The first part of the four-part test asks whether the copyright holder has suffered an irreparable injury. In the past, pre-*eBay*, courts presumed irreparable injury from a finding of liability. However, the Supreme Court in *eBay* made clear that the plaintiff bears the burden on all four injunction factors, including irreparable injury, and courts to have considered the issue post-*eBay* have so held. Therefore, irreparable harm can be established

Continued on next page.

neither solely on the fact of past infringement nor by showing the mere likelihood of future infringement by a defendant, which can be remedied by actual or statutory damages.

(2) Yes. For purposes of determining whether a permanent copyright injunction should issue, irreparable harm is demonstrated either where the defendant has induced and would continue to induce far more infringement than it could ever possibly redress with damages or where the defendant's inducement of infringement renders copyrights particularly vulnerable to continuing infringement on an enormous scale. StreamCast's (D) argument, that copyright infringement can itself never represent irreparable harm where damages—including statutory damages—can be calculated, is not convincing. Some judges have argued that because copyright entails the right to exclude, irreparable harm can occur from mere infringement given the difficulty of protecting a right to exclude through monetary remedies. Others, however, have reasoned that the existence of a right to exclude does not dictate the remedy for a violation of that right. The latter position is more convincing, since a contrary conclusion would come close to permitting a presumption of irreparable harm. Nevertheless, this latter position does not preclude a finding of irreparable harm based on infringement where the qualities of the infringement are such as to require a court, in the exercise of its equitable discretion, to issue an injunction. That is the case here, where certain qualities pertaining to the nature of StreamCast's (D) inducement of infringement are relevant to a finding of irreparable harm. Here, there are two qualities of the infringement that serve as independent bases for finding irreparable harm: (1) StreamCast (D) has and will continue to induce far more infringement than it could ever possibly redress with damages; and (2) MGM's (P) copyrights have and will be rendered particularly vulnerable to continuing infringement on an enormous scale due to StreamCast's (D) inducement. First, given the evidence of massive end-user infringement, it is likely that StreamCast (D) would not be able to pay either actual or statutory damages for past infringement. The amount of infringement that StreamCast (D) could induce in the future is also staggering. Therefore, in this case, StreamCast's (D) likely inability to pay renders damages meaningless and makes equitable relief necessary since MGM (P) has suffered and would continue to suffer irreparable harm absent such relief. Second, a substantial number of MGM's (P) copyrighted works have and would continue to become irreparably exposed to infringement on a tremendous scale due to StreamCast's (D) inducement, which greatly erodes MGM's (P) ability to enforce its exclusive rights. Again, there would be no realistic mechanism for assessing statutory damages for such massive infringement, even through numerous lawsuits against direct infringers—in fact, the need to bring numerous lawsuits by itself is reason to hold that StreamCast's (D) infringement has caused irreparable injury. For these reasons, MGM (P) has satisfied the first part of the four-part test for a permanent injunction. [The other three parts are also satisfied]. The permanent injunction requested by MGM (P) is granted.

ANALYSIS

Unlike a permanent injunction, which resolves the merits of a claim and imposes an equitable remedy because a legal one is inadequate, a preliminary injunction maintains a particular relationship between the parties in anticipation of a decision on the merits, pending completion of the litigation. Therefore, it is arguable that even post-*eBay*, a plaintiff should be absolved of proving irreparable harm at such an early stage and that a showing of a likelihood of success on the merits should give rise to a presumption of irreparable harm. Some courts have taken this position and have assumed the continued existence of a presumption of irreparable harm for preliminary injunctions. Other courts, including the court in this case, however, have taken the position that *eBay* stands for the principle that a presumption of irreparable harm for a preliminary injunction is "contrary to traditional equitable principles," and that such a presumption should not be given effect unless required by statute. Because there is no language in the text of the Copyright Act that would permit a departure from traditional equitable principles, these courts hold that there is no presumption of irreparable harm for either a preliminary or permanent injunction.

Quicknotes

COPYRIGHT ACT Copyright Act of 1976 extends copyright protection to "original works of authorship fixed in any tangible medium of expression, now known or later developed, from which they can be perceived, reproduced, or otherwise communicated, either directly or with the aid of a machine or device." 17 U.S.C. § 102.

COPYRIGHT INFRINGEMENT A violation of one of the exclusive rights granted to an artist pursuant to Article I, Section 8, clause 8 of the United States Constitution over the reproduction, display, performance, distribution, and adaptation of his work for a period prescribed by statute.

ENJOIN The ordering of a party to cease the conduct of a specific activity.

INJUNCTION A court order requiring a person to do, or prohibiting that person from doing, a specific act.

PERMANENT INJUNCTION A remedy imposed by the court ordering a party to cease the conduct of a specific activity until the final disposition of the cause of action.

Universal City Studios, Inc. v. Reimerdes

Motion picture studios (P) v. Computer hackers (D)

111 F. Supp. 2d 294 (S.D.N.Y. 2000), *aff'd sub nom. Universal City Studios, Inc. v. Corley*, 273 F.3d 429 (2d Cir. 2001).

NATURE OF CASE: Action under the Digital Millennium Copyright Act (DCMA) to enjoin defendants' actions.

FACT SUMMARY: Computer hackers developed a computer program that circumvents the encryption system protecting motion pictures on DVDs from being copied.

RULE OF LAW
The focus of injunctive relief is on the defendants before the court.

FACTS: Plaintiffs distribute many of their motion pictures for home use on digital versatile disks (DVDs), which contain copies of the motion pictures in digital form. They protect these motion pictures from copying by using an encryption system called CSS. In September 1999, Jon Johansen, a fifteen-year-old Norwegian boy and two individuals he met under pseudonyms on the Internet, reverse engineered a licensed DVD player and discovered the CSS encryption algorithm and keys. Using this information, Johansen created DeCSS, a program capable of decrypting encrypted DVDs, thereby allowing playback on non-compliant computers as well as the copying of decrypted files to computer hard drives. Mr. Johansen then posted the executable code on his website, informing members of an Internet mailing list that he had done so. The movie studios became aware of the availability of DeCSS on the Internet in October 1999. The industry proceeded to send a number of cease and desist letters to various websites posting DeCSS, some of which removed it from their sites. In January 2000, the film industry brought this action under the DMCA. Defendants responded by engaging in "electronic civil disobedience"—increasing their efforts to link their website to a large number of others that continued to make DeCSS available. Further, defendants contended that their actions did not violate DMCA and, in the alternative, that DMCA, as applied to computer programs or code violates the First Amendment.

ISSUE: Is a permanent injunction remedy appropriate when the activity being enjoined is mirrored by numerous others?

HOLDING AND DECISION: (Kaplan, J.) Yes. An injunction remedy is appropriate when there is a reasonable likelihood of future violations and the plaintiff lacks an adequate remedy at law. The fact that the defendants in this case linked their website to mirror sites in order to assist users of the defendant's website in obtaining DeCSS, despite the injunction barring defendants from providing it directly, suggested a substantial likelihood of future violations absent injunctive relief. In this case, actual damages were nearly impossible to prove. Further, because the DeCSS code remained available to much of the world via Internet postings, among other problems, statutory damages were rendered an inadequate means of redressing the motion picture industry's damages. By concluding that an injunction would be inappropriate in this case simply because many others, at defendant's urging, were posting DeCSS, making an injunction against defendant futile, would have created the wrong incentives for defendants. Defendants confronted with the possibility of injunctive relief would thus encourage others to engage in the same unlawful conduct in order to set up the argument that an injunction would be futile. The court ruled, therefore, that appropriate injunctive and declaratory relief should issue.

ANALYSIS

The defendants in *Reimerdes*, as an expression of their First Amendment rights, linked to other sites to mirror their DeCSS technology after the preliminary injunction. The question arises of whether the permanent injunction violates the First Amendment.

Quicknotes

DECLARATORY RELIEF A judgment of the court establishing the rights of the parties.

ENJOIN The ordering of a party to cease the conduct of a specific activity.

FIRST AMENDMENT Prohibits Congress from enacting any law respecting an establishment of religion, prohibiting the free exercise of religion, abridging freedom of speech or the press, the right of peaceful assembly and the right to petition for a redress of grievances.

INJUNCTION A court order requiring a person to do or prohibiting that person from doing a specific act.

INJUNCTIVE RELIEF A court order issued as a remedy, requiring a person to do, or prohibiting that person from doing, a specific act.

Frank Music Corp. v. Metro-Goldwyn-Mayer Inc.

Copyright owner (P) v. Motion picture licensee (D)

886 F.2d 1545 (9th Cir. 1989).

NATURE OF CASE: Appeal from a reconsideration of the amount of profits attributable to a copyright infringement.

FACT SUMMARY: Plaintiffs challenge the district court's apportionment of damages.

RULE OF LAW
In apportioning damages under Section 504(a) of the Copyright Act, the goal is to award damages proportionate to the contribution of the copyright owner and no more.

FACTS: Frank Music Corp. (P) is the copyright owner and author of *Kismet*, a dramatic musical work. Metro-Goldwyn-Mayer Inc. (MGM) (D) produced a musical motion picture version of *Kismet* under license from Frank (P). From April 26, 1974, to July 16, 1976, MGM Grand presented a musical revue entitled "Hallelujah Hollywood" in the hotel's Ziegfield Theatre. "Hallelujah Hollywood" was largely created by an employee of MGM Grand, who also staged, produced, and directed the show. The show comprised ten acts, four billed as "tributes" to MGM motion pictures. Act IV was entitled *Kismet* and used characters and settings from that musical. Act IV was performed approximately 1700 times, until, under pressure from this litigation, MGM Grand substituted a new Act IV.

ISSUE: In performing apportionment, is it proper to focus mainly on the contributions of the infringer?

HOLDING AND DECISION: (Fletcher, J.) No. The district court erred in weighing the creativity of producers, performers, and others involved in staging and adapting *Kismet* for use in "Hallelujah Hollywood" so heavily. In performing apportionment, the benefit of the doubt must always be given to the plaintiff, not to the defendant. A producer's ability to stage a lavish presentation, or a performer's ability to fill a hall based on the drawing power of her name alone, is not a license to use freely the copyrighted works of others. Thus, apportioning 75% of Act IV to the defendants grossly undervalues the importance of plaintiff's contributions in this case. The district court did not err in finding that 2% of MGM Grand's indirect profit was attributable to "Hallelujah Hollywood." The district court erred in declining to award prejudgment interest. Awarding prejudgment interest on the apportioned share of the defendant's profits is consistent with the purposes underlying the profit remedy. Remanded to enter an award of prejudgment interest.

ANALYSIS

In copyright cases, the exact amount of damages and profits is often difficult to prove with any degree of mathematical certainty. As *Frank Music Corp.* demonstrates, cases where the protected work is incorporated into a new work, with creative contributions added by the alleged infringer, are particularly difficult to apportion.

Quicknotes

COPYRIGHT Refers to the exclusive rights granted to an artist pursuant to Article I, section 8, clause 8 of the United States Constitution over the reproduction, display, performance, distribution, and adaptation of his work for a period prescribed by statute.

COPYRIGHT ACT Copyright Act of 1976 extends copyright protection to "original works of authorship fixed in any tangible medium of expression, now known or later developed, from which they can be perceived, reproduced, or otherwise communicated, either directly or with the aid of a machine or device." 17 U.S.C. § 102.

COPYRIGHT INFRINGEMENT A violation of one of the exclusive rights granted to an artist pursuant to Article I, section 8, clause 8 of the United States Constitution over the reproduction, display, performance, distribution, and adaptation of his work for a period prescribed by statute.

Bouchat v. Baltimore Ravens Football Club, Inc.

Copyright holder (P) v. Pro football team (D)

346 F.3d 514 (4th Cir. 2003), cert. denied, 541 U.S. 1042 (2004).

NATURE OF CASE: Appeal from partial summary judgment for defendant and from judgment on jury verdict for defendant in damages phase of copyright infringement action.

FACT SUMMARY: Bouchat (P), whose unsolicited logo design for the Baltimore Ravens (D) pro football team was inadvertently incorporated in the Ravens' (D) logo and used in all aspects of the Ravens' (D) activities by the Ravens' (D) and its licensing agent, the National Football League Properties, Inc. (NFLP) (D), contended that the district court erred by failing to accord him the benefit of the statutory presumption in the Copyright Act, § 504(b) that an infringer's revenues are entirely attributable to the infringement.

RULE OF LAW
A court may resolve, as a matter of law, that a copyright infringer's revenues are not attributable to infringement where there is no conceivable connection between the infringement and a given revenue stream or where, despite the existence of a conceivable link, the plaintiff has failed to offer anything more than mere speculation as to the existence of a causal connection between the infringement and the claimed revenues.

FACTS: Bouchat (P), an amateur artist, created a winged shield drawing (the "Shield Drawing") as a "Ravens" logo for the pro football team that was moving to Baltimore and that had indicated it was considering "Ravens" as a possible name for the team. Bouchat (P) sent the Shield Drawing to the team once it officially adopted Ravens as its name. The team, the Baltimore Ravens (D), and its licensing agent, the National Football League Properties, Inc. (NFLP) (D), mistakenly used the Shield Drawing in NFLP's (D) production of the Ravens' (D) new logo, the "Flying B." The Flying B was used in all Ravens' (D) activities, including uniforms, stationery, tickets, banners, on-field insignia, and merchandise. Bouchat (P) sued for copyright infringement, and a jury found for him on the issue of liability. Bouchat (P) then sought damages under § 504(a)(1) of the Copyright Act, which renders an infringer liable for "the copyright owner's actual damages and any additional profits of the infringer, as provided by [§ 504(b)]." Section 504(b), in turn, entitles the copyright owner to recover both "the actual damages suffered by him or her as a result of the infringement, and any profits of the infringer that are attributable to the infringement and are not taken into account in computing the actual damages." Bouchat (P) had contended that some portion of essentially all Ravens' (D) and NFLP's (D) revenues was attributable to the infringing use of his artwork. To this end he presented evidence of the gross receipts from all their activities. The district court, however, awarded partial summary judgment to the Ravens (D) and NFLP (D) with respect to all revenues derived from sources other than (1) sales of merchandise bearing the Flying B logo, and (2) royalties obtained from licensees who sold such merchandise (collectively, the "Merchandise Revenues"). In rendering this judgment, the court reasoned that "if the use of the Flying B logo to designate the Ravens (D) could not reasonably be found to have affected the amount of revenue obtained from an activity, the revenue from that activity could not reasonably be found attributable to the infringement." It therefore excluded, as a matter of law, the remainder of revenues (collectively, the "Non-Merchandise Revenues") from the pool of income that the jury could consider in awarding damages. The court further narrowed the scope of the revenues the jury could consider by excluding certain portions of the Merchandise Revenues related to minimum guarantee shortfalls, free merchandise, trading cards, video games, and game programs (collectively, the "Excluded Merchandise Revenues"). In doing so, the court found that there could be no rational connection, or that there was no actual connection in fact, between these particular sources of revenue and the act of infringement. Thus, only those revenues derived from the sale of t-shirts, caps, souvenir cups, and other items bearing the Flying B logo (collectively, the "Non-Excluded Merchandise Revenues") went to the jury for a finding on whether these revenues were attributable to factors other than infringement. The jury found that all the Non-Excluded Merchandise Revenues resulted from non-infringing factors, and therefore denied Bouchat (P) any monetary recovery. Bouchat (P) appealed, contending that the district court failed to give him the benefit of the § 504 statutory presumption that an infringer's revenues are entirely attributable to the infringement—a presumption that he contended could not be resolved on summary judgment. The court of appeals granted review.

ISSUE: May a court resolve, as a matter of law, that a copyright infringer's revenues are not attributable to infringement where there is no conceivable connection between the infringement and a given revenue stream or where, despite the existence of a conceivable link, the plaintiff has failed to offer anything more than mere speculation as to the existence of a causal connection between the infringement and the claimed revenues?

Continued on next page.

HOLDING AND DECISION: (King, J.) Yes. A court may resolve, as a matter of law, that a copyright infringer's revenues are not attributable to infringement where there is no conceivable connection between the infringement and a given revenue stream or where, despite the existence of a conceivable link, the plaintiff has failed to offer anything more than mere speculation as to the existence of a causal connection between the infringement and the claimed revenues. Section 504(b) creates an initial presumption that an infringer's profits attributable to the infringement are equal to the infringer's gross revenue. Once the copyright owner has established the amount of the infringer's gross revenues, the burden shifts under the statute to the infringer to prove either that part or all of those revenues are not profits, or that they are attributable to factors other than the copyrighted work. Despite this burden shifting, there are situations, such as the one at bar, where summary judgment in favor of an infringer with respect to some portion of the infringer's gross revenues is appropriate. That situation is where there is no conceivable connection between the infringement and a given revenue stream, or, where, despite the existence of a conceivable link, the plaintiff has failed to offer anything more than mere speculation as to the existence of a causal connection between the infringement and the claimed revenues. Here, the district court granted summary judgment with respect to both the Non-Merchandise Revenues and the Excluded Merchandise Revenues, thus excluding a large segment of revenues from consideration by the jury as to whether those excluded revenues could be attributable to infringement. Despite the fact that § 504(b) places on the infringer the burden of proving that revenues are not attributable to the infringement, summary judgment was appropriate with respect to both the Non-Merchandise Revenues and the Excluded Merchandise Revenues. Two of the sources of excluded revenues (minimum guarantee shortfalls and free merchandise) had no conceivable connection to the infringement, because revenues from these sources were established by license and could not fluctuate in response to consumer behavior. Therefore, the district court did not err in finding that no rational trier of fact could attribute revenues from those sources to infringement, and, therefore, in removing the revenues from those categories from the jury's consideration. As to the remaining Non-Merchandise Revenues and the Excluded Merchandise Revenues, even though there was a conceivable connection between those revenues and the infringement, Bouchat (P) offered only speculative evidence of a causal link between the infringement and the revenues that earned from these sources, and because the Ravens' (D) and NFLP's (D) request for summary judgment was supported by unrebutted evidence demonstrating that these revenues were not, in fact, in any way attributable to the infringement, there was no issue of material fact for consideration by the jury. Therefore, the district court did not err in granting summary judgment as to these categories of revenue. Finally, contrary to Bouchat's (P) contention, the court did properly instruct the jury that the Ravens (D) and NFLP (D) had the burden of proof on the damages issues. Affirmed.

DISSENT: (Widener, J.) The district court erred by refusing to instruct the jury that the Ravens' (D) and NFLP's (D) profits were deemed attributable to the alleged copyright infringement unless they proved otherwise—despite being asked to do so by Bouchat (P). Precedent requires not only that the court inform the jury that the defendants bear the burden of proof, it also requires that the court expressly inform the jury that they must presume all profits are attributable to the infringement unless the defendants prove otherwise—which the district court failed to do; merely stating that the defendant bears the burden of proof is not enough. The district court also erred by limiting its instructions on the award of profits under § 504(b) to an explanation of the special verdict form. The court read each question from the verdict form and then gave a brief explanation of what the question meant. When combined, these two errors require reversal; otherwise, the fundamental purposes of trial by jury are disserved.

▶ **ANALYSIS**

Bouchat (P) could not elect to receive statutory damages because he had not registered his copyright at the time of the infringement, and he also did not seek actual damages, since if there were any, they were nominal. Regardless of his actual damages, however, Bouchat (P) was entitled to the defendants' profits attributable to the infringement because the award of profits is intended to "prevent the infringer from unfairly benefiting from a wrongful act" and not to compensate the copyright owner. However, when awarding such indirect profits, the goal is to award damages proportionate to the contribution of the copyright owner and no more.

Quicknotes

BURDEN OF PROOF The duty of a party to introduce evidence to support a fact that is in dispute in an action.

COPYRIGHT ACT Copyright Act of 1976 extends copyright protection to "original works of authorship fixed in any tangible medium of expression, now known or later developed, from which they can be perceived, reproduced, or otherwise communicated, either directly or with the aid of a machine or device." 17 U.S.C. § 102.

COPYRIGHT INFRINGEMENT A violation of one of the exclusive rights granted to an artist pursuant to Article I, Section 8, clause 8 of the United States Constitution over the reproduction, display, performance, distribution, and adaptation of his work for a period prescribed by statute.

Continued on next page.

DAMAGES Monetary compensation that may be awarded by the court to a party who has sustained injury or loss to his person, property or rights due to another party's unlawful act, omission or negligence.

PARTIAL SUMMARY JUDGMENT Judgment rendered by a court in response to a motion by one of the parties, claiming that the lack of a question of material fact in respect to one of the issues warrants disposition of that issue without going to the jury.

Los Angeles News Service v. Reuters Television International, Ltd.

Independent news organization (P) v. Television news agency (D)

340 F.3d 926 (9th Cir. 2003), cert. denied, 541 U.S. 1041 (2004).

NATURE OF CASE: Appeal from part of a damages award in a copyright infringement suit.

FACT SUMMARY: When the Los Angeles News Service (LANS) (P) sued Reuters Television International, Ltd. (D) for copyright infringement, the latter argued that the use by its London bureau of LANS's (P) copyrighted videotapes was not actionable because the Copyright Act does not apply extraterritorially except where an act of infringement is completed entirely within the United States.

RULE OF LAW
The Copyright Act does not apply extraterritorially except where an act of infringement is completed entirely within the United States and such infringing act enabled further exploitation abroad.

FACTS: Los Angeles News Service (LANS) (P), an independent news organization, granted to Reuters Television International, Ltd. (D) a license to broadcast LANS's (P) copyrighted video of the beating of Reginald Denny. Reuters (D) subsequently made another videotape of the beating and transmitted it to Reuter's (D) bureau in London (to which the license did not extend), which in turn distributed it via "feed" to its own subscribers. The transmission of the copyrighted material to London was done from New York. When LANS (P) sued Reuters (D) for copyright infringement, the federal district court granted the latter summary judgment, holding, inter alia, that no liability could arise under the Copyright Act for acts of infringement that occurred outside the United States, although awarding damages for the act of copying in New York which constituted a domestic act of infringement. LANS (P) appealed the extraterritorial finding.

ISSUE: Does the Copyright Act apply extraterritorially only where the act of infringement is completed entirely within the United States and such infringing act enabled further exploitation abroad?

HOLDING AND DECISION: (O'Scannlain, J.) Yes. The Copyright Act does not apply extraterritorially except where an act of infringement is completed entirely within the United States and such infringing act enabled further exploitation abroad. The import of this principle, as set forth in prior decisions, counsels a narrow application of the exception to the general rule of nonliability for extraterritorial infringements. The constructive trust rationale preserves a territorial connection. Moreover, no rational deterrent function is served by making an infringer whose domestic act of infringement, from which he or she earns a profit, unless it leads to widespread extraterritorial infringement, liable for the copyright owner's entire loss of value or profit from that overseas infringement. This is particularly true if the overseas infringement is legal where it takes place. Moreover, the resulting "over-deterrence" might chill the fair use of copyright works in close cases. Accordingly, LANS (P) can only recover any profits or unjust enrichment from domestic infringers, on the theory that the infringers hold such profits in a constructive trust for LANS (P). However, to permit LANS (P) to recover damages other than Reuters' (D) profits or unjust enrichment, would improperly permit LANS (P) to recover damages for extraterritorial acts of infringement. Affirmed.

ANALYSIS

As the court in the *Los Angeles News Service* decision makes clear, profits from an overseas infringement may be recovered on the theory that the infringer holds them in a constructive trust for the copyright owner only if the actual act of infringement has occurred within the United States.

Quicknotes

COPYRIGHT Refers to the exclusive rights granted to an artist pursuant to Article I, section 8, clause 8 of the United States Constitution over the reproduction, display, performance, distribution, and adaptation of his work for a period prescribed by statute.

COPYRIGHT ACT Copyright Act of 1976 extends copyright protection to "original works of authorship fixed in any tangible medium of expression, now known or later developed, from which they can be perceived, reproduced, or otherwise communicated, either directly or with the aid of a machine or device." 17 U.S.C. § 102.

COPYRIGHT INFRINGEMENT A violation of one of the exclusive rights granted to an artist pursuant to Article I, section 8, clause 8 of the United States Constitution over the reproduction, display, performance, distribution, and adaptation of his work for a period prescribed by statute.

INTER ALIA Among other things.

SUMMARY JUDGMENT Judgment rendered by a court in response to a motion by one of the parties, claiming that the lack of a question of material fact in respect to an issue warrants disposition of the issue without consideration by the jury.

Zomba Enterprises, Inc. v. Panorama Records, Inc.

Music publisher (P) v. Karaoke disc seller (D)

491 F. 3d 574 (6th Cir. 2007).

NATURE OF CASE: Appeal from award of statutory damages in action for copyright infringement.

FACT SUMMARY: Panorama Records, Inc. (D), which sells compact discs containing unlicensed songs for use in karaoke machines, contended that any infringement on its part of Zomba Enterprises, Inc.'s (P) copyrights did not merit the statutory damages award rendered by the district court because its infringement was not willful; the district court abused its discretion; the award violated the Eighth Amendment; and the award violated due process.

RULE OF LAW
(1) Copyright infringement is "willful" where as a matter of law the infringer recklessly disregards the copyright holder's property rights and its reliance on a fair-use defense is objectively unreasonable.

(2) A court does not abuse its discretion in awarding statutory copyright damages where the court recognizes that it has discretion and the record does not support a finding that the court failed to exercise this discretion.

(3) Statutory copyright damages awarded in a civil action cannot violate the Constitution's Eighth Amendment as an excessive fine where the government neither prosecutes the action nor participates in the award.

(4) A statutory copyright damages award does not violate due process where it is not so severe and oppressive as to be wholly disproportioned to the offense and obviously unreasonable.

FACTS: Panorama Records, Inc. (Panorama) (D) created and sold special CD + G (compact disc plus graphics) discs for use in karaoke machines. The discs contained songs recorded by musicians hired by Panorama (D). The songs previously had been made popular by another artist, and some of the songs were copyrighted. The discs also contained the lyrics for each song, which scrolled across a screen as the music (sans vocals) played. Each of these "karaoke packages" contained nine or ten songs, with two tracks for each song, one track released with audible lyrics and one without. Panorama (D) did not receive licenses to use the songs. Zomba Enterprises, Inc. (Zomba) (P), a music publisher that held copyrights on some of the songs used by Panorama (D) in its karaoke packages, discovered Panorama's (D) unlicensed use and sent Panorama (D) a cease-and-desist letter specifying the licensing terms on which it would permit Panorama (D) to use its copyrighted songs. Although Panorama (D) contacted Zomba's (P) attorney about the letter, it neither ceased distributing the karaoke packages nor licensed the songs. After Zomba (P) brought suit for copyright infringement, asserting 30 counts of such infringement, Zomba (P) and Panorama (D) entered into a consent order in which Panorama (D) agreed "to be restrained from distributing, releasing or otherwise exploiting any karaoke package containing compositions owned or administered by" Zomba (P). However, within a week of entering the consent order, Panorama (D) resumed distributing karaoke packages that contained Zomba (P) copyrighted songs. After a year where this conduct went unabated, Zomba (P) moved for sanctions. The district court concluded that Panorama's (D) infringement was willful, and accordingly awarded Zomba (P) $31,000 for each of the twenty-six infringements at issue, for a total of $806,000. In reaching this decision, the court found that the maximum $30,000 per infringement for non-willful infringement was insufficient, but that the $150,000 per infringement for willful infringement was too high. The court of appeals granted review.

ISSUE:
(1) Is copyright infringement "willful" where as a matter of law the infringer recklessly disregards the copyright holder's property rights and its reliance on a fair-use defense is objectively unreasonable?

(2) Does a court abuse its discretion in awarding statutory copyright damages where the court recognizes that it has discretion and the record does not support a finding that the court failed to exercise this discretion?

(3) Can statutory copyright damages awarded in a civil action violate the Constitution's Eighth Amendment as an excessive fine where the government neither prosecutes the action nor participates in the award?

(4) Does a statutory copyright damages award violate due process where it is not so severe and oppressive as to be wholly disproportioned to the offense and obviously unreasonable?

HOLDING AND DECISION: (Moore, J.)

(1) Yes. Copyright infringement is "willful" where as a matter of law the infringer recklessly disregards the copyright holder's property rights and its reliance on a fair-use defense is objectively unreasonable. For infringement to be willful, it must be done with knowledge that one's conduct constitutes copyright infringement. Thus, one who has

Continued on next page.

been notified that his conduct constitutes copyright infringement, but who reasonably and in good faith believes the contrary, is not willful. Panorama (D) contends that it held a good-faith belief that the copying here at issue was a fair use. This is not enough, since even if it held such a good-faith belief, that belief must also be reasonable. Here, Panorama's (D) continued selling of karaoke packages after the consent order was entered indicates a reckless disregard for Zomba's (P) rights, and accordingly, that Panorama's (D) reliance on its fair-use defense was objectively unreasonable. Under the consent decree, Panorama (D) agreed to cease infringing Zomba's (P) copyrights and, implicitly, to suspend its reliance on the fair-use defense at least temporarily, so that Panorama (D) lacked any legal justification for continuing to distribute copies of Zomba's (P) copyrighted works after the consent decree was entered. Affirmed as to this issue.

(2) No. A court does not abuse its discretion in awarding statutory copyright damages where the court recognizes that it has discretion and the record does not support a finding that the court failed to exercise this discretion. Here, the district court recognized that it had "wide discretion in determining the amount of statutory damages to be awarded, constrained only by the maximum and minimum amounts." The court found that the maximum statutory amount of $30,000 per work for non-willful infringement was insufficient because of Panorama's (D) willfulness, but that the maximum award of $150,000 per infringement was excessive, given the dollar amounts involved in the case. Because the court nowhere indicated it lacked discretion, and given the court's findings, the record does not support a finding that the court abused its discretion. Affirmed as to this issue.

(3) No. Statutory copyright damages awarded in a civil action cannot violate the Constitution's Eighth Amendment as an excessive fine where the government neither prosecutes the action nor participates in the award. The Supreme Court has explained that the word "fine" in this context means a payment to the government. Therefore, the Eighth Amendment does not constrain an award of money damages in a civil suit when the government neither has prosecuted the action nor has any right to receive a share of the damages awarded. Accordingly, Panorama's (D) argument fails. Affirmed as to this issue.

(4) No. A statutory copyright damages award does not violate due process where it is not so severe and oppressive as to be wholly disproportioned to the offense and obviously unreasonable. In the punitive damages context, the Supreme Court has held that an award greater than 100 times the amount of compensatory damages awarded violates due process. While not setting a bright-line ratio, the Court has expressed a preference for a single-digit ratio. However, it is uncertain whether the Court's precedent in the punitive damages area applies to statutory damages awards. Given this uncertainty, precedent governing statutory awards controls. Such precedent has held that an award of statutory damages violates due process where it is so severe and oppressive as to be wholly disproportioned to the offense and obviously unreasonable. This review, however, is extraordinarily deferential, and under such review, an award that was 113 times the amount of actual damages was upheld. Thus, given that the Supreme Court previously countenanced a 113:1 ratio, it cannot be said that where, as here, the ratio is 44:1 that the damages are unacceptable. Affirmed as to this issue.

ANALYSIS

In punitive damages cases, due-process challenges must consider three "guideposts": (1) "the degree of reprehensibility of the" defendant's conduct; (2) "the disparity between the harm or potential harm suffered by [the plaintiff] and [the] punitive damages award"; and (3) "the difference between this remedy and the civil penalties authorized or imposed in comparable cases." In these cases, the courts attempt to determine whether the punitive award is an irrational and arbitrary deprivation of the defendant's property, and thus is a less deferential standard of review than the one employed by the court in this case. However, some courts have suggested in dicta that the Supreme Court's precedent in the punitive damages area could apply to statutory damages awards in class actions where the case is sufficiently serious.

Quicknotes

CEASE AND DESIST ORDER An order from a court or administrative agency prohibiting a person or business from continuing a particular course of conduct.

COMPENSATORY DAMAGES Measure of damages necessary to compensate victim for actual injuries suffered.

COPYRIGHT INFRINGEMENT A violation of one of the exclusive rights granted to an artist pursuant to Article I, Section 8, clause 8 of the United States Constitution over the reproduction, display, performance, distribution, and adaptation of his work for a period prescribed by statute.

DAMAGES Monetary compensation that may be awarded by the court to a party who has sustained injury or loss to his person, property or rights due to another party's unlawful act, omission or negligence.

DUE PROCESS The constitutional mandate requiring the courts to protect and enforce individuals' rights and liberties consistent with prevailing principles of fairness and justice and prohibiting the federal and state governments from such activities that deprive its citizens of life, liberty, or property interest.

Continued on next page.

FAIR USE An affirmative defense to a claim of copyright infringement providing an exception from the copyright owner's exclusive rights in a work for the purposes of criticism, comment, news reporting, teaching, scholarship or research; the determination of whether a use is fair is made on a case-by-case basis and requires the court to consider: (1) the purpose and character of the use; (2) the nature of the work; (3) the amount and substantiality of the portion used; and (4) the effect of the use on the potential market for, or value of, the work.

GOOD FAITH An honest intention to abstain from taking advantage of another.

PUNITIVE DAMAGES Damages exceeding the actual injury suffered for the purposes of punishment of the defendant, deterrence of the wrongful behavior or comfort to the plaintiff.

Fantasy, Inc. v. Fogerty

Copyright owner (P) v. Singer/songwriter (D)

94 F.3d 553 (9th Cir. 1996).

NATURE OF CASE: Appeal from the award of attorneys' fees in a copyright infringement action.

FACT SUMMARY: The district court found that Fogerty's (D) victory on the merits furthered the purposes of the Copyright Act, and it awarded him attorneys' fees.

RULE OF LAW
An award of attorneys' fees to a prevailing defendant that has furthered the underlying purposes of the Copyright Act rests in the sound discretion of the district courts, and such discretion is not limited by a requirement of culpability on the part of the losing party.

FACTS: On July 26, 1985, Fantasy, Inc. (P) sued Fogerty (D) for copyright infringement, alleging that Fogerty's (D) song "The Old Man Down the Road" infringed the copyright on another Fogerty (D) song, "Run Through the Jungle," which Fantasy (P) owned. On November 7, 1988, the jury returned a verdict in favor of Fogerty (D). Fogerty (D) moved for award of reasonable attorneys' fees. Fogerty's (D) motion was denied by the district court upon a finding that Fantasy's (P) suit was neither frivolous nor prosecuted in bad faith. This court affirmed, finding that then-existing precedent precluded an award of fees in the absence of a finding that the suit was frivolous or prosecuted in bad faith. The Supreme Court reversed and remanded, and the case was then remanded to the district court for further proceedings. The district court granted Fogerty's (D) motion with regard to attorneys' fees.

ISSUE: Must a court find some "culpability" on the part of the plaintiff pursuing the suit before it can award a fee to a prevailing defendant whose victory on the merits furthers the purposes of the Copyright Act?

HOLDING AND DECISION: (Rymer, J.) No. An award of attorneys' fees to a prevailing defendant that has furthered the underlying purposes of the Copyright Act rests in the sound discretion of the district courts, and such discretion is not limited by a requirement of culpability on the part of the losing party. Exceptional circumstances are not a prerequisite to an award of attorneys' fees; district courts may freely award fees, as long as they treat prevailing plaintiffs and prevailing defendants alike and seek to promote the objectives of the Copyright Act. The reasons given by the district court in this case were well founded in the record and were in keeping with the purposes of the Copyright Act. Thus, the district court acted within its discretion in awarding a reasonable attorneys' fee to Fogerty (D). The case was remanded to the district court for calculation of the attorneys' fee.

ANALYSIS
Eligibility for attorneys' fees is subject to a requirement of timely registration under the Copyright Act.

Quicknotes
COPYRIGHT ACT Copyright Act of 1976 extends copyright protection to "original works of authorship fixed in any tangible medium of expression, now known or later developed, from which they can be perceived, reproduced, or otherwise communicated, either directly or with the aid of a machine or device." 17 U.S.C. § 102.

COPYRIGHT INFRINGEMENT A violation of one of the exclusive rights granted to an artist pursuant to Article I, section 8, clause 8 of the United States Constitution over the reproduction, display, performance, distribution, and adaptation of his work for a period prescribed by statute.

Positive Black Talk Inc. v. Cash Money Records Inc.

Recording company (P) v. Recording company (D)

394 F.3d 357 (5th Cir. 2004).

NATURE OF CASE: Appeal from denial of attorney's fees in copyright infringement action.

FACT SUMMARY: After the rap artist known as Juvenile (D), his recording company, Cash Money Records Inc. (CMR) (D), and their distributor, Universal Records (Universal) (D) prevailed in defending a copyright infringement suit brought by another rap artist known as D.J. Jubilee (Jubilee) and his recording company, Positive Black Talk Inc. (PBT) (P), Juvenile (D), CMR (D), and Universal (D) sought attorney's fees, which were denied by the district court. Juvenile (D), CMR (D) and Universal (D) claimed that the district court had abused its discretion in denying their request for attorney's fees for successfully defending the copyright infringement claims against them.

RULE OF LAW
A court does not abuse its discretion in denying a request for attorney's fees for successfully defending a copyright infringement claim where the court has based its decision on factors such as frivolousness, motivation, and objective reasonableness.

FACTS: In 1997, the rap artist known as D.J. Jubilee (Jubilee) recorded a song that contained the phrase "back that ass up." He titled the song "Back That Ass Up," and his recording company, Positive Black Talk, Inc. (PBT) (P) released the recording in early 1998. The rap artist known as Juvenile (D) also recorded a song that contained the phrase "back that ass up" in 1997, and his recording company, Cash Money Records Inc. (CMR) (D) entered into a national distribution deal with Universal Records (Universal) (D) and the song was released in late 1998 under the title "Back That Azz Up," selling over four million copies. PBT (P) brought suit against Juvenile (D), CMR (D), and Universal (D) for copyright infringement, and they counterclaimed for, inter alia, violation of the Louisiana Unfair Trade Practices Act (LUPTA). A jury found for Juvenile (D), CMR (D), and Universal (D) on PBT's (P) copyright infringement claim and on their LUPTA counterclaim. Although the court granted Juvenile's (D), CMR's (D), and Universal's (D) request for attorney's fees in prosecuting the LUPTA claim, it denied their request for successfully defending against the copyright infringement claim. In making its ruling, the district court recognized that an award of attorney's fees to the prevailing party in a copyright action, although left to the trial court's discretion, "is the rule rather than the exception and should be awarded routinely." The court of appeals granted review.

ISSUE: Does a court abuse its discretion in denying a request for attorney's fees for successfully defending a copyright infringement claim where the court has based its decision on factors such as frivolousness, motivation, and objective reasonableness?

HOLDING AND DECISION: (King, C.J.) No. A court does not abuse its discretion in denying a request for attorney's fees for successfully defending a copyright infringement claim where the court has based its decision on factors such as frivolousness, motivation, and objective reasonableness. In determining whether to grant attorney's fees to a prevailing party, the Supreme Court has adopted an "evenhanded" approach in which no distinction is made between prevailing plaintiffs and prevailing defendants, but the Court has made clear that it has not adopted the British rule, under which the prevailing party is always awarded attorney's fees. Instead, the Court has set forth a non-exclusive list of factors that courts should consider in determining whether to award attorney's fees to a prevailing party. These include, but are not limited to: "frivolousness, motivation, objective unreasonableness (both in the factual and in the legal components of the case) and the need in particular circumstances to advance considerations of compensation and deterrence." The court in this case, while noting that an award of attorney's fees to the prevailing party in a copyright action, although left to the trial court's discretion, is the rule rather than the exception and should be awarded routinely, in the exercise of its discretion determined that an award of attorney's fees in this case was inappropriate. In reaching that conclusion, the district court determined that the litigation brought by PBT (P) was not frivolous, objectively unreasonable, without proper motive, or brought in bad faith. The argument that the court erred in considering frivolity and motivation is wrong in light of the Supreme Court's non-exclusive list of factors to be considered, as is the argument that the court erred in considering only frivolity and bad faith, since the court clearly considered other factors. In addition, the district court considered the possible effect, or lack thereof, that awarding fees would have on deterring future meritless lawsuits, and it determined that this is a rare case in which awarding fees is not appropriate. For these and other reasons, the district court did not abuse its discretion in concluding that the defendants were not entitled to attorney's fees under § 505 of the Copyright Act. Affirmed.

ANALYSIS

Section 505 of the Copyright Act provides: "In any civil action under this title, the court in its discretion may

Continued on next page.

allow the recovery of full costs by or against any party other than the United States or an officer thereof[;] except as otherwise provided by this title, the court may also award a reasonable attorney's fee to the prevailing party as part of the costs." The Supreme Court has reasoned that the language in § 505 that the court "may" award fees "clearly connotes discretion." To encourage the clear demarcation of the boundaries of copyright law, the Court has indicated that defendants who seek to advance a variety of meritorious copyright defenses should be encouraged to litigate them to the same extent that plaintiffs are encouraged to litigate meritorious claims of infringement through awards of attorney's fees, but that such awards are within the courts' equitable discretion.

Quicknotes

BAD FAITH Conduct that is intentionally misleading or deceptive.

COPYRIGHT ACT Copyright Act of 1976 extends copyright protection to "original works of authorship fixed in any tangible medium of expression, now known or later developed, from which they can be perceived, reproduced, or otherwise communicated, either directly or with the aid of a machine or device." 17 U.S.C. § 102.

COPYRIGHT INFRINGEMENT A violation of one of the exclusive rights granted to an artist pursuant to Article I, section 8, clause 8 of the United States Constitution over the reproduction, display, performance, distribution, and adaptation of his work for a period prescribed by statute.

INTER ALIA Among other things.

Glossary

Common Latin Words and Phrases Encountered in the Law

A FORTIORI: Because one fact exists or has been proven, therefore a second fact that is related to the first fact must also exist.

A PRIORI: From the cause to the effect. A term of logic used to denote that when one generally accepted truth is shown to be a cause, another particular effect must necessarily follow.

AB INITIO: From the beginning; a condition which has existed throughout, as in a marriage which was void ab initio.

ACTUS REUS: The wrongful act; in criminal law, such action sufficient to trigger criminal liability.

AD VALOREM: According to value; an ad valorem tax is imposed upon an item located within the taxing jurisdiction calculated by the value of such item.

AMICUS CURIAE: Friend of the court. Its most common usage takes the form of an amicus curiae brief, filed by a person who is not a party to an action but is nonetheless allowed to offer an argument supporting his legal interests.

ARGUENDO: In arguing. A statement, possibly hypothetical, made for the purpose of argument, is one made arguendo.

BILL QUIA TIMET: A bill to quiet title (establish ownership) to real property.

BONA FIDE: True, honest, or genuine. May refer to a person's legal position based on good faith or lacking notice of fraud (such as a bona fide purchaser for value) or to the authenticity of a particular document (such as a bona fide last will and testament).

CAUSA MORTIS: With approaching death in mind. A gift causa mortis is a gift given by a party who feels certain that death is imminent.

CAVEAT EMPTOR: Let the buyer beware. This maxim is reflected in the rule of law that a buyer purchases at his own risk because it is his responsibility to examine, judge, test, and otherwise inspect what he is buying.

CERTIORARI: A writ of review. Petitions for review of a case by the United States Supreme Court are most often done by means of a writ of certiorari.

CONTRA: On the other hand. Opposite. Contrary to.

CORAM NOBIS: Before us; writs of error directed to the court that originally rendered the judgment.

CORAM VOBIS: Before you; writs of error directed by an appellate court to a lower court to correct a factual error.

CORPUS DELICTI: The body of the crime; the requisite elements of a crime amounting to objective proof that a crime has been committed.

CUM TESTAMENTO ANNEXO, ADMINISTRATOR (ADMINISTRATOR C.T.A.): With will annexed; an administrator c.t.a. settles an estate pursuant to a will in which he is not appointed.

DE BONIS NON, ADMINISTRATOR (ADMINISTRATOR D.B.N.): Of goods not administered; an administrator d.b.n. settles a partially settled estate.

DE FACTO: In fact; in reality; actually. Existing in fact but not officially approved or engendered.

DE JURE: By right; lawful. Describes a condition that is legitimate "as a matter of law," in contrast to the term "de facto," which connotes something existing in fact but not legally sanctioned or authorized. For example, de facto segregation refers to segregation brought about by housing patterns, etc., whereas de jure segregation refers to segregation created by law.

DE MINIMIS: Of minimal importance; insignificant; a trifle; not worth bothering about.

DE NOVO: Anew; a second time; afresh. A trial de novo is a new trial held at the appellate level as if the case originated there and the trial at a lower level had not taken place.

DICTA: Generally used as an abbreviated form of obiter dicta, a term describing those portions of a judicial opinion incidental or not necessary to resolution of the specific question before the court. Such nonessential statements and remarks are not considered to be binding precedent.

DUCES TECUM: Refers to a particular type of writ or subpoena requesting a party or organization to produce certain documents in their possession.

EN BANC: Full bench. Where a court sits with all justices present rather than the usual quorum.

EX PARTE: For one side or one party only. An ex parte proceeding is one undertaken for the benefit of only one party, without notice to, or an appearance by, an adverse party.

EX POST FACTO: After the fact. An ex post facto law is a law that retroactively changes the consequences of a prior act.

EX REL.: Abbreviated form of the term "ex relatione," meaning upon relation or information. When the state brings an action in which it has no interest against an individual at the instigation of one who has a private interest in the matter.

FORUM NON CONVENIENS: Inconvenient forum. Although a court may have jurisdiction over the case, the action should be tried in a more conveniently located court, one to which parties and witnesses may more easily travel, for example.

GUARDIAN AD LITEM: A guardian of an infant as to litigation, appointed to represent the infant and pursue his/her rights.

HABEAS CORPUS: You have the body. The modern writ of habeas corpus is a writ directing that a person (body) being detained (such as a prisoner) be brought before the court so that the legality of his detention can be judicially ascertained.

IN CAMERA: In private, in chambers. When a hearing is held before a judge in his chambers or when all spectators are excluded from the courtroom.

IN FORMA PAUPERIS: In the manner of a pauper. A party who proceeds in forma pauperis because of his poverty is one who is allowed to bring suit without liability for costs.

INFRA: Below, under. A word referring the reader to a later part of a book. (The opposite of supra.)

IN LOCO PARENTIS: In the place of a parent.

IN PARI DELICTO: Equally wrong; a court of equity will not grant requested relief to an applicant who is in pari delicto, or as much at fault in the transactions giving rise to the controversy as is the opponent of the applicant.

IN PARI MATERIA: On like subject matter or upon the same matter. Statutes relating to the same person or things are said to be in pari materia. It is a general rule of statutory construction that such statutes should be construed together, i.e., looked at as if they together constituted one law.

IN PERSONAM: Against the person. Jurisdiction over the person of an individual.

IN RE: In the matter of. Used to designate a proceeding involving an estate or other property.

IN REM: A term that signifies an action against the res, or thing. An action in rem is basically one that is taken directly against property, as distinguished from an action in personam, i.e., against the person.

INTER ALIA: Among other things. Used to show that the whole of a statement, pleading, list, statute, etc., has not been set forth in its entirety.

INTER PARTES: Between the parties. May refer to contracts, conveyances or other transactions having legal significance.

INTER VIVOS: Between the living. An inter vivos gift is a gift made by a living grantor, as distinguished from bequests contained in a will, which pass upon the death of the testator.

IPSO FACTO: By the mere fact itself.

JUS: Law or the entire body of law.

LEX LOCI: The law of the place; the notion that the rights of parties to a legal proceeding are governed by the law of the place where those rights arose.

MALUM IN SE: Evil or wrong in and of itself; inherently wrong. This term describes an act that is wrong by its very nature, as opposed to one which would not be wrong but for the fact that there is a specific legal prohibition against it (malum prohibitum).

MALUM PROHIBITUM: Wrong because prohibited, but not inherently evil. Used to describe something that is wrong because it is expressly forbidden by law but that is not in and of itself evil, e.g., speeding.

MANDAMUS: We command. A writ directing an official to take a certain action.

MENS REA: A guilty mind; a criminal intent. A term used to signify the mental state that accompanies a crime or other prohibited act. Some crimes require only a general mens rea (general intent to do the prohibited act), but others, like assault with intent to murder, require the existence of a specific mens rea.

MODUS OPERANDI: Method of operating; generally refers to the manner or style of a criminal in committing crimes, admissible in appropriate cases as evidence of the identity of a defendant.

NEXUS: A connection to.

NISI PRIUS: A court of first impression. A nisi prius court is one where issues of fact are tried before a judge or jury.

N.O.V. (NON OBSTANTE VEREDICTO): Notwithstanding the verdict. A judgment n.o.v. is a judgment given in favor of one party despite the fact that a verdict was returned in favor of the other party, the justification being that the verdict either had no reasonable support in fact or was contrary to law.

NUNC PRO TUNC: Now for then. This phrase refers to actions that may be taken and will then have full retroactive effect.

PENDENTE LITE: Pending the suit; pending litigation under way.

PER CAPITA: By head; beneficiaries of an estate, if they take in equal shares, take per capita.

PER CURIAM: By the court; signifies an opinion ostensibly written "by the whole court" and with no identified author.

PER SE: By itself, in itself; inherently.

PER STIRPES: By representation. Used primarily in the law of wills to describe the method of distribution where a person, generally because of death, is unable to take that which is left to him by the will of another, and therefore his heirs divide such property between them rather than take under the will individually.

PRIMA FACIE: On its face, at first sight. A prima facie case is one that is sufficient on its face, meaning that the evidence supporting it is adequate to establish the case until contradicted or overcome by other evidence.

PRO TANTO: For so much; as far as it goes. Often used in eminent domain cases when a property owner receives partial payment for his land without prejudice to his right to bring suit for the full amount he claims his land to be worth.

QUANTUM MERUIT: As much as he deserves. Refers to recovery based on the doctrine of unjust enrichment in those cases in which a party has rendered valuable services or furnished materials that were accepted and enjoyed by another under circumstances that would reasonably notify the recipient that the rendering party expected to be paid. In essence, the law implies a contract to pay the reasonable value of the services or materials furnished.

QUASI: Almost like; as if; nearly. This term is essentially used to signify that one subject or thing is almost analogous to another but that material differences between them do exist. For example, a quasi-criminal proceeding is one that is not strictly criminal but shares enough of the same characteristics to require some of the same safeguards (e.g., procedural due process must be followed in a parole hearing).

QUID PRO QUO: Something for something. In contract law, the consideration, something of value, passed between the parties to render the contract binding.

RES GESTAE: Things done; in evidence law, this principle justifies the admission of a statement that would otherwise be hearsay when it is made so closely to the event in question as to be said to be a part of it, or with such spontaneity as not to have the possibility of falsehood.

RES IPSA LOQUITUR: The thing speaks for itself. This doctrine gives rise to a rebuttable presumption of negligence when the instrumentality causing the injury was within the exclusive control of the defendant, and the injury was one that does not normally occur unless a person has been negligent.

RES JUDICATA: A matter adjudged. Doctrine which provides that once a court of competent jurisdiction has rendered a final judgment or decree on the merits, that judgment or decree is conclusive upon the parties to the case and prevents them from engaging in any other litigation on the points and issues determined therein.

RESPONDEAT SUPERIOR: Let the master reply. This doctrine holds the master liable for the wrongful acts of his servant (or the principal for his agent) in those cases in which the servant (or agent) was acting within the scope of his authority at the time of the injury.

STARE DECISIS: To stand by or adhere to that which has been decided. The common law doctrine of stare decisis attempts to give security and certainty to the law by following the policy that once a principle of law as applicable to a certain set of facts has been set forth in a decision, it forms a precedent which will subsequently be followed, even though a different decision might be made were it the first time the question had arisen. Of course, stare decisis is not an inviolable principle and is departed from in instances where there is good cause (e.g., considerations of public policy led the Supreme Court to disregard prior decisions sanctioning segregation).

SUPRA: Above. A word referring a reader to an earlier part of a book.

ULTRA VIRES: Beyond the power. This phrase is most commonly used to refer to actions taken by a corporation that are beyond the power or legal authority of the corporation.

Addendum of French Derivatives

IN PAIS: Not pursuant to legal proceedings.

CHATTEL: Tangible personal property.

CY PRES: Doctrine permitting courts to apply trust funds to purposes not expressed in the trust but necessary to carry out the settlor's intent.

PER AUTRE VIE: For another's life; during another's life. In property law, an estate may be granted that will terminate upon the death of someone other than the grantee.

PROFIT A PRENDRE: A license to remove minerals or other produce from land.

VOIR DIRE: Process of questioning jurors as to their predispositions about the case or parties to a proceeding in order to identify those jurors displaying bias or prejudice.

Casenote Legal Briefs

Administrative Law	Breyer, Stewart, Sunstein & Vermeule
Administrative Law	Cass, Diver & Beermann
Administrative Law	Funk, Shapiro & Weaver
Administrative Law	Mashaw, Merrill & Shane
Administrative Law	Strauss, Rakoff & Farina (Gellhorn & Byse)
Agency & Partnership	Hynes & Loewenstein
Antitrust	Pitofsky, Goldschmid & Wood
Antitrust	Sullivan & Hovenkamp
Bankruptcy	Warren & Bussel
Business Organizations	Allen, Kraakman & Subramanian
Business Organizations	Bauman, Weiss & Palmiter
Business Organizations	Hamilton & Macey
Business Organizations	Klein, Ramseyer & Bainbridge
Business Organizations	O'Kelley & Thompson
Business Organizations	Soderquist, Smiddy & Cunningham
Civil Procedure	Field, Kaplan & Clermont
Civil Procedure	Freer & Perdue
Civil Procedure	Friedenthal, Miller, Sexton & Hershkoff
Civil Procedure	Hazard, Tait, Fletcher & Bundy
Civil Procedure	Marcus, Redish, Sherman & Pfander
Civil Procedure	Subrin, Minow, Brodin & Main
Civil Procedure	Yeazell
Commercial Law	LoPucki, Warren, Keating & Mann
Commercial Law	Warren & Walt
Commercial Law	Whaley
Community Property	Bird
Community Property	Blumberg
Conflicts	Brilmayer & Goldsmith
Conflicts	Currie, Kay, Kramer & Roosevelt
Constitutional Law	Brest, Levinson, Balkin & Amar
Constitutional Law	Chemerinsky
Constitutional Law	Choper, Fallon, Kamisar & Shiffrin (Lockhart)
Constitutional Law	Cohen, Varat & Amar
Constitutional Law	Farber, Eskridge & Frickey
Constitutional Law	Rotunda
Constitutional Law	Sullivan & Gunther
Constitutional Law	Stone, Seidman, Sunstein, Tushnet & Karlan
Contracts	Ayres & Speidel
Contracts	Barnett
Contracts	Burton
Contracts	Calamari, Perillo & Bender
Contracts	Crandall & Whaley
Contracts	Dawson, Harvey, Henderson & Baird
Contracts	Farnsworth, Young, Sanger, Cohen & Brooks
Contracts	Fuller & Eisenberg
Contracts	Knapp, Crystal & Prince
Copyright	Cohen, Loren, Okediji & O'Rourke
Copyright	Goldstein & Reese
Criminal Law	Bonnie, Coughlin, Jeffries & Low
Criminal Law	Boyce, Dripps & Perkins
Criminal Law	Dressler
Criminal Law	Johnson & Cloud
Criminal Law	Kadish, Schulhofer & Steiker
Criminal Law	Kaplan, Weisberg & Binder
Criminal Procedure	Allen, Hoffmann, Livingston & Stuntz
Criminal Procedure	Dressler & Thomas
Criminal Procedure	Haddad, Marsh, Zagel, Meyer, Starkman & Bauer
Criminal Procedure	Kamisar, LaFave, Israel, King & Kerr
Criminal Procedure	Saltzburg & Capra
Debtors and Creditors	Warren & Westbrook
Employment Discrimination	Friedman
Employment Discrimination	Zimmer, Sullivan & White
Employment Law	Rothstein & Liebman
Environmental Law	Menell & Stewart
Environmental Law	Percival, Schroeder, Miller & Leape
Environmental Law	Plater, Abrams, Goldfarb, Graham, Heinzerling & Wirth
Evidence	Broun, Mosteller & Giannelli
Evidence	Fisher
Evidence	Mueller & Kirkpatrick
Evidence	Sklansky
Evidence	Waltz, Park & Friedman
Family Law	Areen & Regan
Family Law	Ellman, Kurtz & Scott
Family Law	Harris, Carbone & Teitelbaum
Family Law	Wadlington & O'Brien
Family Law	Weisberg & Appleton
Federal Courts	Fallon, Meltzer & Shapiro (Hart & Wechsler)
Federal Courts	Low & Jeffries
Health Law	Furrow, Greaney, Johnson, Jost & Schwartz
Immigration Law	Aleinikoff, Martin & Motomura
Immigration Law	Legomsky
Insurance Law	Abraham
Intellectual Property	Merges, Menell & Lemley
International Business Transactions	Folsom, Gordon, Spanogle & Fitzgerald
International Law	Blakesley, Firmage, Scott & Williams
International Law	Carter, Trimble & Weiner
International Law	Damrosch, Henkin, Murphy & Smit
International Law	Dunoff, Ratner & Wippman
Labor Law	Cox, Bok, Gorman & Finkin
Land Use	Callies, Freilich & Roberts
Legislation	Eskridge, Frickey & Garrett
Oil & Gas	Lowe, Anderson, Smith & Pierce
Patent Law	Adelman, Radner, Thomas & Wegner
Products Liability	Owen, Montgomery & Davis
Professional Responsibility	Gillers
Professional Responsibility	Hazard, Koniak, Cramton, Cohen & Wendel
Property	Casner, Leach, French, Korngold & VanderVelde
Property	Cribbet, Johnson, Findley & Smith
Property	Donahue, Kauper & Martin
Property	Dukeminier, Krier, Alexander & Schill
Property	Haar & Liebman
Property	Kurtz & Hovenkamp
Property	Nelson, Stoebuck & Whitman
Property	Rabin, Kwall & Kwall
Property	Singer
Real Estate	Korngold & Goldstein
Real Estate Transactions	Nelson & Whitman
Remedies	Laycock
Remedies	Shoben, Tabb & Janutis
Securities Regulation	Coffee, Seligman & Sale
Securities Regulation	Cox, Hillman & Langevoort
Sports Law	Weiler & Roberts
Taxation (Corporate)	Lind, Schwartz, Lathrope & Rosenberg
Taxation (Individual)	Burke & Friel
Taxation (Individual)	Freeland, Lathrope, Lind & Stephens
Taxation (Individual)	Klein, Bankman, Shaviro & Stak
Torts	Dobbs, Hayden & Bublick
Torts	Epstein
Torts	Franklin & Rabin
Torts	Henderson, Pearson, Kysar & Siliciano
Torts	Schwartz, Kelly & Partlett (Prosser)
Trademark	Ginsburg, Litman & Kevlin
Wills, Trusts & Estates	Dukeminier, Sitkoff & Lindgren
Wills, Trusts & Estates	Dobris, Sterk & Leslie
Wills, Trusts & Estates	Scoles, Halbach, Roberts & Begleiter

CPSIA information can be obtained
at www.ICGtesting.com
Printed in the USA
FSHW020231210819
61218FS